# EXPOSITION OF THE BEATITUDES

## The Saint's Happiness

## Jeremiah Burroughs

Monergism Books

# contents

# Reader

Although all men desire happiness, and nothing is more necessary to be known, there are great misconceptions about it. It is not found in sensual pleasures; if it were, Dives would have been happy (Luke 16), and those who worshiped their appetites would have found fulfillment (Philippians 3). It is not found in honors, for then the Dragon and the Beast would have been happy (Revelation 13:4). It is not found in riches (James 5:1). It is not found in moral virtues, as the heathens would have been happy in that case, and Paul in his Pharisaism (Philippians 3:6). It is not found in knowledge (Ecclesiastes 1:18), nor in the contemplation of divine things, for then Balaam would have been happy (Numbers 24:3, 4), as well as Plato, whose thoughts were of such nature. It is not found in any of these, but in what the Lord Christ has laid down and explained in this work. Some deny that saintship and happiness can be experienced in this life, but David refutes the former (Psalm 16:3), and Christ the latter. It is true that perfect happiness cannot be achieved in this life due to the presence of sin, vanity, and misery in every condition and thing we enjoy. The best of men experience more wormwood than wine. However, there is a true blessedness in this life, which lies in the qualities, actions, and sufferings that have a clear, certain, and strong tendency toward perfect happiness. It can be called "Seminal" or "radical" blessedness. Examples of such blessedness are the Beatitudes mentioned here and elsewhere in the Holy Scripture, such as delighting in the Law of God (Psalm 1:2), fearing the Lord (Psalm 112:1), and being undefiled in one's conduct (Psalm 119:1). Such men are blessed, not simply because of the qualities they possess, things they do, or sufferings they endure, but because these lead to and culminate in perfect blessedness in the end.

Reader, the times are perilous. A sentence of death hangs over most, if not all, of your comforts. You do not know how soon you may be stripped of your apparent happiness. If you do not possess a share in these Christian Beatitudes, you are a miserable man. Your life is a dream, and your death will be dreadful. Presented to you is not the happiness that the world considers blessed, or what you may think is so, but what the blessed Son of the blessed God Himself has declared and will prove to be in life and death. Consider and deem as your blessedness that which the Lord Christ Himself regards and calls blessedness. Then, no matter the challenges, troubles, and changes of the times, you are a blessed man, you shall remain so, and you shall have a blessed end. The Reverend Author of these Sermons, Mr. Jeremiah Burroughs, did so, as it was the subject of his preaching before his death.

These Sermons of his have lain complete and unpublished for thirteen years, up until this very day (for he died on the 14th day of the 9th month, 1646). But with the assistance of those who have taken charge, most of these Sermons have already been printed and are now brought to light. They reveal themselves as the genuine offspring of such a parent, whose spirit is vividly represented within them. Reader, the aim of those who publish them is for you to know, desire, and attain true blessedness in these unhappy times. May your thoughts, affections, and actions align with such a Happiness. This is the earnest desire of:

William GreenhillWilliam BridgePhilip NyeJohn YatesWilliam AderlyMatthew MeadThe 14th of the 9th month, 1659

# SERMON I
## Matthew 5:1

And when he saw the crowds, he went up on a mountain, and after he sat down, his disciples came to him. And he opened his mouth and taught them, saying, "Blessed are the poor in spirit, for theirs is the kingdom of heaven, etc." Matthew 5:1

This chapter, along with chapters 6 and 7, contains a sermon that Jesus Christ preached on the Mount. It is the most extensive and comprehensive sermon recorded in Scripture – the sermon of Christ Himself. As a minister of Christ, I pondered what could be more suitable for me to preach about than the sermon of Christ. Therefore, if God permits and as long as I have life, strength, and liberty, I intend to go through this entire sermon of Christ for your benefit. It would be negligence for a minister to preach someone else's sermons, but to preach Christ's sermon is faithfulness. In 2 Corinthians 5:20, the ministers of God are described as ambassadors of Christ, speaking to the people as if Jesus Christ Himself were speaking in His place. They are to regard themselves as coming to the people in Christ's stead. If we must preach as if Christ were preaching, what could be more fitting than to preach what Christ Himself has preached? This sermon, spanning three whole chapters, was preached by the Son of God Himself, the one who possesses the wisdom of the Father, holds all the treasures of wisdom, and has been in the Father's bosom for all eternity. He knows the Father's mind, His heart, and the counsels of His will regarding humanity's eternal state. He was sent by the Father into the world to fulfill this purpose – to proclaim His mind and will to the children of men.

Oh, what attentiveness is required as you hear this sermon of Christ being repeated, explained, and applied to you! We have infinite reasons to thank God for the way in which we can know His mind through Jesus Christ, His Son. In former times, the Lord revealed His mind to men through various means. But now, as the Apostle says in Hebrews 1, "He has spoken to us by His Son," whom He appointed as the heir of all things and through whom He made the world. Jesus Christ is the brightness of God's glory and the exact representation of His being. Oh, the blessedness of those who live in the times of the Gospel, where God speaks to us through His Son! Christ has come from the Father to make Him known to us. No one knows the Father except the Son and those to whom the Son chooses to reveal Him. Surely, there are great things to be known about the mind of God when the second person of the Trinity is designated by the Father to come and preach His mind to humanity. If we hear news of a friend who has come from a distant land to share important information with us, and we know that this friend is wise, faithful, and speaks only the truth, we eagerly gather around to listen. Sometimes, even if someone returns from the army after a significant battle, and we know they have a good understanding of events and are trustworthy, how eagerly do we seek to be with them and hear the news! But here, my brethren, we have Jesus Christ coming from God the Father, fully knowing the mind of His Father, and sent by Him into the world to make known all the counsels of God that were hidden from the beginning of the world. This news concerns our eternal condition, for that is the essence of the Gospel – good news brought by Christ. Therefore, I implore you to listen, for God says, "This is My beloved Son, in whom I am well pleased. Hear Him."

Now, as I begin and intend (God willing) to continue preaching what Christ says, it is crucial that as long as I stick to His words, you hear Him in them. It will greatly aggravate your sin if you do not pay attention to what will be preached now, for it is the sermon of Jesus Christ that will be expounded. It is the fullest sermon of His that we have recorded. In Hebrews 12, you can see the weight the

Holy Spirit places on this – that God has revealed Himself to us through His Son. He says, "See that you do not refuse Him who speaks. For if they did not escape who refused Him who spoke on earth, much more shall we not escape if we turn away from Him who speaks from heaven." Here in this chapter, Christ speaks from heaven. Although He was physically on earth at the time, we are to consider Him as speaking from heaven. The subject of our attention, fear, and reverence is the sermon of Christ. May we carry this thought with us as we hear Him preaching from these chapters.

All I will do at this time is preface this sermon. There are six aspects to consider in this sermon:

Firstly, since we find this sermon recorded not only in Matthew but also in Luke, we must inquire whether they are the same or not. If they are the same, one will shed light on the other, as the substance of the sermon is nearly identical.

Secondly, we must determine when Christ preached this sermon and the occasion for it.

Thirdly, we should identify the location where He preached it.

Fourthly, we need to know the audience to whom He preached.

Fifthly, we must understand the manner in which He preached.

Sixthly, we should grasp the sermon's scope – what it primarily aimed to achieve. These six points will pave the way for what follows.

Regarding the first point: whether it is the same sermon that Luke records, I notice that interpreters often struggle with it. However, if you read the sermon itself, you will find that although it is not recorded as extensively as Matthew does, the substance is the same, and the wording is nearly identical. In Luke 6:20, it is written, "He lifted up His eyes on His disciples and said, 'Blessed are the poor,'" and so on, just as it is here. The reason for doubt is that in Matthew, it is mentioned that Jesus chose His disciples in chapter 10 and sent them out. But in Luke, it is stated that He chose His disciples before this sermon was preached in chapter 6, verse 13. You will find that the twelve were sent out first, and then the sermon was preached. That is the difference. Secondly, Matthew states that Jesus Christ went up to the mountain and taught His disciples (verse 1). But Luke says that He came down with them and stood on a level place, and He lifted up His eyes on His disciples and said, etc. Matthew says He sat, and Luke says

He stood on the level place. Therefore, some interpreters claim it was a different sermon. However, these differences can be easily addressed.

Regarding the first point: Although Luke presents it as occurring after the sending out of the Twelve, and Matthew seems to indicate it happened earlier, we can reconcile this. Even though Matthew records it in Chapter 10, it does not mean that the events described in Chapter 10 necessarily happened before those in Chapter 5. The Scripture often does not chronologically order events but arranges them thematically. In this case, Matthew had a reason to mention Christ's teachings before addressing the sending out of the disciples in Chapter 10. Thus, it being in Chapter 10 does not negate the possibility of it occurring earlier in Chapter 5.

As for the second point, concerning Matthew stating that Jesus was on the mountain and Luke mentioning Him coming down to the plain, the answer is that it is not stated here in Matthew that He came down to the plain to preach. Instead, it is mentioned that after sending out His disciples, Jesus came down to the plain, and the people came to Him. After spending the entire night on the mountain, as we will see shortly, Jesus sent out His disciples and then encountered a great multitude of people. He performed healing miracles among them and then returned to the mountain, withdrawing from the crowd to preach to His disciples and those who had gathered with Him. So, while it is said that He was on the plain and stood there, indicating that He stood while the multitude was with Him, He later, according to Matthew, withdrew to the mountain again and preached. Thus, there is no substantial objection that would negate it being the same sermon. These two apparent differences can easily be reconciled. Therefore, since the substance of the sermon is the same, we will assume it is one and the same. The different Gospel writers will mutually enhance our understanding.

Now, let us inquire about the second point: the time when Christ preached this sermon. To shed light on this, we must turn to Luke. Although it is not mentioned in Matthew, it will provide valuable insight. The night before this sermon, Jesus spent the entire night in prayer. In Luke 6:12, it is written, "And it came to pass in those days that He went out to the mountain to pray, and continued all night in prayer to God." It was the night before this sermon was preached.

This scripture justifies lengthy prayers on extraordinary occasions. Although in ordinary circumstances, it is more appropriate to keep family prayers short, on exceptional occasions, extended prayers are warranted. Jesus Christ Himself prayed all night, setting an example for His ministers to pray for people while others sleep or engage in other activities. Christ devoted an entire night to prayer.

Now, you may wonder about the occasion that prompted Him to spend the whole night in prayer before preaching this sermon. The reason appears to be the task He had to accomplish the following morning: choosing and sending out His disciples. As stated in verse 13, "When it was day, He called His disciples to Himself; and from them, He chose twelve whom He also named apostles." He had the significant responsibility of selecting twelve apostles who would travel and preach the Gospel, one of the greatest tasks since the beginning of the world. Christ considered this a weighty and important undertaking. Therefore, in preparation for this momentous work, He spent the entire night in prayer, seeking God's guidance and equipping Himself for the task ahead.

You can see from this that the work of the ministry is a great undertaking. Some may consider it insignificant, but Christ regarded it as significant. He made solemn preparations before choosing His apostles and spent the entire night in prayer. Therefore, those in the ministry should view it as a mighty and solemn task. They should recognize the weight of the work they are called to do. Similarly, when people are selecting or calling a minister, they should approach it with reverence and not trivialize it. Instead of hastily deciding, they should dedicate ample time to prayer and seeking God's guidance. While the appointment of civil officers or those who assist the civil authorities may not require the same level of solemnity, when it comes to choosing individuals who will exercise the power of Christ in administering ordinances, it should be done with great solemnity. This was the practice from the beginning. Even the appointment of a deacon (Acts 6) involved prayer and the laying on of hands, and for elders, who have a greater role in exercising the power of Christ, prayer, fasting, and the laying on of hands were observed (Acts 14). It is a solemn and significant task, and all ministers of God should consider Christ's prayer as part of their preparation for ministry. They should reflect on it and have faith in the blessing that comes with it. Furthermore, when Christ said in John 17:20

that He prayed not only for those present but also for all who would believe in the future, it is certain that His whole night of prayer was not solely for the twelve apostles but for all who would enter the ministry and preach the Gospel of Christ to the end of the world. Now, having spent the entire night in prayer, the first thing He does in the morning is to choose His twelve apostles. Afterward, when He sees the multitude approaching Him, He withdraws a little and begins to preach. He delivers an excellent and remarkable sermon, which we are about to discuss. Despite having stayed up all night and expended Himself in prayer (which is physically demanding), Christ does not prioritize His physical well-being. Those who are overly concerned about Him would have urged Him to rest instead of wearing Himself out. However, the next morning, He seizes the opportunity to preach.

Teaching us that ministers of the Gospel should not be overly concerned about their physical well-being, constantly whining and complaining about their weak bodies, or being overly cautious about exerting themselves. If there is an opportunity for service, they should be ready to seize it, even if it means tiredness and exertion. What if it shortens their lifespan a little? Isn't it better to accomplish a great deal of good in a short time than to achieve little good over a long period? Accomplishing much in a short time brings greater comfort. A person's life should be measured by their service, not by the number of years they live. Christ preached this lengthy sermon (the longest we know of), and it was delivered the morning after He had spent the entire night in prayer.

Furthermore, let us observe the remarkable sermon that Jesus Christ preached after such a dedicated prayer. It was a truly heavenly sermon. Also, consider the prayer He had shortly before His death, from John 14 onwards for two or three chapters. Those passages contain some of the most profound aspects of Christ's teachings recorded in Scripture. Therefore, ministers should pray more, and they will preach better. The key to being a good preacher is fervent prayer. Ministers should come to the pulpit with the fragrance of prayer still lingering, for those are the sermons that are warmed in their own hearts. They come to offer the milk of the Word, and just as nurses warm the milk before feeding it to a child, the milk of the Word that is warmed by a minister's heartfelt prayer is most nourishing to the people.

Moreover, we can also note that the way to be filled with the Holy Spirit, to be filled with heavenly truths and a deeply spiritual disposition, is to be devoted to prayer. Spending time in purposeful prayer will help not only ministers but also Christians to be filled with the Holy Spirit and divine truths. Consider that this sermon was preached the morning after Christ had spent the entire night in prayer. This adds to the excellence of the sermon and serves as a special motive for your attention and reception of the sermon's message. Surely, a sermon delivered immediately after such a prayer must contain remarkable substance. This leads us to the second aspect to consider as a preface: the timing of this sermon.

The third preface to this sermon is the place where it was delivered, for everything in Scripture has its significance. According to my text, Jesus went up to the mountain. He had already been on the mountain in prayer, then descended to interact with the people, and later returned to the mountain to preach.

Why on the Mountain?

Some believe it was to fulfill the prophecies in various scriptures about preaching the Gospel on the mountain, such as Isaiah 40:9 and Joel 3:18. However, these are mere conjectures. Others allegorize the idea, emphasizing how ministers should have a heavenly disposition when preaching. But I don't fancy straining Scripture beyond what I believe to be the Holy Spirit's intended meaning. Therefore, the only consideration is the convenience of the mountain as a secluded place. With a crowd around Him, Christ couldn't speak as freely for edification, so He retreated to the mountain where He had spent so much time in prayer. Christ didn't wait to preach in the synagogue or the temple. No, He preached wherever it was suitable to address the people. It's not necessary for there to be a consecrated place for the preaching of the Word.

Which mountain was it, you may ask?

Some have thought it was the Mount of Olives, but that's impossible because Christ was in Upper Galilee at the time, about 40 miles away from Jerusalem. Mount Olivet is as close to Jerusalem as Islington is to the City. Hence, Jerome and others believe it was Mount Tabor. Certainly, this justifies that preaching can take place in any location where ministers have the opportunity and where there can be peace and edification. People have two mistaken notions: some think certain places are so profaned by unholy activities that preaching should not take place there, while others believe certain places have been excessively associated with superstition, and due to the superstition surrounding them, preaching should not occur there. They refuse to attend a sermon because of the place's superstition. Truly, this understanding helps us counter both notions.

Regarding the profane, there is nothing done in any place that defiles it so much that preaching would be unacceptable to God. Even if it were a former playhouse, if there is no more suitable location available, the work of preaching would not be defiled. Shall so many souls perish because they lack a consecrated place to learn about God and Christ? It's a sorrowful thought. This mountain (if it is indeed Mount Tabor, as both Jerome and others believe) was as unsuitable a place as a playhouse. Christ preached this sermon there, a place likely to be tainted by superstition and idolatry. I find mention of this place in the prophecy of Hosea, in Chapter 5, Verse 1: "Hear this, you priests! Pay attention, Israel's house! Listen, royal house! For the judgment applies to you because you have been a snare at Mizpah and a net spread out on Mount Tabor." The meaning of this is that when the ten tribes deviated from the true worship of God in the temple at Jerusalem and established their idols in Dan and Bethel, there were some who were more godly and devout than others. They couldn't be content with worshiping there and felt the need to go to Jerusalem. However, the laws of the king and the priests were against it, and no one could worship in Jerusalem without risking punishment. Nonetheless, many still went, so the priests and others set up watchers to observe those who went up to Jerusalem to worship, just as there have been men assigned to watch when people leave their parish churches, even if there was no preaching at home. Since those going to Jerusalem had to pass through Mount Tabor, watchers were stationed there, hence the mention of a net spread on Tabor. Surely, this place was profaned to the utmost degree, and yet, in spite of that, Christ went and preached this sermon on Mount Tabor. It was as wicked an act to set watchmen to spy on those going to the true worship of God in Jerusalem as it was to stage a play. Nevertheless, as I said, Christ came and preached on the mountain.

And so, regarding any superstition associated with places, the synagogues of the ten tribes and the locations they established for their worship and teaching were greatly corrupted, as they set them up in opposition to the true worship of God in Jerusalem. Yet, Christ would preach wherever He went, regardless of how those places had been misused. He didn't concern Himself with that but took the present opportunity to do His work—to preach the Word. That's the first point.

Secondly, it reminds us that all ministers of God should seize every opportunity to do good. That's the third consideration in this preface.

The fourth consideration is, who are these auditors mentioned in the text? "And seeing the multitude, He went up into the mountain." Now, I confess that some interpret this sermon of Christ as being directed at the multitude that gathered around Him. They believe that Christ was moved with compassion to preach to them because He saw such a large number of people. It is indeed true that a gracious heart and godly ministers are deeply moved when they see a multitude coming to listen, especially when they show a willingness to attend. It is an incredibly moving sight that stirs any minister's heart in the world. We see at other times that Christ's heart was greatly moved upon seeing a multitude of people, as in Matthew 9:36: "But when He saw the multitudes, He was moved with compassion for them, because they were weary and scattered, like sheep having no shepherd." Then He said to His disciples, "The harvest truly is plentiful, but the laborers are few. Therefore, pray the Lord of the harvest to send out laborers into His harvest." When Jesus Christ looked upon a multitude, the text says He was moved with compassion, thinking to Himself, "Lord, what will become of these thousands of souls who know so little about God and the heavenly things?" Therefore, He said to His disciples, "Pray that laborers may be sent into the harvest. These people are willing to hear; the regions are ripe for harvest. Oh, pray for faithful ministers to be sent into the harvest!" The sight of a multitude is truly moving, inspiring preaching and prayer for God to send faithful ministers to preach to them. Indeed, the sight of a multitude is an object of envy for many, as in the past, faithful ministers were silenced due to envy, which goes against the spirit of Jesus Christ. However, I can't base any doctrinal point on this because, at this time, I believe Christ went up into the mountain and separated Himself from most of the people. As the text says, "And seeing the multitude, He went up into a mountain, and when He was set, His disciples came to Him." Perhaps some others joined, but not the majority of them. In Luke 6, where the same sermon is recorded, it says, "He lifted up His eyes toward His disciples and said, 'Blessed are the poor, etc.'" So it's likely that, instead of spending His time with the multitude at that moment, He withdrew to speak to His disciples. Why? Because His main focus was on His disciples, on sending out the twelve and commissioning them as apostles. While preaching to the multitude was indeed good and the heart of Christ was always open to all occasions, now He would attend to the work He had at hand, speaking to His apostles whom He was about to send out.

From this, we can note that individuals must attend to their present work and not be consumed with thoughts of potentially doing greater good in another way, which may cause them to neglect the current work God has called them to. Let us focus on the work we are presently engaged in and not be distracted, thinking that another task may be more beneficial. If this is our current work, then let us dedicate ourselves to it and entrust our efforts to the blessing of God.

And then secondly, we can see from this that Christ holds a special regard for His ministers. He withdraws from the multitude to speak to them. He did not prohibit anyone from coming, but His intention was to address His ministers. Christ recognises the great importance of His ministers; He knows that much depends on them. As mentioned later in this chapter, He refers to them as the salt of the earth, suggesting that the world would decay and deteriorate without them. He also calls them the light of the world, indicating that the world would be in darkness without the light of the Word. Ministers should be filled with light and, in turn, enlighten others. They should be filled with the will of God, just as Epaphras is mentioned in Colossians 4. He prayed for the people to be filled with the will of God. Oh, it is a remarkable thing for a minister to be filled with the will of God, like a sail filled with the wind!

Those who are most instructed by Christ are the most suitable to instruct others. Christ starts preaching to them so that they may preach to the people. Those who have not had Jesus Christ preach to their hearts cannot effectively preach to the hearts of others.

Furthermore, Christ saw that the work was very challenging. The ministry is demanding, and that is why Christ spends a significant amount of time praying for them and instructing them. They were to be set as a light on a hill, with the eyes and scrutiny of others upon them, observing their every move. They would bear the brunt of everything, and if there were any perilous tasks, they would have to face them. The work of God is truly difficult. As Luther once said, "What is it to preach? It is to attract the envy of evil people." This is why Christ made thorough preparations for His apostles before sending them out. That concludes the fourth aspect to consider in the preface to Christ's sermon—the audience He had.

And then the fifth aspect to consider in the preface is the manner in which Christ preached. There are three observable things:

Firstly, Christ sat and preached.

Secondly, He opened His mouth and spoke.

Thirdly, He fixed His eyes upon His disciples, as mentioned in Luke 6.

But now, secondly, we have two aspects to consider: First, that Christ sat down and opened His mouth to speak. As for sitting down, when Christ preached, He would sit rather than stand as preachers do nowadays. It was the common practice among the Jews for preachers to sit down. In Matthew 23:2, it is said, "The scribes and the Pharisees sit in Moses' seat." Christ instructs the people to hear them and obey their words while not imitating their actions. In Matthew 24:3 and Matthew 26:55, it is also mentioned that Christ sat down to preach. He would stand up when reading the Law but sit down when preaching. Likewise, in Luke 4:20, we see the same pattern. In all these instances, we can observe that sitting down was the customary way of preaching. Some may find significance in this, but I believe it was merely a cultural gesture. Christ observed the prevailing practice of sitting down during preaching at that time. Just as French ministers preach with their hats on, conforming to their customs when among them, so did Christ sit or stand as per the prevailing custom in different churches.

You may wonder, does this justify conforming to ceremonies in churches? After all, Christ conformed to the ceremony of sitting. So why was there such controversy over kneeling during the sacrament?

To answer that clearly, you must understand the distinction between ceremonies. If a ceremony is purely natural or civil and aids in the worship of God in a natural and civil manner, then we should conform to the customs of the churches wherever we go. However, when a ceremony acquires a spiritual purpose and when man's institution imparts some spiritual significance to it, as was the case with our ceremonies, then we must not conform to them unless we want to sin against Jesus Christ and our consciences. These ceremonies begin to involve worship when they take on spiritual meanings and are instituted as such. But if a ceremony has nothing more than what its nature naturally contributes to the worship of God, then there should be no contention. It is unnecessary for us or the churches of God to argue about such matters. However, when ceremonies acquire a religious purpose, as stated in the Common Prayer Book to "stir up the dull minds of men," they become sinful. That is why Christ observed the Jewish ceremony of sitting down—it served as a natural aid.

Secondly, Christ opened His mouth and spoke. You might ask why this is mentioned. How else could He speak to them?

Firstly, there is speaking without necessarily opening one's mouth. In Hebrews 11:4, it speaks of a speaking without opening the mouth. It says, "By faith Abel offered unto God a more excellent sacrifice than Cain, by which he obtained witness that he was righteous, God testifying of his gifts: and by it he being dead yet speaketh." So, there is a form of real speaking apart from verbal expression. Some believe that this was a metaphorical reference. Just as Christ preached through His life, ministers of God should continually preach through their holy lives before the people.

Secondly, the phrase "opening the mouth" is used in Jewish expression to signify not only speaking but also having something weighty to say. In Job 32:20, Elihu says that he is full of matter and has excellent things to say, and he declares that he will open his mouth to speak. In English, we use similar expressions. For example, when we pay close attention to something, we say, "I saw it with my own eyes," which means we noticed and considered it carefully. Similarly, if someone wants to convey their serious attentiveness, they might say, "I heard it with my own ears," indicating that they listened attentively and took note. So, Christ opened His mouth to speak, not merely to speak, but to deliver great and weighty messages.

Thirdly, this signifies that the mouth of Christ was like the door to a rich treasury. Jesus Christ possessed a rich treasury in His heart, and His mouth served as the door to access those riches. When Christ opened His mouth, He shared the precious truths you will hear in this sermon. It should be the same for us. Our mouths should be like doors that release the treasures of heavenly truths we have acquired. Just as merchants trade for heavenly treasures in heaven, ministers of God, especially, should have hearts filled with heavenly treasures. When they come to preach, they simply open the door of this treasury— their mouths— to share the valuable heavenly truths. Oh, if only all our mouths were like that! This is the significance of the expression "Christ opened His mouth." It is a mercy, my brethren, that Christ opened His mouth to speak to the people and proclaim the great things of God. It is also a mercy that the mouths of faithful ministers are opened to speak and show people the mind of God. We should be grateful for this privilege. In the past, many ministers had their mouths shut, even though they possessed rich truths in their hearts. The door was locked and barred, preventing the people from benefiting from their words. I believe that England, among all reformed churches in the world, accumulated great guilt by silencing faithful ministers. But thanks be to God that He has silenced those who silenced the mouths. I recall during the time of Chrysostom, the godly people professed that they would rather have the sun withdraw its beams than have Chrysostom's mouth shut. Such was the excellence of Chrysostom's preaching. They reasoned that if the door to the treasury of John Chrysostom's heart were closed and locked, if they could not benefit from it, it would be better to receive no benefit from the sun itself. So, let us consider it a great mercy that the mouths of faithful ministers are opened to speak to you. That concludes the second aspect of Christ's preaching—the fact that He opened His mouth.

And then the third aspect is that He focused His gaze on those He spoke to. The Holy Ghost notes this in Luke 6:20, where it says, "He lifted up His eyes upon His disciples." Surely, my beloved, the eyes of Christ radiated with wisdom, and the glory of God shone through His eyes. In Revelation 1:14, we find that Christ's eyes were like flaming fire. Wisdom makes a person's face shine, and often there is great majesty in the countenance of a minister. There is much significance in the mutual gaze between the minister and the congregation. Therefore, because Christ desired His words to have a greater impact, the text says that He lifted up His eyes upon His disciples and looked at them. Such a gaze has great power in terms of reprimand and warning. Many times, a guilty conscience cannot bear the piercing gaze of a minister. In Acts 13:9, we read about Paul, when Elymas the sorcerer tried to turn the proconsul Sergius Paulus away from the ministry's work on his heart. Paul was preaching, and the proconsul began to be stirred and listen to what Paul had to say. Then Elymas came and attempted to hinder the proconsul. In that moment, Paul, hoping to win over such an influential person for the work God had set before him, fixed his eyes upon Elymas and spoke to him in a severe manner. It was as if he were saying, "You wretch, you child of the devil, full of deceit, how dare you seek to obstruct the Word from reaching such an important man? You child of the devil!" Sometimes, there is great power in the eyes of a minister of the Word. We also see that when Peter denied Christ, Christ looked at him, and Peter went out and wept bitterly. Much was communicated through the gaze of Jesus Christ, and many times the eyes of a minister of God carry great meaning.

Now then, my brethren, this brings us to the conclusion of this sermon for now. I implore you, as we preach through this extensive sermon of Jesus Christ, to realize that His eyes are upon all of you. Why should we not perceive it now just as they did back then when Christ said, "He who hears you hears me"? This sermon is the very one that Christ Himself preached, and just as He lifted up His eyes to His audience at that time, you should know that Jesus Christ lifts up His eyes upon all of you, and His gaze will be upon every heart throughout the preaching of His sermon. Oh, Christ enters the congregation to observe this person and that person, to see how they will receive His word. If you remember this throughout our journey, it will be of great benefit to you. Remember that the eyes of Jesus Christ will be upon you, watching your conduct throughout. And that concludes the fifth aspect by way of preface.

# SERMON II.
## Matthew 5:2

And he opened his mouth, and taught them, saying, Matt. 5:2

The sixth point is to demonstrate the purpose of this sermon, which primarily consists of three things.

First, to reveal the true essence of blessedness and who truly qualifies as blessed.

Secondly, to elucidate the spirituality of the Law, or the spiritual enlightenment that comes through the Gospel's illumination. Christ aims to demonstrate how the duties of the Law are elevated to a higher level by the Gospel. The Gospel does not annul these duties but reveals a more spiritually elevated way of life than what was generally understood under the law. Our Saviour intends to redirect people from finding satisfaction in external acts of righteousness, prayers, or any other means, or from refraining solely from external sins.

And thirdly, to provide a forewarning about false teachers. These are the three main topics of the sermon. Many other things are interwoven within, but regarding the first topic, it is to reveal the essence of true blessedness. Christ begins with "blessedness" on His lips, repeating "blessed" again and again.

From this, we can draw these brief observations:

Firstly, it is Jesus Christ who teaches us where true blessedness lies. If we desire to know how to be happy and blessed, we must turn to Christ. Human wisdom alone cannot attain it. Among the philosophers, there were a hundred and eighty opinions regarding human happiness, and some count even more. They were merely beating around the bush, but it is the Christian who catches the bird. It is only through Christ that we can understand how to be happy. Christ has come from the Father's bosom to reveal the eternal counsels of the Father regarding humanity's ultimate purpose. Since the fall, mankind would never have come to know their true purpose and the good that God intends for them if Christ had not come from the Father's bosom to declare it. Oh, the poor and insignificant things in which people place their happiness when they do not know Jesus Christ and remain ignorant of Him. When Christ is revealed, people's thoughts and hearts are elevated and expanded. They seek happiness in a different manner than they did before. Let us give thanks to God for Jesus Christ, through whom we come to understand where our ultimate purpose lies, that supreme good for which God has made human nature capable.

Secondly, it is the aim and purpose of the ministry to show people how they can attain blessedness. This sermon was preached primarily to the apostles when they received their commission, as I explained previously. When Christ speaks so much about blessedness to them, it is to prepare them to go out and preach it to the world. Oh, it is through the ministry of the Word that people learn how to find happiness. The harm it does is merely to show them how they can be eternally blessed. How poor and miserable are those who live without the ministry of the Word? In what pitiful things do they place their happiness? When you come to attend the ministry of the Gospel, you should regard it as a message from God that shows you the path to eternal happiness. It is called the Gospel that is preached, good tidings. It brings tidings from heaven about how your souls and bodies can become eternally happy. Approach the ministry of the Word with such a disposition. Those who forsake the ministry of the Word forsake their own mercy, the means by which they may find happiness. How debased are people's hearts to value it so little that they cannot even endure a little cold in the morning to attend the ministry appointed by God to reveal happiness to those whom God intends eternal good.

Oh, the transformations that many have experienced through the ministry of the Gospel! Sometimes, in just thirty minutes, the Word has completely turned their hearts around. Their hearts had been pursuing vain and worthless things for happiness, seeking solace only in those things they believed would bring them happiness. Yet, through the ministry of the Gospel, truths have pierced their hearts and brought about a radical change. They would not trade what they have found in the ministry of the Word for ten thousand worlds. They have come to hear the Word with carnal, materialistic, vain, and sensual hearts, focusing solely on earthly matters and base and trivial things. However, in attending the Word, flashes of light have shone upon them, revealing the true good of a rational being, the purpose for which God created man, and the infinite good that the human soul is capable of. As a result, they have scorned and dismissed all those sensual delights and vanities in which they previously placed their happiness. Therefore, learn to understand the purpose of the ministry of the Gospel, and that is the second general observation.

The third observation from Christ's overall purpose is this: By examining what Christ declares as constituting blessedness, we can learn that there is a significant difference between God's perspective on true happiness and the world's perspective. If we consider the eight Beatitudes presented here, we will see that they are entirely contrary to the world's judgment.

Firstly, if the world were asked who is blessed, they would never have said that the poor are blessed. They would consider the poor to be miserable. However, Christ holds a different opinion: "Blessed are the poor in spirit, for theirs is the kingdom of heaven." The world would say, "Blessed are the rich; they are truly happy." In Malachi 3, we call the proud happy, but here it says, "Blessed are the poor."

—— Then secondly, if you were to ask the world who the blessed ones are, they would never tell you that those who mourn are blessed. Certainly, if there are any blessed individuals in this world, they must be those who live joyous and merry lives. But no, says Christ, it is quite the opposite. Blessed are those who mourn. Christ's judgment contradicts the world's judgment.

—— Then thirdly, if you were to inquire about the happy ones, the world would say it is those who refuse to be wronged and have the power to seek justice. If anyone wrongs them, they will know it. The world would consider them happy. But no, says Christ, blessed are the meek. Those who are willing to endure wrongs and respond meekly to those who abuse them. The world thinks that person is a fool for tolerating wrongs, but in Christ's judgment, they are blessed.

—— And then fourthly, if you were to ask the world who the blessed ones are, surely they would say it is those who indulge in all kinds of delicacies, those who can satisfy themselves. But no, says Christ, blessed are those who hunger and thirst. Hungry and thirsty souls are the blessed souls.

—— And then fifthly, if you were to ask the world who the blessed individuals are, they would say it is those who hoard their wealth, thinking it wise to keep what they have and not let it go. But no, says Christ, blessed are the merciful. If a person has great wealth and resources and uses them for good purposes, they are blessed.

—— Furthermore, if you were to ask the world who the blessed ones are, they would never choose the pure in heart. The world believes that the blessed are those who follow their lusts and satisfy them to the fullest. But no, says Christ, blessed are the pure in heart, the Puritans.

—— And then, blessed are the peacemakers. The world believes it is happiness for those who stand their ground and defend their rights. But no, blessed are the peacemakers who would rather relinquish their rights than disrupt the peace.

—— Above all, the world would never have thought that the persecuted were blessed. But no, says Christ. Now, I appeal to your consciences, whether you would have ever believed that blessedness consisted in these things if we had not received it from Christ. Thus, we have seen that there is a significant difference between Christ's judgment and the world's judgment regarding true happiness.

It is of great importance for ministers and young disciples of Christ to divert their hearts from earthly blessedness and consider where true heavenly blessedness lies. This sermon (as I mentioned before) is what Christ preaches to ministers when He sends them to preach to others. It is also for other disciples who have recently converted. Christ had been engaged in His public ministry for two years before this sermon, and many had embraced the profession of Christ. However, despite their commitment to Christ, they encountered nothing but troubles and afflictions in this world. Recognizing their potential vulnerability,

Christ takes care to fully instruct and inform them that even though they may remain in a lowly and persecuted state in the eyes of the world, there is a blessedness that surpasses all these hardships. Indeed, in the midst of suffering, they can experience the greatest happiness. This is what Christ wants ministers and young disciples to understand, as it will redirect their focus away from external matters. They are likely to encounter afflictions and troubles, and therefore, Christ wants them to be spiritual. If their hearts are entangled with the world and sensual pleasures of the flesh, they are unlikely to have a significant impact in their preaching. But those who see a happiness beyond these things are likely to do the greatest good in their ministry.

And as for you who are young, if you are not fully informed of this when you first commit yourselves to Christ, that no matter the afflictions and miseries you endure in the world, there is a happiness in which you can be blessed, you will not remain steadfast in the profession of the Christian faith. In a short period, you will be offended and cast it all aside.

Christ does not say, "You ought to be poor in spirit, you should hunger and thirst, and be meek." No, He does not approach it that way. Instead, He commends what should be in them, rather than exhorting or threatening the opposite. From this, we can learn a valuable lesson: It is a useful and profitable approach for ministers of the Gospel to cultivate love for what is one's duty by demonstrating its excellence, glory, and the happiness that accompanies it. That should be the focus, rather than solely burdening them with the duty or exhorting and threatening them for failing to fulfill it. Although these aspects have their place and time, ministers of the Gospel should primarily aim to convince people that there is blessedness in fulfilling their duty. If we can not only persuade people to do what God requires but also make them love what God requires, showing them its excellence and the blessedness that comes with it, then we will win their hearts to the duty and to Christ forever.

And there is another note regarding the scope of Christ's message of blessedness: Christ does not begin His sermon by saying, "Blessed are those who believe in Me and are godly and righteous." Why does Christ not speak generally about blessedness in relation to righteous people, believers, and saints? Instead, He focuses on the poor, those who mourn. This is because Christ tailors His message to His present audience, those to whom He is preaching. This doctrine is more suitable for His disciples because they were likely to be most troubled by poverty and the afflicted conditions they were likely to face. Therefore, Christ strives to assist them in the area where their chief temptation is likely to lie. He emphasizes the blessedness of the poor and those who mourn rather than simply stating that believers and the righteous are blessed. It is a great skill for a minister of the Gospel not only to preach the truth but also to adapt to the specific needs of the audience, speaking words that are timely and suited to their conditions. A minister should not strive to preach solely based on what might showcase their depth and excellence but rather what is most appropriate for the people they are addressing. These are the notes we can derive from the general scope of Christ's sermon: Christ begins with this kind of blessedness—blessed are the poor. It is wise to follow Christ's judgment rather than our own when it comes to blessedness. We should listen to what the blessed God says about what constitutes blessedness rather than the opinions of wretched and miserable individuals.

"The poor"—they are the blessed ones. In other words, blessedness, in this context, refers to being participants in the chief good for which humans were created and being filled with all the good that their natures are capable of. That is where blessedness lies.

Now, "the poor in spirit" may lack certain worldly possessions, but they are partakers of what truly matters—the highest good of humanity—and will undoubtedly be filled with all the good that their souls and bodies are capable of. These are the blessed ones.

"The poor"—blessed are the poor. The Greeks had two words to denote a poor man. First, πτωχός, which refers to someone lacking necessities without which they cannot survive. The other word, πένης, signifies someone who only possesses the bare necessities to sustain life and soul, as we say, to keep them together.

The word used here in the text does not describe a person who just has enough to sustain themselves but rather someone deprived of what is necessary. They lack something essential, and they perceive this lack as a threat to their well-being. That is the characteristic of the word—blessed are the poor.

"The poor," but not all poor. Blessed are the poor in spirit. Some poor individuals are cursed and miserably poor in every sense. They bring poverty upon themselves through idleness, wickedness, prodigality, and the squandering of resources when they are young and have the opportunity to save for future needs. Such individuals spend everything immediately, leaving themselves and their families on the brink of perishing due to poverty. Christ does not pronounce them blessed; they are cursed poor. In Luke 6:20, Christ says, "Blessed are the poor" when looking upon His disciples. A person may be poor in this world yet be cursed and miserable in relation to God. They are more miserable in God's eyes than in the eyes of other people. Oh, how many poor people do we find living without God in the world, profane and ungodly, swearing and unclean? They are among the most ungodly people on Earth, and it is dreadful to witness. They are likely to be miserable in this life and for all eternity. Such poor individuals should not assume that because they are miserable here, they have experienced their hell and will not be miserable hereafter. No, that is not the case. If you can read, you may find in the Epistle of Jude that some were consumed by fire from heaven and yet were condemned to eternal fire afterward. Similarly, there are those whom the Lord has forsaken in this world and who are likely to be forsaken for all eternity in the world to come.

But you may say, "This offers little comfort to the poor." Little comfort? Are there any here seeking comfort? Do you expect comfort from the word? If any poor person desires comfort from the word, I would be reluctant to let this pass without adding something. Therefore, so that you may not be discouraged in your poverty, take comfort in the following:

Firstly, you, the poor, have souls as precious as the greatest monarchs on Earth. Your souls are equally valuable and capable of experiencing the same glory as the emperors, kings, and queens of the world. That is something significant.

Secondly, you, the poor, have equal access to God, and heaven is open to you just as it is to the most powerful rulers on Earth. If you have the heart to seek it, there is as great a possibility for you to attain a crown of glory in the highest heavens as there is for the mightiest monarch living on this Earth. That should give you hope.

Thirdly, let me tell you that, in some respects, you, the poor, are even closer to eternal blessedness. If you are not wicked and ungodly and have the desire to pursue true blessedness, you are more likely to attain it than the great ones of the world. Your temptations are not as overwhelming as theirs. Poverty tempts you to despair and to resort to desperate measures, but there is greater danger in the temptations that riches bring—the temptation to satisfy our lusts and to be proud, haughty, and scornful.

Fourthly, you, the poor, have a lesser account to give compared to the rich people of the world.

Fifthly, the Scriptures reveal that God has chosen the poor of the world. While He has chosen some who are rich, His thoughts throughout eternity have been fixed upon the poor. In 1 Corinthians 1:26, the apostle writes, "For ye see your calling, brethren, how that not many wise men after the flesh, not many mighty, not many noble, are called: but God hath chosen the foolish things of the world to confound the wise; and God hath chosen the weak things of the world to confound the things which are mighty; and base things of the world, and things which are despised, hath God chosen, yea, and things which are not, to bring to nought things that are." The poor have the Gospel preached to them.

Sixthly, as God has chosen the poor, He has appointed the preaching of the Gospel especially for them. In Luke 14:21, Christ sends His servants to call in the poor, the maimed, the halt, and the blind. Christ invites them. And in Matthew 11:5, the Gospel is preached to the poor. Therefore, if the Gospel is intended to be preached to the poor, it is undoubtedly intended to be preached to this congregation. Oh, that God would grant even you, the extremely poor and those lacking proper clothing or other necessities, the desire to come and listen to the preaching of the Gospel, without making excuses. Come and partake of the bread of life. You may not be invited to the tables of the rich, but God has invited you to His Table, to the supper of the Lamb.

Seventhly, we find in Scripture that there are very few who receive an inward call, and yet the poor are among them. "For ye see your calling, brethren, how that not many wise men after the flesh, not many mighty, not many noble, are called: but God hath chosen the foolish things of the world to confound the wise; and God hath chosen the weak things of the world to confound the things which are mighty" (1 Corinthians 1:26-27). Therefore, the poor have a unique opportunity to experience God's calling.

Eighthly, in addition, if you come in response to the call of the Gospel, the Lord will not overlook you in the slightest because you are poor. On the contrary, the Lord will hold you in high regard and cherish you as much as His soul clings to you. You will experience communion with Him, just like even the greatest godly emperors do. I know what you may say—great emperors and kings, even the wicked ones. Yes, that's true. But I meant even when they are godly. Consider a godly king and a humble, godly alms-person. This humble alms-person can have as much communion with God, and God can accept their service just as much as that of a prince, even if he is godly. You see, God doesn't place as much importance on the magnitude of the work being done as He does on the faithfulness and sincerity of our hearts in carrying out our work. Oh, I wish that God would sanctify your poverty to you so that you would consider the following: "Well, I am a poor and miserable creature in this world, and there is little hope that I will achieve great things here. Let me pursue spiritual riches instead. Although I am likely to be outwardly miserable, why can't my soul, and even my body, be blessed in the end? Why can't I be blessed with God and His Christ forever? If I were able to preach to this congregation and all the poor in it, and if it were proclaimed that there would be a sermon on a specific day to reveal how all the poor in this parish could become wealthy individuals and live in abundance all their lives, I have no doubt there would be a sufficient audience of poor people. And let me assure you, in the name of God, that if you were to come and listen, or if you could persuade those you know to come and listen, we can show you ways in which it is possible for you to be blessed for all eternity, to possess greater riches than if God were to make you kings and queens. So much so that it could be said, not only in a general sense, "Blessed are the poor," but "Blessed is this poor man who resides in this street or in such a humble, smoky dwelling." Even the angels of God may regard you as a blessed individual if you have the heart to attend to the Gospel, which reveals the path to blessedness. Blessed are the poor.

But indeed, blessed are the poor in spirit. However, not every poor person, and not every poverty of spirit, is blessed. There is a poverty of spirit that is evil and accursed. A person can possess a poor and cursed spirit because they genuinely have a poor spirit. By that, I mean someone who has a low, base, and sordid spirit, whose focus has sunk down to low, earthly, sensual things as their highest and greatest good. They have no aspirations beyond eating, drinking, and satisfying their fleshly desires. Here lies a person with a poor spirit—a truly low spirit. But this poor, low spirit is sordid, base, and accursed. Often, you see poor people who fixate on the menial things they are engaged in as their sole objective. For example, you may observe a poor woman scraping in a dust heap or dung hill for an entire hour. It's not the poverty itself that makes her miserable, but rather when that becomes her sole objective. If she can earn sixpence or a shilling a day, she considers herself blessed and focuses on nothing higher. You might say, "This is indeed a poor spirit." Well, to be honest, such poor spirits are found among the people of this world, including the princes and great ones. Many of them solely pursue the satisfaction of their flesh—eating, drinking, and indulging in impurity—as that is most suited to their spirits. These are men of poor, low, and base spirits. The Lord desires His saints to possess low spirits in a godly sense, meaning to be humble. However, the Lord also desires His servants, in another sense, to possess high and lofty spirits, in which nothing in the world can satisfy their spirits except God Himself. Now, that is a person with a high spirit. Such an individual acknowledges their unworthiness even for the tiniest morsel of bread, yet declares that even if God were to grant them the entire world, it would not satisfy them as their portion. They must have God Himself, they must have heaven, eternity, and glory. This person possesses a truly elevated spirit, and in comparison, all other individuals in the world have poor, base, and low spirits. Therefore, not everyone who is poor in spirit is blessed in this way.

But who then? What kind of poverty of spirit brings blessings?

To understand that, you must know this: When it is said, "Blessed are those who are poor in spirit," it means that when a man or woman (as some interpret it) willingly embraces a low and poor condition if it pleases God. They are willing to give up everything, even if they possess great wealth, if God calls for it. They are ready to live humbly. Now, when God grants a person a comfortable lifestyle with abundance and prosperity, they have all their needs met. But this soul says, "It's true, I have received these blessings from God, but God, who searches all hearts and converses with our spirits, knows that in my spirit, if the Lord were to call for all these blessings as a testament to His truth, I am here ready to part with all these outward comforts. I am prepared to live on bread and water all my days, to live in the same destitution as the poorest beggar, as long as the Lord is glorified through me. I bear witness to being truly poor in spirit. It may be that I am not poor in terms of my wealth. I acknowledge that the Papists place great emphasis on this concept of being poor in spirit, suggesting that one should vow poverty. However, God does not require that. Instead, whenever He calls for your wealth or any of your comforts, you should be willing to surrender them at His feet. That is what God expects from every person. So, as I continue, I ask you, who possess wealth and enjoy its benefits, do you find such a disposition in your hearts that if it came down to it, you would willingly give up your entire estate rather than deny even the smallest truth of God? Would you let go of all your wealth rather than commit even the slightest sin against your conscience? Would you value bearing witness to the truth more than living in worldly abundance? If you can truly embrace this mindset, then you are truly poor in spirit, even in the midst of your abundance. True grace does not lie in voluntarily casting away our wealth and riches; rather, it lies in wisely managing our possessions while we have them and being willing to part with them when God calls for it.

Secondly, blessed are the poor in spirit. This refers to a spirit that is willing to submit to God in a low condition when one is placed in such a state. First, it includes those who are willing to be poor if God so desires. Secondly, it includes those who are already poor in terms of their outward circumstances. They have a poverty of spirit that corresponds to their outward poverty. Their spirits submit to God's sovereignty and they are willing to glorify Him in the manner He has set for them. They do not envy those in higher positions, nor do they complain or resent God for the diverse distribution of His gifts—some having much and others having little. No, they recognize that God, through His providence, has brought them to their current condition, and they submit to His hand. They are content to glorify Him in their humble state and faithfully fulfill the duties required of them in their lowly circumstances. Many poor people think, "If only I were as rich as others, then I could truly glorify God." But in their current situation, they are agitated and anxious, seeking various means to provide for themselves. They cannot bring themselves to glorify God in their lowly state. However, if you can find it in your heart to submit to God in your present humble condition, blessed are you, for you are truly poor in spirit. This disposition of your spirit, the willingness to glorify God, is of greater excellence than if God were to make you the chief of a parish or the ruler of a kingdom.

Thirdly, blessed are those who are poor in spirit, not merely in words, expressions, or outward appearances. Many will complain about themselves, declaring their weakness, poverty, and worthlessness, but God knows that their hearts are full of pride. If others were to think of them or speak of them in the same way they speak of themselves, they would not tolerate it. Thus, though they may be poor in words, they are not poor in spirit. Some may live modestly and present themselves as poor, but inwardly their spirits are not humble. They may outwardly adopt a humble lifestyle, believing that pride only lies in clothing and material possessions. However, the true source of pride is found in the spirits of men. Therefore, blessed are those who are poor in spirit, those whose wills, affections, and understanding are humbled before God. Blessed are those who possess a genuine poverty of spirit.

In the fourth place, and more importantly and primarily, blessed are those who are poor in spirit. This refers to those who truly understand and recognize their spiritual poverty. Now, this is a crucial point, the very point that Christ promises blessedness to.

Regarding this, there are three things I will address:

Firstly, I will explain what spiritual poverty is that those who are poor in spirit perceive and are aware of.

Secondly, I will discuss how a heart that is poor in spirit behaves or the various workings of such a heart.

Thirdly, I will explain why such a heart is esteemed as blessed by Jesus Christ.

As for where this blessedness lies, it will become evident in the promise: "For theirs is the kingdom of Heaven."

I will briefly explain the first point to you: What is the spiritual poverty that such a soul sees and is aware of?

Concerning its spiritual condition, such a soul perceives itself as truly destitute.

First, it recognizes that it lacks all true spiritual goodness that would benefit it in relation to God and its own happiness. It sees this clearly. Just as a poor person sees themselves as poor, that is, lacking all the outward comforts others possess and being devoid of necessary things that others have, similarly, one who is poor in spirit perceives their condition in this manner. They say, "O Lord, although when You created man, You made him rich, placing him in paradise and fashioning him according to Your own Image, by which he was the ruler and great heir of all the world, now I am deprived of all good things, especially spiritual good. I am deprived of Your Image; I have nothing of Your spiritual Image within me. I lack any spiritual life that would enable me to have union and communion with You, which would lead to eternal life. I am completely devoid of every good thing that could make me in any way acceptable to God. Now, here is a poor individual who, when they can see it and be convinced of it, understands that they lack every good thing that could make them acceptable to God. They do not possess a single trace of it. They may have an estate and outward comforts in their family, but what do they have in relation to God? How do things stand for them in connection with the infinite and glorious first being of all things? Well, naturally, they are deprived of all. There has never been a person so poor that they did not have a single rag to cover themselves. That is how poor they are in terms of their spiritual condition. Oh, for a person who possesses the riches of the world to recognize themselves as a miserable, poor, and undone individual! This is not an ordinary occurrence, which is why you will find that in Luke 6, Christ opposes the poor to the rich of the world because so few of the wealthy can be convinced of their spiritual poverty.

A poor person, as you know, faces many difficulties that others do not. They endure many miseries. Therefore, a second aspect of this spiritual poverty is for the soul to perceive and be aware of the spiritual evils upon it. It is not only a matter of lacking the Image of God and spiritual life, but it also involves recognizing the misery within the mind, the opposition of the will and heart to God, and the multitude of corruptions in the soul. Oh, the anguish that rests upon me, the darkness of my mind! There is no shortage of vermin that continually surrounds me. Every misery that poor people endure is seen by those who are spiritually poor, just as they are seen within themselves.

Furthermore, the third aspect that renders someone poor is this: Even if they have many miseries, they cannot be extremely poor if they are capable of working for their livelihood. True poverty arises when a person has numerous miseries and is unable to work to sustain themselves. Similarly, although we have lost the Image of God, if we were able to do something to aid ourselves, we would not be so destitute. However, when a person recognizes themselves as utterly miserable and incapable of doing anything to enrich their soul, they are genuinely poor. It is comparable to an individual who has lost everything and subsequently becomes lame, rendering them unable to work or do anything to support themselves. Such a person is genuinely poor—when their labor is lost, along with their possessions. Thus, even if I am unable to labor, if I have friends who can assist me, I am not in utter destitution. In terms of our spiritual condition, who is your friend to offer relief or assistance? Is it God or Christ who should help you? Well, God is a stranger, and you have no connection to Christ in yourself. You must not consider God in terms of who He is in Himself because you are an enemy of God. Scripture declares that we are enemies of God and strangers to the covenant of grace. As such, you are genuinely a poor creature with no one to turn to for help. Even all the angels in heaven cannot aid you, and all the people in the world cannot help you in your wretched condition.

Fifthly, let's consider a scenario where a person has no friend to assist them, and they are unable to work. However, if they possess some form of excellence within them, there is hope that others will recognize their worth. Perhaps they have exceptional abilities, even if they can currently accomplish little due to weakness. This represents our spiritual poverty. We are in a wretched state—devoid of friends, incapable of doing anything—and we lack any worth that would garner God's or the angels' regard. We are inherently worthless creatures, thus further emphasizing our poverty.

Sixthly, even if a person were so impoverished that they cannot do anything presently, there may still be hope if they could potentially do something in the future. However, in our spiritual poverty, we are burdened by debt. As soon as we acquire anything, our creditors may seize it all. Suppose God were to grant us abilities that enable us to perform good deeds. Yet, everything we can do would not suffice to atone for the past. Even if we could perfectly obey God's law now, what would happen to the accumulated debts? God's justice demands satisfaction, and He has decreed that no soul shall be accepted unless His infinite justice is appeased. Now, the soul truly sees its extreme poverty, acknowledging that the debt must be paid in full. If a person has experienced bankruptcy and lost their estate, they may still hope to reach an agreement with their creditors and rebuild their life. Thus, they are not utterly destitute. However, if they realize that the debt must be fully repaid with no possibility of compromise, they would conclude that their life will indeed be impoverished. Those who are spiritually poor recognize this within themselves. They are indebted, and all their efforts can never suffice to satisfy the accumulated debts.

Seventhly, let's imagine a person who receives something to sustain them temporarily, but they must rely on continuous charity. This represents poverty. Similarly, a spiritually poor soul understands that it must live in perpetual dependence. Even if God grants them some ability to act, they require a constant influx of His grace to utilize what they have. They recognize themselves as truly destitute, possessing nothing within themselves. Even if something is bestowed upon them, they do not know how to make use of it without the assistance of another. Thus, the soul perceives its state as dependent on continual grace, needed in every moment. When we consider these seven aspects together, we realize the true extent of our poverty—being deprived of all spiritual good, burdened by spiritual miseries, unable to work, lacking friends, devoid of worth, burdened by debt, and relying on constant grace. Oh, what a destitute creature I am! When a person comprehends and becomes aware of this, they are truly poor in spirit. However, this is not the entirety of the matter.

Next, it is crucial for a person to exhibit behavior that aligns with this state of being poor in spirit. We will discuss this further later.

# SERMON III

## A Description of a person with a poor spirit

"Blessed are the poor in spirit," etc. Matthew 5:3

S everal points have been addressed as a preface to this remarkable sermon by Christ. You have heard its purpose—to reveal where true blessedness resides, a matter in which people are greatly deceived, leading to significant misconceptions. Indeed, what Christ proclaims as blessed is in direct opposition to worldly notions of blessedness. Blessedness entails the enjoyment of the ultimate goal and the highest good attainable for rational beings. It is proper to rational beings—blessed are the poor in spirit.

There are individuals with base and poor spirits who are far from blessedness. Firstly, there are those whose sole focus and aims revolve around money and lowly, unworthy things. They do not aspire to anything higher than satisfying their bodily desires for food, drink, and pleasure. God, Christ, Heaven, Eternity, the Gospel, and the Word are mere concepts to them. However, when presented with money, food, and drink, they consider themselves happy. Such individuals possess a base and poor spirit since their aspirations align with base and poor things. In contrast, the spirits of the Saints are elevated, although they acknowledge their unworthiness to receive even a morsel of bread. They recognize that Heaven and Earth are insufficient to be their portion.

Secondly (to add a few more examples of a person with a base and poor spirit), consider someone who becomes easily discouraged when facing any slight difficulty while embarking on an excellent task. This person has a poor spirit. Some individuals do not even set their aims on any excellent work; they do not possess any thoughts or intentions for excellence. However, if they witness others engaging in valuable work, they may be motivated to initiate a task with inherent excellence. Yet, at the slightest sign of difficulty, they quickly become disheartened, abandon their efforts, and give up. This exemplifies a person with a poor and base spirit, someone hindered either by foreseeing difficulty or discouraged upon encountering any opposition—even if it is a mere fancy. Some individuals who have commenced a religious journey or embarked on a public endeavor for the Church or the Commonwealth become discouraged at the first sign of mockery or opposition and promptly withdraw. These are individuals with poor spirits.

Furthermore, there are those who are selfish, narrow-minded individuals concerned solely with their own welfare. They disregard the well-being of the public and only focus on their personal interests. These individuals also possess poor, base spirits and fail to attain the level of excellence displayed by many pagans.

Lastly, consider those who are easily led astray like fools by every temptation. They succumb foolishly to each insignificant temptation, leading themselves to destruction. Even if a person's conscience convicts them against certain actions, they lack the ability to resist temptation. If their companions invite them to an alehouse or tavern, they cannot resist the allure. A person who is unable to withstand temptation and is easily swayed like a fool towards self-destruction possesses a poor, base spirit. Such individuals lack natural excellence of spirit. Sadly, this is a common occurrence among those who hold themselves in high regard, yet they are individuals with poor and mediocre spirits. This poverty of spirit plaguing many is a curse from God, and it is a heavy curse when such individuals occupy positions of influence. They become obstacles to much good and perpetrate much mischief. It is a wretched curse for kingdoms or countries when, by divine providence, individuals with no spirit of excellence but rather poor, base spirits find themselves in positions of power. Wherever this occurs, it is a grievous affliction, and thus we have reason to pray that those in positions of power possess spirits befitting their responsibilities, rather than being individuals with sordid and low spirits. However, those with poor spirits are not the ones who are blessed as described here.

Who, then? In my previous sermon, I mentioned three or four types of individuals with poor spirits who are blessed. But let's move on to a matter of great importance that is closely related to the words spoken. The poverty of the saints, even godly men who possess grace, is still evident. Now, being poor in spirit means apprehending and being aware of one's spiritual poverty, along with other aspects mentioned earlier. However, even if God has granted grace, there is still a significant level of poverty.

Firstly, the grace one possesses requires continual supply. No Christian can rely on their existing grace without fresh supply. Unlike Adam, who could live off the initial stock of grace he was given, God does not entrust Christians with that stock. It is held by Christ. This is the condition of even the strongest godly individuals—they must daily and continually go to Christ for new supply in order to survive. This is the impoverished state we find ourselves in compared to Adam. It can be likened to a person who was given a stock to trade with but proved to be a poor steward, losing everything and going into debt. Now, their father takes pity on them and sets them up again but places the stock in the hands of a trustworthy friend. The son must give an account and receive money from the friend every day because the father no longer trusts him. This is our condition. In Adam, we received a stock of grace and God enabled us to trade with it for His purposes. But humanity fell, and now the Lord sets up those chosen by Him to engage in godly pursuits. However, God does not trust us with His stock of grace. It is now in Christ, our head, and we must obtain daily supply from Him. This represents the poverty-stricken condition we are in—this spiritual poverty even among the saints.

Secondly, the poverty of the saints lies in the fact that their graces are limited. Even though godly men and women have been bestowed with grace, for the most part, it is so meager that they can scarcely determine if they possess any at all. Their poverty is evident because, despite having grace, they cannot discern whether they truly have it. Although God has given them grace, they often doubt its presence in their hearts. Their grace is like a small spark buried within a pile of embers, requiring much searching before it can be seen. They frequently scrutinize their hearts, examining and seeking that one spark of true grace. It is evident that they are poor.

Thirdly, even the godly are perpetually needy. We usually say that those who are constantly in want and always complaining are poor people. In this sense, all godly individuals are consistently needy, always lacking and frequently expressing their need. While they have reasons to be thankful, they also have cause for self-complaint. They are poor.

Fourthly, their services are of poor quality. When they assess their duties and services, they see how unworthy they are to be presented to the infinitely great and glorious God. They are ashamed of their best services due to their poverty. They recognize the unbecoming nature of offering these services to such a God. They are impoverished in their duties and services.

Fifthly, even at their best, they are weak and impoverished. Their actions are often mixed with corruption and evil, deserving rejection. Their services are indeed feeble. Without the covenant of grace, the righteousness of Christ, and His merits, everything that comes from the best person in the world would be considered filth and dung by the Lord.

Sixthly, the saints are impoverished in that they are easily overcome or unsettled by minor temptations. While they may not be as foolishly led astray by every evil temptation that would ruin them, they are still poor in spirit because even small temptations unsettle and disturb them. It is all too common that when God, through His grace, puts them in a good state, they are quickly thrown off balance by a slight temptation. You must be aware of those times when you had communion with God, but a minor disturbance in the family immediately affected your state of mind. How could the soul that was recently with God and enjoyed such communion be so easily disturbed by trivial matters? This displays a poor spirit. Even the saints are easily thrown off balance and unsettled by minor temptations.

Seventhly, the saints are further impoverished in that they have little ability to help others. Only a few godly individuals have the capacity to do more than simply maintain their own existence, as the saying goes. It is already a struggle for them to survive and maintain peace with God. Being able to be useful to others among whom they live is a rare occurrence. Many godly people exert great effort just to sustain what they already possess, constantly fearing that they may perish one day. They live in constant poverty, thinking, "Even though I have enough to eat today, I don't know where my next meal will come from, or if I'll even have it next week." They believe they will eventually become destitute. Most godly people live in such poverty that they are of little use to others and must struggle to provide for themselves. This is the poverty of spirit. First, we have examined our spiritual poverty in its natural state. Now, let us consider the spiritual poverty of the saints.

You may argue that being poor does not make one blessed; That's true. It is part of their misery to be poor. However, blessed are those who truly understand and are aware of their spiritual poverty, who come to know and deeply feel this poverty. There are few in the world who truly grasp the extent of their poverty. Where can you find a man or woman who comprehends the poverty we are in by nature? And even in terms of poverty regarding the weakness of grace or other aspects, it is often overlooked. But blessed are those who apprehend and are aware of it. Therefore, to understand who the blessed individual is that Christ speaks of, we must consider the behavior and workings of the heart in the sight and awareness of this spiritual poverty, which makes them truly blessed. There are several particulars to briefly go over.

Firstly, a person who is truly poor in spirit regards themselves as vile and insignificant, regardless of any outward excellence they possess. They may have a higher estate or a more comfortable life compared to others, but they consider themselves wretched in their spiritual state. They recognize that there are poor servants of God who, despite living in meager circumstances, honor God more in one day than they do in a month or even a year. They perceive themselves as lower and more insignificant than those who excel in grace. This is an excellent quality—a person who has exceptional abilities yet sees others with greater grace considers themselves lower and more insignificant. Such an individual is poor in spirit and pronounced blessed. Some people are proud of their vices, but the poor in spirit are humble when they see their own graces. While carnal hearts are inflated with what should bring them shame, a gracious heart sees enough in their graces to humble themselves. They find humility in their love, knowledge, and faith—their best qualities. Blessed are those who, in their poverty, possess humility.

Secondly, they do not consider it a great loss if they do not receive the same respect and honor as others. Even if God's providence grants respect, honor, and encouragement to others, they do not envy or trouble themselves over it. They have no reason to expect the same encouragements as others because they understand their lowly nature. They recognize their poverty and do not expect the same treatment. Such individuals are content with what they have and do not seek worldly recognition.

Thirdly, someone who is poor in spirit is one who marvels at every little good they receive, considering it to be significant. They are grateful and full of wonder for every mercy, while also acknowledging that their afflictions are not as severe as they could be. This contrasts with the world, where people are troubled by the magnitude of their afflictions and find their mercies to be insufficient. But a person who is poor in spirit marvels at the abundance of their mercies and the mildness of their afflictions. They do not grumble or complain; instead, they wonder at the tender way in which God deals with them.

Fourthly, a person who is poor in spirit is often in a state of craving. They are prayerful individuals, constantly seeking God's assistance like a beggar seeking alms. True poverty of spirit is often accompanied by a great commitment to prayer. God always listens to their pleas, and He never tires of such beggars. In Proverbs 18:23, it is said that the poor use entreaties, and in Proverbs 10:14, we find similar sentiments. On the other hand, those who can live without prayer, going through day after day without seeking God, have little communication with Him. They have become proud and self-sufficient. But blessed are the poor, those who recognize their need and constantly approach the Throne of Grace. God hears their prayers abundantly.

Fifthly, the poor are the ones who appreciate and extol free grace. They view everything they have as a result of free grace and overlook themselves and their own deeds. While they engage in various duties, they do not dwell on them but instead focus on the grace they have received. They do not rely on anything other than free grace, which they greatly admire. These individuals truly honor free grace.

Sixthly, the person poor in spirit is one who is emptied of themselves. They do not dare to rely on anything within themselves for their spiritual and eternal well-being. Instead, they are delivered from themselves and recognize their own undoing and insufficiency. They are empty of self and every creature, preparing themselves to trust solely in the grace that comes from outside of them, the grace of God revealed in Christ through the Gospel. They do not place the weight of their eternal state on anything within themselves or anything they can accomplish. Rather, they rely solely on the grace of God. This is the behavior of someone poor in spirit who is truly blessed. They commit themselves to God, trusting in Him. Just as the poor in Psalm 10:14 commit themselves to God, emptying themselves and entrusting their souls and ways to Him, not relying on their own wisdom but seeking divine guidance, especially in matters concerning their eternal well-being. In Zephaniah 3:12, it is said that the Lord will leave in their midst an afflicted and poor people who will trust in His name. It is the poor who commit themselves to God and trust in His name. Blessed are these poor individuals who, recognizing their own emptiness, vileness, wickedness, and inability to help themselves, surrender themselves to the grace of God revealed in the Gospel. They commit themselves and all their ways to be guided by God, willingly relying on alms for their present and eternal state. It is in the nature of humans to seek some righteousness of their own, which is why they cannot find comfort. Those with awakened consciences can find no comfort until they are able to do this and that, perform their duties in a particular way, and conquer their corruptions in a specific manner. But God wants you to come before Him as a beggar, with nothing at all, completely stripped, even of your rags. Just as many poor people are proud of their very rags, the hearts of men are proud even if all they have is their civil righteousness. But the Lord will strip you of everything and make you come before Him naked, willing to rely on alms for eternity. It is challenging for a person to rely on alms for a short time, but to rely on alms for the rest of their life is even more difficult. Yet, someone poor in spirit is so aware of their own poverty that they can fully commit themselves to God, content to rely on alms for eternity. Blessed are these poor individuals.

Seventhly, a person who is poor in spirit is willing for God to choose their condition. We often say that beggars cannot be choosers. I am now speaking of someone whose spirit matches their spiritual poverty. If you are spiritually poor, do not think that you have the privilege to choose. No, you must not choose your comforts, abilities, worth, wages, or the timing and means by which God will come to you. Instead, you must leave it all to God. The only thing you should do is look up to God and say, "Lord, have mercy on me." But how and when and to what degree and measure? That is entirely up to God. My soul's desire is that the Lord would have mercy on me. Many reveal that they lack poverty of spirit because when they seek God's mercy and do not experience the immediate comfort they desire, their spirits become discontented, even with God Himself. Such a spirit is not humbled. But blessed are the poor in spirit who prostrate themselves before the Lord, willing to be found by God. They say, "Here I am," and allow God to do with them as He pleases. They completely surrender themselves to His mercy and do not expect to have any say in their desires.

Eighthly, those who are truly poor in spirit look at others whom God has blessed with a remarkable abundance of grace and bless them in their souls. They consider their condition to be elevated. A person poor in spirit resembles poor individuals who, upon seeing those with great houses and substantial incomes, declare them to be truly fortunate. Similarly, those who are poor in spirit do not regard the rich and honorable of this world as the most excellent. Instead, they look upon those who possess the greatest abundance of grace and bless them. They think, "How happy would I be if I could walk with God as they do, if I could conquer my corruptions as they do, if I could value and benefit from the word as they do! How blessed would I consider myself!" This is a commendable poverty of spirit.

Ninthly, blessed are the poor. The poor in spirit are those who are willing to wait. Even if God does not respond according to their desires, they remain content to wait upon Him. God will choose what He will give them, and they are willing to wait. This is mentioned in Zechariah 11:11, where it says, "And it was broken in that day; and so the poor of the flock that waited upon me knew that it was the word of the Lord." Men of means and wealth, when they come to a door for business and cannot obtain what they desire immediately, will leave and not wait. Why? Because they are rich and, in accordance with their wealth, they are proud. On the other hand, a person who is poor and comes seeking alms is content to wait, especially when they know that there is no other door for them to go to at that time. If they believe they may obtain it elsewhere, they will not wait. However, if they come seeking alms and must receive it there or nowhere else, they are then content to wait. Similarly, those who are truly poor in spirit are content to wait at God's gates, knowing that there is no other door where they can receive their alms except at the gates of God. Perhaps you have been seeking God for a month, half a year, or even a year, yet have found nothing. But if you can receive mercy at last, your condition is blessed. This is what a person with a poverty of spirit will say, and they will be content to wait all the days of their life.

Tenthly, someone who is poor has an awe-inspiring respect for God and His word. They are struck with reverential fear of the greatness of God and the authority of His word. This is stated in Isaiah 66, where it says, "To this man will I look, even to him that is poor and of a contrite spirit, and trembleth at my word." The contrite and the poor, those who tremble at God's word, are mentioned together. When they come to the word and hear it explained, they view it as possessing a fearful authority. They consider the word to be above them, and their hearts tremble, fearing that they may not show the proper respect to the word. When a promise is revealed, they tremble, fearful that they may not belong to it. The divine brilliance they see in the word, which is so much greater than themselves, causes their hearts to fear and tremble before the Lord. This is a person who is poor in spirit. It is the opposite of the boldness found in individuals who think they have something to rely on. But one who is poor in spirit sees nothing within themselves that can support them against anything found in the word. No, it is the word that must prevail, regardless of the outcome for their present or eternal state. The word must prevail, and therefore they give an awe-inspiring and reverential respect to the word when they hear it.

Eleventhly, someone who is poor in spirit also possesses a tender heart that melts at the word. Even a small thing from God's word will immediately strike them and cause their hearts to melt. You can observe this in truly poor men and women (not your ordinary vagrants and rogues who feign poverty out of idleness). When you speak to them, you will find a spirit of tenderness within them. Almost anything you say will cause their hearts to melt. Likewise, someone who is poor in spirit has a tender heart towards the word. Even a small thing from

God affects them, and they do not resist the word as others do. They do not have a heart that rebels against the word as others do. When the word comes, their spirits yield to it. When all these qualities mentioned above are combined, it becomes evident who the blessed man or woman is that our Saviour Christ pronounces as such.

Now if you ask why it is that God regards and respects those who are poor in spirit, let me share a word or two.

The primary reason why the Lord holds such regard for them is because this disposition best serves God's great design of glorifying Himself in the world, specifically through the exaltation of His free grace. God desires glory from humanity, but what kind of glory? The magnification of free grace. That is the glory God desires above all else. He desires the glory of His power, wisdom, bounty, and patience, but the glory of His free grace in His Son is what brings Him the greatest delight. Among all dispositions in the world, the poverty of spirit serves God's purpose and design best. Hence, it is not surprising that God highly esteems it.

Secondly, such a disposition makes the soul conformable to Jesus Christ. We know that Christ was willing to be poor. Scripture tells us that Christ emptied Himself, willingly setting aside His glory and taking the form of a servant. When Christ sees a spirit that conforms to His, He regards it and says, "Here is one who is like-minded with Me. I was willing to be poor, and so is this person. I was willing to empty Myself and be anything for the glory of My Father. And here I see a poor creature who is willing to let go of everything they possess and surrender themselves for the glory of My Father and Me." Oh, blessed are these poor individuals! But how few of them can be found in the world! Most often, we find people with spirited hearts—joyful, haughty, proud, pompous, inflexible, rebellious, and bold in their wicked ways. They despise this kind of poverty of spirit. Their hearts are lifted up, and they depend on themselves, standing firm in their own path. It is true, as stated in Isaiah 66, that the Lord who dwells on high in heaven looks upon the poor and contrite. He gazes upon them. But where can God find such objects, such individuals for Him to behold? How few such people exist in the world! The proud and haughty in spirit are cursed. The Scripture speaks of dreadful things against them. However, I am not here to address them, nor am I willing to delay the comfort Christ has for those who are poor in spirit by turning aside to speak to those with proud and haughty spirits. Therefore, I will address the opening of what Christ means when He says they are blessed. Many things could be said to explain their blessedness, but for now, I will share only one Scripture that applies to those who are poor in spirit. To those who are in God's presence today and whose consciences testify that they experience such spiritual workings, I will provide only one text to encourage you until the next day when we will consider what Christ says about you—that yours is the kingdom of heaven. The text is found in Luke 4:18, which says, "The Spirit of the Lord is upon me because he hath anointed me to preach the gospel to the poor; he hath sent me to heal the broken-hearted, to preach deliverance to the captives, and recovering of sight to the blind, to set at liberty them that are bruised, to preach the acceptable year of the Lord." After reading this passage, Christ closed the book. Christ enters the synagogue, and when a book is opened, He finds this passage from Isaiah—a prophecy about Himself. The meaning is this: God the Father anointed Jesus Christ, appointing Him solemnly to the task of coming into the world and preaching good news to the poor in spirit. It is as if God said to His Son, "Son, I have many poor servants in the world who are poor in spirit and aware of their own wretchedness and poverty. Now I appoint You and anoint You to go and proclaim to them the joyful news of salvation. Be sure to comfort them. Speak peace into their lives. Pour oil into their wounds and provide relief and refreshment. I see that they are on the verge of despair, but You must encourage them. I appoint You to this task." Thus, you may declare these individuals blessed when God the Father, from all eternity, sets Jesus Christ apart and appoints Him to this office, ensuring His care for you, your comfort, and your assistance. Christ would be unfaithful in His work if He did not preach comfort to you. This is how much God cares for the poor, even as He seemingly disregards, neglects, scorns, and dismisses the wealthy ones of the world. He sends them away empty-handed. But for those who are poor in spirit, He has given Christ the charge to oversee them. Even if nothing else were said but this, that you have such a promise—that Christ, upon coming into the world, must preach glad tidings to you—it would be an abundance of mercy. In essence, the very essence of the Gospel is to proclaim glad tidings to the poor. Moreover, we will demonstrate that this is a significant aspect implied by "theirs is the kingdom of heaven." It not only means that they will go to heaven when they die but also that the kingdom of heaven, often representing the ministry of the Gospel, belongs in a special way to those who are poor in spirit.

# SERMON IV

## Promises to the Poor in Spirit

Blessed are the poor in spirit, etc. - Matthew 5:3

I will now briefly provide you with a few promises from Scripture for those who are God's poor, and then proceed to the blessedness that Christ proclaims for them—that theirs is the kingdom of Heaven. Now, let's consider the promises for the poor.

First, God thinks about them. Your friends may not think of you. You may be a poor man or woman, and yet godly. You may have wealthy friends who have an abundance and lack nothing, but they do not think of you. However, if you are one of God's poor, as described earlier, God thinks of you (Psalm 40:17).

Secondly, the Lord looks towards the poor with contentment. He not only thinks of you but also keeps His eye on you. When poor men pass by others, they hardly receive a glance. But God's eye is constantly upon the poor for their good. This is evident in Isaiah 66 where it says, "He looketh to the contrite and poor."

Thirdly, He looks upon them without overwhelming their hearts with His dreadfulness. In Isaiah 66, it begins with the declaration, "The heaven is my Throne, and the earth is my footstool," highlighting His glorious nature. A poor soul may think, "How glorious is God! His glory will overwhelm my heart. How can I stand before Him?" Yet, even though Heaven is His Throne and Earth is His footstool, He looks upon those of a poor spirit who tremble at His Word. It's as if He says, "Let no poor soul be intimidated by My glory, for it is for their good and not harmful to them."

The fourth promise is that the Lord prepares His goodness for the poor (Psalm 68:10). Perhaps you do not currently receive the mercy you desire, but God is preparing mercy for you and preparing you to receive it.

Fifthly, the Lord hears the poor. Poor people may petition others without being heard, while the rich can often get their requests granted. However, the Lord hears the poor. There are many Scriptures attesting to this (Psalm 69:33; 109:22; 86). The Psalmist even emphasizes his poverty and neediness as a reason for God to hear his prayers.

Sixthly, the Lord will not allow the expectations of the poor to be frustrated. Poor individuals may wait and wait, only to fail in the end. But if you have a poor spirit, the Lord will not let your expectations be in vain (Psalm 9:18).

Seventhly, the Lord will not forget the poor (Psalm 9:12). Others may forget them, even after granting their petitions, but the Lord will never forget the poor. There are many similar promises made by the Lord to those of a poor spirit. However, let us now focus on one promise in the text that encompasses them all: "Theirs is the kingdom of Heaven." This promise incorporates all other promises into one.

Now, let us explore the depths of these words. From what is apparent at first glance, we can derive three or four observations: Blessed are the poor in spirit, for theirs is the kingdom of Heaven.

Observation 1: God loves to honour those who are willing to humble themselves. God does not say here, "Blessed are the poor, for their sins are pardoned," or "Blessed are the poor, for the promises of the Gospel belong to them." Instead, He declares, "Blessed are the poor, for theirs is the kingdom of Heaven." It is a kingdom that belongs to them. God bestows honour upon the poor. This may seem contradictory, but Christ affirms it. If a poor person were promised, "You shall be provided for. You shall never lack as long as you live," that would be good. However, it goes beyond that—they shall have a kingdom. Christ Himself proclaims to broken hearts who consider themselves unworthy of even the smallest crumb of bread, "Theirs is the kingdom." It is no less than a kingdom prepared for them. Therefore, do not have such a poor spirit as to have low aspirations. Even though you are poor in comparison to yourself, lift up your heart and aim for nothing less than a kingdom. Many poor people would consider themselves happy if they were given a hundred pounds of land per year. But for those who are poor in spirit (as spoken of here), it is not a hundred pounds of land per year or worldly possessions; it is nothing less than the kingdom of Heaven that satisfies their souls. That is the first observation—God loves to honour those who are willing to humble themselves. Other Scriptures align with this, such as Luke 22:28, which says, "Ye are they which have continued with me in my temptations, and I appoint unto you a kingdom." This appointment of a kingdom is a result of their willingness to endure and suffer loss for Christ's sake. However, I won't dwell on these observations, as they are merely points of connection.

Observation 2: True blessedness does not lie in worldly possessions. "Blessed are the poor" does not mean they will receive worldly riches, honour, or promotion. No, blessed are the poor because theirs is the kingdom of Heaven. There is nothing in this world that can make them blessed. True happiness must be sought beyond this world. You do not know what true happiness for an immortal soul entails if you expect to find it here in this world.

Observation 3: The present tense indicates that the saints of God find present comfort, not just future rewards. They do not rely solely on the assurance of future blessings. They find present comfort to sustain their hearts in their poor and humble condition in the eyes of the world. It is often said that good people who are insignificant in the world will be rewarded by God in the future. But what do poor souls have to comfort themselves with in the present? Christ affirms that theirs is the kingdom of Heaven. Taken together, this is enough to uphold your soul in your current state and provide comfort, causing the angels in Heaven to regard you as a blessed creature. The pure in heart are said to see God, but the poor in spirit possess the kingdom of Heaven. Christ uses the present tense because He recognizes that those who are poor in spirit need immediate comfort.

Obs: 4. Heaven is now accessible to the saints, providing true comfort. But they must still look to Heaven in the future. No, they can experience it now.

Luke 17:21 provides a notable Scripture in this regard: "The kingdom of Heaven is within you." It currently resides within the saints. This statement may appear paradoxical, but it is undeniably true. No soul will ever go to Heaven without Heaven first coming down to them. None on Earth will be glorified among saints and angels in Heaven unless it can be said of them that the kingdom of Heaven is within them.

You may ask, "What does that mean?" I will further explain as we consider the main promise: theirs is the kingdom of Heaven. Our main objective is twofold:

First, we must clarify the meaning of this phrase—what Christ intends by the kingdom of Heaven.

Secondly, we need to apply the concept of the kingdom of Heaven to those who are poor in spirit. I won't discuss the overall glory of God extensively, but only as it relates to the poor in spirit. Christ has a specific intention in mind—one that is particularly applicable to the poor in spirit. I will demonstrate this by exploring three types of poor individuals who will find comfort in the treasury of the kingdom of Heaven. This will become clearer as we explain what the kingdom of Heaven is and how it applies to these three groups of poor people.

Let's begin with the first point: the kingdom of Heaven.

The kingdom of Heaven primarily refers to the glory that the saints will experience for all eternity. It represents the state of the Messiah, the king of Heaven. I'm referring to the state of the Messiah after His advent into the world and all the blessings He brings with Him. That is the kingdom of Heaven mentioned here. There are two aspects to consider: the kingdom of God's power, where He rules over the world, and the kingdom given to His Son, the Mediator. It is the latter that is referred to here. Initially, God reigned over the world He created, but sin corrupted His creation, preventing Him from receiving the glory He intended. Consequently, the Lord established a new world—a spiritual and heavenly realm—to glorify Himself in a more spiritual and heavenly manner. He appointed His Son as the King of this new world, a world that the Scripture refers to when it says, "All old things are done away, and all things are become new." This new world begins with the work of grace in the hearts of the saints and culminates in eternal glory. Jesus Christ is the King of this world, while the old world, tainted by sin, is destined for ruin. Before Christ's incarnation, there were glimpses of His glory revealed to the forefathers. However, compared to what was to come after the Messiah's arrival, this kingdom had not yet been established. The administration of things during the time of the Law is not referred to as the kingdom of Heaven. The Jews eagerly awaited the Messiah's kingdom—the very kingdom of Heaven mentioned in this text. As the Messiah's advent drew near, He sent John the Baptist as a forerunner to announce His coming and the imminent arrival of a new kingdom in the world. Therefore, John declared, "Repent, for the kingdom of heaven is at hand." He did not mean, "Repent, for you will go to Heaven and be glorified with God." Instead, it was as if he said, "Oh, now the kingdom of the Messiah is near. Within a few months, Jesus Christ will appear as King, and the Gospel will be made clearer to you. Repent, therefore, and turn away from your wickedness so that you may partake in the blessings of the Messiah's kingdom when it is established." It is also mentioned that since the time of John the Baptist, the kingdom of heaven suffers violence. This confirms that the kingdom of Heaven existed during John's time. The meaning behind this statement is that John, as the herald of this kingdom, ignited a fervent desire for it within people's hearts. Even though the kingdom had not yet been fully established, their hearts burned with zeal. They resolved to strive for it with determination, overcoming all difficulties and opposition. They were determined to have their share in the blessings of the Messiah's kingdom, no matter the cost. During that time, the kingdom of Heaven suffered violence. John Baptist merely spoke of that kingdom, yet people's hearts blazed with passion for it. Now, where are our hearts when a Gospel minister not only declares that the kingdom of Heaven is near but that it has come? This King has come, ascended, triumphed in Heaven, sits at the right hand of the Father, and governs and rules His Church. When we call upon people to repent, for the kingdom of Heaven is at hand, it should also suffer violence. It is a blessed thing when it can be said that Heaven has suffered violence since the time of a particular minister. Previously, people's hearts were detached, concerned only with worldly matters—accumulating wealth, eating, drinking, and entertainment. However, upon hearing the preaching of the kingdom of Heaven, this kingdom of Heaven suffers violence. The zealous take hold of it by force. This kingdom of Heaven represents the state of the Gospel. It is in this sense that Christ said, "Allow little children to come to me, for to them belongs the kingdom of

Heaven." He did not mean that only some of them will go to Heaven. Rather, He meant that just as in the time of the Law, He included not only believers but also their children in the privileges of that administration and the blessings it contained. Therefore, do not think that now, as I establish a new kingdom, I will accept believers but reject their children. No, allow them to come to me, for the kingdom of Heaven belongs to them. They are members of this kingdom I am establishing, just as they were members of the Jewish Church and beneficiaries of its administration. They will likewise be members and participants in the state I am currently establishing, along with its privileges. Therefore, let them not be excluded from this Gospel state any more than they were excluded from the state of the Law and its benefits. This interpretation of the text is significant, especially for encouraging believing parents regarding their children and their participation in the sacrament of baptism.

Sometimes, the term "kingdom of Heaven" is used to refer to specific aspects of the Gospel, such as the preaching of it. For example, the parable of the sower describes the kingdom of Heaven as a man sowing his seed, representing the administration of the Gospel through preaching. This preaching of the Gospel is one element within the broader concept of the kingdom of Heaven. At other times, the kingdom of Heaven refers to the transformative work of the Gospel in a person's heart. For instance, the kingdom of Heaven is compared to a mustard seed, symbolizing the powerful effect of the Gospel in growing from something small to something great. This is the essence of the kingdom of Heaven—the state of the Messiah. Therefore, when Christ says, "Blessed are the poor in spirit," He is proclaiming the blessedness that belongs to those who embody the qualities of the Messiah's state and experience the blessings associated with it.

Furthermore, the kingdom of Heaven is sometimes used to refer to the Church and its privileges. For instance, Jesus said, "I will give you the keys of the kingdom of Heaven," emphasizing the significant role of the Church and its privileges within the kingdom of Heaven. The Church's privileges, administrations, and ordinances are blessings within the kingdom of Heaven, and those who are poor in spirit will partake in all these blessings.

Now, let's explore why it is called the kingdom of Heaven.

Firstly, it is called the kingdom of Heaven because Christ, the King, originates from Heaven.

Secondly, it is distinct from and opposed to the kingdoms of the world. It is not of this world, as Christ Himself declared.

Thirdly, it is called the kingdom of Heaven because Christ currently reigns from Heaven.

Fourthly, the mode of His governance is spiritual and heavenly, rather than external.

Fifthly, it will ultimately lead both the soul and body to Heaven. Therefore, the entire administration of the Messiah's rule and governance is referred to as the kingdom of Heaven.

Christ, as the King, bestows immense blessings within this kingdom. Firstly, it is Christ the Mediator who gives you laws. If you are under the Gospel, having become a subject of Christ through faith, He gives you laws directly. The Jews received their laws (the Ten Commandments) through the mediation of Moses. However, you receive your laws for guidance and righteous living directly from Jesus Christ. Although what Moses required of people in the past is the same as what Jesus Christ now commands, receiving the laws from a Mediator has its advantages. It is true that Moses was a type of Christ even in this aspect, but you receive the laws more fully from the Mediator, Jesus Christ. Thus, your laws for righteous living come directly from Him. This is a point of contention concerning the law, but it is of little edification. The debate revolves around whether we receive our laws from Moses or Christ. Those who speak against the law, in a dispute, can only argue that we are freed from the law as given by Moses. However, this argument is irrelevant because whether we have the law from Moses or not, we are bound by the same obligations that were imposed on the people in the time of the law. It is insignificant whether it comes from Moses or Christ; the fact remains that we have the law and are bound by it with the same strength, provided it comes from the hands of Christ. We can be satisfied in knowing that we have the moral laws of justice and equity in this kingdom of Heaven. Indeed, they are given in a different manner by the Mediator, with greater strictness, spirituality, and expansion. As our King later states in this chapter, He did not come to destroy the law but to fulfill it, to open it up. He says, "You have heard that it was said, 'You shall not commit adultery.' But I say to you that everyone who looks at a woman with lustful intent has already committed adultery with her in his heart." Christ expounds upon the law and elevates its requirements. There is great comfort in having your law come from Jesus Christ. Additionally, you can take comfort in knowing that He will not be so exacting as to demand all the penalties prescribed by the law for its violation, as was required under Moses' administration. During Moses' time, specific penalties were imposed for breaking the law. However, God now reveals more grace, not strictly enforcing the curses upon every transgression. Moses delivered the law with the understanding that the people would consider themselves cursed if they transgressed any part of it. Although Christ's redemptive work was partly revealed to aid believers during that time, it remained largely unknown. As a result, the majority of people regarded themselves as accursed if they violated any aspect of the law. In the kingdom of Heaven, there is the blessedness of having laws given to you by someone who loves you more than His own life. He willingly laid down His life for you, the very person who receives the law. It is a tremendous comfort to have laws given by someone who loves you so dearly. Moreover, He is the Judge of the law and will bear all the penalties for its violation. He loves you more than His own life. Such knowledge brings great comfort.

The second aspect of the blessedness of the kingdom of Heaven is that Jesus Christ now reigns in the hearts of His saints through His Word and Spirit more fully than in the times of the Law or in any other conceivable way. It is true that there was a general work of God on the hearts of the heathens in terms of their moral virtues, but there was no ruling of their hearts by the Scepter and Spirit of Jesus Christ the Mediator. Even though some believers in the time of the Law experienced the sanctifying work of the Spirit to a certain degree, it was generally meager and insufficient compared to the pouring out of the Spirit in abundance within this kingdom. This fuller, clearer, more powerful, and excellent outpouring of the Spirit was reserved for the coming of the Messiah, who established His spiritual government in the hearts of His people. This is a concept that we struggle to grasp. We understand that certain duties are required of us and we attempt to fulfill them, but we fail to recognize Jesus Christ exercising His authority in our hearts, enabling us to fulfill His requirements as stated in His Word.

Thirdly, all dealings between God and believers take place within this kingdom and do not extend beyond it. What I mean by this is that when you have offended God and He has something to say to you regarding your transgression, the matter should not be taken to the Court of strict Justice. No, it must remain within this kingdom—the kingdom of the Messiah. It is a privilege of someone living in a particular kingdom that they cannot be summoned to another kingdom to answer for their fault. If they were in another kingdom, they might face severe consequences, but within this kingdom, the laws are more favorable, providing comfort. Thus, if you, as a believer, were under the kingdom of God's power, merely acknowledging Him as the Creator of Heaven and Earth and ruling over the world, any offense on your part would result in eternal death. This fate awaits all individuals who are solely under the kingdom of God's power. In this context, they are considered as God's creatures, subject to His power and dealt with accordingly. Every offense is met with exact justice, resulting in punishment, even death. However, once a believer enters into the kingdom of the Messiah, they enjoy other privileges. When a believer offends, they do not stand trial in that Court—specifically, the kingdom of God's power. Instead, they are to answer before the Court of Jesus Christ, with Christ serving as the Judge. Christ deals with believers through His administration, which He received from the Father. Thus, believers can confidently stand before God, despite their offenses and weaknesses, knowing that all transactions occur within this kingdom and not outside it. This brings great comfort to those who are poor in spirit. Indeed, blessed are the poor in spirit, for the kingdom of Heaven is theirs. The kingdom of Heaven—the kingdom of the Gospel—belongs to them. This is the blessedness they receive through the kingdom of the Gospel—that all dealings between God and them occur within this kingdom. Likewise, all of God's dealings with them happen through the Messiah. Everything they offer to God is through the Messiah. Therefore, in their relationship with God, they have nothing to do apart from their King. Their King undertakes all matters concerning them in their relationship with God. If you have entered into this kingdom, your King—Jesus Christ, who is both God and man—has taken responsibility for all things pertaining to you in your relationship with God. Thus, you are blessed because the kingdom of Heaven belongs to you.

Consequently, all the mercies that come from God are delivered through Christ to you. They reach you through the means of this King, and it is through

His right that you possess them. For instance, when there is a matter to be resolved between two kingdoms, the transactions occur between the two Kings. Ordinary individuals do not engage in such transactions between kingdoms. Similarly, there are, in a sense, two kingdoms—the kingdom of God as the Creator and the kingdom of the Messiah. All the things we receive from the kingdom of God's power as the Creator are mediated by Jesus Christ. We receive them through the right of our King. Moreover, if afflictions befall us due to our offenses or sins against the work of creation, and we deserve punishment, God as the Creator does not directly afflict believers. Instead, He entrusts the task of correction to Christ. The afflictions that occur within this kingdom are of a different nature than the afflictions inflicted upon those who are under the kingdom of God's power. The latter are the result of vengeful wrath, while the former are administered by Christ the Mediator and delivered in a different manner. Therefore, being within this kingdom is abundant with blessedness.

Thirdly, being in this kingdom provides you with protection. Even if you are poor and insignificant in yourself, Jesus Christ, the Son of God, undertakes to protect you, deliver you from evil, and supply all your needs. This is the duty of a King, and those who are subjects in a kingdom greatly benefit from the protection offered by their ruler. To be in a kingdom and denied its protection would be a great misery. However, in the kingdom of Christ, there is no denial of protection for any of His subjects. He protects them all and provides for every need within His kingdom. While earthly kings may neglect the protection of their subjects, if they were to deny protection, there might be other means for individuals to protect themselves. Yet, the saints in the kingdom of Christ have no other source of protection but their King.

Fourthly, Christ takes care of all the provisions necessary for every individual soul. As a King, He doesn't oversee every household, but He does provide for each soul.

Fifthly, in this kingdom, Christ undertakes to conquer all the enemies that oppose your spiritual and eternal well-being. Christ is your King, and He will not relinquish His power or faithfulness. Therefore, He will subdue your enemies—sin, death, the devil, and all adversaries of the Church will eventually be defeated.

Sixthly, as a King, Christ establishes ordinances, imparts gifts, and adminis-
ters various ministries. All the ordinances, gifts, and ministries of the Church are
given by Jesus Christ as its King, and as one who is poor in spirit, you have the
right to partake in them. It is not only those who possess an elevated level of grace
who are entitled to participate in the ordinances. Even if you are merely aware
of your spiritual poverty, you have the right to partake in all the ordinances.
However, while you have the right, you must also engage with the ordinances
in a manner appropriate to them. All the gifts of the saints belong to you, and
you benefit from all the ministries within this kingdom.

Seventhly, the entire world is brought under the subjection of this kingdom.
The kingdom of the Father—the kingdom of power through which the Lord
rules over the created world and upholds it through providence—is all aligned
with and supports the kingdom of the Messiah. Understanding this is of great
significance, for it reveals that every act of God in ordering heaven and earth
is directed towards advancing the kingdom of the Messiah and promoting the
spiritual well-being of those within this kingdom. Therefore, blessed are you,
for the kingdom of Heaven belongs to you.

Eighthly and lastly, this kingdom will ultimately allow you to reign with
Christ. To some extent, you already share in Christ's reign. All the subjects
of Christ's kingdom are made kings and priests to God. Furthermore, in a
glorious manner, they will be granted the opportunity to reign with Christ. In
Revelation 3:21, it is stated: "To him who overcomes I will grant to sit with
Me on My throne, as I also overcame and sat down with My Father on His
throne." This verse is difficult to understand, but it clearly depicts two thrones
mentioned by Christ—His Father's throne and His own. Christ affirms that He
sits with the Father, ruling together with Him. However, Christ also promises
that believers will be granted the privilege of sitting on His throne, just as He sits
on His Father's throne. There is a specific throne that belongs to Jesus Christ,
and all the saints will sit with Him upon it. This concept is also mentioned
in other Scriptures, such as Matthew 19:28 and Luke 22:30, where Christ
tells His disciples, who have shared in His temptations, that they will sit with
Him, judging the twelve tribes of Israel. They will also partake in His kingdom,
sharing meals and fellowship with Him. These Scriptures seem to imply a special
and glorious condition that the saints will eventually experience before fully

inheriting the highest heavenly glory. They will sit on the Lord Christ's throne and participate in judging. While the highest heavens do not require a judging throne, there will be a time for judging the wicked and ungodly. The saints will reign with Christ in a glorious manner, and ultimately, they will enter Heaven itself and possess all the glory that Christ has obtained through His sacrifice. Therefore, even though you currently deny yourself the abundance of worldly wealth and are willing to endure the hardships, contempt, and troubles associated with a lowly state, remember that it is for My sake that you embrace poverty. Perhaps you could attain worldly riches like others, but be content with a humble condition for the sake of the things of this world. Trust in Me, for there is a kingdom reserved for you—the kingdom of Heaven. Although this kingdom may currently appear poor, just like you are poor in spirit, it is a humble and seemingly insignificant kingdom. Its glory is spiritual and can only be perceived with a spiritual eye, not a carnal one. However, as My chosen ones, those who have received My Spirit, you can comprehend the excellence of this kingdom and the numerous privileges it entails. Therefore, strive to endure your lowly condition quietly. Even though you may be lacking in abilities and plagued by weaknesses, take comfort in the fact that you are among those who sit with the Messiah. The good of the Gospel belongs to you, and the Father, Son, and Spirit have grand intentions to elevate this glorious kingdom to its pinnacle. It has already begun within your souls, and you will undoubtedly experience its fulfillment in the fullness of its glory. In Daniel 7:24, this kingdom is referred to as the kingdom of the saints that will prevail in the world. Indeed, there is a kingdom of Christ that will prevail in the world, regardless of any opposition it faces. Earthly kings may rage, and the nations may devise futile plans, but the Lord will establish His King on His holy hill, and the saints within this kingdom of Christ will ultimately prevail in the world. This kingdom will undoubtedly progress. My brethren, the Scriptures speak of the good tidings of the kingdom. The few points I have discussed here are some of the good tidings associated with the kingdom of Heaven. In Acts 1:3, after Christ's resurrection, we learn that He spent forty days with His disciples. You may wonder, "What did Christ do during those forty days?" We have read about many things Christ did before His death, but what do we know about those forty days? Scripture tells us that He spoke to them about the kingdom of Heaven. During that time,

Christ discussed the very subject I am speaking to you about now. He informed them of the blessed and glorious kingdom of the Messiah they were destined for. Although they would be impoverished, despised, and considered nobodies in the world, they were members of that kingdom and enjoyed its privileges. Christ would also make them instrumental in advancing that glorious kingdom. Thus, He taught them about the ordinances, laws, and privileges associated with the kingdom. Consequently, we find that after Christ's resurrection and the outpouring of the Holy Spirit upon their hearts, the disciples no longer fantasized about an earthly kingdom. They abandoned such thoughts and began to understand the true meaning of the Messiah's kingdom, which Christ preached to them during those forty days before His Ascension. These are the key points I have endeavored to present to you regarding the kingdom of Heaven, which is described as the portion of those who are poor in spirit. You may exclaim, "These are indeed blessed things!" However, the task now is to apply them. For the time being, remember what has been said. Understand the significance of the Scripture that urges you to "seek first the kingdom of heaven and its righteousness, and all these things shall be added to you." I have provided a brief overview of the glory of the kingdom of Heaven. Although I have not addressed the felicity of the saints after the day of Judgment, I have provided enough for you to set your hearts on pursuing the kingdom of Heaven. You who have pursued the world and believed that you would be blessed if you could live luxuriously and enjoy a comfortable income, recognize that there is a kingdom that concerns you. As far as we know, this kingdom applies to every soul present here. Therefore, above all else pursue that kingdom so that you may obtain your portion in it.

# SERMON V

## Comfort for the Poor in Spirit

"Blessed are the poor in spirit, for theirs is the kingdom of heaven." - Matthew 5:3

As you may recall, we are currently discussing the first blessedness attributed to those who are poor in spirit. We have extensively covered the subject of this blessedness, examining who the poor are according to Scripture, and emphasizing that they are indeed blessed.

However, we have now reached the point where we explore the blessedness pronounced by Christ upon them: "theirs is the kingdom of heaven." We made several observations from the context, "Blessed are the poor, for theirs is the kingdom of heaven." Christ does not say, "Blessed are the poor, for God will show them mercy," but rather, "theirs is the kingdom of heaven." It is a fitting blessing for the grace that shines most prominently in them. Christ uplifts them from their poverty of spirit and crowns them with the glory of a kingdom—the kingdom of heaven. Yet it is not just any kingdom; it is the kingdom of heaven. In our previous discussion, we established that worldly possessions cannot bring true blessedness; it must be something from the kingdom of heaven. It is noteworthy that Christ does not say, "the kingdom of heaven will be theirs," as

He says of others, such as "Blessed are the pure in heart, for they shall see God." No, He declares, "theirs is the kingdom of heaven."

Christ assures the poor that they cannot wait, for they have immediate needs. He promises not only what they will have after death, but a kingdom that they can possess in the present—"theirs is the kingdom of heaven."

We have begun to explore the nature of this kingdom of heaven and the various meanings of the term "kingdom" in Scripture. However, the main purpose of Christ's words here is to convey the state of the Messiah and the blessings He would bring into the world through His administration. That is the kingdom of heaven referred to in this context. I do not believe Christ intended to focus solely on going to heaven and experiencing glory after death, although that is one aspect among many. His aim here is to emphasize that those who are poor in spirit are blessed because they partake in the present blessedness of God's people during the time of the Messiah's arrival. Therefore, I do not intend to discuss the glory of heaven in this sermon. Any discussion on that matter will be more relevant to verse 10: "Blessed are those who are persecuted for righteousness' sake, for theirs is the kingdom of heaven." For now, I will focus solely on the blessed state of those who are poor in spirit, which involves enjoying the good things in the Messiah's era. That is the meaning of the Scripture that calls for repentance because "the kingdom of heaven is at hand." It is an invitation to turn away from sinful ways and not indulge in our desires as we used to. Repent, for Jesus Christ has come into the world, bringing great glory with Him. Since I aim to conclude within this session, I will skip over our previous discussion and proceed to what remains. Moreover, what remains will build upon some of the points we previously explored concerning the kingdom of heaven. This leads us to the following:

What comfort can be derived from considering the Messiah's arrival in the world? What encouragement does it bring to those who are poor in spirit, and how do they specifically find happiness? This is the focus of this sermon and the aim of Christ's message. Therefore, to further elaborate on this, I will present the following three points.

Firstly, let us consider the comfort for those who are outwardly poor—those who have spirits that align with their outward conditions, who are godly in their poverty, and willingly submit to God in their humble state. What encouragement can they find from the Messiah's state and the kingdom of heaven? I believe Christ intended to speak comforting words to such godly, impoverished individuals, as we can see in Luke 6, where Christ contrasts the rich in this world with the poor in spirit. Therefore, in this scripture, Christ undoubtedly aims to bring comfort to the godly poor.

Secondly, let us consider those who are poor in abilities and gifts, men and women of meager talents who are godly and humbly acknowledge their limited capabilities. What good can they derive from the kingdom of heaven, and what comfort can they find in it?

Thirdly, let us consider those who are poor in grace, those who recognize their spiritual poverty. What blessedness do they receive from the kingdom of heaven?

Firstly, let us address those who are outwardly poor—godly poor individuals. I am speaking directly to you, and I truly believe that Christ is also addressing you. Likewise, He desires His ministers to speak comforting words to you. You are individuals whose outward circumstances have left you lowly and humble. However, as you willingly submit to God's plan for your lives and honor Him in your poverty without complaint, Jesus Christ pronounces you blessed today. He declares that the kingdom of heaven belongs to you. In other words, do not be disheartened by your lowly status in this world, for your spirits align with the condition God has placed you in. The Lord has appointed a kingdom for you—the kingdom of heaven. Although you may not be esteemed in this world, you possess a great deal within the kingdom of heaven.

Now, let us consider several aspects of being poor in this world yet godly. In Luke 12:29-31, Christ addresses those who are outwardly poor in relation to the kingdom of heaven. He advises them, "And do not seek what you are to eat and what you are to drink, nor be worried. For all the nations of the world seek after these things, and your Father knows that you need them. Instead, seek his kingdom, and these things will be added to you." He further assures them, "Fear not, little flock, for it is your Father's good pleasure to give you the kingdom." When contemplating what to eat and drink, the thoughts of many poor individuals—particularly the godly poor—revolve around how they will provide for their families. However, Christ instructs them not to be anxious about such matters. Even those to whom Christ spoke faced severe hardships, perhaps comparable to the struggles encountered by the godly poor who hear me today. Yet, they were urged not to worry. Why should they not be concerned about what they would eat and drink? Because, as Christ states, "all these things the nations of the world seek after, and your Father knows that you need them." Instead, they should seek the kingdom of God, and everything necessary for their well-being would be provided. Christ emphasizes, "Fear not, little flock, for it is your Father's good pleasure to give you the kingdom." Therefore, focus on the kingdom of Jesus Christ, for if you possess that, you have an abundance. Though you may be a small flock, it brings joy to your Father to bestow a kingdom upon you. Consequently, the awareness that your Father has appointed a kingdom for you and is giving you that kingdom should bring solace to your hearts despite the hardships you face in your impoverished state.

Now, let us consider specific aspects that bring comfort to those who are outwardly poor but godly. Firstly, reflect on the fact that the King of the kingdom of heaven, Jesus Christ Himself, experienced poverty. You may speak of the kingdom of heaven, but in the meantime, we endure difficulties in this world. However, remember that you are not enduring greater hardships in this world than the King of the kingdom you have been translated into. Jesus Christ Himself, the great Prince and King of Heaven, was poor in this world. Therefore, the realization that your King shares the same humble circumstances and experiences as you should be a tremendous source of support. It is akin to a general saying to his soldiers, "Continue, even if all you have to drink is water. Remember, you drink the same as your general." Likewise, Christ can rightfully say to you, the poor in spirit, "Why are you dismayed by your poverty? Am I not poorer than you? Perhaps you have a modest house, but consider what is said of Christ: 'Foxes have holes, and birds of the air have nests, but the Son of Man has nowhere to lay his head.'" Christ did not even have a home to call His own. Your diet may seem humble and modest, lacking the bountiful dishes enjoyed by others. In John 21:5, after His resurrection and when His suffering for sin had ended, Christ came to His disciples and asked, "Children, do you have any fish?" He did not inquire about the specific types of dishes they possessed, but simply whether they had anything at all. This emphasizes Christ's contentment with whatever was available. Additionally, 2 Corinthians 8:9 tells us that "though he was rich, yet for your sake he became poor, so that you by his poverty might become rich." There is no godly person in Scripture who was in a poorer condition than Christ, in many respects. Therefore, take comfort in the knowledge that your King, both then and now, willingly subjected Himself to a state of poverty. This should alleviate any murmuring thoughts regarding your own impoverished condition. Remember, the kingdom of heaven is yours. If you truly comprehend the meaning of the kingdom of heaven and consider who the King of this kingdom is, understanding that His own state was marked by poverty, it will dispel any discontentment you may feel towards your humble circumstances. My kingdom is not of this world, says Christ. So, even if you lack the worldly riches, know that Christ Himself did not possess them either.

But secondly, consider this: Christ's poverty was to sanctify your poverty. Merely considering that our Captain or King suffers alongside us is something, but no poverty or suffering of a King or Captain can remove the curse of his subjects' sufferings. However, the poverty of Jesus Christ, the Heir of this kingdom, was meant to take away the curse of your poverty and sanctify it. When you hear that He was poor in this world, you can exercise your faith, saying, "Lord, this was to sanctify my poverty." Indeed, poverty itself is a curse, but for the godly, the curse is removed through the poverty of Jesus Christ. Just as the death of Jesus Christ sanctified the death of the godly, removing the sting of death, so too are their poverty and afflictions sanctified by the poverty and afflictions endured by Christ Himself. Therefore, in this kingdom, you can find comfort and goodness.

Thirdly, this kingdom of heaven is primarily comprised of the poor in the world. The mere consideration of this fact is immensely helpful for those who are outwardly poor. I admit that there are occasions when rich individuals are also subjects of this kingdom, as mentioned in Mark 15:43, where it is said that an honorable counselor waited for the kingdom of God. Great men may become subjects, but ordinarily it is the poor who are the subjects of this kingdom.

Then fourthly, the Lord has orchestrated things in such a way that the significant events in this kingdom of heaven have been carried out by the lowly and poor, not by the great ones of the world. The Lord Christ has not relied heavily on the great ones of the world to advance His kingdom.

From this, it follows in the fifth place that poverty is not a hindrance to attaining the highest position in this kingdom of heaven. While poverty may hinder one from attaining high positions of honor in a worldly kingdom, a poor person in the kingdom of heaven can reach the same high degree as the richest individual. Therefore, when choosing officers for the church, there should be no consideration of a person's wealth. I acknowledge that when selecting officers for the state, a poor person, though possibly wiser than someone of means, may not be the ideal choice, as it is not suitable for someone without means to have control over others' estates. However, when it comes to the kingdom of heaven, where matters concern solely spiritual power and dealing with consciences rather than estates or outward liberty, the selection of officers should not be influenced by wealth. The kingdom of heaven is not concerned with worldly possessions or social status, but solely with dealing with individuals' consciences in regard to their spiritual well-being and their path to heaven. Therefore, in the church, considerations of a person's wealth should not outweigh the slightest trace of godliness and understanding in matters of the kingdom of heaven. It is indeed a carnal approach to focus on the chief of the parish without considering their godliness or lack thereof. If the chief possesses the same godliness and understanding as others, then they should be chosen as an officer. However, it is wrong to allow wealth to be the deciding factor when there is a lack of godliness and understanding. Such an approach only serves to align the state of the kingdom of heaven with the world. In contrast, those who are poor in this kingdom are just as capable of reaching high positions as anyone else. This is a great source of help and comfort for the godly poor who partake in the kingdom of heaven, as they enjoy all the privileges associated with this kingdom. Although they may not have the privileges of a worldly kingdom in terms of wealth and status, they can fully partake in the privileges of the kingdom of heaven.

Sixthly, even those who are outwardly poor but godly have a rightful claim to all things in this world as far as it is good for them. It is said of Abraham in Romans 4:13 that he was the heir of the world. This is spoken of Abraham as a believer, and every believer is a child of Abraham and therefore inherits Abraham's blessings. Hence, every believer is an heir of the world. All things belong to you, and you belong to Christ, and Christ belongs to God. You may wonder why, if believers have the right to all things, they do not possess them. The answer lies in their condition; they are not in a state that allows for possession.

However, all things work for their good in one way or another. Just as all the kingdoms of the world are subject to Jesus Christ and are surrendered to Him for the advancement of His kingdom, all things in the world are surrendered to the saints for their benefit, as they partake in the kingdom of heaven.

Seventhly, in this kingdom, there are spiritual riches that can fully compensate and are infinitely superior to all outward riches. You may think that if the state were to provide you with a certain amount, you would be a happy person. However, valuing the riches of the world more than the things of the kingdom of heaven is a mark of a carnal heart. The things of the kingdom of heaven make you rich in faith, holiness, promises, your relationship with God and Christ, and the enjoyment of the Holy Spirit and His gifts and graces. These things are abundantly shared within the kingdom of the Messiah, even more so than in the times of the Law. Back then, being poor was a greater evil because spiritual riches were not as abundantly communicated by God. Instead, those spiritual riches were reserved for the coming of the Messiah. Consequently, God was more lenient with the outward estates of individuals during the times of the Law. If you had lived during the times of the Law, it is likely that you would not have been as poor. However, on the other hand, it is unlikely that you would have had the same measure of grace, the same manifestations of God to your soul, as you have now. Therefore, it is well for you to be in the kingdom of heaven, where there is such abundant communication of spiritual riches.

Eigthly, from all these considerations, it follows that the great temptations that trouble those who are poor and godly can be alleviated through the contemplation of the blessings of the kingdom. What are these temptations, you may ask? There are three significant temptations that afflict those who are poor and godly, temptations that are not as troubling for those who possess wealth.

Firstly, I am afraid that God is against me and does not bless me in anything I undertake. This fear and bondage have already been addressed.

The second temptation is feeling despised due to being in a poor condition. No, you are a king. You have been translated into the kingdom of His dear Son and have a share in His kingdom. Therefore, do not listen to the temptation that arises from contempt and being despised. Does the world not regard you? The Lord God highly regards you, for He has given you a kingdom.

Then there is a third temptation: feeling useless in the world. However, this text will address that temptation. The kingdom is yours, and as you have heard, the Lord Christ advances His kingdom through the poor. So do not be troubled by your perceived uselessness in the world. This is the eighth support for those who are outwardly poor and humble in spirit, in line with their poverty.

The ninth support is this: eventually, even the poor and godly will possess all things. I find scripture to support this in Revelation 21:7. Some may doubt such a claim, but by comparing different passages, it becomes clear that it does not refer to the glory in the highest heaven, but to another glory. "He who overcomes will inherit all things, and I will be his God, and he shall be my son." There will come a time when they will possess everything, and they will certainly receive abundant honor. In Zechariah 9:16, there is an excellent expression of the honor God will bestow upon His saints when speaking of the kingdom of Christ. The Lord their God will save them in that day, and they will be as precious stones in a crown, lifted up as an ensign upon His land. This promise applies to all the saints. There is a coming time when they, who may currently be despised and clothed in rags, will shine as brightly as the sun. Just as you see the sun in the sky, your poverty-stricken body, which lacks food and proper clothing, will soon shine as brightly as the sun in the firmament. Concerning possession of worldly things, consider Matthew 19:29: "And every one that hath forsaken houses, or brethren, or sisters, or father, or mother, or wife, or children, or lands, for my name's sake, shall receive an hundredfold, and shall inherit everlasting life." The passage does not speak solely of being rewarded in heaven; it goes beyond that. In addition to everlasting life, they shall receive a hundredfold. You may argue that in another Gospel, the hundredfold is mentioned alongside persecution, as in Mark 10:30. However, if you carefully examine the promise, you will find it even more extensive: "He shall receive an hundredfold now in this time, houses, and brethren, and sisters, and mothers, and children, and lands." You may say that receiving a hundredfold means receiving grace worth a hundred times the value of their lands. Yet, you see that the Holy Spirit mentions specific things like houses and lands. Nevertheless, there is a passage that seems to contradict this. It states that they will receive houses and lands (and the like) in this time, but with persecution, and in the world to come, eternal life. It mentions persecution, so how can these two ideas coexist? To answer that, I genuinely believe that this is a correct interpretation: the phrase "with persecution" in your book is translated from the Greek word "meta," which does not always mean "with" but can also mean "after." There are various instances where "meta" signifies "after" rather than "with." For example, in Mark 8:31, it is translated as "after three days, He shall rise again." Therefore, you can use the same justification to translate the other phrase, that they shall receive houses and lands a hundredfold after enduring persecution. Determining how, when, and in what manner the Lord will fulfill this is challenging. The fulfillment of prophecies often serves as the best interpretation of them. However, it seems evident to me that the Scripture indicates that it is part of the kingdom of Jesus Christ, which He will eventually bring His people to enjoy. Whatever good things are to be enjoyed here will be part of the reward for His people. This reward is bestowed in a spiritual and holy way, not in a sensual way as some may have dreamed. This is the blessing for those who are poor in their outward circumstances and possess spirits in harmony with their condition.

Now, there are many who are troubled by their limited abilities. However, if they possess spirits that are in harmony with their abilities and are willing to honor God with them, the kingdom of heaven also belongs to them. But for now, I will leave them aside and address the third group: those who are poor in grace.

Firstly, if you have only a small amount of grace and feel poor and insignificant, do not be troubled. You are blessed because, first and foremost, you have been delivered from the power of darkness and translated into the kingdom of heaven. As stated in Colossians 1:13, "He has delivered us from the power of darkness and conveyed us into the kingdom of the Son of His love." Though there may be much darkness in your mind, the power of darkness has been taken away, and you have been brought into the kingdom of God's dear Son. In Matthew 12:28, Jesus states that the casting out of demons is a result of the kingdom of God coming. Before the coming of the Messiah, demons had dominion over people. But now, the kingdom of heaven has come to your soul, and the devil can no longer reign over you. The devil may still trouble you when you are melancholic or in darkness, but all those who possess even the smallest amount of grace, no matter how poor they may be, have the kingdom of heaven.

This means that the power of the devil has been cast out, and you will never be under the dominion of darkness again.

Secondly, the limited abilities of anyone cannot hinder them from understanding the highest things in the kingdom of heaven. It does not depend on one's abilities. In fact, those with limited abilities are often chosen to confound the wisdom of the world. Even those with humble abilities may have a greater understanding of the things of the kingdom of heaven than the greatest scholars in the world.

Thirdly, a remarkable comfort for those who are aware of their small measure of grace is that, being in the kingdom of heaven, they are no longer required to answer for their wrongdoings in the court of divine justice. If you were in the kingdom of God's power solely as the Creator, you would have to answer for all your offenses in the court of God's justice. However, having been translated into the kingdom of God's dear Son, you will answer for all your failures there and not be hauled before the court of divine justice. This is a great help for those who are poor in grace, and it is a privilege of being in this kingdom.

Fourthly, Christ Himself, your King, is both your Judge and Advocate. It is a blessed thing to be in such a kingdom, especially when you realize your own faults and weaknesses. O you who are poor in grace, yet are in the kingdom of heaven, know that Jesus Christ, your King, will be your Judge, determining your eternal destiny. He will also be your Advocate, pleading for you. Therefore, do not let the poverty of your grace discourage you or cause you to despair.

Fifthly, the righteousness of your King is your righteousness when you enter this kingdom. In 1 Corinthians 1:30, it is written, "But of Him you are in Christ Jesus, who became for us wisdom from God—and righteousness and sanctification and redemption." When you enter the kingdom of the Messiah, you receive a privilege that no subject in any earthly kingdom can possess. There may be subjects in other kingdoms who have good kings, but the goodness of their king is not their own goodness. However, you are in a kingdom where the King is perfectly righteous, and His righteousness becomes your righteousness. Even though you are poor and your corruptions may overcome you, you are blessed, for you are poor in spirit and have entered a kingdom where the righteousness of the King is your righteousness. This is the fifth comfort of being in this kingdom.

Sixthly, the wisdom of your King also becomes yours. Jesus Christ, your King, possesses all the treasures of wisdom and knowledge. He has become wisdom to us, so do not let the insignificance of your abilities discourage you.

The seventh comfort is this: if you have entered this kingdom, then the little grace you possess, no matter how small, will be upheld for eternity. It is a special aspect of the glory of the kingly power of Jesus Christ to uphold the graces in the hearts of His people. This makes them more enduring than all the grace Adam had in his state of innocence. Adam had perfection in his state of innocence. Now, although you are weak and poor and may think that if Adam fell, you will fall even more, you are in a kingdom where the power of Christ, your King, is exercised in upholding the little grace you have. In 2 Timothy 4:18, there is a comforting passage: "And the Lord will deliver me from every evil work and preserve me for His heavenly kingdom. To Him be glory forever and ever. Amen!" It is as if the text is saying, "The Lord has already brought me into the possession of the kingdom of heaven, and He must preserve me until I come to enjoy it fully." You may fear certain temptations and believe they will overcome you, but take heart, for it is the kingly power of Christ to preserve the little grace you have until you enter His heavenly kingdom. Your situation is similar to that of David. After being anointed, David was persecuted by Saul to the point where he said, "I shall perish one day by the hand of Saul." However, if he had faith to believe the promise that was made to him, he would never have reasoned in such a manner. Likewise, many souls who are anointed for this heavenly kingdom, often think, "Certainly, I shall perish by the hand of this corruption." Remember that you are an anointed one, and it is the power of Jesus Christ to uphold the little grace you have. This is another benefit and fruit of being in this kingdom.

And then, in the eighth place, know that being brought under this kingdom, even if your grace is poor, you are as perfectly justified before God as Abraham, Isaac, Jacob, David, Paul, Peter, or any other strong saints who have ever lived. Your grace may be poor in terms of sanctification, but in terms of justification, it is as rich and glorious in this kingdom as the grace in the justification of any godly person who has walked the earth. Indeed, this can be considered as the fruit of the kingdom of heaven. During the time of the Law, this aspect was not fully revealed. It was such a great treasure of God's goodness that it was reserved to be unveiled when the Messiah was to come into the world. The treasury existed before, but the opening of this treasury of justification, I say, was reserved for the arrival of the Messiah. The Messiah has come to open this rich treasury of justification and to assure all those who are poor in spirit, troubled by the poverty of their grace, that although they may be poor in terms of sanctification, they are perfectly justified, just like any other godly person. Isn't it a blessedness to be a member of the kingdom of heaven? Oh, it should greatly stir the hearts of men and women to seek after the kingdom of heaven.

Ninthly, know that the right to your inheritance in this kingdom, as well as the very peace and joy of this kingdom, is not forfeited by your failures. In Romans 14:17, it is written that the kingdom of God is righteousness, peace, and joy in the Holy Spirit. As long as you are in this kingdom, you possess righteousness and peace, and you have reasons for joy.

And then, in the tenth place, surely you will be perfected soon. Judgment will be victorious. Satan will be trodden under your feet, and all imperfections will be swallowed up by perfection. The seed that is in you now will come to fullness. Although you may be weak now and not love God as much as you desire, soon you will love, delight in, glorify, and fear God as much as you desire.

Furthermore, in the eleventh place, all the ordinances in this kingdom belong to you, and you should not be deprived of them if there is any grace of Christ in you. Indeed, one must be cautious when entering this kingdom. If I had time, I would have spoken a word or two on that matter. No one who has no grace at all should claim the benefits of this kingdom. However, one who is poor in grace must not refrain from coming to the ordinances or praying out of fear. No, you should rather come, for all the ordinances belong to you. The kingdom of heaven is yours. Therefore, whenever you look upon any ordinance of the Word or sacrament, you may think, "Well, this is the ordinance that Jesus Christ has appointed for the building up of my soul and the strengthening of my grace." Therefore, come to it in such a way that it strengthens your grace.

Twelfthly, by entering this kingdom, you gain free access to heaven. Just as those who live in the city have free access to various parts of the world that others do not, those who remain in the world and are still in their natural state are banished from the presence of the Lord. They do not have the freedom to trade for grace, comfort, happiness, and glory in heaven as the saints do when they enter this kingdom. Through Jesus Christ, you may trade to heaven every day and have the privilege and right to enrich yourself in heaven. Even if you are poor when the trade for heaven is open, why should you be discouraged by the little grace you have? Oh, blessed are you, for you have this privilege in the kingdom.

The last thing I shall speak of now is that in this kingdom, the Spirit is poured out in much greater abundance than before. Do not be discouraged if you have not yet experienced a great work of grace in your heart. In this condition, the Spirit of God is communicated in a far more abundant manner than in the time of the Law. During the time of the Law, only David and those who were to be employed in public work might have expected it. But even if you are not employed in any public work, you can expect to be glorious in grace in this world. We have the promise that the feeble shall be as David, and those of the house of David shall be as the Angel of the Lord. There will be a time when the gifts of the saints will be elevated, and they will have clearer and deeper understanding of the mysteries of godliness than ever before. One significant hindrance to the growth of grace in those who are poor in spirit is their lack of faith to act upon the promises that are made regarding the outpouring of the Spirit in the times of the Messiah. If evildoers know how to give good things to those who ask, how much more will the Lord give His Spirit to those who ask Him? Considering these things is a great help to those who are poor in spirit, revealing their blessedness. And what binds all these together is that in this kingdom of heaven, the Lord desires His people to be delivered from the spirit of bondage. As there is a spirit of bondage, there is also a spirit of adoption, a free spirit to come into God's presence. The Lord does not want His people to be afraid of His presence but wants them, those who are apprehensive of their spiritual poverty, to look upon themselves as the children of this kingdom and to approach their Father with freedom of spirit. Now, my brethren, I have shown you the blessedness of those who are poor in spirit. I wish that I had spoken only to those who are poor in spirit. I confess that discussing such matters in these wanton times can make one fear and tremble. However, even if only one person who is poor in spirit benefits from it, although there may be a thousand hardened individuals in this congregation, God will accept that. In the meantime, you who are of poor spirit and truly humbled before God, consider the cost of your comfort. Perhaps it has caused the hardening of many hundreds in this congregation to even speak of such a thing. But says God, let it cost the hardening of many; your comfort is so dear to Me that I desire it despite this. Therefore, take these things and make use of them to further your sanctification. We have a very notable Scripture for cautioning against the misuse of these things in Hebrews 12:28. We have received a kingdom that cannot be shaken. So, what then? Shall we take liberty and live loosely? No, says the Scripture. Therefore, let us have grace, whereby we may serve God acceptably with reverence and godly fear. The Scripture makes this use of it: Therefore, what? Therefore, let us not be wanton, but let us serve Him with reverence and godly fear, for our God is a consuming fire. In 1 Thessalonians 2:12, it is written: "That you would walk worthy of God who calls you into His kingdom and glory." Walk as those who are partakers of the kingdom of heaven. Walk above the world. Let it not appear that you possess the same base and low spirits as the people of the world. Instead, walk worthy of the kingdom to which the Lord has called you.

# SERMON VI

## Godly mourners shall be comforted

Blessed are those who mourn, for they shall be comforted. - MATTHEW 5:4

On the last day, you may recall that we spoke about the first Beatitude, the blessedness of the poor in spirit, and what Christ meant when He said that theirs is the kingdom of heaven. We explained that the kingdom of heaven does not solely refer to going to heaven after death, although that is true. The main purpose of Christ's statement here is to show that even the poor in spirit shall partake in the blessings of the Messianic era. With the Messiah coming into the world and establishing a new kingdom different from what was before, the poor in spirit shall become participants in that kingdom, enjoying all its privileges. I will not revisit the detailed exposition of the privileges of that kingdom. The main focus of the previous sermon was to apply it to the poor in spirit and to demonstrate the blessedness that they receive from this kingdom. The Lord has chosen the poor in this world so that they may partake in the kingdom of heaven. Therefore, it is a great encouragement for Gospel ministers to preach about the kingdom of heaven to congregations that have many poor individuals. I wish that the poor in this congregation could hear about the blessings of the kingdom of heaven. I believe that if the poor in this place could be exposed to the Gospel, I would have as much hope of doing good here as in any other place in the kingdom. The Gospel itself is often referred to as the kingdom of heaven because it reveals the great things pertaining to the Messianic kingdom. So, to those of you who are poor and have come here, be encouraged to continue coming. And I urge you to encourage your poor neighbors and friends as well, telling them that even if they are extremely poor, if their spirits are poor and humble in accordance with their poverty, the kingdom of heaven is open to them too. Share with them what you have heard about the kingdom of heaven from the Gospel and the blessed things it offers. Then there is great hope that God intends to bring many in this congregation to His blessed kingdom.

The preaching of the Gospel is likened to casting a net, and it is referred to as the kingdom of heaven. We have a vast sea in which to cast the net, but it seems that those whom I would most like to capture in the net, the poorest and most humble, seldom come within its reach. I mean the poorest and most lowly people. Oh, you who are rich and hold positions, take measures to bring in the poor so that they may come into this net. When we cast the net, that is, when we preach the Gospel, may it be to them as if the kingdom of heaven has come near to them.

And you, young ones, listen attentively to the things concerning the kingdom of heaven. When you come home, ask your parents and guardians about the meaning of the kingdom of heaven, how poor people can become kings and priests unto God. We have even more reason to encourage young ones to inquire about this because as soon as the kingdom of heaven began to be known, the young ones were eager and deeply affected by it. Compare these two passages of Scripture: Mark 11:9-10 and Matthew 21:15. There you will find that the children and young ones were shouting "Hosanna to the Son of David!" And when the chief priests and scribes saw the wonderful things that Jesus did and heard the children crying out in the temple, saying, "Hosanna to the Son of David!" they were greatly displeased. Now compare this with Mark 11:9-10: "Those who went before and those who followed cried out, saying, 'Hosanna! Blessed is he who comes in the name of the Lord! Blessed is the kingdom of our father David that comes in the name of the Lord! Hosanna in the highest!'" They cried out "Hosanna in the highest" because of the kingdom of the Messiah that was coming. It is said that the chief priests and scribes were troubled by this. Carnal hearts may be troubled to see young ones so enthusiastic about the kingdom, but the Lord stirred them up to be affected by the kingdom of the Messiah, and Christ justifies them. Jesus said to them, "Have you never read, 'Out of the mouth of babes and nursing infants you have perfected praise'?" This is for the honor of Jesus Christ that young ones shall cry "Hosanna," etc. Everything that has been said about the blessedness of the poor should teach us to highly esteem those who are poor in spirit. Even though they are despised by the world, do not despise them. "Blessed is he who considers the poor" (Psalm 41:1). In James 2:5, it is said, "Has not God chosen the poor of this world to be rich in faith and heirs of the kingdom which He promised to those who love Him?" But you have despised the poor. Be careful not to be guilty of despising any of Christ's little ones. Those who are poor in spirit are highly esteemed by Jesus Christ, so do not treat them lightly. There are many more things that can be said about the promises made to the poor, namely, the kingdom of heaven. Now we come to the second Beatitude.

"Blessed are those who mourn, for they shall be comforted."

In Luke's account, you will find it presented in a different order, and various copies have it differently. There are two or three Beatitudes set in a different order there. But regarding the essence itself, it is one of the strangest paradoxes in the world: "Blessed are those who mourn." Among all the affections, sorrow is the least beneficial to human nature. Nature gains something from the affections of love, joy, desire, hope, and even fear, but sorrow weakens nature. Yet Christ addresses this and says, "Blessed are those who mourn." It is more than saying, "Blessed are those who grieve." Chrysostom, commenting on this passage, says that it does not merely mean blessed are those who grieve, but blessed are those who mourn. The word translated as "mourn" here signifies an exceedingly great mourning, like the mourning that takes place at the death of friends. When someone buries an intimate friend, a dear child, or a close relative, what great mourning there is in the eyes of the world! But Christ says, "Blessed are you in that moment." If you are godly and my disciples, you are blessed in that mourning, even if your mourning is the greatest in the world. It is in the present tense: "You who mourn," indicating its continuation. Even if you mourn constantly, even if you find yourself in a sorrowful state and live in it all your days, still you are blessed for mourning. The world is all about merriment and splendor. Oh, blessed are those who are merry, who can drink wine from bowls, adorn themselves with rosebuds, sing to the harp, and invent musical instruments like David. They are considered the blessed ones in the world. But we see that Christ's judgment is completely contrary. Blessed are those who mourn. Surely, not all those who mourn are blessed.

First, there is a foolish mourning in which men and women are not blessed. They mourn without knowing the reason, and this is not blessedness but folly.

Secondly, there is a natural mourning, when one mourns solely because their circumstances have worsened and they have experienced some misfortune. This type of mourning does not possess blessedness.

Thirdly, there is a worldly mourning. Worldly sorrow leads to death. Mourning over the loss of worldly possessions, considering it the greatest loss of all, is not blessed; it leads to death.

Fourthly, there is an envious mourning, when people mourn and grieve over the good fortune of others. Surely, this is not blessed but cursed.

Furthermore, there is a devilish mourning, when men and women mourn because they cannot indulge their desires.

Lastly, there is a hellish, desperate mourning when people mourn in despair. This is hellish and not blessed. Such mourners are not blessed.

But who, then, are blessed? Those who mourn. That is, those who, by the providence of God, find themselves in a mournful condition. They may be deprived of many comforts in this world that others possess, or they may be afflicted by the hand of God and find themselves in a sad state. Yet, their hearts submit to God's will and sanctify His name in these circumstances. These are the blessed ones. We must clarify the meaning of the previous verse, "Blessed are the poor." It does not refer to all the poor, but to the poor in spirit. Similarly, "Blessed are those who mourn" refers to those who mourn in spirit, whose spirits are humbled before God and honour Him in their mournful condition. Their condition may be low, but their hearts are even lower than their condition. These are the blessed ones, especially those who direct their mourning towards the right object. They mourn for sin as the greatest evil, not only for their own sins but also for the sins of others, recognizing the lack of honour given to God in the world. They take to heart the afflictions of the Church, mourning not only for their own afflictions but also for the afflictions of the Church. Blessed are those who mourn in this way.

Next, all those who mourn in a gracious manner.

You may ask, when does one mourn in a gracious way and manner?

First, when one experiences any form of suffering, the heart willingly surrenders to God, honouring Him in that condition into which He has placed it. This surrender is not forced but voluntary.

Secondly, those whose mourning is regulated by grace. Their mourning is guided by faith, love, and hope. They do not mourn as those who have no hope. Grace governs their mourning, setting boundaries for their waves of sorrow.

Thirdly, when mourning leads the heart to long for God. They mourn not primarily because comfort is gone, but because they are deprived of something good that could help them progress in their relationship with God. Their souls mourn after God in the midst of any affliction.

Fourthly, those who mourn have a great concern for fulfilling the responsibilities of their mournful condition. This is a crucial aspect to consider in the blessedness of mourning. Those who mourn take into account the duty that God requires of them in that particular condition. Ordinary men and women are often preoccupied with their afflictions, their thoughts constantly focused on them. But in gracious mourning, the soul is concerned about the work. It is not a sullen mourning but a mourning that is active and stirring. The heart is engaged. In John 16:20, it is compared to a woman in labour. Jesus says, "You will weep and lament, but the world will rejoice. You will be sorrowful, but your sorrow will turn into joy." A woman experiences sorrow during childbirth because her time has come. But as soon as she delivers the baby, she forgets the pain, overwhelmed with joy that a child is born into the world. This illustrates that the mourning of the saints should resemble the sorrow of a woman in labour, with some good coming out of it. This is a valuable meditation for us. When we find our hearts burdened with sorrow, we should consider the purpose of our labour. We can never find comfort in our mourning unless we bring forth something through our sorrow. Even if the Lord keeps them mourning throughout their lives, they are blessed.

For they shall be comforted; comfort will come. Now, the reason for this blessedness arises, first, from the mourning itself—secondly, from the promise. Surely, it is a blessed thing to be such a mourner.

First, because the lower our hearts are in submitting to God in this mournful condition, the greater is our reverence for God, who has brought us into this condition. The Lord brings His people into a mournful condition. And the lower their hearts are in submission to God, the greater is the respect they show to Him. There is a great deal of grace exercised in a gracious mourning.

Secondly, a mournful condition, when governed by grace, brings much good to the soul. It eradicates the rankness in the hearts of individuals. Naturally, there is rankness in everyone's heart, especially when they indulge their fleshly desires. Like weeds that grow vigorously in the summertime, winter frosts nip the weeds and keep them in check. If it is a prolonged frost, it kills them. Similarly, a sanctified mournful condition has the power to kill the vermin, to kill our lusts. It serves as a special means of mortification in the soul. Therefore, blessed are those who mourn and conduct themselves graciously in a mournful condition.

Thirdly, it delivers from many temptations. You may think that a life of merriment and extravagance is the only happy life. But know that there are far more temptations in that life than in a mournful condition. It is true that temptations exist in a mournful condition—temptations to despair or to resort to unlawful means to alleviate the situation. However, the temptations in a jovial condition are more in line with a person's nature and, therefore, more dangerous. Hence, blessed are those who are kept in a mournful condition if God grants them the ability to sanctify His name in it.

Fourthly, those in a mournful condition are blessed because God has chosen that condition for them at the most opportune time. When a person is sick, bitter things are more appropriate than sweet things. We are all frail and ailing creatures, and it is a great mercy of God to select a mournful condition, with its bitterness, for us at this stage of our lives, rather than sweet and indulgent things. If God subdues your heart so that you are willing to accept this, blessed are you. For you now mourn when it is most fitting to mourn—a mournful state is suitable for us considering the conditions we face in this world. You may desire jollity, much like a poor sick person yearning for sweet delicacies. But blessed are you if you are willing to submit to God's choice for you.

Fifthly, and most importantly in this text, they shall be comforted. This is only to make the comforts sweeter for you when they do arrive. The Lord is simply shaping your soul according to His own will and leading you to greater comfort. Just as when a person intends to build a grand structure, the stones that they primarily use for construction are hewn and polished to be comely and suitable for the building, while other stones are not given the same attention. So, it is an indication that the Lord has great things in store for you, great comforts. He is now preparing you in your mournful condition for significant comfort. You shall be comforted.

For first, there is a time coming when all tears shall be wiped from your eyes. Just read Revelation 7 from verse 14 to the end, and you will discover what is promised to God's people who endure a mournful condition in this world.

Moreover, not only will all tears be wiped away, but you shall also receive the fulfillment of all the promises. It is challenging to overlook the numerous promises found in Isaiah 35:10 and chapter 51:3, among others. As you continue reading through the book of God, you will encounter many similar promises. And among these promises is the assurance of Christ's second coming, as mentioned in John 16:20. This serves as great comfort, for Christ declares that although you weep and lament now, you will be comforted. Jesus Christ promises that upon His return, you shall have the privilege of enjoying His presence and all the blessings He has obtained through His blood. Rest assured, if you ever become a partaker of all the good that Jesus Christ has acquired through His sacrifice, you will lack no comfort.

Furthermore, your comfort will be proportionate to your sorrow. Just as it is said of the whore of Babylon, "so much as her pleasure has been, so much torment give her." In contrast, as much sorrow as you have experienced for the sake of Christ's name, you will receive an equal measure of joy and comfort. Christ has prepared many mansions in His Father's house, and He has comforts ready in proportion to all your sorrow and mourning. It is possible that if you had a more comfortable life in this world, you might have less comfort reserved for you in the hereafter.

"They shall be comforted."

But when will they be comforted? When will this comfort be bestowed upon them? They shall be comforted when the wicked are sorrowful. Isaiah 65:13 describes the contrasting conditions of the saints and the ungodly. The Lord God says, "Behold, my servants shall eat, but you shall be hungry; behold, my servants shall drink, but you shall be thirsty; behold, my servants shall rejoice, but you shall be ashamed; behold, my servants shall sing for joy of heart, but you shall cry for sorrow of heart and wail for vexation of spirit." Therefore, you shall find comfort when the ungodly are put to shame.

Secondly, you shall be comforted when the Lord imparts His choicest mercies to you. During this time of your life, the Lord does communicate with you, but only to a limited extent compared to what He intends. This present life is not the opportune time for experiencing true comfort. Consider what Abraham said to Dives: "Son, remember that in your lifetime you received your good things, and likewise Lazarus evil things; but now he is comforted and you are tormented." It is far better, my brethren, not to seek our comforts and rewards in this life because it is not the time for God to unveil the fullness of His mercy. All the things of this world are but a few crumbs. I recall Luther's words regarding the entire Turkish Empire: it is merely a crumb of bread that the Master of the house throws to the dogs. They have their crumbs here, but there will come a time when God will bestow His choicest mercies, opening all the treasures of His grace and sharing them with His saints. They shall be comforted.

Lastly, we shall find comfort when we are more capable of receiving it than we are now. This is the best time to be comforted. Blessed are those who mourn, for they shall be comforted. And this comfort that the mourners will receive...

Shall be, first and foremost, a pure comfort. We may experience some sweetness in life, but it is often mixed with poison or other troubles. However, the comfort promised to the mourners will be pure, free from danger and the troubles of this world.

Secondly, these comforts are spiritual in nature. By this, I do not simply mean that they will provide comfort to the soul rather than satisfying carnal desires, as most worldly comforts do. It goes beyond that. These comforts will primarily originate within the soul and radiate to the body. Our current comforts usually begin with external factors and bring comfort to the heart through bodily sensations. But the comforts of the saints will first be experienced in their souls and then extend to their bodies.

Furthermore, these comforts are divine. All comfort ultimately comes from God in one way or another, but the comfort promised here will come directly from God Himself. Our current comforts are often received indirectly, through various channels. However, the comforts of the saints will be directly from God. They will be in alignment with His nature and bring Him joy. Your joy in worldly pleasures, such as drinking, merriment, and revelry, may bring you temporary happiness. But does God find joy in these things? No, true comfort for the saints is found in the consolations of the Almighty. If your comfort is holy and gracious, it brings joy not only to your own heart but also to the heart of God. There is joy in heaven, and God rejoices with you. No comfort should satisfy a heart that has communion with God unless it bears the evidence that God rejoices alongside your joy. So, seek this assurance in the midst of your joy.

Thirdly, it is a complete comfort. Ask, and you shall receive, so that your joy may be full. It would be insufficient to say, "Blessed is a sick person, for they shall have health." That would be a weak expression because health is merely the removal of sickness. However, when Christ says, "Blessed are they that mourn, for they shall be comforted," He means that they will experience a fullness of comfort that will far outweigh any sorrow they have endured. They will enter into the joy of their Master, rather than the joy entering into them.

Moreover, this comfort is strong. It can withstand any affliction or opposition, as stated in Hebrews 6:18.

Fifthly, it is an eternal consolation. As mentioned in 2 Thessalonians 2:16 and 2 Timothy 2:11, it is a faithful saying that if we have died with Christ, we shall also live with Him. If we suffer, we shall also reign with Him. Mourning is like a seed that will undoubtedly yield a harvest. In Psalm 97, it is referred to as a seed: "Those who sow in tears shall reap in joy." Similarly, in Psalm 126, the same concept is expressed. The mourning of the saints is their sowing season, and a harvest will surely come.

Furthermore, the Lord takes pleasure in communicating Himself to His saints, and therefore, they must be comforted. God rejoices in being called "The God of all comfort," and He comforts us in all our tribulations.

They must indeed be comforted because God has made promises to that effect. Additionally, God the Father has anointed Jesus Christ to be a Comforter, as stated in Isaiah 61. Just as Jesus Christ was appointed by God the Father to proclaim good news to the poor in spirit, He was also anointed to bring comfort to those who mourn. It is as if God says, "I appoint you, my Son, for this task," and we can be certain that Christ will faithfully fulfill His role as Comforter.

Lastly, they shall be comforted because the Holy Spirit, who is equal with the Father and the Son and is glorious in His work, derives His name from this very purpose. The Holy Spirit, known as the Comforter, has the same glorious essence as the Father and the Son. If the works of the Father and the Son are glorious—such as the creation of all things and the redemption of mankind—then the work of the Holy Spirit must also possess a corresponding glory. Therefore, it is inevitable that you will be comforted as long as the Holy Spirit exists, as His work must be glorious.

Oh, the stark contrast between the comforts of worldly hearts and those of the saints! Your comfort comes from indulging in drink, gambling, and other carnal pleasures. But what difference is there between finding comfort in a pint of beer or a game of cards and finding comfort in the Holy Spirit, whom God the Father and the Son have appointed to be your eternal Comforter? And you, who disregard the comforts of the saints and prefer to satisfy your carnal desires through eating, drinking, and playing, what does the language of your soul say? "Lord, let me find comfort in food and drink rather than in the work of the Holy Spirit." We hear from Your word that the Holy Spirit is designated by Yourself and Your Son to be the Comforter of the saints. Yet, these are the comforts you have no interest in. You would rather indulge in earthly pleasures and take a chance on whether you will have any share in the comforts of the Holy Spirit. But despite this, those of you with mournful spirits, who continue to mourn and deny yourselves the sensual comforts that others indulge in, do not be discouraged. Instead, bless yourself in your God, bless yourself in the assurance that Christ has promised you comfort.

I have briefly touched upon the main points that shed some light on the interpretation of these words. However, I had intended to provide further application, specifically addressing the people of God and offering some help in their comfort. If Jesus Christ has declared that they shall be comforted, it is the responsibility of all people to provide comfort to them, especially the Ministers of Christ. I will now speak a few words concerning what applies to all of us based on what has been discussed.

Firstly, we can see the immense value of religion and godliness. It has the power to bring comfort to the most mournful conditions in the world. Even if a person has lost everything they possessed, if they are godly, religion will reveal how they can still find blessedness in that situation. The blessedness of the godly is not contingent on their circumstances. While others in the world may lament and be filled with sadness over their losses, you can find satisfaction in knowing that you have not lost your happiness. You may have lost your wealth and external comforts that once brought you delight, but your blessedness does not reside in worldly pleasures; it resides in your relationship with God. Therefore, do not shy away from godly sorrow just because it brings trouble and affliction. Do not be deceived by the temptations of Satan, which keep many souls in bondage and prevent them from walking in the ways of God. Some people, upon embracing godliness, fear that they will never experience joy again. But we see that there is an abundance of comfort proclaimed by Christ Himself, even in the duty that seems contrary to mirth. "Blessed are those who mourn, for they shall be comforted." If your enemies prevail against you and hold you captive, your blessedness remains intact because of your godliness. If your body is plagued by sickness and severe pain, you can still be blessed in your godliness. Even if you have lost your friends, you are still blessed. Therefore, do not be afraid of godliness simply because it may bring some trouble and sorrow. Many men and women fear to embrace godliness because they believe it will take away their joy. Do not be fooled by this temptation. It is true that religion may bring about certain sorrows and afflictions that you did not experience before. You may suffer more for the cause of God, and you may feel greater remorse for your sins. Religion may bring additional outward sorrows and afflictions. However, the comforts it brings far outweigh the sorrows. Therefore, do not hesitate to be one of Christ's mourners, for Christ has committed Himself to comfort you. Just as Egypt had more venomous creatures than other countries but also had more remedies to cure them, religion may bring sorrows and troubles, but it also offers abundant healing and help.

# SERMON VII

## The Folly of Those Who Seek Only Mirth

"Blessed are they that mourn: for they shall be comforted." - Matthew 5:4

Here, we rebuke the vanity and foolishness of those among us who are solely focused on mirth and jollity. They cannot seem to be happy unless they are immersed in worldly joy and merriment. They place their happiness in these temporal pleasures. How contradictory is your judgment compared to that of Jesus Christ! Christ says, "Blessed are those who mourn." Why? Because they shall be comforted. But you say, "Blessed are those who are merry, who have an abundance of worldly delights." Yet the Spirit of God says in Ecclesiastes 7:2, "It is better to go to the house of mourning than to go to the house of feasting." Now, which of these two shall we believe? Will we believe your base and carnal heart that places all its happiness in joviality? Or will we believe the wisdom of God, who declares that it is better to go to the house of mourning? If a man had said this, you would have considered him a fool. Which of you would choose to find delight in an abundance of creature comforts and worldly company rather than in the house of mourning? But the Holy Spirit settles the matter. He states that the house of mourning is better than the house of laughter because the heart is made better through sadness. The house of mourning brings much good to the soul that does not come from the house of laughter. Laughter often corrupts the heart, whereas sorrow often improves it.

Consider this: What if this dreadful woe pronounced by Christ Himself, in Luke 6:25, were to be your portion? "Woe unto you that laugh now, for ye shall mourn and weep." Your time of sorrow is yet to come. When you see men living grandly and merrily in the world, yet offering no service to Jesus Christ, and being unproductive in their positions, you may say of them, "Alas, here are men who rejoice now, but they shall mourn and weep. Their time of mourning is approaching." How much better would it be to mourn now than to have an eternity of mourning? If you give yourself to pleasure and let your heart pursue vanity in your youth, then all your sorrow will accumulate and overwhelm you in despair. You, in your youth and strength, expend your energy on vanity. Know that your sorrow is accumulating, ready to descend upon you all at once and sink you into everlasting despair. How can you expect that God would look upon you with favor when you are so full of sin and wickedness? Will it be well with you in the end? There are so many precious saints in the world who would not knowingly sin against God for all the wealth in the world. They make it their greatest concern and endeavor to honor God in their generation. Even if they are occasionally overcome by weakness, they go on mourning throughout the day. Are these saints kept in a state of mourning while you rejoice? While you find pleasure and allow your heart to be fully satisfied by worldly pleasures? Know that you, too, must mourn deeply.

The mirth that these men experience arises from ignorance. The mirth you indulge in is a result of your ignorance of your true condition. You are in darkness. Woe to the mirth that has no foundation other than ignorance! Furthermore, these men take advantage of their conscience when it is asleep or numbed. It would be impossible for them to be so merry and carefree if they did not take advantage of their conscience when it is dulled and numb. For if their conscience were awake, it would condemn them and say, "You are engaging in activities that are not rightfully yours." Cursed be any comfort that cannot stand with a clear conscience, and cursed be your joy if it cannot coexist with thoughts of death and judgment. Such mirth cannot be good. I urge you to consider this.

Whenever you have serious thoughts of God, of death, and of eternity, your joy is dampened. Even when you are fully immersed in pleasure, if your conscience reminds you of the eternal condition, you experience secret qualms. Therefore, you have reason to suspect that any joy and mirth which cannot stand with thoughts of God and eternity is sinful. Beware that you do not share the fate of the one who sought pleasure and satisfaction in the creature but found nothing to satisfy him at the time of his death. Take heed, lest that become your portion. Son, remember that in your lifetime you had your good things, but now you are tormented.

The main thing I want to emphasize in this text is the third use, which is for comfort and consolation. I want to fully align with the mind of Christ in this matter and do as He did—to comfort those who mourn. That will be my work for the rest of the time. You are blessed by the Lord if you truly mourn, and I will now speak.

First, I offer comfort to those who truly mourn. Secondly, I will address an objection that may arise. Thirdly, I will provide guidance on how mourners should carry themselves in their state of mourning to find comfort.

It is an excellent thing to comfort mourners. In the 29th chapter of Job, it is said that finding one who can speak a word in season to the weary is as rare as finding one out of a thousand. This is part of the office of Jesus Christ and the Spirit of Christ, and it brings glory to humanity. Surely, it must be a great and glorious work to be part of the office of Jesus Christ and the Spirit. The Spirit is not only a convincer but also a comforter (John 16:18), and this brings glory to humanity. While some people rejoice in causing others sorrow, that is a cursed thing. It is even more wicked to bring someone into sorrow and then rejoice in it. Pericles, on his deathbed, had friends who spoke of his virtues, the authority he held, and the victories he had won. But he remarked that they had forgotten to mention the best and most noble thing about him—that no Athenian had ever worn a black gown because of him. That was his glory, and we should be cautious not to bring others into a state of mourning, so that we can say that we have never made anyone sad or heavy.

If we have done so, we should humble ourselves and confess it to God, seeking His forgiveness. God delights in comforting people, not in grieving those who mourn. If God does not take pleasure in grieving them, then surely we should not either. They cannot wrong us to the extent that we should be provoked to grieve them, especially considering how often we wrong God. God Himself says (Lamentations 3:33) that He does not delight in causing grief to the children of men. Now, let me speak more directly to you who are spiritual mourners. Take comfort in these points:

First, if your mourning is sincere, your tears and sorrows are far better than the wine of the worldly. Your tears are more pleasing to God than the mirth of wicked men could ever be. It is better to be in your condition than in the condition of others. Your tears are precious to God, especially if they arise from a genuine godly sorrow. There is nothing more precious to Him, second only to the blood of Jesus Christ, than tears that come from a right principle of godly sorrow.

Secondly, consider this for your comfort: If you had not been mourning, you might have been sinning. You could have been engaged in activities that would darken the glory of God. Now, which is better? Judge for yourself. The curse of all your afflictions has been taken away by Jesus Christ. The bitterness of sorrow has been removed from you. Your mourning is based on a misunderstanding. You have a right to comfort, even if you do not perceive it. You mourn because you do not realize your right to it. So, what is there to discourage you or prevent you from finding comfort? The curse of every affliction and the evil of sin have been eradicated.

Thirdly, consider that all your sorrows are measured out by God, who is your Father. You are not at the mercy of wicked men, who determine how much you should mourn or when you should mourn. You are under the care of God, your Father. If you, as parents, had the power to deliver your children from anything that could harm them, wouldn't you do it for their good? Now, you are under God's care, and you will not sorrow or weep one tear more than your Father deems necessary for your well-being. God takes note of all your sorrows. He collects all your tears in a bottle, and He Himself is afflicted in all your afflictions (Isaiah 53:9). God is aware of all our miseries, even if others may overlook them. Often, when any of the saints are under dark clouds and in an afflicted condition, they are frowned upon, even though they were previously favored. But God does not act that way. You may not be fully aware, but God is even more sensitive than you are. He is more aware of your sufferings and takes care of you.

Fourthly, find comfort in the fact that Christ himself experienced sorrow. By sharing in your sorrow, you are becoming more like Jesus Christ. So why should you consider it a burden when you are being conformed to His likeness? In fact, Christ's sorrows were meant to sanctify your own. He sorrowed so that your sorrows could be sanctified. If God ordained Christ, His beloved Son, to be a man of sorrows, then your condition is not as bleak as you think. You are, in fact, conforming to Christ in this. So why should we hesitate to be like Christ? Didn't God think it worthwhile to make Christ a man of sorrows for your sake? And yet, you consider it too much to bear sorrows in order to be conformed to Him.

Fifthly, take comfort in knowing that you have a stake in the God of all consolation. The darkness of your condition cannot hinder your connection to God. You have comfort in the promise, which is as certain and sure as if you already possessed it. You will undoubtedly receive it in the future, and there will come a time when you will have full consolation. God will hold the wicked accountable for their merriment. They will answer for causing others to be sad, and they will have to give an account for all their joyful hours. Their mirth will become a bitter portion when God charges the weight of guilt upon their souls. Oh, what a difference there will be between you and them on that day! You have mourned for a few days and will find comfort in the end, while they have rejoiced for a few days but will face an eternity of sorrow.

Sixthly, it may be that some of you are saying, "It's true, there is great comfort and precious consolation in these words. But my afflictions are immense. They are greater than others. If I were afflicted as so-and-so is, I could bear it. If I had the burden that someone else carries, I could be content and submit to it." For your comfort, know that this perspective may arise more from the disorder of your spirit than from the weight of the affliction itself. The disorder of your spirit may be great, and that causes the burden to feel heavy. The affliction itself may not be as great, but your heart is unwilling to surrender to it. If your heart were willing to submit to the hand of God, the affliction would become easier to bear.

Furthermore, remember that your afflictions are mixed with many blessings. None of you can claim to have purely afflictions. They are always mixed. God could have brought upon you pure afflictions, absolute miseries, and deprived you of any glimpse of mercy. But even in your darkest hours, you have some consolations—more mercy than affliction. I am confident that no one here in this gathering, even if their afflictions seem the greatest, has a shortage of mercies.

And then consider that God suffers more from your sins than you can suffer from His hand in your afflictions. Even the slightest dimming of His glory is a greater evil than any affliction you can endure. This should strengthen your spirit, knowing that God suffers more. Therefore, you should not be unwilling to endure something when God Himself suffers more than you.

Seventhly, if you desire comfort, consider this: God comforts His saints in a way that may not be sensed but can be embraced through faith. Exercise your faith and draw comfort through it. Place your faith in the promise and let that bring forth the comfort of the promise. Sensory perception is not the means by which God comforts His people, and if we seek comfort in a sensual manner, we deceive ourselves. Therefore, strive to derive comfort from the exercise of faith. In fact, we should value the comforts that arise from the exercise of our own graces more than those that come from tangible experiences. When you cannot find comfort in the created things, know that it is God you are dealing with, and that is your comfort. God has not appointed the creature to be the object of your comfort, but Himself. Therefore, when you seek comfort in the creature rather than in God, you undervalue Him and go astray in your search for comfort. In Isaiah 51:12, God says, "I, even I, am He who comforts you. Who are you that you should be afraid of a man?" Consider that God speaks to you in this way: "I am the one who comforts you. Why are you troubled? Look to God saying this to you. Why are you downcast, O poor soul? Is there not more comfort in My word, in My power, than in anything that causes your distress?" In Isaiah 57:19, God says, "I create the fruit of the lips—peace, peace, to him who is far off and to him who is near." You may not see how you can be comforted, and therefore, because you cannot see it, you think it is impossible. But when you cannot see comfort, remember that God can create comfort for you. Look upon God as the Creator of comfort and do not succumb to discouragement. God would rather recreate His first work of creation than let you, a true mourner, lack comfort. He will create comfort for you. This should strengthen your faith and sustain your soul in the darkest times of despair. There is nothing too difficult for God. Just as He created all things out of nothing by the power of His word in the beginning, do you think He is unable to create comfort for you now? If God begins His work, do not fear your comfort.

Lastly, suppose your condition is such that no one in the world has ever been in a similar situation. Yet, you can still find comfort. I suppose there is not a single person in this congregation who has experienced the same level of spiritual or physical trouble as you, or perhaps even worse. But even if it were true that no one has ever been in the same condition as you, there is still comfort for you in this Scripture: "Since the beginning of the world, men have not heard, nor perceived by the ear, neither has the eye seen, O God, beside You, what You have prepared for him who waits for You" (Isaiah 64:4). If you have a heart to wait upon God in your mourning condition, He has mercy and comfort prepared for you, beyond what anyone can comprehend. Oh, this should encourage you to wait upon God. Even though we may not know the nature of the comfort, God does. And thus, I have endeavoured to open this box of consolation within this section, which is the first aspect of this use.

The second is to answer a question that may be raised: But you may ask, the promise here says, "They shall be comforted." But I fear this doesn't apply to me. I have mourned for a long time and yet cannot find comfort. I have been in a state of sadness, and I cannot see the promise being fulfilled for me. How should I sustain myself in this situation?

First of all, have you truly mourned? Perhaps you have sinned more than you have sorrowed. Examine your heart carefully. Have your sins outweighed your sorrows? Therefore, do not be disheartened. What is this sorrow compared to eternal sorrow? What is this small measure of mourning compared to an eternity of misery? Remember that you are delivered from the peril of eternal perishing. Let this thought sweeten all your sorrows. Although your condition may be sad, you are saved from eternal damnation.

Secondly, consider that faith makes future comforts present to you. This is the glory of faith and its essence. It has the power to make a promised mercy that seems distant appear present. Just as Abraham, by faith, saw the day of

Christ in the distant future, faith can bring a mercy to your soul, making it present even if it seems far away. Just as despair makes hell and the impending wrath appear present to the wicked who have enlightened consciences burdened with the weight of their sins, so faith can make a promised mercy certain, even though it may not be possessed yet. If you have no comfort, no glimpse of love in your communion with God, search your spirit to see if there are any clusters of Canaan's grapes within your soul. This is a sign that you will have more if you have any at all. Even if you only have a spark of divine love, know that you will have more. But if you cannot discern any hint of God's presence, remember that we now have the Word and the ordinances. Why do we have these if not to support our spirits? This was what David relied on to sustain his heart. In Psalm 119:49-50, he said, "Remember the word to Your servant, upon which You have caused me to hope. This is my comfort in my affliction, for Your word has given me life." The Word of God is sufficient to uphold the soul even in the darkest times of sorrow. When you find little comfort in your senses, turn to the Word and retrieve it through faith.

Thirdly, consider that it is not strange to be without comfort for a long time. Even the most precious saints, who have served God faithfully, have been kept in darkness for extended periods without comfort. Though they have rendered much service to God, their hearts have been distant from Him in terms of comfort. We see this in the words of Heman in Psalm 88:7, 14-15, "Your wrath lies heavy upon me, and You have afflicted me with all Your waves. The terrors of the Almighty overwhelm me; Your terrors have brought me to the brink of destruction." Heman was truly a man of sorrows. This is the experience of a godly and wise person. Similarly, David expressed his longing for comfort in Psalm 119:81-82, saying, "My soul faints for Your salvation; I hope in Your word. My eyes fail from searching Your word, saying, 'When will You comfort me?'" Even though you may read the Scriptures that have comforted others, if you cannot find solace for yourself, if they do not bring you peace, do not think that God has never dealt with anyone like you. No, the Scriptures testify to the experiences of others who have faced similar trials.

Fourthly, consider that all this time, while comfort may seem distant, your sorrow is actually working to bring about greater consolation. Your afflictions are laying the groundwork for even greater comforts. When comfort finally arrives, you will see why it was worth the wait. You will have no reason to complain but rather to thank God for the delay, knowing that you would have been undone had comfort come earlier. It was the sentiment of Mr. Bates, while in prison, to bless God for not being in his own or his enemies' hands in terms of sorrow and affliction. If he were in his own hands, he would have come out of trouble too soon. If he were in his enemies' hands, they would have kept him in trouble for too long. But he knew that he was in God's hands, and God knows when it is best to deliver him. Therefore, patiently wait on God, even if comfort may tarry. When it does come, you will see that it was worth waiting for. Even if you must wait until death, even if you do not experience comfort until the last hour, eternity will compensate for the delay.

Fifthly and finally, consider that this is a time for mourning, and we know that things are reasonable and best in their appointed time. This is a Christian's planting season. In the world, we will face trouble, and through many tribulations, we will enter into Heaven. Just as a farmer is willing to endure storms and hardships during the planting season with the knowledge that the harvest is forthcoming, so even though you now sow in tears, there will be a time of reaping in joy.

But here is something that troubles many souls. I would be willing to wait until God comes if I were assured that this promise applies to me. This would truly uplift my heart. I would gladly serve God to the best of my ability, endure any affliction, and consider myself fortunate if He would employ me in anything, if only I were certain that the promise is mine. However, I fear that this promise belongs to others and has nothing to do with me.

In response to this, we should strive to have our mourning in a gracious disposition, and then we can be sure to receive comfort. This leads me to the third point I mentioned regarding the guidelines.

The third point in this context is as follows: How can we order our mourning in such a way that it brings us comfort? How can I conduct my sorrow in a manner that brings me the assurance that the promise is meant for me? How can our consciences affirm that we are blessed by this promise? Even though others may see us as sad and heavy-hearted, how can we carry ourselves in such a way that they may say, "These individuals are blessed, even though they are in a sorrowful state"? Now, I urge you to take note of these guidelines.

First and foremost (which I particularly want you to focus on), in your mourning, make sure to maintain good thoughts about God. No matter what troubles you face, do not let them give rise to doubts or harbor resentment towards God. The saints have always endeavored to restrain their hearts from falling into this state. In Psalm 43:5, observe how David reproaches his own heart and admonishes it. He secretly checks and reins it in, saying, "Why are you cast down, O my soul? Why are you disquieted within me? Hope in God, for I shall yet praise Him, the help of my countenance and my God." It is beneficial when we have any reasoning within our hearts about the sadness of our circumstances to lay this conclusion at the foundation: "Yet God is good to Israel; yet God is good." Although I am in misery and sorrow, God is good to His saints, to those in a sorrowful condition. Those who are in such a condition tend to reflect and meditate on their sorrows and afflictions in their thoughts. But when you do so, be sure to establish this foundation first: "Yet the Lord is good." Before you even contemplate your sorrows, affirm that the Lord is good, and His counsels are sure and steadfast. David was deeply troubled in his spirit in Psalm 73:1, yet see how he establishes this conclusion: "Truly God is good to Israel." Therefore, you should also say, "Yet the Lord is good to my soul," regardless of what your senses, temptations, or Satan may make you believe. Yet God is good to Israel, yet God is good to my soul. Similarly, in Jeremiah 12:1, the prophet declares, "Righteous are You, O Lord, when I plead with You; yet let me talk with You about Your judgments." Notice how he affirms God's righteousness before he reasons with Him about his circumstances. He justifies God by saying, "You are righteous, O Lord." Only then does he proceed to discuss the matter. Therefore, when thoughts arise in our hearts about our sorrowful conditions, when we ponder and reflect on them, let us be sure to say, "You are righteous, O Lord." We can then consider our afflictions and weigh them in the balance, but this principle must be firmly established at the core. In a similar vein, consider the psalmist in Psalm 89, from verse 38 to the end. It recounts a somber tale, yet he begins by praising the mercy of God and exalting it above all. After lifting his faith to the heavens in the exaltation of God's mercy, he then considers his own sorrows and the sorrows of the Church. When the heart is firmly grounded in God's love, in the covenant, and in His mercy, then we may freely express our sorrows. But before you allow your heart to indulge in sorrow, make sure you first contemplate the love of God. Conclude with the acknowledgment of God's goodness. In the final verse of the psalm, after the account of the sorrowful story, the psalmist concludes, "Blessed be the Lord forevermore! Amen and Amen." He emphasizes it with two asseverations, as if to ensure that it is duly noted: God is good from the beginning, and even though there is a bitter part in the middle, he concludes, "Blessed be the Lord." Let us adopt the same reasoning. Even though my condition is very sad, and I hardly know what to think of myself, God forbid that I should hold negative thoughts about Him. No, I will say, "Yet the Lord is righteous." Perhaps you have witnessed the saints enduring difficult trials for the sake of God and His cause, and your spirits may begin to rise, leading you to question God's faithfulness and love towards His people. May this never be the case for any of you. Remember these Scriptures and let them be the conclusion of your hearts in the most sorrowful state you may find yourself in: "Blessed be the Lord forever. Amen and Amen."

Secondly, be sure to acknowledge all the mercy you receive from God in the midst of your afflictions. Do not let any affliction overshadow the mercy bestowed upon you. It is disheartening to see how often a few afflictions hinder the recognition of the many mercies that the saints experience. Just as a small object can obstruct the sight of the eye, like a penny placed upon it preventing one from beholding the sun or the sky, a minor affliction can darken the soul and hinder it from perceiving a multitude of mercies. Every little trouble obscures God's mercies. We should be cautious of this and make sure to include our mercies alongside our afflictions. Whenever we recount our sorrows, we must number our mercies alongside them. In Psalm 103:2, even while David was fleeing for his life, we see the wondrously sweet disposition of his spirit, full of praises. He exclaims, "Praise the Lord, O my soul, and forget not all His benefits." Offering praise to God in a sad condition is a melodious song to the Most High.

Thirdly, beware of adopting a sullen and ill-tempered disposition, whether towards God or others, in your sorrows. It is quite common for individuals in troubled conditions to add stubbornness to their mourning. However, we must strive to avoid this, recognizing it as a great evil, and instead cultivate a peaceful and gentle spirit. When people are pleased, they are merry, cheerful, and of good temperament. But when they are afflicted, in pain or sorrow, they become rough and ill-tempered, making it difficult for others to speak with them. This disposition is highly undesirable, and God does not approve of it in times of sin or trouble.

Fourthly, refrain from determining that comfort will never come during sorrow simply because you do not presently experience it. Do not say that comfort will never come because it is absent in the present moment. Moreover, when comfort does arrive, many are so obstinate that they refuse to accept it, as they wish to prove their own determination right. God says to such a soul, "Peace be to you," but the soul responds, "This news is too good to be true; I will not receive it because I want to uphold my determination." Similar to Rachel, who refused to be comforted, many individuals reject comfort from the Word in their spiritual distress. This is unkind treatment towards God. In Job 15:11, "Are the consolations of God too small for you?" Know that the Lord expects you to gratefully accept even a crumb of mercy that He offers. Consider your unworthiness, acknowledging that you are undeserving of God's comforting word. However, if the Lord brings His consolations of free grace, welcome them. Bless God that you can receive mercy on any terms. Like the woman of Canaan who said, "Even the dogs eat the crumbs," say, "I am but a dog, yet Lord, let me have a portion as a dog, and I will gratefully accept it from Your hands." Oh, be thankful for the smallest mercy, for it is the surest way to receive more. In His own time, the Lord will bestow further mercy upon you.

# SERMON VIII

## How mourners should order their mourning

"Blessed are they that mourn, for they shall be comforted." - Matthew 5:4

When you find yourself in a state of mourning, be careful not to envy those who are not in the same sad condition as you. Even though you may lack many desired comforts, bless God for others who have them. It is a sign of a good disposition and a positive preparation for comfort when you can sincerely thank God for the comforts others enjoy. However, it is common for hearts troubled with sorrow to become envious, especially if they are in a lowly and afflicted state. But beware of such a mindset, as it will intensify your sorrow and make it more bitter for you.

Lastly, in accordance with your mourning condition, engage in much prayer. Be sure to couple abundant prayer with abundant sorrow. Never allow your heart to indulge in excessive sorrow that cannot coexist with ample prayer. Whatever your state may be, even if you claim that it forces you to mourn, remember this timeless rule for those who wish to mourn in a Christian manner: there must be a proportion of prayer to sorrow. If there is little prayer, there should be little sorrow; if there is much sorrow, there should be much prayer. I have found in Scripture that mourning and praying are often linked. As the Apostle James says, "If any man be afflicted, let him pray." In Hosea 12, it is written concerning Jacob that "he wept and made supplication," connecting weeping and supplication. The same connection is made between affliction and praying. In the book of Judges, it is mentioned that the people of God mourned and wept to such an extent that the place was named Bochim, and they sacrificed there to the Lord. Sacrifice is mentioned alongside mourning. If one's mourning renders them unfit for sacrifice, it also makes them unfit for prayer. Surely, such mourning is not a godly sorrow. If it hinders you from praying, if you cannot pour out your soul freely before God as you do in other times, beware of such mourning. In Ezra 9, there is a remarkable passage where the holy man Ezra, in great affliction and sorrow, sat in astonishment. However, in verse 5, he says, "At the evening sacrifice I arose from my heaviness." When the time came for him to offer sacrifice, he rose from his heaviness. His mourning did not hinder him from fulfilling his duty. When your heart is constricted in mourning, regardless of the reasons you give for your mourning, whether it be your unworthiness or sinfulness or any other excuse, if it restricts your heart in prayer, it is not a godly sorrow. Add much prayer to much mourning. When someone approaches you and you constantly complain about your afflictions, and you mourn more than your neighbors, do you pray more than your neighbors? Do you pray as much as you complain? Is there a proportion between your praying and complaining? If there is no proportion between your praying and complaining, then be silent, complain no further, but pray more. Many other rules could be provided, but we will leave them and proceed to the more spiritual sense of the text.

Blessed are those who mourn.

I have discussed those who find themselves in a state of mourning and conduct themselves graciously within that condition. I have explained how they are blessed and how they shall be comforted. However, there is a more spiritual aspect to the text. If those in any mourning condition behave graciously, they are blessed and will be comforted. Therefore, I will focus on those who mourn for sin, making it the object of their mourning— their own sins, the sins of others, and the afflictions of the Church. Those who mourn for these reasons are truly blessed, and they shall be comforted.

Regarding these individuals, I do not intend to extensively consider the topic or discourse on godly sorrow. Instead, I will provide some insight into spiritual mourners who grieve over their sins and the sins of others. First, I will explain what true mourning for sin entails.

Firstly, true mourning for sin occurs when a soul mourns because it is against God. As David proclaims in Psalm 51:4, "Against thee, thee only have I sinned." While David had sinned against Uriah, his kingdom, and his own soul, he acknowledged that above all, he had sinned against God. This truth deeply affected him. David reiterates, "thee, thee only have I sinned," as if to say, "O Lord, I am not primarily concerned about the negative consequences of my sin, but what truly troubles me is that I have sinned against such a blessed God as you are. I have gone against your blessed will, and that pierces my heart." This is godly sorrow—mourning not so much because the sin is against oneself, but because it is against the beloved God whom the soul adores.

Secondly, true mourning for sin involves grieving over it as the greatest evil. As written in Romans 7:24, "O wretched man that I am! Who shall deliver me from this body of death?" Paul never bemoans his sufferings, despise or losses in the world. Instead, he cries out concerning his sin. His greatest sorrow is for sin.

Thirdly, true mourning for sin also involves approving of the Law that forbids that sin. The afflicted heart acknowledges the Law of God as holy, just, and good, even in the midst of the affliction caused by sin. As stated in Romans 7:12, "Wherefore the law is holy, and the commandment holy, and just, and good." Though the soul recognizes its wretchedness and vileness, it approves of the Law. Many individuals are troubled by their sin, yet their spirits are against the holiness of the Law that forbids that sin. They may wish that such a Law did not exist or that it did not reveal God's threats against their sin. However, a truly mourning heart, sensitive to the evils caused by sin through the Law, says, "I would not wish for the absence of such a Law. I bless God that I have come to know the Law, and I not only recognize it as a righteous Law but also as a good Law." This is the third aspect of true mourning for sin.

The fourth aspect is that true mourning for sin leads the heart to Jesus Christ. If you are troubled by sin, mourn, and believe that your mourning alone can satisfy God, your mourning is only carnal and natural. Many individuals, when troubled by their sin, mistakenly think that God will be satisfied solely by their mourning. However, no matter how much you mourn, even if you mourn your heart out for thousands of years, it could never satisfy God's justice. Your mourning will amount to nothing unless it drives you to Jesus Christ for satisfaction to God's justice. Mourning for sin that leads the soul to Christ—that is the blessed mourning. Conversely, if anyone finds satisfaction solely in their mourning, thinking that God will accept them without their hearts being drawn to Christ, their mourning will fade away and come to nothing.

Fifthly, true mourning for sin entails the heart's rejection of sin. It is not mourning for sin while continuing to live in sin, but rather, genuine and gracious mourning for sin leads to an eternal separation between the soul and sin. Every individual naturally has a connection between their soul and sin. However, when God afflicts the soul for sin, causing it to mourn in a godly manner, the soul becomes so aware of the evil of sin that it permanently severs the bond between sin and the soul. If sin has become so bitter to me through God's grace, then farewell to it forever. Although I may fall due to weakness, I will renounce sin. It sets the soul against sin for all time.

Sixthly, true gracious mourning for sin is a voluntary work within the soul. It is not imposed upon the soul, but rather, in a gracious manner, the soul willingly and freely applies Scriptures that make sin burdensome. It does not turn away from those Scriptures or truths. Instead, when it hears any truth or reads any Scripture that highlights the weight of sin, it willingly and gladly applies them. It rejoices in coming across any truth of God that reveals the evil of its own sin. This is a genuine and free form of mourning. Conversely, some individuals mourn desperately, compelled to do so against their will. However, when the heart can freely embrace the Word and genuinely thank God for opening its eyes to understand the evil of sin, and for applying those truths that have made sin burdensome, that is true and gracious mourning. Many individuals are troubled by sin despite their hearts rebelling and trying to rid themselves of God's truths. They seek solace in worldly company, engaging in activities such as playing or drinking, in an attempt to push away those truths. However, a gracious man or woman, when confronted with a truth that troubles them for their committed sins, goes alone and blesses God for that truth. They say, "Blessed be the time when the Lord revealed the evil of sin to my soul. May the Lord continue to impress these truths upon me." They consider it a great mercy. This is the sixth aspect of true mourning.

Seventhly, and finally, a gracious mourner for sin cannot be satisfied with anything other than the removal of the guilt and defilement of sin. A person who mourns for sin in a natural or forced manner may be satisfied if God grants them peace or removes the anguish and fears from their conscience. However, a gracious mourner for sin seeks satisfaction only in the cleansing of sin's guilt through the blood of Christ and the sanctification of the soul by the Spirit of Jesus Christ. This is the sole source of comfort for their heart.

In summary, I have briefly outlined what constitutes gracious mourning for sin. Although a more extensive exploration of these seven aspects could have been undertaken, I have only provided a glimpse. Now, those who mourn in this manner for sin are blessed for several reasons.

Firstly, they greatly honour God. The sovereignty, holiness, and justice of God are honoured when a lowly creature, who has offended the sovereign, holy, and righteous God, mourns for its committed sins. In such a state of mourning, God perceives Himself as honoured. In contrast, when a sinner obstinately persists in prideful and stubborn sinning, they defy the Almighty God and deny Him the honour He deserves. Yet, when the Word of God breaks down such a sinner, afflicting them for their committed sins, and the sinner humbly prostrates themselves before the Lord, mourning and lamenting over their sins, the name of the great, holy, and just God is exalted. Blessed are those who exalt the name of God in this manner. You should have honoured God through obedience, but you failed and dishonoured Him through disobedience. If your heart is now willing to honour God through mourning, there is blessedness.

Secondly, mourning for sin is a blessed thing because it is an evangelical grace. It is what is promised in the Gospel. When Christ says, "I will send the Comforter," you might wonder, "What is the purpose of this Comforter? To comfort us by convicting us of sin?" Indeed, the role of the Comforter is to convict the world of sin. Although it may seem paradoxical, it is the Comforter's way. Therefore, mourning for sin is blessed. There is nothing more evangelical than faith and repentance. Mourning for sin, as I have described it, is not a legalistic act or a work of the Law. The Law does not take notice of mourning for sin. Rather, it is a work of the Spirit of God, the comforting Spirit, to convict the world of sin. By the way, when you hear preaching that penetrates your heart and convicts you of sin, do not be vexed or troubled by it. This is the Holy Spirit, the Comforter, performing His first work—convicting the souls that will be saved of their sin. Therefore, embrace it and bless God for it. Now the Holy Spirit comes to pave the way for comfort in my soul. In Zechariah 12, it is written, "I will pour out on the house of David and the inhabitants of Jerusalem a spirit of grace and supplication. They will look on me, the one they have pierced, and they will mourn for him as one mourns for an only child." This mourning is a fruit of the spirit of grace and supplication promised to be poured out in the Gospel era. The first sermon we hear of Christ preaching is, "Repent, for the kingdom of heaven is at hand." He instructs His disciples to preach in the same manner. Preaching that elicits mourning for sin is an evangelical preaching. It is a fruit of the spirit of grace promised in the Gospel era. A congregation upon whom the Lord pours out this spirit of grace, causing them to look upon Christ whom they have pierced with their sins and mourn over Him, is blessed. The abundant fruit of the Gospel is manifested within them.

Thirdly, those who mourn for sin are in a blessed condition because they have acquired proper judgement. Their understanding is enlightened to discern what is truly good and evil, and their spirits are in the right disposition. Previously, they were blind and ignorant, unaware of God, themselves, and matters pertaining to their eternal well-being. But now they comprehend the essence of good and evil. Formerly, their hearts were hardened, rendering them impervious to the impact of divine truths. However, their hearts have softened graciously and are now in the right disposition. Therefore, they are blessed.

Fourthly, mourning for sin assists in alleviating other sorrows. While we reside in this world, we will encounter numerous sources of sorrow. We must grieve over something. The sorrow for sin diminishes the impact of other sorrows. Those who are deeply affected by the wrongfulness of their sins are not greatly perturbed by other afflictions. The awareness of sin overshadows the pain of other sorrows.

Fifthly, it is a means to prevent eternal sorrows. Surely, every soul must come to understand the meaning of sin at some point in their lives. No sinner on Earth can evade this experience. Sorrow for sin is inevitable. It is determined in Heaven that all individuals must die, just as it is predetermined that all must experience sorrow. If repentance is necessary, sorrow becomes an essential component. Therefore, it is far better to grieve for sin while there is a chance of pardon than to mourn for sin when there is no hope of remedy. If you spend your days here in frivolity and merriment, never experiencing the weight of sin on your spirit, you are destined to endure eternal sorrows and bear the burden of your sin for all eternity. However, blessed are those who mourn now, who comprehend the burden of their sins. By experiencing the weight of sin now, they feel it at a time when there is hope of deliverance from this evil for all eternity. Thus, they are undoubtedly blessed. Consider how many thousands of men and women have lived carefree lives, proceeding through their existence with hardened hearts, never becoming aware of their sins. Yet, on their sickbeds or at the point of death, they cry out in anguish over their sins, only to find that the Lord has withdrawn from them. Now, I would ask such individuals, would you have considered it a blessed thing if you had carried the weight of sin on your soul before, during your healthy and strong years? On their sickbeds and at the point of death, they exclaim, "Oh, how fortunate it would have been if I had known the evil of sin earlier! How blessed it would have been if, during the times I spent in revelry, mirth, and taverns with certain companions, I had devoted those moments to mourning for my sin. How blessed it would have been if I had been alone with God, lamenting for my sin! How happy it would have been for me! I would now have comfort and peace in my sickbed." Yet, I was led astray by my senses and my flesh, seeking to gratify the desires of the flesh. I thought, "Let me live joyfully and extravagantly for a while." And now, the weight of sin descends upon me. I feel its burden, and I cry out for the Lord's mercy. The sins of my merry gatherings come to mind—my oaths and violations of the Sabbath, my indulgence in drunkenness and immorality, my lies, and my neglect of God and His worship. It would have been better for me to have been a mourner earlier. Therefore, blessed are those who mourn.

Lastly, it is a disposition that prepares one for the grace of God. None taste the sweetness of God's grace in Christ more than those who mourn for sin. A single drop of mercy is incredibly sweet. It is worth more than countless worlds. The application of a single drop of Jesus Christ's blood to the soul is profoundly sweet. Such a disposition is blessed. We preach Jesus Christ and the glorious mysteries of grace and salvation to you time and again. However, many thousands regard these precious truths with little importance. You hear them and depart, your hearts unaffected. Yet, if you were among those who mourn, you would treasure even the crumbs that fall from the table. Those truths that are currently disregarded would be highly esteemed. They would be worth more than thousands upon thousands of worlds to you. Therefore, blessed are those who mourn, for they possess the disposition to value Jesus Christ, the great work He has accomplished in the world, and the supreme purpose of God the Father. This purpose has been His chief work and His great design throughout eternity—to magnify Himself. Blessed are those who possess such a disposition, valuing the glory of God in Jesus Christ.

Seventhly, there is another reason why those who mourn are blessed: the abundance of promises made to them. This is one comprehensive promise, although there are numerous others throughout Scripture that offer comfort to those who mourn. Simply reading Psalm 34:18 and Isaiah 57:15 would be enough to bring comfort to the mourners. They are in a blessed condition because they shall be comforted.

Firstly, they will be absolved of the sins for which they mourn. Yes, you are absolved, and one day you will come to know that you are freed from those sins. The sins that weigh on your heart will never be held against your soul. This is a blessed assurance, be certain of it. Perhaps the Holy Spirit has not yet come upon you to seal this in your soul, but you are one upon whom the Holy Spirit will descend, making it clear and certain to your soul. Your pardon is already sealed in Heaven, and it will be sealed in your conscience. Just as I can regard a condemned criminal as a blessed man if I know that his pardon has been sealed, even if he himself is not yet aware of his blessedness, those who understand the Word of God and comprehend His revealed will in the Scriptures know that you are a blessed individual, and you will come to know it one day.

Secondly, not only will you be assured of your absolution, but your mourning for sin will cause God to have compassion on you in your afflictions. The Lord will bring sweetness to your afflictions. The reason why our afflictions are so bitter is because sin is not bitter enough. However, for those who bear their sin as a burden, they will experience the Lord's compassion in all their afflictions.

Thirdly, you will find comfort in the fact that your very mourning for sin will be a blessing to help you overcome the very sin for which you mourn. This is certain: either a person's sin will put an end to their mourning, or their mourning will put an end to their sin. If one continues in sin, they will cease to mourn. However, if they do not cease to mourn, they will cease to sin. Mourning for sin possesses a special efficacy that aids in overcoming the sin for which you mourn. The bitterness you now experience acts as a specific means to combat the lingering worms within your soul.

Lastly, above all, you are blessed if you mourn for sin because one day you will be completely freed from sin. You will no longer sin against God. Won't that be a blessed time? Won't it bring you comfort? Certainly, such a time exists. To delve into these specific points with supporting Scriptures would require a significant amount of time, which I am not willing to do here. Instead, let us continue exploring Christ's sermon.

Now, by way of application, let's address some important points. Firstly, what will happen to those who rejoice in sin? Those who find pleasure and delight in sin, who sin and laugh in their wickedness, who make sin their source of entertainment and ultimate joy in the world? There are many individuals whose greatest delight lies in indulging their sinful desires and lusts. Oh, what a dreadful condition they are in! The wickedness of their souls is truly terrifying. Is there nothing else that brings joy to their hearts apart from that which opposes the blessed God Himself? Nothing else that caused Jesus Christ to suffer to the point of death, sweating drops of blood, and crying out, "My God, my God, why have you forsaken me?" Beware, for such individuals are reserved for eternal sorrows. If Jesus Christ pronounces those who mourn for sin as blessed, then surely those who rejoice in sin are cursed.

Furthermore, mourning for sin is not synonymous with melancholy. To mourn and be troubled by one's sin is not to become heavy-hearted and melancholic. The weight of sin laid upon the soul is the work of the Spirit of God, who intends to bless this soul for all eternity. Therefore, do not view it as foolish for people to be troubled by their sin. Allow me to provide two examples: one against melancholy and one against folly. Let's begin with melancholy. Who, according to Scripture, had more sorrow for sin than David? Read his Penitential Psalms: Psalm 38, Psalm 51, and Psalm 6. David experienced the burdensome weight of sin and mourned over it. Yet, the text states that David had a ruddy complexion and an active spirit. Now, for folly, consider Psalm 88. I have not come across any psalm that demonstrates the sorrow and affliction of a godly individual more than Psalm 88, penned by Heman. In 1 Kings 4:31, Heman is depicted by the Holy Spirit as one of the wisest men on earth. Yet, in Psalm 88, we witness him engulfed in sorrow and affliction, particularly due to sin. Therefore, mourning for sin is not folly but blessedness. It is the work of the Spirit of Christ. However, the main focus is to address those who are mourners.

Firstly, let me share with you the comforts that are found in Scripture, providing comfort to your soul. Comfort is available in various ways. Firstly, know that you are dealing with a God of infinite grace and mercy. While you may perceive God as filled with wrath and justice, you are actually engaging with a God of boundless mercy, who delights in showing mercy. You are dealing with a God whose mercy is His greatest glory. His grandest purpose is to magnify His free grace. Therefore, take solace in your mourning for sin. Consider this: if a child has a loving and merciful father and mother, and the child privately enters a room, wringing their hands, mourning and lamenting over their inability to please their parents, grieving over any actions that may cause them sorrow, it would deeply affect your hearts to witness this display of genuine sorrow and mourning from your child. The compassion you feel towards your child stems from the compassion that the Lord, who is an infinite ocean of mercy, has poured out upon you. Even if you were to gather all the compassion of all the parents in the world, it would be nothing more than a drop compared to the infinite ocean of God's mercy. Therefore, the Lord regards your mourning and your inability to do more to please Him, acknowledging that your actions cause Him grief. He sees your mourning, holds His bottle, and every tear shed in your mourning for sin is collected in God's bottle.

Secondly, know that you are dealing with God in a covenant of grace. If you were to approach God solely as the Creator and yourself as a creature, in the context of the covenant of works, you would be undone, and all your mourning would be in vain. Even if you were to wail for your sin throughout your days, God would pay no heed. However, you are dealing with God in the covenant of grace, which He has established with poor sinners through Jesus Christ. In this covenant, your mourning for sin is accepted. When you come into the presence of God, burdened by the guilt of your sin and considering His holiness and righteousness, little comfort may be found. However, when you approach God through the mediation of His Son, and in the context of the covenant of grace, you will grasp the true meaning of this covenant. The Lord has set apart a people for Himself, not dealing with them based on their own merits but sending His Son to make satisfaction on their behalf. All God's dealings with them are through His Son, and their approach to God is accepted only through His Son. Understanding this brings great comfort and solace. After Adam's fall, our condition was such that God could have forever rejected us, paying no attention to any mourning for sin. However, it is through the redemptive work of Christ's blood that mourning for sin is regarded by God. You are not dealing with God based solely on your own merits but through His Son, who presented His sorrows to the Father on behalf of your soul.

Thirdly, understand that Jesus Christ has made a sufficient atonement for sin. In other words, the Lord Jesus Christ has rectified all the harm that sin has caused to God. The Lord has not suffered more harm from your sin than He has received honour through Christ's suffering for sin. Your sin may have been grave and greatly offended God, but the Lord Jesus has paid the price for all that wrongdoing. Now, when there is a means of atonement, when I approach God seeking forgiveness for my sin and assistance in overcoming it, I know that God will never suffer any harm from my sin that has not already been reconciled through the blood of His Son. If I were dealing with God on His own terms, I might think that the Lord would eventually take vengeance on me, even if He is currently patient with me. However, now that I understand the true meaning of atonement that Jesus Christ has accomplished and the price He has paid, I see a way in which all the harm my sin has caused to God has been rectified. This realization cannot help but uplift the heart greatly.

# SERMON IX

## The Comforts of Mourners for Sin

"Blessed are they that mourn, for they shall be comforted." - Matthew 5:4

To proceed, fourthly, know that it is God's very way of bringing sinners to eternal life to lead them in a path of mourning for sin. Just as the Israelites were brought out of the captivity of Babylon, which served as a type of God bringing sinners out of the captivity of sin, He said, "With supplications and weeping will I lead them." It is the method God employs to draw sinners to Himself. The way to Jerusalem, which symbolizes the vision of peace, passes through Bethani, the house of sorrows. Christ Himself took that path when He journeyed to Jerusalem. Throughout all ages, God has led His servants to true comfort through the way of sorrow. The route to the valley of Beracho, the valley of blessing, is through the valley of Bacah, the valley of tears. In these indulgent times, some believe they have discovered a new route to comfort. May they find success with their new approach to comfort. Some think that there is a quicker way to comfort than the one Christ has presented here in His Word. They consider His preaching, in this Sermon of His, that the way to comfort is through mourning, to be legalistic. If you regard Christ as a legalistic preacher for proclaiming that the blessed ones are the mourners who shall receive comfort, then you may cherish your thoughts. If you dare to rely on the comfort you have obtained by other means, then proceed with your audacity. However, Christ presents this way and declares that those who mourn are the ones He takes it upon Himself to comfort. Christ is anointed to preach glad tidings to the mourners.

Fifthly, take solace in knowing that it is the work of the Spirit, sent into the world as the Comforter, to convict of sin (John 16:8). As Christ promised the coming of the Comforter, He explained the role of the Comforter. The first task of the Comforter is to convict souls of their sinful state, to bring awareness of their condition outside of Jesus Christ, to illuminate their wretched condition. The Spirit, even the comforting Spirit, convicts, according to the text. One might have expected that, in accordance with human ways, it would be the spirit of the Law, a legalistic spirit, that convicts of sin. Yet, it is the Spirit, the comforting Spirit, that convicts of sin. Therefore, if you lack this conviction of sin, no matter how much you may speak of the comforts of the Holy Spirit, there is undoubtedly a misunderstanding within you. For when the Holy Spirit comes to comfort, He first enters the heart to convict of sin. Therefore, you, whose spirit is convicted of sin, of the unbelief that resides in your heart, and is convicted powerfully to the point of being deeply affected, this should be a comfort to you. O Lord, through Your mercy, I am not only on the path that You lead those whom You have purposed to save, but I also experience the work of the Comforter. I hope He has come to my soul, for He has convicted me of my sin, and I find my heart affected by sorrow for my sin in a way different from before.

Sixthly, another source of comfort for those who mourn for sin is that the Lord values your mourning. You may think that you can do little for God, as you have a wretched and sinful soul, and you are weak and unable to do much. But if you can mourn, know that such mourning (as has been explained) is a sacrifice to God, as acceptable as any offering you can present to Him. In Psalm 51, it is said, "The sacrifices of God are a broken spirit; a broken and contrite heart, O God, you will not despise." Such mourning is equivalent to all sacrifices. Therefore, even when you have no offering to present to God, if you possess a broken spirit for your sin, God highly values that. Let me tell you this: there is nothing that God values more than the tears of a broken heart, that which springs from a contrite spirit. It is a blessing, for godly sorrow arises from both faith and a sense of sin. I can confidently say that, next to the blood of Jesus Christ, nothing is esteemed higher by God than this. Therefore, you can find comfort in the present.

Seventhly, know that although in our eyes the difference between sins is significant, and rightly so, as we should strive to consider our sin in all its enormity and aggravations, when it comes into the hands of Jesus Christ for satisfaction, great and small sins do not make such a difference in His work of mediation. If you spill water in a house from a pail, it creates a great mess, but there is not much difference if you pour it into the Thames. Similarly, though the difference of sin weighs heavily on our consciences, when it comes to the infinite sea of the mediation and satisfaction of Jesus Christ and the grace that is found there, the difference is not so significant. Oh, may only those who mourn for sin hear this, so that the hearing of it may lead others to have their hearts broken as well.

Eighthly, for your comfort, know this: as long as receiving comfort from the Word makes you aware of your unworthiness, that sense of unworthiness should not hinder you from taking comfort. It is a certain rule that when taking comfort makes me more aware of my unworthiness, that sense of unworthiness should not prevent me from embracing comfort. This is a common concern that troubles those who mourn; they fear that taking comfort would be presumptuous. But remember this rule: if taking comfort makes you more aware of your unworthiness, that sense of unworthiness should not hinder you from grasping onto comfort. Let this be both a rule of guidance and encouragement for those who mourn for sin.

Furthermore, there are various rules to assist those who mourn in managing their spirits while seeking comfort.

The first rule is to strive for a quiet and patient heart. Sorrow can be tiresome to our flesh and blood, but when the sorrow is for sin, it is accompanied by the grace of God. Therefore, if mourning for sin leads to impatience, frustration, and agitation, it is not right. Mourning for sin should have a sweetness to it and should make you patient under God's hand, waiting for the time when He will speak comfort to your soul. You may find yourself in a condition where you are aware of such a great evil upon you that no creature in heaven or earth can comfort you. In such a state, resolve to wait for the day of goodness, for the time of love, when God will speak peace to your soul. And in the meantime, commit to waiting upon Him, using all the means at your disposal until your last breath, regardless of the outcome. Let this be a guiding principle for how to direct your heart when you are in a state of mourning.

And then a second rule is this: Do not just dwell and fixate on the pit of despair you find yourself in. Even while mourning for sin, even if you don't yet have assurance that your sins are forgiven, look up to the promise. You may think it doesn't apply to you, but fix your gaze upon it. Look up to the brazen serpent if sin has stung you, just as those who were bitten in the wilderness looked up to the brazen serpent. Present the Covenant of Grace to your soul, for just as the presentation of the Law has the power to terrify the heart, the presentation of the Gospel has the power to draw the heart to it. There is a vivifying quality in the grace of the Gospel when it is beheld. It is not merely an object for the eyes or understanding; there is power in it. It enters the heart to work upon it. Many who mourn allow their hearts to sink and only consider the darkness of their souls, but they do not lift their eyes to the graciousness of the promise. We have an excellent Scripture for this in Psalm 86:4-5. David says, "Rejoice the soul of your servant, for to you, O Lord, I lift up my soul." That's the way to find joy. You pray to the Lord, longing for Him to bring joy to your soul, and yet you let your soul grovel on the ground. But rejoice the soul of your servant, for to you, O Lord, I lift up my soul. This Scripture is extremely valuable to those who mourn for sin, for nothing reveals more fault in mourners than their desire for joy in their hearts while allowing their hearts to remain low. They do not stir themselves up or strive to lift up their souls. David says, "For to you, O Lord, I lift up my soul." And in verse 5, "For you, Lord, are good and ready to forgive, and abundant in mercy to all who call upon you." The Lord is ready if you can only lift up your soul and be ready. Therefore, beware that the anguish and trouble of your soul do not hinder you from looking upon the promise, from listening to the promise that is made to you. In Exodus 6:9, we find that when Moses spoke to the children of Israel, the text says, "They did not heed Moses." Why? What did Moses come for? He came to bring them a message of comfort, but they did not listen to him because of their anguish of spirit and cruel bondage. The anguish of their spirits and the cruel bondage prevented them from listening to Moses. Be cautious that you, as a mourner for sin, do not find yourself in the same condition when it's time for me to apply the promise to you. Do not let your anguish of spirit and cruel bondage prevent you from heeding what is said to you. It is not good for a person crossing a narrow bridge over a great and deep river, especially if they have a weak head, to keep looking at the river and contemplating its depth and the abyss they would fall into if they were to slip. Such constant staring would be enough to make them fall. Instead, let them look straight ahead to the shore and proceed as carefully as they can. Once they have reached the shore, they can then look back safely and thank God for their deliverance. It should be the same for a heart afflicted by sin. While you mourn and see it as a dreadful abyss ready to swallow you, you are fixated on it, which puts you in danger of being consumed. But the truth is, when you are on this precipice (for the work of repentance is akin to a precipice), you are to look at the promise, at the grace of God in the Gospel that is offered to you. And when you have reached the shore and are able to apply the promise of grace, then you may look back at the dreadful abyss that almost swallowed you and give thanks to God for His deliverance.

And then a third rule in seeking comfort is this: Do not be more concerned with obtaining comfort for yourself than with the glory of God. Even when you mourn for sin, strive to have your heart in such a frame that you are as concerned and careful about the glory of God as you are about finding comfort for yourself. We have experienced that many who are greatly afflicted by their sin are solely focused on comfort. They long for someone to speak words of comfort to them, and no words are acceptable unless they bring immediate comfort. But in the meantime, they are little aware of the dishonour God has endured or how God should receive honour. In contrast, a heart that is rightly influenced, when it apprehends the evil of sin, is equally preoccupied with the dishonour that their sin has brought to God. They contemplate how this dishonour can be rectified. They think, "If I were to continue living in a way that dishonours this blessed God, what would become of me? How much better would it have been if I had never been born than to live dishonouring a God who is so glorious in Himself and infinitely worthy of all honour from His creatures." It is good when the honour of God occupies your heart, and you are concerned about it. Because you cannot mend that breach, you listen to what you hear in the Gospel of Christ. But you are also careful that any rule that opposes your sin or helps you in obedience to God is embraced by your heart as eagerly as the rules that bring immediate comfort. Let me explain this using a simile to ensure better understanding: Many with weak stomachs, on the verge of collapse, long for something invigorating. They seek hot drinks, thinking that these will provide them with more energy and heat, suiting their condition. However, the truth is that hot drinks only scorch and deplete them, making them weaker and weaker, and depleting their natural heat. But a wise physician, when he comes and inquires about their intake, will tell them that they have spoiled themselves. They should have purged the ill humours in their bodies, taken broths and other things that may not be as hot, but gradually strengthen their constitution, nourish them, and produce good blood. Good blood, in turn, raises good spirits, and those are the best spirits. While one might experience a temporary surge of heat from hot drinks, it does not last. But if one can acquire heat from good blood, that will endure, and the person will live and become strong. This principle applies to Christians in every way. Some are very aware of their sin and long for all comfort. They desire only to hear about Christ and His free grace, and nothing else satisfies them unless it directly brings them comfort. Well, perhaps that might provide temporary heat, but the truth is that this heat fades away and comes to nothing. On the other hand, if a wise physician for the soul applies the word that can purge the evil from their hearts, the word that carries the essence of sanctification and walking with God in the path of holiness, and if they are encouraged to embrace those things alongside the free grace of the Gospel, where Christ is presented not only as a Priest offering sacrifice but also as a King ruling in the heart, that will produce good blood. Therefore, be concerned about the glory of God, about how you should live to His praise, as much as you are concerned about finding comfort for yourself. Otherwise, the eager pursuit of comfort for yourself may lead to your downfall.

Fourthly, and then furthermore, you must seek comfort in order to obtain grace, rather than seeking grace solely for the purpose of comfort. There are those who seek grace only because it brings them comfort and eases their conscience, but they have no genuine love for grace apart from its potential to bring personal comfort. However, a godly soul seeks comfort to enhance and advance grace. They desire comfort because it will enlarge their heart for God. The more peace they experience in their soul, the more it will further the grace within them. Therefore, they seek comfort. On the other hand, a hypocrite seeks grace only because they cannot have comfort without it. The true seeker of God's comfort desires it to facilitate the growth of grace within them.

Fifthly, the last rule I would give to mourners is this: If you are unable to exercise a faith of assurance, try to exercise a faith of adherence instead. This is something anyone can do. You may say that only believers can do this, but you do not know whether there is already a seed of faith in your heart. Let your condition be as sorrowful as can be imagined. You claim to be a wretched sinner, and we will grant that. Yet, even in this very moment when you view yourself as such a vile sinner, there is nothing preventing you from exercising a faith of adherence. That is, casting your soul upon the free and full grace of God in Christ and clinging to it. You may ask, "But can I presume? Do I have any right to it?" I say this: No soul has any right to the promise of grace other than by casting themselves upon it, which grants them the right. Now, it may be that you do not have the faith of assurance, which concludes, "Well, Christ is mine, and because I know this, I will trust and believe in Him." However, you can still do this: I see the promise offered to wretched and sinful creatures. Although I do not know if He is mine, I will venture my soul and eternal state upon it. I will lie here and entrust my soul to the free grace of God in Christ for forgiveness, sanctification, salvation, and all that is good. This is the path to finding comfort. Endeavour to exercise an act of faith in adherence, cleaving to it, even if you cannot exercise an act of assurance. I have spoken these words in an attempt to comfort mourners. For Christ promises that they will find comfort. If I can bring this promise, spoken by Christ in this sermon, to just one soul, it will be sufficient. Even if some may harden their hearts and misuse what is said, it will be enough, and Christ will accept it. If the promised comfort can be brought home to even one soul through this sermon, Christ says, "You shall be comforted." And how can this be achieved if not through the Word? Therefore, it is right for you to come and listen to the Word. It may be that you have come to hear the Word many times, but it has not comforted your soul. There has been no union between the Word and your soul, and so you have departed without comfort. Nonetheless, come again and again. Do not say that it is in vain for you to attend the Word because you have already heard, I am certain, as precious truths as any can be heard, and you have not found them comforting. Well, even though they have not comforted you at that time, there has not yet been a connection between your heart and those truths. Still, come again and again, and eventually there will be a connection between the Word and your soul. In one sentence, the Spirit of God may implant something in your soul that you have not experienced in your entire life. Oh, one may say, "I find my heart troubled and mourning for sin. I long for comfort, and God knows I have read the Word, where I find precious and excellent truths. But they do not reach my heart." Well, I will continue to come and wait, hoping that the angel will come and stir my heart. Even if it has not happened yet, eventually you will be able to say, like Mr Glover speaking to his friend Austin, "Oh, he has come! He has come!" So, persist in using means, waiting for the Word to come and connect with your heart so that you may find comfort. Now, I cannot say for certain if it is the comfort of Jesus Christ that has comforted my soul in my mourning condition. Oh, if only I knew whether it is His comfort or not. Well, let me give you two or three signs to discern whether it is the comfort of Jesus Christ or not.

Firstly, if your joy and comfort are the joy of the Lord, then it becomes your strength. As Nehemiah said to the people, joy brings strength, and comfort brings strength to your soul. For instance, can you say, "Through God's mercy, although I was weak before and could not overcome certain corruptions, since God has spoken peace to my soul, I have found more strength in my heart to overcome my corruptions than ever before"? If your comfort has such an effect, it is from God. If it leads you towards Him, it comes from Him. If it is a delusion or a fancy, it will not produce these results. Hypocrites are exposed in this regard as much as in anything else. When they are in terror, they are cautious of sin and diligent in their duties. However, when they have peace, they become more careless. It is different for those whose hearts are sincere with God.

Secondly, the true comfort of Christians is sustained by that which initially produced it. Just as in nature, what begets a thing also nourishes it, so it is with the human heart. Whatever nurtures your comfort is what brought forth your comfort, and what brought it forth will also nourish it, and nothing else. Therefore, if your comfort is truly spiritual and originates from the Spirit of Jesus Christ in your heart, nothing will nourish your comfort more than Jesus

Christ Himself. This will create within you a longing for more communion with Him. Hypocrites may have comfort, but what sustains and maintains their comfort are external things they possess, the esteem of the world, their talents and abilities, and earthly pleasures. However, the comforts of the saints are sustained by higher principles. The Scriptures compare their joy to the light of the sun, which cannot be sustained by low and base things like the light of a candle. Therefore, if you find that the light in your soul is sustained by principles that are above, by the Sun of Righteousness shining into your heart, then it is true comfort.

Thirdly, if your comfort is of such a nature that it governs all other comforts in your heart, particularly the comfort of hoping for the forgiveness of your sins, then it is genuine. The comforts of a hypocrite, although they may experience great joy, cannot overpower their natural comfort, nor can they displace the corrupt joy that was already present in their souls. However, the joy of the saints is different. It overrules natural joy and eradicates corrupt and sinful joy. Just as the light of the sun extinguishes the light of a kitchen fire and dims the light of a candle, the light and warmth of true comfort in the soul will displace the carnal joy previously experienced. As Augustine said, "How sweet it is to be without such sweetness." There was a time when I thought I could not imagine living without the sweetness of certain sinful desires. But now, how sweet it is to be without them. Many of you may live merrily, but the joy you have is nothing more than joy in base and low things—a corrupt joy. However, if you were to experience the comforts of the Holy Spirit, it would supplant that joy, leaving no room for the corrupt joy that currently satisfies your heart. This concludes my address to those who are mourners. However, I have a few more words to speak.

Firstly, I address those who have not yet experienced such mourning, and secondly, I will speak to the saints, encouraging them to mourn further since Christ promises such comfort. For those who are reluctant to mourn, there is a group of people who are afraid of mourning, thinking that it will lead them to despair if they give in to mourning for their sins in any way. Consequently, when their hearts are touched by the Word, they strive with all their might to dismiss it, resolving never to return to hear it again if it penetrates their consciences and cuts deep. They cannot sleep as peacefully that night as they did before.

They regard mourning for their sins with such apprehension, as if it were the most wicked thing in the world. Oh, deluded soul, you are utterly mistaken. Remember this text and understand that, if you acknowledge this to be the book of God and these to be the words of Christ, you may know that you are mistaken. Christ declares that those who mourn are blessed. If you desire to become a blessed person, be receptive to the spirit of mourning. If the Spirit of God begins to approach your soul through the Word, be willing to open your heart to Him, embrace it, and cherish that Word. Recall this text, speaking figuratively, from the book of Daniel, chapter 7, verse 28: "My thoughts greatly troubled me, and my countenance changed, but I kept the matter in my heart." This is an instructive passage. Daniel had something revealed to him by God. Granted, your situation differs from Daniel's, but God had conveyed a message to him, and the text states that his thoughts troubled him, and his countenance was visibly affected. Did he cast it aside? No, he kept the matter in his heart. I firmly believe that when some of you come to hear the Word, there are moments when something pierces your spirits, troubling your thoughts. When you lie awake on your beds at night, there is something that troubles your hearts, and you seek the company of others to distract yourself from it. Oh, no! Rather, you should hold on to it. How do you know if the Lord is now in the process of making you blessed? Previously, you had been on a path leading to wrath and misery, in a cursed way. Now, the Lord Christ is drawing near to bless you, as far as you know. You have an opportunity for blessedness that, if rejected, may never come again. If you disregard the Word that is beginning to work in your heart, the Lord may decree that it never strikes your heart again, and that the Spirit never accompanies this Word again. Then, when you seek comfort on your sickbed, this Scripture may be held against you: "Blessed are those who mourn, for they shall be comforted." You will regret having rejected the ways of the Spirit that would have led you to mourn. If you desire comfort on your sickbed and deathbed, be willing to mourn and continue in the work of the Holy Spirit when it begins to stir your heart in a mournful way over your sins. Do not be deterred by any notion, even if some may teach a new way to completely abandon mourning. Know that it is the old way in which the saints of God have previously walked. Embrace this, and to help you embrace it, here are a few instructions.

Firstly, it is advisable for those whose hearts are troubled by their sins to find solitude, to remove themselves from the presence of others and retreat. Whenever you feel your heart beginning to be troubled, take time alone to meditate on your sin and bring the matter before God in the privacy of your soul. It is worth noting the excellent example we can learn from Peter when he committed his great sin and Jesus looked upon him. As you know, the text says, "He went out and wept bitterly." However, I discovered in the Gospel of Mark, chapter 14, verse 72, it is mentioned that "when he thought thereon, he wept." The term translated as "thought thereon" in the original language signifies any kind of violence a person inflicts upon themselves. Some translations render it as "cast himself out," indicating a forceful act of separating oneself from company. Peter had had enough of them. So, when you feel the Spirit of God beginning to stir and work in your heart, cast yourself out from the company, as it were, and diligently engage your thoughts in matters that may further affect your heart.

Secondly, present God to your soul to the utmost extent possible. Consider that you are dealing with an infinite God in all your ways. Present God and Christ to your soul. You may say, "I dare not." But do not be afraid of this. One day, you will behold the Lord in His glory. Therefore, present the Lord to your soul now in His glory.

Thirdly, do not be content with any duty until you find your heart starting to break. Call yourself to account. Now, I am praying to God, and I can say, "Forgive us our trespasses as we forgive them." But do I find my heart mourning for them? I refer to my own sins. Do I acknowledge them with bitterness and trouble of soul? Oh, it would be an excellent disposition not to cease until you sense some movement in your heart. You may object, "But I cannot get my heart to stir. God knows I would give a great deal if, every time I approached God's presence, I could lament and mourn for my sin. Oh, but I cannot." It is good that you acknowledge your desire to do so, whereas there are some who think that once they become believers, they need not mourn. To refute this mistaken opinion, understand this: After the assurance of the pardon of sin, more mourning is required and typically preached by the saints than before. I can even provide you with a remarkable example from David. You will find that after David had sinned, and the prophet came to convict him of his sin, David confessed his sin. The prophet, speaking in God's name, told him that the Lord had forgiven his sin. However, a considerable time later, when David composed Psalm 51, you will see that he began mourning afresh, even though his sin had already been forgiven, and he was aware of it. Take a close look at Psalm 51 and observe the title that David gives to the Psalm: "To the chief Musician, a Psalm of David, when Nathan the Prophet came unto him after he had gone into Bathsheba." So, Nathan had come to David before he wrote this Psalm. When Nathan confronted him, he assured David that his sin had been forgiven. Yet, David wrote this Psalm and lamented his sin with bitterness. He cried out to God to restore the joy of his salvation, so that the broken bones might rejoice. Even though he had received that message from God that his sin was forgiven, his very bones were broken. If the Lord were to send a messenger from heaven to inform you, man or woman, that all the sins you have ever committed throughout your life are freely forgiven, what would you do? Truly, upon hearing such news, you have every reason to retire to your closet this evening and lament your sin. If possible, let your tears flow tonight, as David says, he made his bed swim with tears. Therefore, the assurance of the pardon of our sin does not hinder mourning for sin. It simply makes our mourning more sweet and infused with the gospel. To assist you in attaining such a heart of mourning, look up to God and seek the spirit of mourning. As mentioned in the latter part of Zechariah 12, "I will pour the spirit of grace and supplication upon them, and they shall look upon me whom they have pierced, and they shall mourn for him as one mourns for his only son and shall be in bitterness for him as one is in bitterness for his firstborn." Notice that God has promised not only comfort to mourners but also mourning to sinners. Therefore, you are not excluded. The promise is boundless: "I will pour out the Spirit of grace and supplication, and they shall mourn." So, cry out to the Lord and plead His promise. Also, remember the promise, "I will take away the heart of stone and give them a heart of flesh." God's promise is not contingent on certain conditions or individuals but is a free and absolute promise.

Furthermore, it is beneficial to engage with those who are broken-hearted Christians. Being in the company of such individuals will make you reflect and think, "Lord God, someone who lives so righteously and graciously possesses a broken heart. I, on the other hand, have a wretched heart, yet I cannot find my heart breaking." The fellowship of these humble and contrite hearts will greatly aid you.

Lastly, if you cannot mourn, then mourn that you cannot mourn. This will be acceptable to God. You may say, "I cannot command my heart to mourn for sin as I desire." However, can you not go to God and lament and complain about this as the greatest evil that afflicts you? Say, "Lord, I consider this dull and hard heart of mine to be a most fearful evil upon me."

And finally, do not permit yourself to find joy or comfort in anything in this world until you experience a broken heart for your sin. If your heart does not yield in mourning for sin, then it shall not rejoice. Do not allow it to indulge in vain mirth and joy until it breaks. Although you may have previously taken pleasure in certain company and in the use of worldly delights, it is true that it is lawful for a person to find comfort. However, is it suitable for someone like me, who can never mourn for my sin? No, let this be charged upon my heart: first, strive to be affected by sin and mourn for sin. Then, I hope I will find more comfort in both God and His creation than before.

Lastly, take great care not to sin after mourning. If you desire to possess a mournful heart as described in my text, guard against sinning. When God begins to wound your heart for your sin, above all times, you need to be vigilant and cautious. Do not permit yourself to willfully sin again after mourning.

# SERMON X

## An Exhortation to Mourners for Sin

"Blessed are they that mourn, for they shall be comforted." - Matthew 5:4

I have just a word or two of further exhortation regarding the topic of mourning for sin.

It is an exhortation even for those who have already mourned for sin to continue in their mourning, to make it an ongoing practice. I mentioned earlier that the assurance of the pardon of sin does not hinder mourning for it; rather, it should promote it, as was the case with David. Therefore, you who are the people of God, God expects you to mourn for sin. You understand how sin is a violation of God's holiness and His blessed will more than others. You are aware of the price paid for the purchase of its pardon. Therefore, mourn, for your sins grieve the Spirit of God more than others. While the sins of other men may provoke God's Spirit, your sins grieve God's Spirit. Your sins do more harm than others, so mourn. You comprehend the immense damage sin causes in the world. It burdens the entire creation, and should you not be aware of the evil that remains in your hearts? You know that sin is a greater evil than any affliction.

Therefore, carry the weight of sin with a heavy heart for as long as you live. God does not have much time left to glorify Himself in your sorrow. It will not be long before you are delivered from your sin. However, as long as you have this body of sin, God expects you to mourn. God expects you not only to mourn for your own sin but also to mourn for the sins of others. Blessed are those who do so, for they shall be comforted.

Firstly, we are to mourn for the sins of others. We have remarkable Scripture to support this. In Ezra 9:3, we witness the lamentable state Ezra was in due to the sins of his people. He tore his garments and sat down astonished because of their sins. David, in Psalm 119:53, expressed horror gripping him when he observed the wicked forsaking God's law. His heart was struck with horror at the wickedness of men abandoning God's law. In verses 136 and 158, he says, "Rivers of water run down my eyes because they keep not thy law" and "I beheld the transgressors and was grieved because they kept not thy word." David's spirit was in a blessed state when he penned this Psalm, and we see how affected he was by the sins of others. In the famous passage in Ezekiel 9, we find that God takes note of those who mourn for the sins of the places where they live. If we turn to the New Testament, we find numerous examples. The apostle Paul, in 2 Corinthians 12, expresses his intention to mourn and bewail those who have sinned when he visits them. In 2 Peter 2:7, it is said of righteous Lot that "his soul was vexed," and in verse 8, it is stated that "he vexed his righteous soul from day to day with their unlawful deeds." The Greek word used in these passages indicates oppression, as much as a burden that oppresses the soul. The sins of others were burdensome to Lot's soul, causing him distress. That is the meaning of the word. We find the same word in Acts 7:24, where it speaks of Moses helping the man who was oppressed. The word used there is "καταπονουμένῳ," the same as used for Lot's vexed soul. Lot's soul was troubled by the wickedness he witnessed, feeling oppressed by it, just as sickness weakens a person. That is the meaning of the first word in verse 7. Then, the second word in verse 8, "vext," is better translated as "cruciate" in the original. It signifies tormenting a person on a rack. It is as if the Holy Spirit is saying that the wickedness of those among whom Lot lived put his gracious soul on the rack. He experienced the torment of a person on a rack due to the sins of those around him. As for you, the wicked and ungodly, do not assume that you will only suffer for your own sins. You will suffer because of the anguish you cause the godly. Do not believe that your sins do not concern them at all. They indeed wrong them. Suppose you saw a man striking your father in the street, and you approached him to ask why he did it, and he responded, "What's that to you? I did not strike you." But he struck your father. Likewise, when you sin, you dishonor their God, their Father. This is a form of crucifixion to them.

The reasons, therefore, why we must mourn for the sins of others as well as our own are as follows. Firstly, it is because the blessed God is greatly dishonoured. Oh, how it must pierce the heart of a godly person to witness the dishonouring of God, whom their soul loves. God, who is infinitely blessed, glorious, and worthy of all honour from all creatures, is dishonoured by lowly and wretched worms. There is a story of Cræsus' son who was mute all his life until he saw a soldier attempting to kill his father. The affection he had for his father broke the barriers of his speech, and he cried out, "Why do you kill Cræsus?" Likewise, when we witness the dishonouring of our beloved God, it must inevitably pierce our hearts.

Secondly, our love for others should cause grief. Why? Because when we see others sinning against God, we witness them causing harm to themselves. Doesn't it grieve you when you see individuals harming and destroying themselves? When you hear of houses on fire and the excruciating pain they endure, you mourn for it. It would even soften the hardest heart in the world. You can never witness a person as miserable as one consumed by sin. Sin makes them the most wretched creature in the world. Therefore, if you have any love for your brother, mourn for their sin.

Thirdly, the sins of others bring much evil into the world. What is the cause of the evils present in the world if not the sins committed within it? As long as you live in this world, you cannot help but share in the miseries caused by sin. As Ecclesiastes 9 says, "One sinner destroys much good." So, what do many sinners do? Like vapors ascending imperceptibly but descending in noticeable storms and tempests, the sins of the world may ascend unnoticed, but they will come down in grievous storms.

Fourthly, there is cause for mourning for the sins of others because whenever you see someone commit a sin, you must consider that the root of that sin is in your own heart. It is said of Bradford that he never saw a person commit a sin or heard someone swear an oath (or the like) without saying, "God be merciful to me, a sinner." He recognized the root of that sin within his own heart. It is true that the Lord has restrained you from committing such heinous sins, but the root of those sins still exists in your heart. Therefore, you have cause to mourn when you see sin in others. Blessed are those who mourn in this way.

Firstly, this demonstrates sincerity and reveals much of the Spirit of God. Mourning for the sins of others displays more sincerity than mourning for our own sins, even though there is more reason to mourn for our own sins than for others.

Secondly, by mourning for the sins of others, you free yourself from their guilt. How can you, living in a nation or family, be free from the sins of those you interact with if you do not mourn for them? However, when you mourn for the sins of others, you free yourself from their guilt. This is especially true when you mourn for the sins of those related to you. For instance, suppose there is a godly child whose eyes have been opened to see their own sins, and they mourn for them. But they worry and wonder if God will show them mercy, considering they come from a lineage with a father or mother who is profane, a drunkard, a swearer, or a scoffer. Now, as a child, you have no means of being delivered from the guilt of your parents' or forefathers' wickedness except through mourning for them. If God has rescued you from a wicked lineage, He expects you to mourn and lament for the sins of that lineage. Similarly, if you live in a wicked family, and God's judgments may befall the family due to its sin, you cannot free yourself from their guilt except by mourning for their sins, as well as your own. Blessed are you if you do so. If you mourn for their sins, the Lord will not punish you for their sins.

Thirdly, blessed are those who mourn for the sins of others because, through this, they make themselves suitable instruments for God to use in opposing the sins of others. There are no individuals more fitting for God to employ in His service, to halt the progression of others' sins, than those who take those sins to heart. Therefore, above all others, individuals in public positions, those God uses to curb wickedness, should be deeply exercised in the grace of mourning for the sins of others. You, who God has placed as leaders in parishes, towns, or cities, entrusted with the responsibility of restraining sin in your communities, if your hearts are not moved by the sins prevalent in your surroundings, you will be ill-suited instruments for God's honour and the prevention of sin. It is no wonder that people in such positions care little about the consequences of their actions, allowing things to go astray for personal gain. But blessed are those who mourn for the sins of others, for they are the instruments God employs and delights to use in His service.

And then they shall be comforted—those who mourn in this manner.

Firstly, in times of public calamity, they shall find solace. Take Jeremiah, for instance, a great mourner for the sins of others. In Jeremiah 15:11, the Lord promises him protection during such times of distress. Read Jeremiah 9 for a more detailed account. Jeremiah bitterly laments, wishing for his head to be waters and his eyes a fountain of tears, and he longs for a cottage in the wilderness. Although he mourns partly for the slain of his people, he also mourns for their sins. In Jeremiah 15:11, God assures him that he will find refuge. The famous passage in Ezekiel 9 instructs a person with a pen and inkhorn to mark all those who mourn for the sins of others. God takes notice of them and promises mercy, providing for them despite the calamity befalling their surroundings.

Secondly, you shall be comforted by knowing that all the wickedness of humanity will be subdued. A time will come when God will no longer be dishonoured by the sins of people as He is now. The refuse will be cast aside, and there will be rejoicing at the righteous judgments executed upon the wicked. While we mourn when we witness God being dishonoured by the wicked among us, there will come a time when we no longer mourn their sin but rejoice in God's righteous judgments upon them. Blessed are those who mourn, for they shall be comforted.

Therefore, by way of use, let us deeply consider the sins of those around us—not only in our parishes and families but also the sins of the nation. I will mention just a few instances, but even those who struggle with meditation will easily recognize numerous others.

Firstly, let us mourn for the great injustice prevailing in our midst today. There is ample cause for mourning due to oppression and injustice. Isaiah 59:11-15 describes how we roar like bears and mourn sorely like doves. Why? Because we expect judgment and salvation, yet they seem distant. Verse 14 continues, "Justice is turned away backward, and justice standeth afar off: for truth is fallen in the street, and equity cannot enter. Yea, truth faileth; and he that departeth from evil maketh himself a prey: and the Lord saw it, and it displeased him that there was no judgment." The sin of injustice is further aggravated by the present time. The Lord has, by His outstretched arm, delivered us from oppressors. Yet now, we oppress one another. The cry for the sin of injustice must be reaching the heavens like never before. However, some may complain without valid cause. Woe to us! There is significant cause for mourning due to widespread injustice among us.

Secondly, mourn that Christ is not embraced more widely. We have unprecedented opportunities to welcome Jesus Christ into our lives, as fair as any throughout history. Jesus Christ is presenting Himself to us in the most inviting way, yet a spirit of malignity has risen among us. We seem ready to declare, "We will not have this man to reign over us." Mourn for the ignorance and profanity of the people in our land. Despite the liberty of the Gospel (unlike ever before), many turn away from it, judging themselves unworthy of eternal life and spurning the grace of the Spirit. Romans 9:2 reveals Paul's deep concern for his countrymen, to the extent that he could wish himself cut off from Christ. He was troubled by their ignorance and rejection of Christ. One would expect that, given the wondrous works God has done to bring us the liberty of the Gospel, people would eagerly embrace it. Yet, we find the opposite—a vile spirit against godliness has emerged among men.

Thirdly, mourn the divisions among us. The devil realizes he cannot easily lure many towards profanity and Popery as before. Therefore, he now seeks to spoil religion through divisions, even among the godly. Satan's cunning is most evident in this. Many are affected by the divisions in the land, but it is often because others do not share their opinions. Their mourning is self-serving, as they desire to claim all esteem, honour, dignities, and preferments without any accountability. They cry out against divisions, but their lamentation is mostly selfish. There is a lack of genuine spiritual mourning for the sins that cause divisions among us.

Furthermore, mourn for the abuse of our liberty, the wantonness prevailing in our society. The Lord has granted us more freedom than our ancestors ever had or could have imagined. Yet, what an abuse of this liberty! People indulge in all kinds of licentiousness, using the plea for true liberty of conscience as an excuse. They blaspheme and commit wickedness.

Mourn, too, for the unthankfulness that pervades our society. Because we do not have everything exactly as we desire, we are quick to say, "Nothing has been done." Such an ungrateful statement is abhorrent. God has done immeasurable things for our nation, worth more than your life or the lives of ten thousand others. To claim that nothing has been done because it does not align with your desires is a wretched display of ingratitude. Reflect on this and let it pain you.

Lastly, mourn for the scandals and stumbling blocks present among us. Many who profess religion cast stumbling blocks in the paths of those seeking righteousness, causing them to abhor the ways of godliness due to their wicked lives.

And lastly, let us mourn for the failures of good men when they face trials. This is a grievous evil that we witness in our time. Never before has there been a kingdom where so many godly individuals held positions of power in government and ministry. Yet, oh, the shortcomings we observe in them. Many of them follow the same principles as their predecessors but in different ways. We see the truth of the saying, "Put men in power so they can have power over others." We witness their strange spirits, even in those we once thought had broken hearts and mourned for the sins of others in positions of authority. Together with their brethren, they used to fast, pray, and cry out to Heaven against the wrongdoings of those in power just a few years ago. Now, as they hope to obtain the same power, they are treading the same path as their predecessors. My brethren, I speak these things with a sense of duty, laying them on our hearts to bewail them with bitterness in our souls. I do not say this to reproach anyone, as there is enough reproach already. Instead, we should mourn for these failings. God forbid that we should speak in a manner of reproach. No, let our words be words of lamentation, for these failings have been greatly detrimental to God and the public good. If we could set aside our quarrels for a while and mourn together, reformation would progress in a different manner than it does now.

Moreover, there is another evil to mourn: men mourn because they cannot have their own way, and their mourning stems from a spirit of revenge. Many times, even their fasting becomes a fast for strife. We should mourn for our own mourning.

Now, let us turn to the final point in my text. Blessed are those who mourn for the afflictions of the Church. It is evident in Scripture that the saints often mourn greatly for the sufferings of God's people. Nehemiah, for instance, though at the royal court with a high position and in a state of ease with abundant riches, appeared sad. He did not want the king to be surprised by his sorrow while the Church was in such a dire state. A significant passage in Luke 19 describes how Jesus wept as He approached Jerusalem, grieving for their sins and the impending misery. He lamented, "If you had known, even you, especially in this your day, the things that make for your peace! But now they are hidden from your eyes." Note that Jesus did this at a time when He was not personally undergoing great affliction. In fact, in the very next verses, it is depicted that people cut down branches, spread their garments in the way, and hailed Him with cries of "Hosanna to the Son of David! Blessed is He who comes in the name of the Lord! Hosanna in the highest!" Jesus received great honour at that time. Yet, His heart was not solely occupied with the honour bestowed upon Him; He was still moved by the miseries of others. As He approached, He wept. This should teach us that, regardless of our own favourable circumstances—whether our tables are well-furnished, and we receive honour and respect from others—we should not allow these comforts to dampen our concern for the afflictions of our brethren. Romans 12 commands us to weep with those who weep and mourn with those who mourn. Hebrews 13:3 states that we must even consider ourselves as being in bonds with those who are in bonds. We should be affected by their sufferings as if we were experiencing them ourselves. This is what God requires of us. The examples of Jeremiah, David, the prophets, and Paul, among others, serve as reminders of this duty. It would be endless to list all the examples found in Scripture. But blessed are those who mourn. There is ample reason for us to do so.

Firstly, those in afflictions are not just strangers; they are our brethren, close to us, the saints of God.

Secondly, we have the same root within ourselves. Can you, in all conscience, believe that such men should be in a state of affliction while you feel nothing yourself? Shouldn't you, with all that you possess, experience the same hardships? Is there any reason why these excellent saints, who have served God so faithfully, should be cast out of their homes, while you sit at a table filled with abundance, surrounded by your wife, children, and a well-furnished house in peaceful conditions? What reason can be given? Is there not as much in you to provoke God as there is in them? Have you done more for God than they have? If you do not have a heart of adamant, this thought should break you.

Yet, there is another reason. Consider the dishonour God experiences through the afflictions of His people. Truly, the Lord suffers when they suffer. In all their afflictions, He is afflicted. As the Church declines, the wicked gloat and triumph, and wickedness prevails. This should touch your heart. God, in a manner of speaking, declines, and His cause declines with the suffering of the saints. The glory of God is intertwined with the well-being of His people, and He suffers in their afflictions.

You might ask, if God suffers, why does He allow the saints to be so afflicted? To that, I answer: The Lord permits their afflictions to distinguish between the true and the false. He also brings glory to His name in various ways. However, even though God brings praise through the sufferings of the saints, we should still mourn and lament because, in the meantime, God is suffering, and these afflictions greatly dishonour Him, although He, in His infinite power, can derive honour from them.

Furthermore, if you only consider the magnitude of the evils in these times, you will see that now is the time to mourn for the afflictions of others. Those who stand as witnesses for the truth have every reason to prophesy even in sackcloth. If only we understood the woeful evil and miseries of war. It is an evil that contains an abundance of evils within it. It is the cup of God's anger, and its wine is as red as blood. It is a mixed wine, its ingredients being murder, robbery, rape, deflowering, cruelty, torment, famine, and pestilence. These are the elements in this cup. Although we may sit quietly in our homes and not experience the dreadful evils of this civil war, others can testify. If only you could see the mournful miseries they have witnessed: people of good standing and reputation, who lived comfortably and were prominent saints, now driven from their homes like beasts. If only we could see what has happened in Ireland. They cry out to us, "O you who pass by, is it nothing to you, all you who pass by? Behold and see if there is any sorrow like my sorrow." It would be of great use to expose the woeful misery of others. But let me show you how blessed are those who mourn for the afflictions of others. They are blessed.

Firstly, they possess much of the Spirit of Christ within them. Their spirit resembles that of Jesus Christ when He lived on earth, and that was a blessed spirit.

Secondly, they demonstrate that they are members of the same body. If you can hear of the woeful evils suffered by the churches and not mourn, it is evident to the whole world, and God tells you in your conscience, that you are but a dead member, not a living member of the body of Jesus Christ. However, when your hearts are affected by the miseries of the churches, you have assurance in your souls that you are living members of Jesus Christ.

And blessed are you because, in this, you walk with God. You follow God's ways. When God shows mercy to His church, you can rejoice. And when God is in a season of affliction, you mourn. This is walking with God, having our hearts respond according to the different aspects of God's providence. Blessed are those who walk with God.

"You shall be comforted." That is,

Firstly, know that there will come a time when God's people will be delivered from all their sorrows. Every tear will be wiped away from their eyes. There will be no more prickling briars or grieving thorns. This is promised to the saints, and I believe this time must come even in this world. The saints will be honoured just as they have been dishonoured, and wicked men will no longer persecute them. Instead, the wicked will be brought under their dominion. There is a day when the saints will have victory over the wicked and the ungodly. You who mourn for the afflictions of the saints shall find comfort in this. "O you afflicted one, tossed with tempest and not comforted, behold, I will lay your stones with colourful gems." Yes, the foundation of the Church will be like that, a burdensome stone to all who persecute it. "Arise, shine; for your light has come! And the glory of the Lord is risen upon you." This is what the Lord says to the churches: "Comfort, comfort My people! Speak comfort to Jerusalem, and cry out to her, that her warfare is ended, that her iniquity is pardoned." Such a time will come when the people of God will be comforted, and the saints will rejoice in the salvation of God, saying, "This is our God; we have waited for Him, and He will save us." Indeed, such a time will come.

Moreover, there are many promises for those who mourn for the afflictions of the saints. In Psalm 41, it is declared, "Blessed is he who considers the poor."

Those who consider the afflicted are blessed. In Isaiah 57:18, the Lord promises to restore comforts to His church and to those who mourn with her. Both the church and her mourners will be comforted. In Isaiah 66:10, there is a promise to those who mourn with the people of God. They will rejoice. And in Zephaniah 3:18, there is a promise for those who consider the reproach of the solemn assembly to be a burden. God will gather them. The saints of God are reproached and persecuted, while others may rejoice. However, those who find it burdensome will receive a gracious promise from the Lord.

Again, those of you who mourn for the afflictions of the saints are blessed. For when God brings affliction upon you, He will acknowledge your souls in the day of affliction. If your children, dear wives, or anyone close to you should be afflicted, you can confidently go to God and pray, "Lord, comfort me in my affliction, and comfort my wife, my children, my father, my mother in their afflictions." You can find comfort because you mourned for the afflictions of His children. God will say, "Here is someone who is afflicted. What about the man's child or wife who is facing affliction? Ah, I remember when my children were afflicted, and they mourned for my children. Now that their children are afflicted, I will take it to heart and have compassion on them in their affliction." Therefore, blessed are those who mourn.

Now, let's apply this message. First, it should serve as a rebuke to the jollity of people's spirits in these sad times. It is wicked to have a carnal, jolly spirit during such solemn moments. Certainly, God gives you permission to find comfort and rejoice in Him. You may argue that we are commanded to rejoice always, and that spiritual joy and mourning can coexist. However, know that God expects you to temper your carnal joy. I will present two Scriptures that are quite severe against those who are merry and jolly in times of sorrow. The first is from Isaiah 22:12: "And in that day did the Lord God of hosts call for weeping and mourning, for baldness and wearing sackcloth. But behold, joy and gladness, slaying oxen and killing sheep, eating meat and drinking wine: 'Let us eat and drink, for tomorrow we die!' Then it was revealed in my hearing by the Lord of hosts: 'Surely this iniquity will not be atoned for you until you die,' says the Lord God of hosts." This Scripture is alarming for those who indulge in the flesh during these times. I implore you, if you believe that this Scripture is the word of God, to lay it upon your hearts and consciences when you return home. God says, "When I called for mourning and weeping, there was instead joy, gladness, mirth, and drinking of wine. This iniquity will not be atoned for until you die." God will not forgive it. It is spoken of as an unpardonable sin, although I believe it is not as unforgivable as the sin against the Holy Ghost. Nevertheless, even if God grants you a heart to see its evil, you may suffer consequences in this world. Just as the Lord dealt with Moses, He would not listen to him and commanded him to speak no more on the matter, leading to his death in the wilderness. The Lord cannot help but look upon such individuals with indignation. He asks, "Shall I chastise my own dear children, while this worthless person only cares about eating, drinking, and making money? I will not tolerate this," says God. It will not be atoned for until they die. Oh, my brethren, if there was ever a time for weeping and mourning, it is now. Not having a heart that mourns during these times is a sign that your heart is hardened against the fear of God. If ever this text of Christ was applicable, it is in these mournful times, where those who mourn are declared blessed, and on the other hand, those who do not mourn will certainly be cursed by Christ when they stand before Him.

The other Scripture is from Amos 6, where the Lord laments that they drank wine from bowls and indulged in music and all kinds of merriment. But, He says, there was none who remembered the afflictions of Joseph. Joseph may have been imprisoned, sold, and endured various afflictions, but what did it matter to them? They did not even remember. Woe to them.

# SERMON XI

## How to Mourn for the Afflictions of Saints

"Blessed are they that mourn: for they shall be comforted."-
Matthew 5:4

B ut now, my brethren, the topic I will address is how we should mourn
for the afflictions of the saints, so that we may mourn sincerely for their
afflictions. Some may say, "We are affected, and God forbid that we should not
be grieved when we hear about the Church's afflictions. It truly saddens our
hearts to hear about the plundering of so many good people and how they are
displaced from their homes." However,

First, there can be a natural mourning for the afflictions of others, which is
not the blessed mourning spoken of here. To understand the difference between
natural and spiritual mourning for the afflictions of the Church, consider these
three or four key points, which I will briefly mention.

But now, my brethren, I shall speak about how we should mourn for the
afflictions of the saints, so that our mourning may be genuine and heartfelt.
Some may argue, "We are affected, and God forbid that we should not grieve
when we hear about the Church's afflictions. It truly saddens our hearts to

hear about the bloodshed and devastation in countries. As human beings, we cannot help but be affected. However, are we primarily moved by spiritual considerations? Are we most affected because the saints are suffering, because their freedom to practice their faith is taken away, because the enemies of God's people prevail, and because religion is being trampled upon? Do we mourn for these reasons? These are truly mournful times. Many people mourn out of fear of external dangers or due to heavy taxes. They grieve because things are not as they used to be. But spiritual mourning is founded on spiritual grounds."

Secondly, spiritual mourning leads to fervent prayer. As mentioned earlier, those who are in a sorrowful state themselves should engage in much prayer. Likewise, those who mourn for the afflictions of the churches, if their mourning is of a spiritual nature, will pray fervently for the churches. I appeal to your consciences regarding this matter. Often, you hear distressing news about the suffering of your brethren. Perhaps you will say, "Lord, have mercy upon them." But have you ever secluded yourself and poured out your soul before God in secret, interceding for the churches of God? Or perhaps you have done so occasionally, but is it a regular practice for you? When you hear of the afflictions of the churches, are your hearts deeply affected to the extent that you prostrate yourselves before the Lord in prayer? Such deep sorrow in prayer signifies spiritual mourning. Feeling a heaviness in your spirits upon hearing bad news may be natural, but breaking your spirit before God in prayer for the church is truly spiritual. Considering that the churches now suffer more than ever before, are your prayers for them more fervent than before? This is spiritual mourning, and blessed are those who mourn in this way, for their mourning drives them to prayer and enlarges their hearts in prayer.

Thirdly, if your hearts are spiritual in your mourning, then whatever God spares you from experiencing—such as not having to endure the same suffering as others—it will motivate you to be more earnest and willing to spend your strength in serving and doing for God. If your hearts were truly affected as they should be for the churches, you would reason as follows: "How do they suffer in their estates, bodies, and liberties? They are compelled to expend their strength and resources in suffering. However, Lord, you do not call me to spend my strength and resources in that same way of suffering as you call my brethren to. Yet, Lord, I willingly offer my strength and resources to be spent for you in acts of service. It is good for us to have our strength and resources spent for God in exercising our graces, rather than being spent in suffering for our sins." When you hear of anyone suffering through any unfortunate circumstance, they suffer greatly for God passively. Therefore, I should be willing to expend my efforts actively for God. This is a compelling argument that your hearts are spiritual.

Furthermore, when your gratitude for being delivered from the heavy afflictions that others endure humbles your hearts as if you were experiencing the same afflictions, it is a good indication of a spiritual state. When you hear about the afflictions of other people, and your sensitivity to their suffering moves you to express thankfulness as deeply as if you were personally afflicted, then your hearts are spiritually attuned. This brings us to the second point: what duties are incumbent upon us when we hear about the afflictions of others while we ourselves are delivered? In other words, what actions should we take in response? I will answer this by stating three duties that are called for in such circumstances.

Firstly, we should diminish our attachment to worldly comforts in this life. When we learn about the sufferings of the churches, we should be willing to forsake a significant portion of our earthly comforts that cater to our fleshly desires. We should be willing to curtail ourselves, as far as possible, for the sake of serving God. It is certainly not permissible for people in times like these, when darkness has enveloped the land and numerous brethren, to grant themselves the same liberty to indulge their fleshly desires as in more favorable times. I could cite several scriptural references to support this, but I will move on to the remaining points.

Secondly, the second duty is to be ready to assist those who are afflicted, to extend ourselves for their comfort. Since Christ has declared, "Blessed are they that mourn: for they shall be comforted," each one of us should strive to fulfill this statement. We should comfort them through our material resources and by any means possible. We should never consider it burdensome to be frequently called upon to show compassion to those in distress, even if we are frequently asked for contributions. We should do so willingly and cheerfully. You cannot fulfill the obligations that God imposes upon you in recognizing the mournful condition of others unless you are willing to lend a helping hand. You cannot pray to God to comfort them without taking His name in vain if you are not also willing to do what you can.

Thirdly, we should mentally place ourselves in the same condition as those who are suffering, considering what we would do if God were to truly subject us to the same circumstances they endure. When you hear about those who have lost their possessions, have been exiled, and are wandering in search of bread—people who were once accustomed to living comfortably—try to imagine yourself in their position. Reflect upon what would become of you if you were in their situation. Suppose you were at the mercy of enemies, as they are. What would become of you? What a dire state you would be in! You may wonder, "Why should we trouble ourselves in this way since God has delivered us? Why should we mentally place ourselves in the same condition as our brethren?"

To that, I respond that God requires this of us. You cannot be as deeply aware of their situation as you ought to be, nor can you fully appreciate the lessons to be learned from their afflicted condition unless you occasionally place yourselves in their circumstances and contemplate what you would do if you were in their position. To support this, I will provide this scripture from Hebrews 13:3: "Remember them that are in bonds, as bound with them; and them which suffer adversity, as being yourselves also in the body." The apostle addresses those who are at liberty, yet he requires them to remember those who are in prison as if they were imprisoned with them. So, those who are currently imprisoned by the enemy should consider themselves as if they were imprisoned alongside them. Likewise, those who have lost everything should imagine themselves in that same condition. Therefore, you must remember them; otherwise, your hearts will be superficially touched by their afflictions if all you can say is, "How cruelly they are treated! May the Lord have pity on them and show them mercy!" But consider this seriously: What if I were in their position? What if it were truly my condition?

But you may ask, what good would come from putting ourselves in their condition? To that, I answer that there are many benefits. If you were to place yourself in their situation and consider what it would be like, you would be led to certain realizations and further duties.

Firstly, if I were in their condition, I would undoubtedly become aware of the futility of worldly pursuits. How vain it is to rely on outward comforts in this world! There was a time when they, perhaps not long ago, enjoyed the same comforts as I do now. Yet, in a single night, everything was stripped away from them, leaving them with nothing and burdened by sorrowful afflictions. Surely, they cannot help but think to themselves, "The pursuit of worldly pleasures is futile. Trusting in any earthly comfort is foolish, as it can be swiftly taken away without warning." Let me also come to this realization now.

Secondly, if I were in their condition, my conscience would undoubtedly accuse me of abusing the mercies I had received. Suppose all my comforts were taken away, just as theirs were. Would not my conscience immediately confront me and remind me of how I had misused those mercies? Would it not point out that I failed to utilize my wealth for God's purposes as I could have? Those of you who currently possess comfortable estates may think that since they are your own, you can use them as you please. However, if God were to suddenly take away your possessions through some unforeseen event, your conscience would be the first to hold you accountable for misusing your wealth. It would also remind you that you did not use your resources to honor God as you could have. Imagine if God allowed the enemy or a fire to sweep away everything in a single night—do you not think that your conscience would reproach you, saying, "I could have made better use of these resources for God"? When a mercy is taken away from someone, it is common for conscience to accuse them of misusing that mercy. For instance, when a man buries his wife, the first thing his conscience tells him is, "I did not fulfill my marital duties as I should have." Similarly, when any mercy is lost, conscience has more freedom to accuse one of misusing that mercy. Therefore, if you were in their condition, I believe your conscience would be more forthright in addressing you. This is the second thing that conscience would do if you were in their situation.

Thirdly, putting yourself in their condition would result in a reduction of your outward comforts but an enlargement of your duties. I strongly believe that, in general, our brethren in those regions where the enemy has wrought havoc (excluding those who are foolish) are more diligent in their religious duties than ever before. They do not neglect their sacred responsibilities to the same extent as in the past. Certainly, if you were in their condition, and if the

Lord were to reduce your outward comforts, you would be more diligent in performing your religious duties.

Fourthly, if you were in their condition, you would possess a more serious spirit. Currently, you enjoy outward prosperity and may not deeply consider the state of your relationship with God. However, if God were to suddenly strip away all your comforts, it would undoubtedly lead to serious contemplation. You would ponder the state of your soul in relation to God. While things may be disheartening in the worldly sense, you would question how they stand in light of eternity. Therefore, place yourself in that condition so that the triviality and frivolity of your spirit may be lifted, and you may become as serious as you would be if you were in their condition.

Fifthly, if you were in their condition, you would learn to be content with little. Therefore, imagine yourself in their position and consider this: Suppose God were to take everything from me. If He were to restore even a small portion, I would praise His name. I would be grateful for the bread I have now. Many who once lived as comfortably as you would be grateful for the smallest provisions. Now, place yourself in their condition and bless God for the little you have. In this way, you should identify with those who are in bondage and affliction.

Lastly, you would learn to value peace with God. Those in affliction greatly cherish peace with God and peace within their own consciences. The godly among them think to themselves, "Had we not established peace with God and maintained peace within our consciences, what would we do? But thanks be to God, we have kept our peace with Him, and our consciences are at peace." In these times of war, it is this peace that comforts their hearts. Therefore, place yourself in their condition so that you may learn to value peace with God and peace within your conscience.

And then the seventh and final point is this: if we were to place ourselves in their condition, we would undoubtedly rise against Popery and Tyranny. Suppose we were in Ireland, under the heavy tyranny of those barbarous Papists. It would compel us to rise against the Popish religion and think to ourselves, "Is this the Popish Religion? It is a bloody and wicked religion, a cursed religion is Popery." We would urge our children to despise Popery as long as they live. The cruel treatment of the people there would stir our hearts. The prevailing

Popish party here should provoke us all to rise against Popery and Tyranny. It is
a miserable state when a few men tyrannize over the people. Let us join forces to
cast off the yoke of Tyranny, so that we may be governed by the law and know in
advance when we have transgressed. The recent miseries in these three kingdoms
should stir up the spirits of those who are not foolish or willing to be slaves,
to rise against Tyranny and never allow it to prevail over them again. Placing
ourselves in their condition may lead our hearts to be somewhat affected as theirs
are, and thus we shall be truly aware of the mournful state of our brethren.

To achieve this, it is good for us to frequently confront ourselves with the
great evil of a selfish spirit. Just because I am free and unaffected, should none of
the afflictions of the Churches of God and the sufferings of the countries touch
my heart? How base is the selfish spirit within me! Is my flesh more important
than the flesh of others? Charge this upon your souls in the presence of God,
and it will serve as a means to break your hearts.

Secondly, when you partake in the blessings you have, let your thoughts be
seasoned with considerations of the afflictions of your brethren. As you sit at
your table, reflect upon how you have an abundant feast, but how is it with
others? When you retire to bed and find peace within your home, contemplate
the state of your brethren. When you go about your trade and business in the
streets, think about others. And when you return home to the presence of
your wife and children, remember the condition of your brethren. Therefore,
with every blessing you enjoy, let the thought of your brethren's afflictions be
intertwined with it, just as you season your food with salt. Your blessings will
become much more meaningful if they are seasoned with considerations of the
afflictions your brethren endure.

Furthermore, remember that you are part of the same body as them, as stated
in Hebrews 13. You are subject to the same things they are. How just would it be
for God not to affect me with the miseries of others, and instead bring upon me
equally great or even greater afflictions? The Lord has countless ways to subject
you to as great afflictions as any part of the kingdom has ever experienced. There
is no more dangerous sign that God intends such afflictions for you than being
unsympathetic to the sufferings of your brethren. How easily might the Lord,
through secret treachery or massacres, subject you to woeful afflictions just like
them? Therefore, considering your susceptibility to the same or even greater

afflictions, be sensitive to the miseries of your brethren. Serious contemplation of their sufferings would powerfully impact your heart.

Lastly, consider the words of the Apostle Peter: "If judgement begins at the house of God, what shall become of them that obey not the Gospel of God? And if the righteous shall scarcely be saved, where shall the wicked and ungodly appear?" If many righteous servants of God have had to endure harsh circumstances and go through great difficulties on their path to Heaven, what will become of me? Will I barely be saved? That is, saved through many trials, dangers, and sufferings. Then what will become of me? Where will I stand? My conscience tells me that there is much unrighteousness within me. If God's beloved saints attain Heaven through such trouble, surely there is trouble reserved for me. Such thoughts would break your hearts and lead you to mourn with those who mourn. Blessed are those who mourn in this way, who are sensitive to the afflictions of God's people, for they shall be comforted. And thus, we have concluded the discussion of the second beatitude: "Blessed are the poor in spirit" and "those who mourn."

Now, let us proceed to the third beatitude:

"Blessed are the meek, for they shall inherit the earth."

First, regarding the word "meek," some believe it comes from a Hebrew word that signifies thinness, lowliness, or leanness. At times, it is used interchangeably with humility, as Christ combines them by saying, "Learn from me, for I am humble and meek." The Latin term for meekness is derived from a word that describes a person who is, as it were, silent when wronged. It can also be understood in reference to animals that are not fierce but are gentle and accustomed to human contact. Meekness, as stated in my text, refers to a disposition that is easily entreated, gentle in spirit, and marked by gracious control over the passion of anger. Those men and women who possess self-control to moderate their anger are meek.

Naturally, meekness may arise from a person's bodily constitution. Many individuals are not naturally prone to anger, depending on their physical temperament, while others have a more choleric disposition. Additionally, there is a natural meekness that stems from the strength of reason. Even a rational person can, by virtue of reason, restrain their anger to a great extent. However, true meekness must surpass these natural inclinations, whether arising from bodily temperament or the strength of reason. To understand how meekness goes beyond these, consider the following points.

First, a naturally meek person is meek in some outward situation where others would become angry. However, this natural meekness, which is only from their disposition, does not align with the exercise of the grace of zeal for God. On the other hand, spiritual meekness, being a grace of the Holy Spirit, does not oppose any other grace. That is a certain rule: various vices may be contrary to one another, but no grace can be contrary to another grace. Therefore, those who are spiritually meek are also zealous. They possess spiritual principles that make them meek and able to control their anger in personal matters. Yet, those same principles make them zealous for God. However, when meekness is only natural, arising from bodily constitution or the power of reason, it extinguishes zeal. Those who are meek in this way are not acquainted with the grace of zeal for God. You may encounter individuals who never get angry, even when their children and servants do things that would make you angry. They are patient, quiet, and meek, tolerating everything. You might think this displays true meekness, but it is not. You can discern this because even when their children sin against God, they are not angry. This is not a meekness born of grace. True grace teaches men and women to be meek and gentle when they are crossed personally, but it will never teach them to be meek in a way that they are not angry when God is dishonoured. You will find that those portrayed in Scripture as the most eminent for meekness in personal matters have also been the most zealous in God's cause. Take the example of Moses, who was declared by the Lord to be the meekest man on earth. However, when he descended from the mount and saw that the children of Israel had set up a golden calf idol, Moses was all on fire. He smashed the tablets of stone, which contained the law written by God Himself, in his zeal for God. Moreover, he roused the people to take their swords and slay their brethren. Moses, the meekest man to ever live, exhibited great zeal. Another example is Christ Himself, who presented Himself as a model of meekness, saying, "Learn from me, for I am meek." Yet, when faced with the Scribes and Pharisees, who were adversaries of godliness and deceived the people by equating all religion with outward forms, He pronounced eight woes upon them in Matthew 23, speaking to them in a most scathing manner. No godly person ever preached with greater bitterness. Christ had a bitter anger toward the Scribes and Pharisees, despite being the meekest man. It was a bitterness of spirit, and you will not find anyone more passionately zealous against sin than Jesus Christ. When He witnessed the desecration of God's house, He overturned the tables of the money-changers and fashioned a whip to drive them out of the temple. The zeal for God's house consumed Him. Similarly, Paul, who was very meek, wrote to Timothy instructing him to correct opponents with meekness. Yet, when Paul fixed his gaze upon Elymas, who sought to turn Sergius Paulus away from the faith, he sharply rebuked him as "thou child of the devil" and full of deceit. Paul's words to Elymas were more terrible than any man could speak. This meekness contains a mixture of zeal. When a person can be meek in personal matters, deny themselves, and moderate their anger, yet become all on fire for God's cause, that is true meekness—the meekness that is pronounced blessed here.

However, as it differs from natural meekness, let us inquire into its constituents. It consists in the moderation of anger in six aspects.

First, with regard to the object of anger, it is a grace that enables us to moderate anger in such a way that we are not angry and froward without reason. We are able to give an account of our anger. In true meekness, the heart possesses such power that if I am angry, I can provide a justification for it.

Secondly, it means not being angry about everything.

Thirdly, it entails not becoming angry about what is good—for example, becoming angry when our brethren merely perform their duty. Those who possess meekness of this nature are not truly meek. However, when the soul commands itself not to become angry about anything unless it can give an account of it to God, it demonstrates true meekness. Indeed, many of you think that when you are angry, you are rational. If someone asks whether you are right to be angry, you say, "Yes, I am right to be angry." But can you provide as satisfactory an account of it to God as you do to others? Can you say, "Lord, I was angry, but it was no more than You desired me to be, for it was upon such and such just grounds that I was angry"? Many people become angry with inanimate objects, such as a craftsman becoming angry with his tools and throwing them away. They also become angry with dumb animals. This is the first aspect: moderation of anger with respect to the object. We should not become angry about anything unless we can justify it to God, explaining why we were provoked to anger and why it was appropriate.

And secondly, meekness moderates anger with regard to its timing.

First, it should not be sudden. People tend to be impulsive in the passion of anger, but they should be deliberate. If there is a valid reason for anger, it is better to weigh and consider the matter before expressing anger. Reflect on the situation and, if there is sufficient cause, then let your anger be released. But when people become suddenly angry, their explosive nature is like gunpowder, a small spark igniting a fire within them instantly. The sudden change that often occurs in many individuals, even within a family, is astonishing.

Secondly, anger should not be untimely. Take caution not to let anger arise when you are about to perform your duties. If you have the grace of meekness, you would have enough self-control to say, "Let passion wait until I have finished my prayer." This would be excellent for families. Sometimes, when husbands, wives, and families are about to pray, the Devil presents temptations to provoke their anger. He knows that their prayer will be spoiled if he can ignite their anger. But if meekness has the power to control anger, to make anger serve rather than dominate, then Satan's scheme is frustrated. Suppose a servant, neighbour, or child behaves inappropriately. Even then, you can say to anger, "Stay here until I have finished my prayer, and afterwards, I will address you." The same applies when you come to hear the Word. It is dangerous to give in to anger at any time, but especially on the Lord's Day. If you allow anger to take hold, there is a high chance that you will ruin the Sabbath. Your thoughts will revolve around the wrongs done to you and thoughts of revenge, manifesting your displeasure. Meekness moderates anger, giving one power over their anger so that it is not untimely.

Thirdly, meekness moderates anger in terms of its duration. Many individuals' anger is like the fire of hell—it is kindled once and never extinguished, unquenchable like the fire of hell itself. Their dog days persist throughout the year. You may encounter individuals who, once something occurs in their families that provokes their anger, remain in a state of fury day after day. There are even cases where husbands and wives will not speak to each other for two or three days. This is sinful and far from meekness. If you possess the grace of meekness, it will establish boundaries for anger. Just as you can unleash anger when necessary, you can also control and suppress it. However, many times the winds stir up the waves of the sea, and even when the winds subside, the waves remain agitated and boisterous. Similarly, many individuals, after the cause of their anger has been removed, cannot overcome themselves. It is comparable to children; if they become upset, they cry, and even if you give them what they want, they cannot immediately regain control. The same is true for many people—they are not persistent in other matters, but when it comes to anger, they remain fixed. In any good pursuit for God, they are fickle and inconsistent, but their passion endures. Meekness moderates anger in terms of its duration.

Fourthly, meekness moderates anger in terms of its intensity. If I am angry, I will not be angrier than necessary. Why be so violent, so fierce, so cruel in anger? Some do not know how to be angry without becoming furious. However, someone with a meek spirit may experience anger at times, but their meekness will determine the appropriate measure of anger—just enough, neither more nor less, according to the cause of their anger.

And fifthly, meekness moderates anger by examining its underlying cause. Anger often stems from pride in the heart or from other desires or weaknesses. However, meekness of spirit effectively controls anger so that it does not arise from pride, lust, or weakness. This is how meekness moderates anger.

And then the consequences of anger, oh, the woeful evil effects that result from the anger of individuals. In the span of just one hour, countless acts of sin are committed when people yield to their passions. Sometimes, a person in a sour and peevish mood commits more sin in a single day than someone in a meek and calm state does in a year, or even their entire life. You may do something in one day that will cause you to repent for the rest of your life. Sin is multiplied almost infinitely when we give in to anger. Passion and anger fuel the lusts within people's hearts, and thus they become very active in sin during moments of anger. Just as Moses, in his holy zeal, broke the tablets on which the Law was written, people, in their sinful anger, shatter both the tables of the Law with their disruptive and sinful actions. Reviling speeches, vengeful thoughts, harmful words, and desperate resolutions abound during times of anger. However, when meekness resides in the heart, it restrains anger and prevents it from leading to sinful outcomes. Meekness questions why the Lord has given this affection to the soul. Surely, it is not for the production of such base and sinful effects. The Lord forbid it. Reflect on the evil of anger during times of humility, and humble yourselves for the incredibly wicked effects of your sinful anger. For those who struggle to find material for prayer during private moments of communion with God, simply consider a fit of anger you have experienced. See if there is not enough sin during that time to provide matter for your confessions. Meekness moderates anger by considering the purpose. When angry, one should not be angry for oneself. Sometimes you are angry with a child, but it is for the purpose of showing displeasure against an offense so that the child may amend their ways. The same applies to servants. The Lord, who knows all things, knows that when you express anger towards anyone, be it a man, woman, child, or servant, you aim for their good. You believe that by being gentle towards them and not manifesting your anger, they will be better off. This should be the resolution of every godly parent, master, and so on. Oh, blessed are the meek! Blessed are those who have the power to overcome the passion of anger. They are blessed. I should have discussed many ways in which the meek are blessed here, and they shall be blessed forever. This grace of meekness is extolled as much as any other grace I know, second only to faith itself, which is the great mother grace.

If you are meek, you are like God the Father. When God desired to reveal His glory to Moses in Exodus 33 and 34, was it not a significant part of His glory that He is long-suffering and gracious? It is the Father's glory to be so.

And it is the glory of Jesus Christ to be so. Jesus says, "Learn from me, for I am meek." Christ calls for no other grace to be emulated by His disciples but humility and meekness. Blessed Saviour, why do you not speak of your other excellent graces? You possessed immeasurable grace, and when you wanted your disciples to learn from you, why did you not mention learning confidence from you, or heavenly-mindedness, or despising the world, or any other grace? No, says Christ, if you want to be my disciples, I commend this to you: I am humble and meek. Was that the great commendation of Christ? Yes, the Lord Jesus considered it His glory to be meek. Do you consider it dishonorable? Why would it be dishonorable for you when it was honorable for Jesus Christ? If Jesus Christ regards meekness as His glory, should you not consider it your glory? Oh, blessed are those who resemble God the Father and God the Son.

And they have much of the Spirit of God. What is the Spirit of God compared to more than meekness? When the Holy Spirit appeared upon Jesus Christ, it took the form of a dove. It is said that doves have no gall; they are the emblem of meekness. Therefore, if you want to be like the Father, Son, or Holy Spirit, you must have a meek and gentle spirit. Blessed are those who are meek, for they have much of the Father, Son, and Holy Spirit within them. It is worth noting that in sacrifices offered to God, He does not desire lions, tigers, or other wild creatures, nor birds of prey. Instead, He requires doves, pigeons, lambs, and sheep. The Lord esteems these sacrifices more highly than the perverse and wayward spirits of men. Now, I will provide you with just one Scripture that testifies to the blessedness of meek spirits. Many promises are made to the meek. Here is one great promise in my text, but for now, let me share only this one Scripture. Those who have found goodness through Scripture should eternally bear in mind the need to cultivate meek spirits. This verse specifically applies to women, as they are the weaker sex, and passion and anger arise from weakness. In 1 Peter 3:4, when the Holy Spirit addresses women, urging them to demonstrate themselves as daughters of Sarah, He says, "Likewise, wives, be in subjection to your own husbands, that if any obey not the word, they also may without the word be won by the conversation of the wives, while they behold your chaste conversation coupled with fear: whose adorning let it not be that outward adorning of plaiting the hair, and of wearing of gold, or of putting on of apparel: But how then? Women are often inclined towards such things; therefore, the Holy Spirit mentions these specific points. However, He says, "Let it be the hidden man of the heart, in that which is not corruptible." What is that? What particular instance will the Holy Spirit mention to represent the hidden man of the heart? He says, "A meek and quiet spirit, which is in the sight of God of great price." You cherish fine clothes and ornaments, considering them precious. You think that wearing costly lace and attire makes you valuable. But what are these to God? It is as if the Holy Spirit is saying, "Even if you have the plainest garments, you are just as acceptable to God. He looks into the inward man." Therefore, to see someone adorned with fine clothing but possessing a wayward and perverse spirit is abhorrent to God. He regards such individuals as wearing an ugly garment. However, even if you are dressed modestly, if you possess a meek and quiet spirit—a spirit that arises from the grace of the Spirit of God within you—oh, says the Holy Spirit, this is an ornament, it is of great value to God. It is much esteemed by Him. Oh, be infatuated with it! When a friend visits you, you say, "If only I knew what you love, I would have it for you." Now, women and others, say this to God, "Oh, if only I knew what you love most, I would strive my utmost to ensure that you have it." Behold, here is what the Holy Spirit says to all women, and it is true of men, women, and servants. A meek and quiet spirit is of great value to God. Therefore, even if you cannot remember anything else, conclude that you have previously possessed a wayward and peevish temperament, and oh, the sins you have committed in your waywardness. Yet, the Lord has commended meekness to you. The text states that the meek are blessed, and another Scripture says it is highly regarded by God. May the Lord grant us meek spirits so that we may be blessed.

# SERMON XII

## Meek persons Subjects for Christ to comfort

"Blessed are the meek, for they shall inherit the earth." - Matthew 5:5

G od does not value the worldly treasures of gold, silver, land, possessions, and crowns. These things mean nothing to Him. As stated in Isaiah 40, all the nations of the earth are like a drop in a bucket, less than nothing in His eyes. God does not regard the nations with all their grandeur and glory. However, a meek and quiet spirit is highly esteemed by God. It holds great worth in His sight. Even though the nations of the earth are worth no more than a speck of dust, the meek are blessed.

Furthermore, the meek are blessed because they are the ones Christ is anointed by the Father to comfort and preach good news to. Surely, they are blessed. Just as Christ is anointed by the Father to preach the Gospel to the poor and those who mourn, He is also anointed to preach good news to the meek. In Isaiah 61:1, it is written, "The Spirit of the Lord God is upon me because the Lord has anointed me to preach good tidings to the meek." The truth is, the meek are sad and disconsolate. Therefore, Christ, as designated by the Father, proclaims good news to the meek. Hence, they must be blessed since the Father has sent Christ to preach good news to them.

Thirdly, they are surely blessed because meekness, the ability to moderate and control anger, is considered the glory of God Himself. In Exodus 34:6, when God wanted to reveal His glory, one aspect of it was His ability to moderate His anger when provoked and to be patient with humanity. This is the glory of the Father. Similarly, in Psalm 45:4, a prophetic psalm about Christ, it is stated, "You are fairer than the sons of men; grace is poured upon your lips; therefore God has blessed you forever. Gird your sword upon your thigh, O most mighty, with your glory and your majesty. And in your majesty ride prosperously because of truth, humility, and righteousness." Here, the majesty and glory of Christ are described, and meekness is one attribute that bestows glory and majesty upon Him. Therefore, blessed are the meek.

Meekness is also an evidence of their election and a fruit of God's eternal love towards them. Whenever true Christian meekness is present, we can conclude that the soul was predestined by God from eternity to eternal life. Colossians 3:12 states, "Therefore, as the elect of God, holy and beloved, put on tender mercies, kindness, humility, meekness, and long-suffering." These are the fruits of election. If one desires to demonstrate that they are among the elect of God, they should display mercy, kindness, and meekness, not wealth, natural abilities, or worldly honors. Meekness, loving kindness, and long-suffering are the true indicators of God's election. Hence, they are blessed.

Moreover, meekness is a special fruit of the Holy Spirit in the hearts of the saints, demonstrating His presence within them. Galatians 5:22 provides a comprehensive list of the works of the flesh and the fruits of the Spirit. When describing the fruits of the Spirit, the passage states, "But the fruit of the Spirit is love, joy, peace, long-suffering, kindness, goodness, faithfulness, gentleness, self-control. Against such, there is no law." While many words describe the fruits of the Spirit, most of them are closely related to meekness. Love and a meek spirit bear great resemblance to each other. Meek individuals experience the sweetness of joy like no other. They possess a peaceable disposition. They exemplify long-suffering, gentleness, goodness, and faithfulness. Meekness is present in all these qualities. The Holy Spirit mentions numerous virtues closely associated with meekness to emphasize the excellence of this grace. These virtues resemble one another like kinsmen. Meekness is the fruit of the Spirit, while passion and anger are the fruit of the flesh and the devil. Thus, blessed are the meek.

Meekness also demonstrates magnanimity; it reveals a noble and courageous spirit. Many believe that their passion and obstinacy are indications of a brave and lively spirit. Froward individuals, especially during fits of anger, take great pride in the boldness of their spirits. However, a meek spirit is the most courageous in the world. This is the judgment of the Holy Spirit in Proverbs 16:32, which states, "He who is slow to anger is better than the mighty, and he who rules his spirit than he who takes a city." What greater bravery and magnanimity can be found than in soldiers who conquer cities? We consider them to possess exceptional and courageous spirits. Yet, the meek are regarded by the Lord as the most brave and excellent spirits. "He who is slow to anger is better than the mighty, and he who rules his spirit than he who takes a city." Ruling one's spirit with the grace of meekness is a more courageous feat and is highly esteemed by God. Scripture speaks abundantly about meekness to emphasize how blessed the meek are.

Furthermore, we find that meekness aligns with walking worthily of our calling. Ephesians 4:1 says, "I, therefore, the prisoner of the Lord, beseech you to walk worthy of the calling with which you were called." How can we walk worthy of our calling? The Lord has called us out of darkness into light, and He desires us to walk worthily of this calling. A poor soul may wonder how it is possible for such a lowly creature to walk worthily of such a glorious calling. What can one do to demonstrate walking worthily of this calling? If there is any way to testify to walking worthily of God's glorious mercy, it is by displaying humility, meekness, long-suffering, and love towards one another. This is the path to walk worthily of our calling. It is the path of walking worthily of all the mercies of God, including His deliverance from bondage. When we can forbear one another with meekness, humility, and long-suffering, it is a manifestation of walking worthily of our calling.

Now, I turn to the portion of the text: "For they shall inherit the earth."

It's a peculiar promise, as strange as any we find in Scripture. It goes against worldly logic, defying all rational understanding. "Blessed are the meek," it declares. You might question, "Are they truly blessed? They may gain entry into heaven when they pass away, but in their lifetime, they are likely to suffer great injustice." If we endure wrongs and tolerate those who harm us, we may face an abundance of injustices and swiftly lose everything we possess. This line of reasoning stems from a carnal heart. However, if you dare to trust Jesus Christ, he professes that among all people, it is the meek who will inherit the earth. They will experience a better earthly life than others.

Now you might ask, "Can inheriting the earth truly bring them blessings?" The answer is yes. Inheriting the earth in this context represents great blessedness and serves as a clear indication that God has blessed a person. It doesn't mean they will accumulate worldly riches, but rather that they will possess the earth as children of God. While others may receive earthly possessions through God's generous bounty, and it is not wrong for them to have such things, they do not inherit them as co-heirs with Jesus Christ. Wicked individuals may possess worldly goods bestowed upon them by God to sustain them temporarily, like a judge or prince providing sustenance to a criminal for a few days until their execution. However, they do not inherit these possessions. They lack the rightful ownership that comes with being co-heirs with Jesus Christ. Thus, it is a blessed thing to have all our rights restored in Christ, even in relation to earthly possessions. This love from God originates from the same source as Jesus Christ Himself. Although the things enjoyed are outward and material, those who have the fatherly care of God upon them in this world, providing for their needs and infusing the comforts of creation with the influences of His love, are truly blessed. They recognize God's love in these provisions, and all things in the earthly realm are sanctified for their eternal benefit. Therefore, blessed are the meek.

Furthermore, the Scriptures reveal that Christ has other intentions for His saints on earth. It is said that there will be new heavens and a new earth, a place where righteousness dwells. This blessedness may be fulfilled when the new earth comes into being. In Revelation 5:10, it is written, "And hast made us unto our God Kings and Priests, and we shall reign on the earth." I will not explore the controversies surrounding this matter but accept the words of Scripture as they are presented. It is evident that in some way or another, the saints will reign on the earth. Therefore, the meek will have a significant share in this reign with Christ, even in the earthly realm.

But why the meek and not others? Certainly, all God's people will share in the inheritance of this world. It is said of Abraham in Romans 4 that he was the heir of the world, and thus all the descendants of Abraham inherit his blessings. Each of them, like Abraham, becomes an heir of the world here on earth as well as in heaven. However, there is a particular connection between the promise of inheriting the earth and meekness. Let me explain this in various aspects.

Firstly, the meek are not inclined to engage in disputes as readily as others. They prefer peace and tranquility, and as a result, they enjoy their possessions more comfortably on this earth. Individuals who are quarrelsome, passionate, and prone to litigation often squander their inheritances and destroy the fortunes left to them by their parents. Many possess such dispositions that they would resent contributing a mere five shillings to a good cause, even though they accumulate wealth through legal battles, spending hundreds or even thousands of pounds. Have you not heard them say, "I will have my way, even if it costs me a considerable sum"? Such individuals are obstinate and foolish. However, the meek preserve their wealth and live more prosperously on this earth. This is the first advantage the meek have in inheriting the earth.

Secondly, though they possess only a little, the meek enjoy it with peace and contentment. A simple meal of greens shared in peace is more satisfying than a lavish feast marred by conflict. Consider a poor couple sitting together, sharing a small piece of bread and humble fare, yet living in harmony and meekness. They experience greater comfort on this earth than wealthy individuals who have grand tables but possess froward spirits. These individuals cannot find peace even when their meals are served flawlessly. They complain that the meat is poorly cooked or the bread is improperly baked. They find fault with their servants, saying, "This servant does this and that." Those who are engrossed in worldly affairs and possess froward spirits never truly enjoy the fruits of their labor. Conversely, the meek, though they possess only a little, savor their portion with contentment, peace, and quiet. Consequently, they can be said to inherit the earth more than others. In truth, you cannot fully enjoy the things of the world without inner tranquility.

Thirdly, the meek shall inherit the earth because meekness is a quality that no one wishes to harm. "Who will harm you if you are devoted to doing good?"

Those who live meekly and peacefully within a community will find support in their cause. Therefore, they experience more benefits on this earth than others.

Fourthly, the meek have a greater appeal. For example, if you were seeking a servant for your household, would you not inquire about their meekness and tranquility? If you learned that they were froward and prone to anger, you would hesitate to invite them into your home. However, if you discovered that they possessed a meek and peaceful spirit, you would say, "I want this servant, even if it means paying them higher wages." Here, you can see how the meek inherit the earth more than others. The same principle applies when one seeks a spouse. One of the primary qualities sought in a potential partner is a meek spirit. Even if they lack material wealth, a meek and quiet individual is often preferred. Thus, meekness plays a crucial role in earthly inheritance. If a person were traveling, they would choose an inn where the host and staff possess a peaceful disposition rather than another establishment where such tranquility is absent. Meekness greatly contributes to the inheritance of the earth, even in these matters.

Fifthly, wherever meekness exists, the soul surrenders its cause to God. Regardless of the wrongs a meek individual endures in the world, they entrust their cause to God. In doing so, they experience a great blessing on this earth. Consider this: a meek person possesses an untroubled heart, even in the face of injustice. Consequently, they can interest God in their cause. Once you have involved God in your cause, you are more likely to succeed. It is akin to making a debt the king's responsibility. In such a case, the debt is more likely to be repaid than if you attempted to resolve it through your own strength or by seeking allies. If you can surrender your cause to God with meekness, entrusting it to Him, you are bound to find success. Through this, you will fulfill your desires and wishes, even here on this earthly plane. I can provide an excellent Scripture to support this claim. In Numbers 12, Moses is commended for his meekness. It is said, "Now the man Moses was very meek, above all the men which were upon the face of the earth." Ambrose stated that Moses' meekness brought him greater honor than his mighty deeds. Chrysostom explained why God chose to speak face to face with Moses rather than any other person—it was because of his extraordinary meekness. The Jewish tradition holds that when Moses was about to die, God embraced him and took his soul. Regardless of the accuracy of this tradition, the soul is precious to God. If God were to extract a soul in this manner, it would surely be Moses' soul. Observe how Moses interested God in his cause and how God responded. In Numbers 12, we find that Moses was wronged. Miriam and Aaron spoke against him because of his marriage to an Ethiopian woman. They questioned whether the Lord spoke only through Moses, casting doubt on his status. Yet, Moses did not retaliate or cry out against them. Instead, he remained meek. The Scripture states that Moses was very meek, and as a result, the Lord spoke suddenly, commanding Moses, Aaron, and Miriam to come out to the Tabernacle. The Lord's response was swift. It was as if God declared, "Who is this servant Moses, my meek servant, who has been wronged? I will promptly appear on his behalf." The Lord spoke suddenly, as if bursting forth from heaven. Does it not demonstrate that the less stirred Moses' anger was, the more stirred God's anger became to vindicate him? You, on the other hand, swiftly become angry, but by doing so, you fail to involve God in your cause. However, if you were meek, God's anger would be kindled on your behalf. Do you not think that when God's anger is kindled against those who wrong you, He will rectify your cause more effectively than your own anger ever could? Therefore, I encourage you to adopt the spirit of God's servants from the past, such as Moses and David. Observe how they interested God in their cause and how God responded.

Sixthly, the meek shall receive blessings here on earth because there are numerous gracious promises made to them that offer great mercy to help them in their earthly journey. This promise, found in Psalm 37:11, existed during the time of the Law. Moreover, Christ reveals that the intent of the promise remains intact in the Gospel. Although the promises of outward blessings in other places are generally stated as godliness having promise in this life, Christ specifically singles out particular promises for the meek. In Psalm 25:9, it is written that the meek will be guided in judgment and taught the Lord's way. What an exceptional promise! It holds more value than all your possessions. If you were familiar with Scripture, you would consider this promise to be worth thousands. Show me another Scripture where the qualification of the subject is mentioned twice in so few words. The Lord loves the subject here; it seems He delights in pronouncing the very name. He does not merely say, "The meek will be guided in judgment and taught His way." No, the Lord loves to utter the name, "O the meek, the meek," twice in succession. He loves them, guides them in judgment, and teaches them His way. This promise pertains to guidance and instruction in any matter. For instance, consider a person facing a challenging business situation, unsure of how to navigate their path. A meek individual, when faced with adversity, seeks to quiet their spirit by resting in God. Once their spirit is calm, they turn to the promise, saying, "Lord, haven't You said that You will guide the meek in judgment? You will not abandon them to their own thoughts and spirits. The counsel of the froward leads to ruin, but You guide the meek in judgment. You have promised to guide me in ordering my affairs in this world if I can overcome my anger. And nothing aids understanding and judgment more than meekness and tranquility." In Proverbs 17:27, it is written, "He that hath knowledge spareth his words, and a man of understanding is of an excellent spirit." In the original Hebrew, it says, "A man of understanding is of a cool spirit." Hot-tempered individuals, those with quick tempers and fiery spirits, believe they possess more understanding than others. But the Holy Spirit declares otherwise. The person of understanding has a calm spirit. Meekness offers great advantages in natural ways to help one's spirit, but even more so when there is a promise that God will teach them. There are numerous other promises in Scripture that support this notion. In Psalm 76:9, it is stated that when God arises to judge and save, He pays no mind to froward spirits but ensures He looks after the meek. In Psalm 149:4, it is written, "For the Lord taketh pleasure in his people: he will beautify the meek with salvation." Meekness is a beautiful grace, and the Lord will adorn the meek with salvation. Furthermore, in Isaiah 29:19, there is a promise to the same effect. However, there is one more notable promise in Zephaniah 2:3 when times of calamity befall. It says, "Seek ye the Lord, all ye meek of the earth, which have wrought his judgments; seek righteousness, seek meekness: it may be ye shall be hid in the day of the Lord's anger." You may wonder, "Through God's mercy, I find that I have some control over my anger. But am I meek?" If you seek the Lord, seek meekness as well. It may be that you will be hidden on the day of the Lord's anger. It is as if the Holy Spirit is saying, "If anyone in the world is hidden, it could be you." Oh, these are the individuals who are blessings to the public in the places they reside. The prayers of the meek prevail with God, unlike the prayers of the froward. When you, who are froward, come to seek God, you cannot do so without wrath and doubt. But seek the Lord, all ye meek of the earth. Oh, the promises God has made to those who are meek on this earth. All these promises strengthen the great promise stated here: the meek shall inherit the earth.

Now, the main point discussed thus far has been an explanation to demonstrate how this promise, that the meek shall inherit the earth, is fulfilled. Now we shall turn to its application. Meekness is like salt; we need it in every aspect of our lives. The lives of men and women lack flavor in the places God has put them because of the absence of this grace of meekness.

# SERMON XIII

## A Rebuke of believers lacking meekness

"Blessed are the meek: for they shall inherit the earth." - Matthew 5:5

Now we shall move on to the Application, which I will address in two specific aspects. Firstly, the Rebuke of those who profess to be disciples of Christ, yet we cannot see the mark of the Spirit of Christ upon them, especially in regard to meekness. This is something we should lament and, if possible, extinguish the fire of their passionate spirits with tears. The ones I will direct my words to are those who claim to be willing to be Christ's disciples, to hear Christ. After all, this is Christ's sermon, and He directed it to His disciples. It is not surprising to see those who are worldly, led by earthly spirits, exhibiting frowardness, passion, and pride. However, it is a matter that deeply concerns the Spirit of God when those who are godly display such behavior. It is a direct contradiction to true grace. It is considered a special offense against passion and frowardness, and likewise for meekness. Otherwise, the Spirit of Christ would be grieved, as stated in Ephesians 4:30, "And grieve not the holy Spirit of God, whereby ye are sealed unto the day of redemption." But what actions grieve the

Spirit of God? What should we avoid to prevent grieving the Spirit of God? In verse 31, it is written, "Let all bitterness, and wrath, and anger, and clamour, and evil speaking, be put away from you, with all malice." Instead, be kind to one another, tender-hearted, forgiving one another, just as God, for Christ's sake, has forgiven you. Giving in to passion and frowardness will indeed grieve the Spirit of God. Those of you who have experienced the goodness of the Spirit of God in your hearts should be cautious of frowardness. Strive for meekness and kindness, so that the Spirit of God may delight in you, as it is very much aligned with the nature of the Spirit of God, which is gentle as a dove. I confess that I had considered discussing the futile justifications that many provide for their passion and frowardness. However, I have decided to leave that topic for later, as I plan to address it in verse 22 of this chapter, if God grants me life and freedom to continue with the sermon. But for now, in this use of rebuke, I will focus on conveying to those who profess to be saints that frowardness and a lack of meekness are as contrary to true grace as any other corruption one can think of. They may believe that their angry and passionate natures exempt them from the other corruptions that people indulge in. However, it is important to realize that a hasty and froward spirit, a spirit not governed by the grace of meekness, is, to a large extent, as opposed to true grace as anything imaginable. In fact, the absence of meekness and the presence of passion and frowardness should raise suspicions about the existence of true grace in those individuals. Rather than meekness, they exhibit passion and frowardness. Consider the following points:

First, frowardness and anger are contrary to true grace. What does grace do when it enters the heart? The first thing it does is reveal to the soul its own vileness, wretchedness, and baseness due to sin, as well as the danger it faces because of sin. How contrary it is, then, for a froward and passionate heart to react against the recognition of its own vileness and baseness! Do you not realize that you are a sinful worm, utterly vile and base? Yet you cannot tolerate anything that goes against you, and your heart immediately bursts into flames at the slightest opposition. Surely, you do not know yourself.

Second, the initial lesson that Christ imparts to anyone who enters His School is that of self-denial. This is the ABC of a Christian. "Whosoever will come after me, let him deny himself." How contrary is a froward and passionate spirit to the grace of self-denial, which is the very foundation of a Christian's journey! The first lesson that Christ teaches His students is to deny themselves, not to be fixated on their own minds, wills, and thoughts as they used to be. However, a froward heart is the epitome of self-centeredness. What causes passion to flare up? It is the feeling of being crossed, thwarted in our own will. Yet if self-denial were present, meekness would naturally follow.

Third, when grace enters the heart, does it not reveal to the heart its infinite need for mercy? It brings the heart to the feet of mercy, acknowledging that without divine intervention, it is eternally lost. How does this reconcile with your sight or sense of need for mercy when you possess a froward disposition and cannot tolerate anything in others? Yet you confess that you are in desperate need of mercy yourself.

Fourth, when grace enters the heart, it brings the heart into submission to God, subjecting it to a different rule than it followed before. Subduing the heart of a sinner to God is a primary work of grace. Sinful hearts are naturally rebellious and stubborn in their relationship with God. But this is completely contrary to frowardness and passion. A froward heart desires to be above God and any rule. It cannot keep itself in check and subject to authority. Hence, froward and passionate people often use expressions like "I will" and "I don't care." Their hearts are not subdued to God's authority. On the other hand, a heart that is submissive to the Lord and His authority immediately yields to Scripture. But a froward spirit does not. How contrary frowardness is to true grace.

Fifth, as soon as grace enters, the Spirit of Jesus Christ also enters the soul, making it, to some extent, like Jesus Christ. As I mentioned in my previous sermon when discussing the excellence of meekness, the Spirit of Christ is characterized by meekness. "Learn of me; for I am meek." Thus, your frowardness, which is so opposed to the Spirit of Jesus Christ, contradicts the work of grace.

Sixth, when grace comes, it brings light and wisdom to the soul. Naturally, we are foolish and disobedient, encompassed by darkness. However, no disposition of the soul is in greater darkness than that of froward and passionate people. Passion heightens folly, and such souls are not guided by wisdom. Thus, frowardness is very contrary to the work of grace.

Lastly, you are aware of the promise of the Gospel that it will make spirits meek. When the Gospel comes, the wolf and the lamb lie down together, those who had wolfish spirits. The lion and the ox eat together, signifying peace, love, and tranquility where the Gospel is present. Now, anything contrary to the work of the Gospel is also contrary to the work of grace in the heart. You, who profess godliness, should be aware that there is more danger in a froward and passionate spirit than you realize. Though you may think that because you make a profession, attend sermons, spend much time in prayer, fasting, and longing for ordinances, you surely possess grace. However, you may be mistaken. The frowardness of your hearts may be your eternal ruin. Consider the gravity of your situation. You strongly condemn those who are drunkards, and rightly so, as they are shut out of the Kingdom of Heaven. But is there not as much danger in a drunken passion as there is in drunkenness induced by alcohol? Indeed, the passion that arises from anger often leads to as many and as grave sins as drunkenness caused by beer or wine. You would find it repugnant if someone were to say that you became intoxicated once a year. But how often have you been intoxicated by passion? Such drunkenness can be as offensive to the Spirit of God as being drunk on beer or wine. Therefore, consider it a greater evil than you realize.

But let us move on to the Exhortation.

Blessed are the meek. Let us all learn to cultivate meek and gentle spirits. I recall in Numbers 6 it is said of the Nazirites that, just as they were not to drink wine, they were also not to drink vinegar. The Nazirites were a people consecrated to God, separated from others. All the saints of God are like Nazirites. Like Christ, all who belong to Him are set apart for God's purposes. Now, here is the requirement for all Nazirites: they must not possess vinegar spirits, sour and bitter dispositions. Instead, they should have quiet and meek spirits. This applies to all of us, especially those in subordinate positions. They should display meekness towards their superiors, and those undergoing bodily or spiritual afflictions should exhibit meek and quiet spirits. It is unbecoming for anyone to possess a froward and passionate heart, but particularly those who are facing trials. The Lord sends afflictions to humble and meek them. If they are not meek now, when will they be? We ought to be meek towards our brethren, towards one another, and towards our neighbors. Many people are so accustomed to displaying frowardness and passion towards their servants, children, or spouses that even when dealing with God Himself, they reveal their froward and passionate nature. My brethren, let us learn to appreciate this lovely and admirable grace of meekness. Therefore, in this section, I will present various ways or aids to help you develop a habit of meekness, to conduct yourselves meekly and gently in your respective spheres, so that you may claim the blessing of being the chosen ones of Christ and inherit the earth.

Firstly, if you desire meek spirits, learn to value the peace and sweetness of your spirits. Consider it a precious jewel of great worth, as we previously discussed how God esteemed meekness. To acquire it, you must have a genuine appreciation for the tranquility and peace that meekness brings to the soul. We can say, just as Tertullus the Orator said to Felix, "By thee we enjoy much peace." By meekness, much peace is experienced in the heart. Therefore, Christ says, "Learn of me, for I am meek and lowly in heart, and ye shall find rest unto your souls." There is rest. So, place a high value on the rest and peace of your spirits. Consider the following: if a temptation arises that stirs your passion, should you forfeit the sweetness you have experienced in your spirits just to have your way in that matter? Through God's mercy, I have discovered that when I overcome my passion, I experience the sweetest moments of my life. When I deny myself and practice meekness, oh, the peace in my heart is priceless. Should I lose it for a trivial matter, for a mere trifle? Oh, the poor trifles and toys for which men and women cast aside the peace of their spirits, as if they were worthless! If a person held a golden ball in their hand and someone in the street threw dirt at them, wouldn't it be considered foolish for them to retaliate by throwing their golden ball back at the person, seeking revenge? That is precisely what you do. You possess the grace of meekness in your hearts and have experienced the peace it brings. Yet, when a temptation arises, someone does something displeasing to you and opposes your will, how do you retaliate? You throw away this golden ball, which represents the peace and meekness of your spirits. Do not lose it for something insignificant. That is the first principle.

Secondly, to help us overcome passion and cultivate meekness and tranquility, it is beneficial to make a covenant with God (in the strength of Christ), even if it is for a short period of time. You may consider making this covenant when you wake up in the morning. Think to yourself, "Today, there may be circumstances that could stir my passion and rob me of the comfort of meekness. Well, I will covenant (enabled by God) that, from this day forward, whatever befalls me, I will maintain my composure until night. At least, I will bear it until then. And I will do so for this reason: if there is a valid reason for me to be stirred and angry, I can reserve my anger and deal with it later. I can address it afterward, just as well as I can do it today. But for today, I am resolved to restrain my passion and my will. Even if you think a whole day is too long, commit to it until noon. Resolve that from now until noon, regardless of what happens, you will not exhibit any signs of passion. Instead, you will consider addressing the issue after noon or the next day. One would think this is not an impossible task, even for someone with a quick temper, to be resolved for one day, to endure whatever comes their way. But you may say, "This will not mortify the corruption of passion." Although it may not completely mortify it, you cannot fathom the power of restraining your passion even for a short while. Just as fire can be extinguished by suffocating it, a person who can overcome themselves for one day will experience such sweetness that they will begin to think, "Why not make the same covenant for tomorrow?" And then, after experiencing the sweetness of that day, they will contemplate resolving the same for the following day. Oh, if you could only overcome yourself for a day, you would discover so much good that it would greatly assist you in facing another day.

Thirdly, this covenant alone will not be sufficient unless there is humility for the past. Those who only resolve to undertake a duty without humbling themselves for their previous failings are unlikely to make much progress through their resolutions. Therefore, if you want to overcome yourself and undertake what God requires of you, you must humble yourself for your past failures. Physicians use bitter substances to purge bile, and those who wish to tame wild creatures do so by keeping them in the dark. Likewise, humility for the disorders of passion is a special means of purging out passion and calming and quieting the spirits of men and women. Many of you have been overcome by froward fits, and you have recognized the inconvenience they cause. Perhaps you have thought, "This is not good," and you hope to never do it again. But unless you humble yourself for what you have done, you will fall back into it. This rule applies to all areas of life. Those who resolve to change in a particular aspect, but do not humble themselves for their past actions, will return to their sin. We have a notable example in the people of Israel. If you read the second and third chapters of Exodus, you will find that the people quarreled with Moses because the water was bitter. However, they were not humbled for this. In the sixteenth chapter, they were at it again. Though God showed mercy to them then, when they encountered another difficulty, they became froward and angry once more. And when God delivered them on that occasion, you will find them quarreling again in Exodus 17:2. Therefore, every time a new situation arose, they fell back into their old patterns. Why? Because there is no record of them humbling themselves for their past disturbances. Therefore, you who have froward dispositions, seek solitude and apply the salt tears of humility to your anger. Observe the transformation it brings. Humility for the past is a valuable aid for the future.

Fourthly, if you desire meek and tranquil spirits, beware of the initial stages of passion. When a fire begins, we do not wait until the whole house is ablaze to extinguish it. If a small fire or even smoke is detected in any part of the house, one immediately investigates its source. Likewise, when passion begins to arise, your house, your soul, begins to catch fire. At the first sign, you should be just as committed to extinguishing it as you would be if you saw flames erupting in your house. Perhaps a small amount of water can put out the fire now, but if you wait half an hour, several buckets of water will not suffice. Therefore, treat passion as you would treat poison. Administer a remedy immediately. Do not allow your passion to persist. Consider it a fever, and seize it at its onset. There have been dreadful outbursts of passion that originated from small beginnings and escalated into acts of great violence. I recall reading in the history of Venice about two sons of the Duke of Florence. After a hunting trip, they argued about which of their dogs killed a hare. One claimed, "My dog caught it first," while the other asserted, "No, it was mine." Their argument persisted until one drew his sword and killed his brother. Witnessing his master's murder, the brother's servant drew his own sword and killed the remaining brother. As a result, the Duke lost two sons in one incident.

How often does it happen in your families that a small spark ignites a fire? At first, there may be just a word spoken improperly, which could have easily been overlooked. But no, that word begets another, and that word begets another, and so on, until it grows into a dreadful flame. Beware of the beginning of anger. Whenever anger starts to arise in the family or in your souls, it is time for you to take a look at yourselves. Sometimes you may have friends whose falling-outs begin merely with a change in their countenance. One person thinks, "Surely such a one does not look at me with the same pleasant countenance as before." And from there, suspicions and misinterpretations arise. Then comes distance, followed by listening to tales carried by others, believing and exaggerating them. Then hard words are spoken against one another, followed by ill treatment, leading to violent and intense conflicts and actions against one another. All this could have been prevented if care had been taken from the beginning. Proverbs 14:14 says, "The beginning of strife is like releasing water, so stop contention before it starts." Be cautious of the beginnings of sin if you want to maintain a meek and quiet disposition.

Now, a fifth rule is this: if you want to keep your spirits calm, anticipate that you will encounter things that will go against your will. This helps to prevent anger and quiet our hearts. Just as Anaxagoras said when he heard of his deceased son, "I know that I fathered a mortal." Similarly, when you hire a servant, anticipate their weaknesses beforehand. Certainly, there will be many things done by them that will displease you. When you marry, anticipate that there will be disagreements and displeasure between you and your spouse. Likewise, when you make a friend, anticipate that they have their own flaws and weaknesses. If we anticipate that we will not have all our desires satisfied in this world, it will be a means to calm our hearts. It is no more than what I expected. A soldier going into battle finds peace when facing hardships by thinking, "This is nothing more than what I anticipated." Similarly, when sailors encounter storms at sea, it would be unseemly for them to fret and worry because they knew they were likely to face storms. So, whenever something happens that opposes you, remember that if you had wisdom beforehand, you would think that there would be various things that would go against your will. Now, God is testing me to see whether I will bear these crosses that befall me.

The sixth rule is this: consider your own frailty. Others may provoke and stir up your anger, but you should follow the rule of seeking and granting forgiveness. If you encounter certain things in others that may offend you, it may not be long before they encounter things amiss in you. This is a marvelous help in calming the spirits of those who are truly gracious. In Galatians 6, observe the Apostle's argument: "Brothers, if someone is caught in a sin, you who are spiritual should restore them gently. But watch yourselves, or you also may be tempted. Carry each other's burdens, and in this way, you will fulfill the law of Christ." Bear one another's burdens. Consider that you may also be tempted, and therefore bear one another's burdens. The burden is likely to be mutual. I bear my brother's burden, and my brother is likely to bear my burden. I have a burden that may test his patience as much as his tests mine. So let us bear one another's burdens. It is ordinary for those with the greatest weaknesses to bear with the weaknesses of others, lest they become like a gouty leg that requires constant attention but is useful for nothing. Many proud and haughty individuals expect others to please them, but they seek to please no one. Remember your own frailty.

If any of you say, "But I am not as burdensome to others as they are to me, so there is no equality in bearing his burden because he is likely to bear mine," I beseech you to consider the answer to that. First, everyone tends to think that they are not as burdensome to others as others are to them. Granted, but then observe that it appears you are stronger than your brother. If the heavier end of the burden is upon your shoulder, then you should bear it quietly, for it seems God has made your shoulder more capable of carrying it. It is not more difficult for a person to bear others' offenses against them than it is for them not to be offensive to others. Therefore, bless God when you think that your brother's burden is greater than yours, for it is God's mercy that He has made your strength greater than his. Thus, considering one another's burdens, let us strive to bear them meekly and quietly.

Furthermore, as the seventh rule to help you, strive to maintain peace with God. There is no better way to keep your heart calm than to have peace with God. When all is well between God and your soul, external storms and tempests will not shake it. What disquiets people's hearts is the corruption within, rather than the temptations without. However, the peace that comes from being at peace with God is a topic we may consider further when we discuss the blessedness of being peacemakers. So, I will not dwell on it now.

The eighth rule is this: convince yourself that nothing done in anger cannot be done better without it. The Apostle says, "The wrath of man does not produce the righteousness of God." For instance, if you want to reprove someone, the best way is to do it with meekness. When restoring those who have fallen, do it with meekness, considering yourself lest you also be tempted.

Then it follows, "Bear one another's burdens and so fulfill the law of Christ."
Bear one another's burdens. Consider that you may be tempted, and then bear
one another's burdens. The burden is likely to be mutual. I bear my brother's
burden, and my brother is likely to bear my burden. I have a burden that may
test his patience as much as his tests mine. Therefore, let us bear one another's
burdens. As for correcting your children or servants, do not think that if you do
it without passion, you must not do it at all. That is foolish. You can do it better
without passion than with passion. Therefore, some pagans would not correct
their servants merely because they were angry. If you need to give an answer to
someone who has spoken amiss to you, you can convince them better if you can
overcome your passion. You can reason with your brother much more effectively
without your passion than with it. The truth is, those who have control over
their passion have a great advantage over those they contend with. Consider this:
when your heart is full of anger, it wants to act immediately. But suppress your
passion, and call upon the grace of meekness. Consider that you want to act, but
why can't you act as well without passion as with it? Yes, you can do it better,
and therefore, you will.

In the ninth place, when you feel your anger starting to rise, strive to redirect
it towards another object. Instead of anger, exercise mourning. If someone has
displeased you, whether it be your wife, child, or servant, before giving in to
anger, find a solitary place and lament their sin. They have done wrong, not
only against you but against God as well. If that is the case, mourn for their sin
against God before displaying any anger. Then see how your passion will work
after mourning for their sin. You will find this rule to be of great use. Husbands
and wives who have not lived peacefully or masters in their households should
observe this. When something is done amiss, if it is not a sin against God, then
it is not a significant matter to provoke your anger. But if it involves sin, then be
sure to mourn for it before God. Then, display your passion. Physicians aim to
stop excessive bleeding from one vein by redirecting it to another. Likewise, we
should redirect our affections. A Christian displays wisdom, strength, and skill
in being able to turn their affections this way and that. They can exercise anger,
love, sorrow, joy, and hope. If a person cannot redirect their affections, there is
likely a disturbance. But this is the excellence of a Christian—they have command over their affections and can turn them in various directions. It is good

when dealing with children, who may be stubborn or sulky, not to confront them with rage. Instead, if you can redirect their thoughts to something else, you can bring them out of their sullen mood sooner than by opposing it. The same applies to ourselves; sometimes there is a sullen, froward disposition in our hearts. The remedy may not be to directly oppose it, but to have another object before us to redirect the current of our hearts.

Tenthly, another rule to help against anger is this: do not engage in lengthy discourse. Be cautious during moments of stubborn passion not to let words multiply. Proverbs 8:13 and Matthew 5:22, among other Scriptures, highlight the danger of excessive words during moments of anger, particularly when it leads to vile speech. Words are like wind, but they are the wind that fans the flames of anger to a blazing heat. Proverbs 7:11 describes the loudness of a harlot—a most unbecoming trait for women, even when provoked by anger. They should refrain from being loud in speech, from multiplying words. The whorish woman is characterized by her loudness. Therefore, those who wish to conduct themselves with matronly sobriety and modesty should be cautious of using loud speech. Moreover, when it comes to adding word upon word, it is better to be silent. Consider David's response when dealing with his froward brethren in 1 Samuel 17—he turned away from them and would no longer respond. I confess that turning away in a sulky manner is not good either. Instead, offer a few gentle words and then turn away. Turning away without any response can be just as provoking. Thus, give a gentle answer first and then turn away, resolving not to multiply words at such times. That's another rule.

Eleventhly, if you desire to be free from anger and possess a meek and calm spirit, be cautious of involving yourself in excessive busyness that God has not called you to. The reason for this is that every task will have some aspect that goes against your desires. Therefore, make sure you are only engaged in what God calls you to do, and there you will find God's blessing. When individuals take on more than what God has called them to, it's no wonder their fingers get burnt. It is observed that those who are excessively busy are often irritable. However, when you know that your tasks are aligned with God's calling, and you do them in obedience to God, you can expect God's blessing to bring you peace. Otherwise, there will be many temptations involved.

Twelfthly, be cautious of excessive curiosity. In a household, if a person insists on prying into every aspect of family life, checking every room and monitoring every occurrence, there is a high chance that many things will disturb their peace. You should not take note of every minor fault in a servant or every small offense committed by your spouse or children. You must see without seeing, if you wish to maintain a meek spirit. Foolish and excessive curiosity in scrutinizing every detail of family matters, especially those that do not concern you, is unbecoming. It not only goes against one's dignity but also causes great disturbance within the family.

Thirteenthly, another helpful strategy is to consider whether the current situation is a temptation from the Devil. The Devil holds a grudge against me, and who knows what mischief the Devil is trying to cause me now. If you have enough control over your heart to think in this manner whenever you are in a fit of anger, it is an excellent approach. Recognize that this might be a temptation, and the Devil intends to lead you into sin. Augustine provides a wonderful analogy: Just as a fowler sets his net near a hedge where birds gather and throws stones and sticks into the hedge to scare them, not with the intention of killing the birds but to drive them out of the hedge so they will fly into the net, so it is with the Devil. When the Devil intends to lure you into sin, he says, "I cannot tempt them to commit such sins unless I stir their passion. Let me provoke their anger, and then I can lead them into sin." The Devil's aim is to make you fall into sin. When the Devil stirs up anger (like a fowler throwing stones into the hedge), he cares not so much for your anger but for the evil he wants to bring upon you through your anger. Therefore, simply having the thought that this might be a temptation, and if it turns out to be a temptation to some wicked sin, what would become of me? I would rather sit still and do nothing than allow the Devil to manipulate me.

Fourteenthly, consider the example of God, Jesus Christ, and His saints. It is a powerful method to combat anger and passion—reflect on how meek the Lord is. When God had to deal with Cain, He approached him with gentleness and meekness, asking, "Where is your brother?" Even when Cain responded rudely, God continued in a meek manner, saying, "If you do what is right, will you not be accepted?" Similarly, when God dealt with Jonah—a froward and pettish prophet—He asked him, "Is it right for you to be angry?" when He saw Jonah in a fit of anger. This is a good example for us to follow when dealing with others who have angry spirits. We can ask, "Is it right for you to be angry?" God did not confront Jonah forcefully but approached him gently and meekly. Consider how God deals with His poor creatures. It is no disgrace for you to deal with your servants and children in the same manner they are less injurious to you than you are to God. I could also present to you the example of Jesus Christ. I recall reading about someone who, when asked how they could overcome themselves when faced with wrongs and injuries, replied, "I meditate on the sufferings of Jesus Christ. I reflect on the injustices He endured, yet how He remained as gentle as a lamb and did not open His mouth. I continue meditating until my spirit is quieted. The meditation on the sufferings of Jesus Christ, His wounds, and how He bore them meekly and gently is a special means." I remember Camerarius recounting how some individuals, when consumed by rage, would place a sheep or lamb before them as a means of calming themselves. Similarly, when we are in a fit of anger or a mad rage, let us place before us that meek Lamb, the Lord Jesus, and it will help to calm us. In 1 Peter 2, the Apostle uses the example of Christ to encourage us to maintain a quiet and meek spirit. He reminds us that we are called to patiently endure the wrongs done to us because Christ also suffered for us, leaving us an example to follow in His footsteps. He committed no sin, and no deceit was found in His mouth. When He was reviled, He did not revile in return. When He suffered, He did not threaten but entrusted Himself to Him who judges justly. Simply read this passage and consider the example of Jesus Christ, and it will be a special means to quiet your spirit.

And so, I should have presented the examples of the saints—Abraham, David, Stephen, Paul, and others. But I'll mention just one or two more. I recall the famous example of Calvin's attitude towards Luther, which is particularly relevant to ministers. Despite their differences in judgment and approaches, Luther being of a hot and fiery temperament, and Calvin being more tender, Calvin had this to say about Luther: "Even if Luther were to call me a devil, insult me in any way, I will still acknowledge Luther as the servant of Jesus Christ, and one whom Christ uses as an instrument for much good." Calvin exhibited a sweet and gentle spirit, considering Luther, a man instrumental for God, with such kindness. There is no better way to heap coals of fire upon the heads of those who oppose us than to demonstrate meekness and gentleness towards them.

Therefore, as a conclusion, I urge you to treasure these rules that you have heard. And let me add one more—fifteenthly, be cautious of the next temptation if you desire to exercise the grace of meekness. Even if you forget other rules, remember this one: be wary of the next temptation. Leave with the resolution that you have heard about the excellence of the grace of meekness, how Christ commends it and the wonderful promises attached to it. You have also gained insight into the evil of a froward spirit, which is contrary to meekness, and have received many rules to help you live more peacefully in your family. Now, as you depart, be aware that a temptation may arise tonight. This is the way of the Devil—to tempt you just when you have heard against a particular sin. And when you have been called to a specific duty, a temptation will arise to distract you from that duty. If the Devil can prevail over you after a sermon, he considers that the sermon has been wasted and will not benefit you. So now, after hearing all this about meekness, it is possible that tonight or tomorrow morning, a temptation to frowardness and anger may come your way. There's a high chance you will encounter something that provokes you. If you have the presence of mind to think, "This is the Devil's attempt to nullify the profit of those sermons I heard on meekness," and through God's grace, resolve to resist that temptation, you cannot fathom the amount of good that can come from overcoming the next temptation. However, if the very first temptation overwhelms you and prevails against you, bidding farewell to these sermons, then my efforts on your behalf will have been in vain. I cannot guarantee that you will have the opportunity to hear sermons on this topic again, so take heed and ensure that you do not lose the impact of the word. Leave with the resolve, through God's grace, to apply these truths in the management of your heart and your family life. Let your actions bear witness to the fact that you have heard sermons on meekness. For you women who may have lived in strife with your husbands, and you husbands who may have been harsh towards your wives, may it be evident that you have encountered the blessedness of meekness. Let both husbands and wives incorporate this into their prayers, thanking God for the revelation of this scripture to them.

# SERMON XIV

## Rules and aids to Christian meekness

"Blessed are they which do hunger and thirst after righteousness: for they shall be filled." - Matthew 5:6

On the last day, you may recall that we discussed the conclusion of the third beatitude mentioned by Christ: "Blessed are the meek, for they shall inherit the earth." We concluded with an exhortation to embrace this blessed and precious grace of meekness. We provided various rules to promote the cultivation of meekness. I do not intend to reiterate what was previously said. Instead, I will add one more crucial point that greatly aids in developing meekness, particularly for those who are godly.

Sixteenthly, the absence of this grace brings great dishonor to individuals and their profession. Let those who lack meekness remember their own prayers and expressions before God. This recollection would greatly contribute to our meekness. Consider how you have acknowledged your own unworthiness before God during prayer. You freely express to God how vile, sinful, and wretched you are, recognizing that your sins deserve God's eternal wrath. You wonder how you have escaped damnation. You may continue in this manner during prayer or even in the company of others, speaking humbly about yourself. Yet, as soon as someone crosses your path, you become as froward and angry as anyone else. Are you the same person who, not long ago, stood before God acknowledging your vileness, sinfulness, and wickedness? Did you express astonishment at your deliverance from hell? Are you that individual? If so, when faced with opposition in the world, are you unable to endure it? You claim that you deserve hell, but if a child, servant, wife, husband, or friend opposes you, you cannot tolerate it. If only you could reflect on your expressions before God during prayer, it would cause you to view yourself as despicable and humble your heart when your anger begins to rise. You, who possess a passionate and froward heart, either pray to God in the morning or do not. If you neglect prayer, you reveal yourself to be atheistic. If you do pray, I assume that a significant part of your prayer involves acknowledging your wretchedness, sinfulness, and vileness. Why do you engage in such morning prayers if, when faced with temptation during the day, you yield to anger? If you possessed the self-control to think about your prayer and how incompatible your conduct is with those acknowledgments you made regarding your sinfulness and wretchedness, it would subdue you in the midst of your unruly passion.

Various groups of people should strive for the grace of meekness, but I will address only those in an afflicted condition. In the Hebrew language, the same word signifies both "afflicted" and "meek." This illustrates that those who are undergoing affliction should possess meek and quiet spirits, as God's hand is upon them. However, it is quite the opposite in reality. Often, the most afflicted individuals are the most froward. For instance, many sick people, when ill, become more irritable and froward than at other times, whereas they should exhibit more meekness, quietness, and gentleness under God's hand. Similarly, among the impoverished, reviling communication is often heard. When crossed in any way, they resort to railing and reviling, displaying a proud, froward, and passionate spirit. If God has afflicted you with poverty, it is (if He loves you) to keep your spirit low. If your heart were low, it would also be meek. However, we will move on from meekness and proceed to the following verse, which states, "Blessed are they that do hunger and thirst after righteousness." This notion appears contrary to worldly opinion. The world would rather say, "Blessed are those who are full" rather than "those who hunger and thirst." Yet, the Holy

Spirit pronounces a blessing upon those who hunger and thirst, and a woe to those who are full. In Luke 6:25, it is written, "Woe unto you that are full." Many believe that the greatest happiness lies in having full tables, dishes, cups, and purses. However, the Holy Spirit does not regard such abundance as true happiness. Instead, He pronounces a woe to those who are full, while declaring blessedness upon those who hunger and thirst after righteousness.

Some interpret this hunger and thirst literally, especially when comparing it to what Saint Luke says (as I mentioned at the beginning of this sermon, despite the various objections against it, it appears to be the same sermon) in Luke 6:21. Luke does not mention the word righteousness, but only "ye that hunger now," opposing hunger to those who are full. Therefore, they believe it is meant literally. They understand it as follows: Blessed are those who are godly (this must be understood), who lack bread and drink. They are in such extreme circumstances that they do not have bread to eat or water to quench their thirst. It is as if Christ is saying, "Do not be troubled if you are pushed to such an extreme that you lack basic necessities. This will not hinder your blessedness. You can still be blessed." When you are in great need, you may be inclined to look at those who are well-fed and have abundance and consider them blessed. But do not be deceived. Woe to those who are full! However, you are blessed in your great need and extremities. Some interpret this blessedness as being drawn from the Old Testament, just like the previous beatitude of meekness, which is taken from Psalm 37:11. In a similar manner, this beatitude of hungering and thirsting is derived from Isaiah 65:13. However, my purpose is not to dwell on this interpretation. Therefore, we must go further.

The object of their hunger and thirst in this context goes beyond physical needs. They hunger and thirst after righteousness. However, I confess that even learned interpreters and godly men, such as Calvin and Musculus, do not take these words any further than this: Blessed are those who, in their extreme circumstances, simply hunger and thirst to have what is right and just. They are godly individuals who find themselves in lowly and oppressed conditions, longing for righteous dealings in the world. Their interpretation does not go beyond this point. Calvin, as you know, usually captures the essence accurately and provides a spiritual interpretation. However, in this case, he limits his interpretation to this understanding. Hunger and thirst clearly signify earnest desires that arise from a sense of lack. These desires intensify due to the acute awareness of the absence of the desired object. There are no desires as strong and earnest as those of a hungry or thirsty person. Therefore, those who hunger and thirst after righteousness long for righteous dealings, desiring to be treated justly. Some interpreters believe this interpretation is sufficient. They only speak of hungering and thirsting for their own righteous dealings and the presence of righteousness. However, I believe we can go further in interpreting this righteousness. We can understand it as a hunger and thirst for righteousness to prevail in the world. I truly believe that this is one significant aspect intended by the Holy Spirit. Christ looks upon His disciples and, as if speaking to them, says, "You are likely to encounter many unrighteous dealings in the world. You will witness the prevailing injustice and unrighteousness. However, it will pain and grieve your souls to observe the unrighteousness in the world. You will long for a time when righteousness will prevail and govern among humanity." Blessed are you! Do not involve yourselves in their unrighteous dealings. Instead, when you witness such injustice in others, let your desires be for the time when righteousness will prevail in the world. Blessed are you for hungering and thirsting in this manner. I firmly believe that this is a significant aspect Christ intended when pronouncing this blessedness. Therefore, I must not gloss over it as many do when discussing this blessedness.

I acknowledge that the other interpretations, particularly the righteousness of Jesus Christ and the power of righteousness in one's own heart, are more excellent in themselves. Yet, I doubt whether Christ had those in mind initially, especially when speaking to His disciples who were likely to be in poor and lowly conditions. He begins with those who are poor in spirit. We have already interpreted the meaning of that. Therefore, although you are likely to encounter many unrighteous dealings, you are blessed if you are content with the condition you may face and yet lift your desires to heaven, appealing to God to vindicate your righteousness. It is as if Christ says, "The world will accuse and revile you, calling you troublesome, factious, and turbulent. But you are blessed. Can you appeal to God for your righteousness? Can you desire that while the world reviles and accuses you of hypocrisy, making a show of religion without having any truth within you, God will judge your righteous cause? Blessed are you if you can do so. Do not be overly troubled by these accusations. Instead, hunger and thirst for the time when the Lord will make your righteousness evident." If the world accuses you of self-seeking, implying that all your actions are driven by self-interest, you can appeal to God regarding the righteousness of your heart in those matters. You long for the time when God will reveal the secrets of all hearts, making it evident whether you sought self or His glory. Blessed are you if you can hunger and thirst for the manifestation of God's righteousness in this manner. Even if the world accuses you of partiality or wronging others, you hunger for the time when God will vindicate righteousness. It is common for the wicked to cast aspersions upon the saints of God, seeking to tarnish their holy profession with some form of evil. Yet, if you patiently endure such accusations and long for the time when the righteous God will reveal your righteousness, blessed are you for hungering and thirsting in this way.

Blessed are you, for:

First, you have the testimony of your own consciences when people accuse you.

Secondly, you have the testimony of God. God bears witness for you.

Thirdly, blessed are you, for God is working on your behalf while you endure these accusations.

And one day, you will be satisfied. God will clear your righteousness, and He will make it shine brightly like the noonday sun. Currently, you are being smeared with accusations by wicked individuals. But in Revelation 19:8, it is written that to the Church, it was granted to be clothed in clean, white fine linen, which represents the righteousness of the saints. Although it primarily refers to the righteousness of Christ, it may also have a connection to the righteousness I am speaking of. It is similar to a respectable woman walking on the street and being dirtied by mad people. When she returns home, she has clean linen to put on. Likewise, though the saints may be covered in dirt and have their names tarnished in the world, Jesus Christ has fine linen to clothe them with. They will appear righteous before the saints, angels, and the entire world one day. In Matthew 13:43, there is a promise that the righteous will shine forth like the sun in the kingdom of their Father. They will indeed shine forth with great glory, in addition to receiving a great reward in their Father's kingdom. Currently, they reside in the kingdom of the world, where darkness prevails. But when they enter the kingdom of their Father, they will shine forth like the sun. This pertains to all forms of righteousness, whether it be the perfect righteousness of Christ that they will be adorned with or the perfection of sanctification. It also encompasses the righteousness by which they will be vindicated from all cast aspersions. Blessed are they, for they will be cleared.

Yes, blessed are they, for they will be filled. You will be recompensed for the unjust accusations that are hurled at you now. Your reward will be even greater, increasing your glory. Therefore, consider yourselves blessed when you are unjustly deemed unrighteous, for you will be honoured all the more. This is evident in the notable Scripture in 1 Peter 4:14: "If you are reproached for the name of Christ, you are blessed, for the Spirit of glory and of God rests upon you." God will certainly compensate you for all the suffering you endure in this manner.

Furthermore, those who hunger and thirst after righteousness do not merely desire God to clear their righteousness (though that is one form of righteousness they long for). They also yearn for righteousness to prevail among all people. Blessed are those whose hearts ache when they witness unrighteousness in the world. They are grieved by the sight of this unrighteousness and long for God to appear and establish righteousness as the governing principle in the world. They are pained by the unrighteous dealings among mankind. This is what Christ aims at when He says, "Indeed, you will witness a great deal of unrighteousness, but it will trouble your hearts, and you will long for the time when righteousness shall prevail. Blessed are you."

Firstly, the people of God cannot help but feel anguish in their hearts when they witness unrighteous dealings in the world. This pain is as intense as that of a person who lacks bread. It troubles them more than all their persecutions and afflictions. There is nothing they long for more than the coming of Jesus Christ, not only for their own salvation, but also for righteousness to prevail.

Firstly, when the saints observe unrighteous dealings in the world, they recognize that it greatly diminishes the honour of God. They reason within themselves, "Is not God a righteous God? Then what a dishonour it is to Him for there to be so much unrighteousness in the world."

Secondly, this unrighteousness among men is contrary to their own spirits, for the Lord has instilled righteousness in their hearts. To witness individuals in positions of power or those professing religion behaving unjustly causes them pain. It contradicts the gracious disposition that God has placed within their hearts.

Thirdly, through this unrighteousness, they witness the suffering of the righteous, how precious servants of God are trampled upon, and how wicked and ungodly individuals prosper. It grieves their hearts to see such disorder.

Fourthly, the unrighteousness they observe in the world presents numerous temptations to commit evil. At times, these temptations even prevail over the truly godly, as they did with David, whose righteous soul faltered when he saw the prosperity of the wicked and the afflictions suffered by the godly. When the righteous witness others behaving unrighteously, yet succeeding in their designs, while those who walk according to righteousness suffer greatly, it becomes a significant temptation. They long for the time when this temptation will be removed, along with the dishonour brought upon God, the incongruity with their spirits, the suffering of the saints, and the elimination of this temptation. They cry out, "O Lord, if righteousness were to prevail, then You would be honoured more than ever. We would experience the joy of our hearts, and Your saints would no longer suffer as they do. Deliver us from these temptations."

Fifthly, through unrighteousness, they witness how the wicked are burdened in their hearts. The saints find it grievous to see those engaged in unrighteous ways prosper and become hardened, assuming that God is like them. They long for righteousness to prevail so that the wicked may be ashamed and confounded.

Sixthly, they observe that many become atheists due to unrighteousness, doubting whether God truly rules in the world. Therefore, they plead, "O Lord Jesus, manifest Your governance over the world."

Seventhly, through this unrighteousness, they witness the establishment of Satan's kingdom and the hinderance it poses to the righteous kingdom of Christ. They question, "Lord, will the kingdom of Satan always prevail in the world? O Lord, when will the righteous scepter of Jesus Christ reign among mankind?"

Lastly, this unrighteousness tends to lead to wickedness, ruin, and confusion. They comprehend that unless God appears in His righteousness to rectify these disorders resulting from the unrighteousness of men, everything will descend into ruin and chaos. Therefore, they implore the Lord to hasten and reveal Himself as a righteous God. This is how the saints hunger and thirst after righteousness—to witness righteous dealings in the world. Now you understand what causes their hearts pain, the evil in unrighteousness, and the excellence they perceive in righteousness.

They hunger and thirst after righteousness. They have great desires and offer many prayers to God. They cry out for God to hasten the coming of righteous times. They send up strong pleas to God for righteousness to prevail in the world. How long, how long will it be holy and true, etc.? They send up powerful prayers to God for righteousness to triumph throughout the world. And for their own part, they refuse to engage in any unrighteous ways. They would rather endure any misery than be associated with or partake in any unrighteous actions. Even if they hold public positions with many advantages, they would rather lose everything than involve themselves in unrighteousness. A righteous heart craves righteousness more than bread or drink. Therefore, they will have nothing to do with unrighteousness. Though they live in an unrighteous world, they say, "God forbid that I should be involved in unrighteousness. No, it is righteousness that my soul craves. I will hunger and thirst for it. Therefore, even if I lose all my friends, my wealth, and my material possessions, I will keep my conscience clear and remain a champion for righteousness throughout my life. I will demonstrate that I am not merely playing games with God by hungering and thirsting for righteousness while being unrighteous myself. I will strive to promote righteousness as much as I can so that it may prevail in the world. Blessed are these individuals.

Firstly, they bear the image of God upon themselves at present. If you possess a righteous heart, you have the image of God. Your heart is just like His. The Lord is a righteous God, and so are you. Blessed are you of the Lord because you bear His image.

Secondly, those who hunger and thirst after righteousness bear witness for God in this unrighteous world. Although they live among others who are unrighteous, should the great God have no one to testify on His behalf? Yes, there is a generation of people who stand up to bear witness to God's righteousness. They desire nothing more than righteousness. Oh, blessed are you of the Lord! You are witnesses unto God.

Thirdly, you are blessed because your hunger and thirst for righteousness deliver you from many temptations that others succumb to. Other individuals may have some resolve not to be unrighteous, but when they witness the unrighteousness of others, they are overcome. Their hearts are not as firmly set against unrighteousness as yours, which hungers and thirsts for righteousness. Consequently, when your heart is grieved by the unrighteousness in the world and longs for God's righteousness, you are delivered from temptations that ensnare others. It is a blessed thing to be delivered from temptation.

Fourthly, those who hunger and thirst after righteousness are blessed because they are suitable for public service. They are not individuals who would manipulate righteousness to further their own ends or seek personal gain from public affairs. What use are they? However, those who hunger and thirst above all else for the establishment of righteousness in the world are suitable to be employed in public service. The Lord takes pleasure in employing such individuals. When people realize that their hearts are set on righteousness, they will be eager to employ them. Although some may initially become vexed and irritated by those who strive to maintain righteousness, let these men continue on their unwavering path of promoting righteousness. Eventually, they will receive honour from men. All who interact with them will regard them as blessed individuals who are fit for public service.

Fifthly, they are blessed because they stand against the current of unrighteousness and prevent it from flooding the world. Blessed are those who are willing to resist the stream of unrighteous dealings to prevent its overflow. They bring about much good for others as well as for themselves. The Scriptures affirm the blessedness of such individuals in Psalm 12:5: "For the oppression of the poor, for the sighing of the needy, now will I arise, saith the Lord; I will set him in safety from him that puffeth at him." Truly, the Lord blesses the righteous. Their actions against unrighteousness prevent it from overtaking the world. They are instruments of great good.

Those who hunger and thirst after righteousness are blessed because their desires will be fulfilled. In Proverbs 11:23, it is said, "The desire of the righteous is only good." It is good, and God approves of it. He will fulfill it. There is a time coming when all those who love righteousness will witness the punishment of unrighteousness and the rewarding of righteousness. Currently, you may see some instances where unrighteousness is punished and righteousness is rewarded, but that does not completely fulfill you. There will come a time when you will witness the punishment of all unrighteousness in the world and the rewarding of all righteousness. In Psalm 58:11, it says, "Verily there is a reward for the righteous: verily he is a God that judgeth in the earth." The time will come when all people will be compelled to acknowledge that there is indeed a reward for the righteous, and that God is a just judge. This will fill the hearts of the saints with joy. When God brings every person to account and punishes all unrighteousness in the world, and when He rewards all righteousness, it will bring great satisfaction. Furthermore, all the disorder caused by unrighteous dealings in the world will be set right. God will transform the chaos of confusion into a beautiful and orderly arrangement. You will witness everything being brought into a splendid and harmonious order. Will that not fill you? In the book of Ecclesiastes, Solomon speaks of injustice in chapter 3:16: "Moreover, I saw under the sun the place of judgment, that wickedness was there; and the place of righteousness, that iniquity was there." In the very places where I expected to find justice, wickedness was present, and in the places where I thought righteousness would prevail, I found iniquity. What then? I said in my heart, "God will judge the righteous and the wicked, for there is a time there for every purpose and for every work." Those righteous ones who hunger and thirst after righteousness should cherish this text: "You will be filled." There will come a time when God will judge the righteous and the wicked. There is a time appointed for every purpose and work, and you will be filled.

Moreover, all the desires of every righteous person from the beginning of the world will be satisfied. From Abel, who was killed by Cain, to all the patriarchs, apostles, prophets, martyrs, and saints throughout generations, they all hungered for righteousness. Righteous Abel and the others—yes, their blood cries out to the righteous God to manifest righteousness in the world. "O God, my righteousness," says David and others. When the time comes for every prayer of every righteous servant of God to be heard and granted, surely it will be a blessed time that will fulfill them. Will it not satisfy you to have every prayer of every righteous servant of God from the beginning of the world fully answered and all their desires fulfilled? Surely, this will satisfy you. Blessed are you, for you will be satisfied.

And for the satisfaction of the righteous who cry out to God against the unrighteous dealings in the world, consider some texts of Scripture. There are

many well-known scriptures pointing in this direction, that there is a time coming when righteousness shall prevail in the world. In Isaiah 1:26, it says, "And
I will restore thy judges as at the first, and thy counsellors as at the beginning:
afterward thou shalt be called, The city of righteousness, the faithful city." And
in Isaiah 3:10, it says, "Say ye to the righteous, that it shall be well with him:
for they shall eat the fruit of their doings." Mark, say to the righteous that it
shall be well with them. You who are righteous may be concerned that things
will not go well, but I say to the righteous, it shall go well with them. For they
shall reap the benefits of their righteous actions. If you continue on a righteous
path, committing your righteousness to God, be content and patient. You shall
enjoy the fruits of your deeds, and you shall be satisfied. Here is a promise to
nourish you when others treat you unjustly. It would be endless to speak of all
the scriptures that demonstrate how righteousness will prevail in the world. In
Isaiah 11:4, it speaks of Christ coming to judge the world with righteousness.
In Isaiah 60:17, it says, "I will also make thy officers peace, and thine exactors
righteousness." In Isaiah 61:10, it says, "I will greatly rejoice in the LORD, my
soul shall be joyful in my God; for he hath clothed me with the garments of
salvation, he hath covered me with the robe of righteousness." I could name
nearly twenty scriptures from the prophecy of Isaiah that prophesy a glorious
time of righteousness, where violence and oppression shall be abolished. My
brethren, let us find comfort in this. Despite the violence and wrongdoing that
exists, we hope and believe that the Lord will deliver His people from violence,
wrongs, oppression, and all unrighteousness. The exacter shall be righteousness.
In chapter 60:17, the Lord makes a gracious promise to His Church. He will
turn brass into gold, iron into silver, wood into brass, and stones into iron. He
will make the officers instruments of peace and the exactors embodiments of
righteousness. This is a prophecy of the times of the Church. There will come
a time when the officers who deal with the people of God will bring nothing
but peace, and those exacting from them will be righteousness itself. They will
be as righteous as the people desire. Isn't it a blessed time when all individuals
in positions of power will bring nothing but peace to the saints of God and no
longer wrong them? The Lord will make them righteousness itself. No wonder
Christ expresses this in terms of hunger and thirst, for it will be a glorious time.
Christ knew that a glorious time was coming when righteousness would prevail

in the world. The people of God in those times knew it even more than we do now. They knew that such times were coming. Justin Martyr, one of the earliest Christian apologists, affirms that every Christian believes in the coming of these glorious times. He speaks of the glorious times of the Church and the people of God, in which they will be delivered from the violence, wrongs, and oppression of ungodly men. Every Christian believes it. This interpretation of hungering and thirsting after righteousness may not be common among you, but I am confident that those in the early days of Christianity would have readily embraced it. In 2 Peter 3:13, it says, "Nevertheless we, according to his promise, look for new heavens and a new earth, wherein dwelleth righteousness." This description of the glorious condition of the saints indicates that there will be not only new heavens but also a new earth where righteousness will prevail. According to the promise in Isaiah 65:17, "For, behold, I create new heavens and a new earth: and the former shall not be remembered, nor come into mind." But be glad and rejoice forever in that which I create: for, behold, I create Jerusalem a rejoicing, and her people a joy. This is a time of the restoration of the Church. A verse or two before this, in the same chapter, is the scripture from which my text is taken. It says in verse 13, "Thus saith the Lord, Behold, my servants shall eat, but ye shall be hungry: behold, my servants shall drink, but ye shall be thirsty: behold, my servants shall rejoice, but ye shall be ashamed." My servants who hunger now will be satisfied, while you who are full will hunger. It is evident that Christ referred to such times. Those of you who hunger and thirst for these times, when you search the scriptures, you find promises that although the Lord may allow wicked men and unrighteousness to prevail for a while, there are glorious promises in the scriptures that righteousness will be exalted in the world. You long for these times. Oh, that these times would come! Well, blessed are you, for they will come. They will surely come, and you will be satisfied. It is as if he is saying, there will be times as glorious as you can imagine, and righteousness will prevail to the fullest extent. You will be filled. And in Micah 7:9, it says, "I will bear the indignation of the LORD, because I have sinned against him, until he plead my cause, and execute judgment for me: he will bring me forth to the light, and I shall behold his righteousness." The church laments the severe suffering they endure in those times. The best among them is like a brier, and the most upright is sharper than a thorn hedge. They describe the unrighteousness prevailing in those times. They say, "Trust not in a friend, put not confidence in a guide, keep the doors of thy mouth from her that lieth in thy bosom. For the son dishonoureth the father, the daughter riseth up against her mother, the daughter-in-law against her mother-in-law; a man's enemies are the men of his own house." But then they declare, "Therefore I will look unto the LORD; I will wait for the God of my salvation: my God will hear me." And in verse 9, they say, "I will bear the indignation of the LORD, because I have sinned against him, until he plead my cause, and execute judgment for me." As if to say, Lord, I will not complain, but I will wait for You. I have sinned against You, and even though I do not deserve such unrighteous treatment from men, I acknowledge that I deserve Your use of them as instruments to afflict me. Therefore, I will wait upon the Lord. He will bring me forth into the light, and I shall behold His righteousness. This text should provide us with comfort in the face of unrighteous dealings that occur now. It leads us to the application of it all. Let the consideration of this point remove the stumbling block that causes people to stumble, namely, that God allows unrighteous men to prevail as they do. Do not be offended by this, for there will come a time when righteousness will reign, when the Lord Jesus Christ will appear in His glory and take His throne. He will judge the world in righteousness, as it says in Acts 17:31. This meditation greatly helps the godly individuals I am speaking to. Whereas others, who are not acquainted with this, when they see the unrighteousness prevailing in the world, they will join in and support it. But the saints will continue to stand for righteousness and be on its side. They know that a time is coming when righteousness will prevail. The scriptures speak of the root of the righteous that will prevail and the fruit of righteousness that will come forth from that root, even in the midst of storms and tempests. Secondly, if those who hunger and thirst after righteousness are blessed, then certainly those who are unrighteous are cursed. Cursed are those who seek after unrighteousness. What will Jesus Christ declare over those who seek to promote unrighteousness in the world? If there is anyone here whose conscience tells them that they love unrighteous ways, that they seek to increase their wealth through dishonest means, that they are willing to gain unjustly, know that you are joining forces with this unrighteous world to uphold the kingdom of darkness. Be aware that Christ pronounces a curse upon you. This is implied when He blesses those who hunger and thirst after righteousness. Those who hunger and thirst after unrighteousness are cursed. If you hunger and thirst after ways of unrighteousness and care not how you acquire wealth, you should tremble with fear. The servants of God whom you have treated unjustly cry out to God and report all your unrighteous dealings. God has promised them that their cries will be heard and answered. When these servants of God express their desires to heaven, saying, "O Lord, I have suffered unrighteous treatment from this man or woman," know that these cries are recorded in heaven and will be answered one day. What will become of you then? We read in Acts 24:25 that when Paul preached about temperance, righteousness, and the coming judgment before Felix, even though Paul was a poor prisoner standing before Felix, who sat as a judge, Felix trembled. What was Paul's sermon about? It was about righteousness and the coming judgment. It was as if Paul said, "Though you think you have me in your hands and can do as you please, there is a righteous God who will call everyone to account." Felix, being aware of his unrighteousness, shook and trembled, even when listening to a poor prisoner at the Bar. Now you are here, listening to a poor minister of God proclaim that righteousness will prevail. What will become of you then? Remove from some wealthy individuals all that they have acquired through unrighteous dealings, and they will be left poor indeed. Cursed is an estate and its possessions obtained through unrighteousness. You must relinquish it all. Therefore, let the Lord strike your heart, so that you may be willing to restore and undo your unrighteousness to the best of your ability. Become a friend of righteousness by restoring what you have wrongfully gained and laboring to undo your unrighteousness. Find comfort in the day of Jesus Christ, when He will come to reveal righteousness before men and angels.

And then the final point should have been this: to encourage all the servants of God to continue in the ways of righteousness, to pursue righteousness, and to seek righteousness. In Revelation 22, around verse 11, it says, "He that is righteous, let him be righteous still." Are there any among you whom the Lord has planted the seed of righteousness in your hearts, whose hearts now cling to the love of righteousness? You can say, "Well, let God do with me as He pleases, I will walk in righteousness, I will walk according to the standard. Even though God has placed me in a generation where I see that the majority of men and women are unrighteous, I am determined to walk by the rule of righteousness and entrust everything to God." Take comfort, for you will be satisfied and remain righteous. The Lord, the righteous God, is with you, and Christ, who is your righteousness, is with you to fill your soul with that which will satisfy you forever. Let me share one scripture that demonstrates that both the wicked and the righteous will be satisfied. Proverbs 14:14 says, "The backslider in heart shall be filled with his own ways, and a good man shall be satisfied from himself." Take note, every person will be satisfied in one way or another. The apostate, those who were outwardly religious but resorted to unrighteous means to provide for themselves and their families because they lacked trust in God's provision, well, the Holy Spirit says they will be satisfied. God will fulfill them by allowing them to have their own way. But a good man is satisfied from himself, referring to those who are good and righteous, who walk according to the standard of righteousness. Peace be upon them. They are currently blessed, and they will undoubtedly be satisfied.

# SERMON XV

## Times of Righteousness Promised to the Church

"Blessed are they which do hunger and thirst after righteousness: for they shall be filled." - MATTHEW 5:6

There is great blessedness in hungering and thirsting after righteousness, as I have shown in many instances. When the time comes for God to manifest His righteousness to the world, it will be a truly blessed time. The saints who have a glimpse of this cannot help but long and thirst for that time. The omniscience, wisdom, power, holiness, justice, goodness, and faithfulness of God will be glorified in a manner different from how they are glorified now. Every groan, sigh, and complaint of the saints will be heard by God, and it will be evident that He has heard them. Their appeals to God will be examined and judged, and all their efforts and services will be rewarded. Their sufferings will be compensated. The purpose for allowing so much unrighteousness in the world for so long will be revealed. Their enemies will be subdued and put to shame. Their innocence will be vindicated, secrets will be unveiled, the ulterior motives of individuals will be exposed, misconceptions will be rectified, the futility of worldly wisdom and schemes will be revealed. This will indeed be a blessed time. Oh, when will that time come, say the saints, when righteousness will prevail.

Furthermore, I believe this is the intended meaning here because I find numerous promises in the Scriptures regarding a future state of the Church where righteousness will triumph. For instance, 2 Peter 3:13 speaks of new heavens and a new earth where righteousness dwells. It is evident that this refers to a state of the Church when compared with Isaiah 65:17. In Isaiah 11:4, there is a promise connected to the preceding verses: "But with righteousness shall he judge the poor, and reprove with equity for the meek of the earth." Verse 5 continues, "And righteousness shall be the girdle of his loins, and faithfulness the girdle of his reins." These are promises of Christ. Isaiah is replete with such promises regarding the future state of the Church. In Isaiah 32:16-17, it says, "Then judgment shall dwell in the wilderness, and righteousness remain in the fruitful field. And the work of righteousness shall be peace; and the effect of righteousness quietness and assurance forever." Has this ever been fulfilled? There is a time that the saints long for. In Isaiah 33:5, it states, "The Lord is exalted; for he dwelleth on high: he hath filled Zion with judgment and righteousness." There will be a time when Zion is filled with judgment and righteousness. Additionally, Isaiah 60 contains several expressions that we discussed last time. "I will also make thine officers peace, and thine exactors righteousness." And it continues, "Violence shall no more be heard in thy land, wasting nor destruction within thy borders; but thou shalt call thy walls Salvation, and thy gates Praise." When God makes their rulers righteous and their governors just, violence will cease, and there will be no more destruction. Furthermore, verse 21 states, "Thy people also shall be all righteous, they shall inherit the land forever." This aligns with the previous promise, "Blessed are the meek: for they shall inherit the earth." "Thy people shall be all righteous, they shall inherit the land forever, the branch of my planting, the work of my hands, that I may be glorified." These promises clearly indicate that there will be a time of glorious righteousness. Malachi 4:2 also touches upon this: "But unto you that fear my name shall the Sun of righteousness arise with healing in his wings." Although this verse refers to spiritual healing, it also encompasses outward healing through righteousness. We could spend this entire hour exploring the many promises of righteousness that God will bestow upon His people one day. Those who are godly and understand the mysteries of God, as Proverbs 3:32 states, are aware of this future time when righteousness will prevail. This knowledge prevents them from being swayed by the temptations that lead hypocrites astray. The godly continue on their upright path, eagerly awaiting the fulfillment of righteousness. Blessed are they for various reasons, as we have discussed. Let us now move on from what has been said, or what could be further said, concerning this interpretation. But if God were to manifest His righteousness, who could stand? Even the best among us are conscious of our own unrighteousness. Can we truly hunger and thirst for the time when God's righteousness will be fully revealed? Yes, we can, and this is the privilege of the saints. The more righteous and just God is, the more they long, hunger, and thirst for His manifestation. This is a great privilege. But how is this possible? There is another righteousness that enables them to stand before the infinite righteousness of God: the righteousness of Jesus Christ. So that when the Lord reveals Himself in the full glory of His righteousness to the world, they can stand before Him with joy. Therefore, they hunger and thirst for the righteousness of Jesus Christ, for the righteousness of Christ, the mediator between God and them, the righteousness of justification. Without it, even our God, with whom we must deal, is a consuming fire. Now, as we proceed to address this point, there are several aspects to consider, and we will approach them in this order.

First, let us discuss what this righteousness of Jesus Christ is for which the saints hunger and thirst.

Secondly, we will explore the nature of their hunger and thirst, the inner workings of their hearts as they yearn for this righteousness.

Thirdly, we will examine the desirable qualities of this righteousness, what aspects make the saints desire it so fervently.

Fourthly, those who desire it are blessed. They are blessed in the present.

Fifthly, they will undoubtedly be filled with this righteousness. These are the five points we will elucidate.

To begin, let us clarify what this righteousness is that we are discussing. It is the righteousness necessary for justification, which I would describe as follows.

It is the complete satisfaction of divine justice in every aspect required, whether through punishment for sin or obedience to the Law. This satisfaction is made by the Lord Jesus Christ, who is both God and man, the Mediator of the new Covenant. He serves as the representative for all those whom the Father has given to him and who have put their faith in him. This is the righteousness that Christ declares blessed are those who hunger and thirst after it. While the previous righteousness possessed some beauty, you will see that this righteousness carries greater significance and consequence. Now, we must understand that sin has caused an immense divide between God and humanity. God was determined to have His justice satisfied; otherwise, none of His children would ever be saved. If His justice were not satisfied, they would be in the same lost state as the angels who sinned against Him. Therefore, God declared that punishment must be inflicted for the committed sins, and His Law must be upheld without exception. When God insisted on this, He did not merely say, "You have sinned against Me, and I will forgive you, and that's the end of it." No, God declared, "You have sinned, and I am resolved that My justice shall be honored. Either you will face eternal damnation, or some other way will be found that brings as much honor to My justice as if you were eternally condemned." Man is now in a fallen state, having lost all righteousness. He is incapable of thinking a righteous thought, speaking a righteous word, or performing a righteous action that is acceptable to God. However, God affirmed, "I am determined that My righteous Law will be upheld for your salvation. What a fearful situation man finds himself in, knowing what God demands! In such a circumstance, mustn't all men perish eternally? If this question had been asked in heaven after God revealed His determination, surely all the angels in heaven would have responded, "Then man must perish. We cannot conceive of any way for them to be saved if God insists on this." However, Jesus Christ, the wisdom of the Father, the second person of the Trinity, stepped forward and revealed a way in which God's infinite justice could be satisfied, His Law upheld, and wretched, sinful, corrupt man still saved. The Lord Jesus Christ presented Himself as the head of a second Covenant, saying something along these lines: "Father, all mankind has fallen away from You under the first covenant You made with them. They are now trapped in sin and unrighteousness. But I am willing to be the head of another Covenant. I will act as a Mediator, taking their human nature upon myself. I will provide a way for their salvation that brings as much glory to Your justice as if they were all damned. Your Law shall have no grounds for complaint, as it will receive full satisfaction." Upon this proposal, God the Father and the Son agreed on the way of the second Covenant, known as the Covenant of grace. The Father appointed His Son as the head of this Covenant, representing all those whom the Father has given to Him. It is not intended for the salvation of all individuals, but only those whom the Father has given to Him, who will be represented by Him. The Father ordained that they would hear the Gospel preached in due time. This righteousness would be made known through the Gospel, and by the Holy Spirit, they would come to understand this righteousness. Through faith, they would appropriate this righteousness, as the suffering and obedience of Jesus Christ, which He presents to God the Father, is made over to believers. By faith, they would lay hold of this righteousness and offer it to God the Father as satisfaction. This is the righteousness of Jesus Christ. In this manner, wretched sinners become righteous in Christ. Their sins are imputed to Christ, and Christ's righteousness is imputed to them, as stated in 2 Corinthians 5:21: "For he hath made him to be sin for us, who knew no sin; that we might be made the righteousness of God in him." This is an immensely glorious righteousness, as we will discuss later. Those who are enlightened by the Holy Spirit to grasp the reality, certainty, beauty, necessity, and glory of this righteousness, and whose hearts are set upon it with a hunger and thirst for the assurance of their part in it, for the glorious effects that will arise from it—blessed are those souls. They will be filled with this righteousness. Though they may not yet possess full comfort, assurance, or the glorious fruit of this righteousness, they are presently in a blessed condition while they hunger and thirst for it. This constitutes the second interpretation of this text. Indeed, though the other interpretation relates to the glorification of God, this interpretation carries even greater significance. Whenever you hear from the Word the preaching of the righteousness of Christ or justification through Christ, you can understand its meaning through this concise description.

Now, let us explore the second point, which involves the soul's experience of hungering and thirsting after this righteousness.

To comprehend this, we must consider the origin of this hunger and thirst. It arises from a clear apprehension and deep conviction of four aspects.

First, the soul clearly understands and is thoroughly convinced that it needs righteousness to stand before the holy and righteous God. While people who continue in the common ways of unrighteousness may not pay much attention to their relationship with a righteous God, or if they acknowledge His righteousness, they may not perceive an absolute necessity for righteousness to stand before Him. It is common for individuals who have lived ungodly lives to only think of God's mercy and cry out for it when they sense death approaching. Their thoughts are focused solely on God's mercy and they trust in it. But a soul that comprehends God's ways with sinners and their salvation recognizes not only God's mercy but also the absolute need for righteousness to stand before Him. They understand that no unrighteousness can enter the Kingdom of Heaven, and therefore, if they depart this world as unrighteous souls, even all the mercy in Heaven cannot save them. Their conscience reveals their unrighteousness, acknowledging the unrighteous and ungodly course of their life. Now, as they are about to appear before the great and infinitely righteous God, their soul ponders how it can stand before Him. They realize that they must possess righteousness; otherwise, they cannot stand before Him. This is the first factor that gives rise to hunger and thirst.

Secondly, the soul becomes convinced of the insufficiency and imperfection of its own righteousness. It examines its heart, ways, and life, searching for righteousness. Some may consider themselves more righteous than others, reasoning that if they are to stand before the righteous God, they hope they can because they have not been as wicked and ungodly as others. However, these people are greatly mistaken, and the Holy Spirit has not yet worked in them to reveal the true state of their relationship with God. They do not truly know God or themselves if they hold such thoughts. But when the Lord graciously works in the soul through His Spirit, it examines their life and heart and recognizes that all their righteousness is like a filthy rag. Perhaps their righteousness reaches no higher than mere moral civility. Thus, they possess no true righteousness. Even if their heart is sanctified and their life sincere and holy, this righteousness, being imperfect, cannot enable them to appear before the infinitely righteous God. The overwhelming flame of His burning justice would consume them. If they try to present their imperfect righteousness before this righteous God, it would be like holding up a piece of brown paper to shield oneself from a mighty flame of fire. This realization forms the second aspect.

Thirdly, the soul discovers that there is another righteousness beyond its own—one that surpasses the imperfect righteousness it possesses, rendering it unable to meet the soul's current needs. Even if their righteousness enables them to stand before other people, it means nothing in the presence of God. Therefore, there must be another righteousness, and the Gospel unveils it. The Gospel proclaims that the Son of God was made sin and that atonement is possible through Him. Believers receive Him as wisdom, righteousness, sanctification, and redemption. The soul perceives the certainty of this truth and is empowered to believe it, a work that can only be accomplished by the mighty work of the Holy Spirit within the soul. We can all say that we must be saved by Jesus Christ because we hear it, but to truly believe in the certainty of a righteousness beyond our own, to present it before the Father, requires the power of the Holy Spirit. The Holy Spirit enables the soul to believe in its reality and to comprehend its fullness. The soul sees it as sufficient to satisfy God for any sin, no matter how great. This marks the third aspect.

Fourthly, the soul must also be enlightened regarding how the Gospel imparts this righteousness to the individual. It is true that Jesus Christ, as the great Mediator, works righteousness for sinners. However, the soul wonders how this righteousness can be made its own, enabling it to stand before the Father clothed in this righteousness. This is the final aspect that the Lord reveals to the soul through the Gospel. The soul learns that Christ, along with His righteousness, is freely offered to every wretched sinner. Through belief, by entrusting their souls and eternal destinies to it, fully casting themselves upon this righteousness, it becomes theirs. It becomes their righteousness before the Lord. When the soul comprehends that the Gospel offers Christ and His righteousness freely, and that it is not dependent on the sinner's condition, whether lowly or elevated, they realize that this righteousness is sufficient to engulf all unrighteousness. In comparison to the infinite ocean that can easily consume every drop, all their unrighteousness is insignificant. The soul, therefore, launches itself into this infinite ocean of righteousness, and by an act of God, the Father imputes the righteousness of Jesus Christ to the soul, just as the sin of Adam was imputed to all his descendants. Thus, we see the origin of this hunger and thirst arising from such a work of God.

Now, let us observe how the soul expresses its hunger and thirst for this righteousness.

Firstly, it feels and gains assurance of its need for righteousness. It experiences a profound pain caused by its lack of righteousness. Similar to the intense pain experienced in hunger and thirst, the body longs for relief until it is satisfied. Some may not fully understand the pain of hunger and thirst, although there may be a few who do, and others who have experienced it more deeply in the past. The pain of hunger and thirst is one of the greatest physical pains we can endure, and a person on the brink of starvation would rather face a fire than be without food. Likewise, the soul that understands the nature of God and the infinite necessity of this type of righteousness to appear before Him cannot help but feel faint. It is a throbbing pain in their heart, and until this pain is alleviated, the soul remains in a state of great distress, a truly lamentable state if it comes to comprehend these truths but lacks assurance.

Secondly, until the hunger is satisfied, nothing else matters to the soul. Like a person lacking bread or drink, ready to perish from deprivation, all other offerings mean nothing. They disregard everything else, and nothing satisfies them except bread. Even if someone were to present bags of gold or silver, it would mean nothing to them because they need bread. They might be given splendid suits of satin and velvet, but what use are those if they are on the brink of starvation? Even if they were given all the possessions in the world, without bread, without satiating their hunger, those possessions are worthless to them. This is how it is with the soul that comes to understand the need for this righteousness. While it may possess certain outward comforts bestowed upon them by God, none of those compare to righteousness in terms of the soul's standing before the great God. They must stand before Him to receive the sentence of their eternal destiny, and they are uncertain how long it will be before they face Him. Therefore, righteousness is what they truly need—a righteousness that will be accepted by the infinitely righteous God.

Thirdly, just as nothing matters until the hunger is satisfied, hunger and thirst create a strong desire, so intense that the body is on the verge of fainting if the desire remains unfulfilled. The soul experiences the same state. If they do not possess this righteousness, they will perish. They feel weak and feeble, even dying. Yes, they will die eternally. They perceive themselves on the verge of eternal perdition if they lack this righteousness. There is a fainting in their spirit until this righteousness is obtained.

Fourthly, there are strong endeavors to obtain it in hunger and thirst. We often say that hunger will break through stone walls. No task is considered too difficult when it comes to acquiring bread. If someone is on the verge of starving, they won't stay home just because the weather is bad. If there's bread to be had, they will go and get it. Just like when Jacob heard there was grain in Egypt, the soul that understands the significance of this righteousness and its necessity does not plead or pretend that God's ways are too hard. They don't use the difficulty as an excuse. They don't say, "Leaving behind sinful desires and overcoming the struggles of my heart is hard, very hard. It's hard for me to embark on a new life and follow new paths." Oh, it's hard, very hard for me. Such excuses are not made by a soul that hungers and thirsts after this righteousness. Is it possible to obtain it? The mere possibility is enough for my soul. If the Lord requires certain things, no matter what they may be, I am willing to follow Him diligently, even if it means waiting on Him in the use of ordinances for a long time. The soul exerts its power and makes great efforts, crying out to God and seeking to understand the way of the Gospel more than ever before.

Fifthly, a person who hungers and thirsts is resolute in their desires. Their desires are accompanied by power and determination. They don't set conditions or negotiate terms. Even if the endeavors are challenging, this is the work of grace in the heart that distinguishes it from hypocrisy. When the soul surrenders itself to God, it submits and signs a blank, meaning it allows God to set the terms. The soul is willing to yield and do whatever God requires, just as Paul, with trembling and astonishment, said, "Lord, what wilt thou have me to do?" The metaphorical language illustrates the soul's submission to God. It's not a condition for receiving faith, but it describes how God works in the soul, bringing it to this state of hungering and thirsting for righteousness. This is the condition that Christ speaks of—hungering and thirsting after righteousness. It is true that God deals with each soul differently, with some receiving grace more readily. However, if you have received it sooner than others, don't become arrogant and question why others have to struggle with hungering and thirsting. We don't impose this as a legal requirement. We simply acknowledge that this is the way God works in some souls, keeping them in a state of hunger and thirst for a long time, until they come to know that they partake in this righteousness and their hearts are broken.

Sixthly, something quite notable is that the soul remains unsatisfied in its hunger and thirst until this righteousness arrives. A child who merely plays with food or whose belly is full may cry out for something they see. But you can easily distract a child with a rattle when their belly is full. However, if they are truly hungry, no matter what rattles you offer, they will not be satisfied until their hunger is appeased. The same applies to the soul. Many individuals may have some initial awakening in the work of God within them. They begin to realize their need for righteousness, considering their wicked lives and how they will appear before God. They understand that they must make peace with God because of their wickedness. At this stage, they may experience some desires and engage in prayer and attending to the Word for a while. However, note this: after a while, feeling weary and exhausted because they haven't fully obtained God's assurance and the righteousness hasn't been applied by faith, something or someone satisfies them. Their hearts are drawn away from those initial good beginnings. The devil may persuade them that living slightly better than before is sufficient righteousness. They become satisfied with that notion and eagerly engage in many public good works. While these actions are commendable, if they satisfy the soul, I must say that the soul is ruined—eternally ruined if it finds satisfaction in them. The soul that God works upon in a saving manner, when it hungers and thirsts in this way, nothing in the world can satisfy it. Even if the world offers everything, it will not quench the soul's thirst when it is striving after Christ, seeking forgiveness and mercy in Him. The soul pursues God through all means and ordinances, but it doesn't consider these as the righteousness it must offer to God. Instead, it sees them as means through which God reveals righteousness and conveys the work of His Spirit into the soul, leading the soul to the righteousness of Jesus Christ. The soul rests solely in this righteousness. Due to a lack of proper understanding, many thousands stumble in their profession. During their youth, they were reckless, but as they grew older, they lived better lives. They believe that this is conversion. However, it is a mistake to confuse the means of revealing righteousness or conveying the work of the Spirit with righteousness itself. Beware of this error; it is perilous. To all of you who are seeking the righteousness of Jesus Christ, take heed. Be unsatisfied in your hunger and desires. Let nothing quiet your soul except the application of the righteousness of Jesus Christ through faith, enabling you to present the infinite righteousness of the Son of God to the Father for your soul's sake. This is what can truly enable you to stand confidently before the Almighty God. Luther has an excellent expression about the distinction between righteousness. He says, "Righteousness between man and man in a political sense is a very sweet thing, as it upholds the peace of kingdoms. However, if you, because you are a good citizen, a faithful spouse, or a just merchant dealing fairly in your trade, believe that these things make you righteous before God, you have turned the sweetest thing into an abomination that God cannot tolerate." This expression from Luther is highly valuable, so beware. Those of you who are good citizens, acting honorably in your communities, and none of your neighbors can find fault with you, take note. It is true that only those who possess the righteousness of Christ attain this level, but one can attain this level and still miss out on the righteousness of Jesus Christ. If you find satisfaction in this outward, civil, or moral righteousness, if you believe it makes you righteous before God, then you have turned the sweetest thing into an abomination that the Holy Spirit will not tolerate. Thus, you can see the work of the soul in hungering and thirsting after this righteousness. Now, the main thing that remains is to present to you the loveliness of this righteousness—the desirable object that the soul hungers and thirsts for. Through understanding what this righteousness is and the work of God in causing this hunger and thirst, you can see why the soul should earnestly desire it. However, there are many more aspects to highlight—the beauty and excellence of this righteousness, in the hopes of igniting hunger and thirst for it in all your souls. It is certain that every one of you has an infinite need for it. Even those who have never experienced it, if they come to know it, their hearts would be captivated, turning away from other things and fixating on this righteousness. And for those who have some knowledge of it, if they knew it more deeply, their hunger and thirst would intensify even more.

# SERMON XVI

## The Desirability of the Object Longed For

"Blessed are they which do hunger and thirst after righteousness: for they shall be filled." - Matthew 5:6

Now I turn to the third point, which is the desirability of this object. Blessed are those who hunger and thirst after righteousness; it is an exceedingly desirable object, and those who recognize its worth cannot help but long for it—to have a share in it. For

First, through this righteousness, all despairing temptations and thoughts due to our lack of righteousness are removed. Many of you are unaware of the strong despairing thoughts that plague the souls when they realize they must deal with an infinitely great God and see the unrighteousness of their hearts and lives. You cannot comprehend the inner turmoil and war within their thoughts. They would give anything to be freed from the anguish and trouble caused by these sinking despairing thoughts and temptations that afflict their souls. But nothing in the world can remove them except the sight and application of this righteousness of Jesus Christ, as described earlier. Therefore, it is highly desirable.

Secondly, through this righteousness, the soul finds a way to make amends for all the wrong it has done to God through sin. I have wronged God through my sin, and I cannot fathom a way to rectify it. It would be impossible for angels and humans to conceive of a solution. However, the revelation of this righteousness of Christ, applied to the soul by faith, shows a way to completely rectify all the wrong done to God by my sin. Isn't this desirable? Wouldn't you give anything if you had thousands upon thousands of worlds to make it right again? Here is a way to rectify everything. Oh, what a desirable object this righteousness is.

Thirdly, through this righteousness, the law is completely satisfied, and all its claims are answered. The law has nothing to charge against the soul for any transgressions. This is a desirable thing. Being freed from the law as a rule of life is not desirable to a gracious heart. Blessed are those who love your law (as a rule of life); nothing shall offend them. They choose the law for themselves; that is desirable. But the claim that the law makes on the soul and the charges it brings against the soul for breaking it— the soul desires to be delivered from this. It is a severe and dreadful evil to stand before God's law, which possesses infinite justice and has such terrifying charges to lay upon me. Oh, that I could be freed from whatever the law has to charge! Well, this righteousness will do it. It will deliver the soul from all the charges the law may bring. Therefore, in Romans 10:4, it is said that Christ is the end of the law for righteousness to everyone who believes. He is the fulfillment of the law; it finds its perfection in him. You may transfer the demands of the law to your surety, and God will only deal with the surety in this matter. By possessing this righteousness, you are able to give the law whatever it may claim and discharge it of any charges it may bring against you.

Fourthly, through this righteousness, the eternal risk of perishing is completely eliminated. When the soul apprehends this righteousness, it perceives within itself a sense of absolute safety and blessed security. If only this righteousness could be applied to my soul, although it's true that there will still be much unrighteousness in me, I know that this remaining unrighteousness will never jeopardize the eternal fate of my soul. The hazard of eternal perishing is completely gone. Isn't this desirable? What would a troubled soul give to know that the risk of eternal perishing is over, especially those who understand the concept of eternity and sense the possibility of perishing in it? Nothing can satisfy the soul except this. If I were to seek satisfaction for my soul's eternal state and deliverance from the risk of perishing through my own efforts, thinking that I will improve my life and do better (even if everyone does the same), the fears will return to the soul. There will be uncertainty whether I will perish forever or not. Perhaps I will, perhaps I won't. I hope God will accept me, but I cannot be certain. However, when the soul understands that an infinite and glorious righteousness can be applied through the Gospel, it can truly bless itself in Jesus Christ and say, "My soul, return unto thy rest, for the Lord hath dealt bountifully with thee." Even though you are unrighteous in yourself, there is a righteousness that frees you from the danger of perishing. You are undoubtedly safe. This righteousness will surely lead you to eternal life, for there is no condemnation for those who are in Christ Jesus. It is impossible for a soul that God the Father looks upon in the righteousness of His Son, a soul as righteous as a believer is through the righteousness of Christ, to perish eternally or for God to hate them or pour out His avenging wrath upon them. It is impossible; it can never happen.

Fifthly, it is worth hungering and thirsting for this righteousness because through it, we gain access to the throne of grace and can stand boldly before it—before God Himself, before His infinite holiness and justice. We stand not only before God's mercy but also before the very throne of justice. Although I must deal with an infinitely holy and just God, there is a way for me to stand boldly—with holy boldness—before His infinite holiness and justice. Romans 5:1 says, "Therefore being justified by faith, we have peace with God through our Lord Jesus Christ." Through Him, we have access by faith into this grace wherein we stand. By Him, we come to have access even to the tribunal of God's justice. Therefore, there is no need to appeal from the justice seat of God to His mercy seat. It is through His mercy that God provides such a way, that He brings us to it, and that He accepts us in it. This enables us to stand before His justice seat, and our pardon is sealed in the court of justice.

Sixthly, this righteousness is a glorious robe that will cover the souls of the saints, the believers, in the presence of God, Christ, and the holy angels when Jesus Christ and God the Father appear. At the great day, they will be adorned and beautified with this glorious robe. You hear much about the dread of judgment day, the shrill sound of the trumpet, and everyone appearing before the Lord to hear the sentence of their eternal destiny. It may instill terror in some of your hearts. However, this robe of righteousness takes away all the terror of that day. The glorious condition of the saints being clothed with this robe before the Lord... Now those to whom this righteousness is revealed understand the purpose of this righteousness on that day. And that is the sixth aspect in which it appears so desirable.

Seventhly, there must undoubtedly be a most glorious reward for this righteousness, raising the condition of the saints above that of Adam in Paradise, and even in some respect, above the angels themselves. If Adam had remained righteous in Paradise, there would have been a righteousness suitable for such a creature, and the angels possess a righteousness suited to their natures. But here is the righteousness of the Son of God, the righteousness of God-man, and it surpasses the righteousness that Adam had or could have had. It is of a higher nature than the righteousness of the angels in heaven. And now, to have this righteousness made over to the soul as its own righteousness, there must be an expectation of a glorious reward for this righteousness. If Adam had remained righteous, he would have lived, but it does not seem that he would have lived anywhere other than Paradise, in this world. However, this righteousness purchases a higher degree of glory than if Adam had ever remained righteous. The reward for this righteousness must be glorious indeed. And just as the righteousness itself is bestowed upon the soul, so is everything that this righteousness deserves—all the fruits of the Father's good pleasure for the righteousness that His Son offers. They are also made over to the soul, and the soul has a present right to them. When a poor creature comes to understand a righteousness that surpasses the innocence of Adam, that exceeds the righteousness of angels—the righteousness of the Son of God being made over to it—and all the good that this righteousness deserves, all the fruits of the Father's good pleasure for His Son's righteousness, become mine too. Oh, how desirable is this when genuinely apprehended by faith.

Eighthly, this righteousness is a perfect righteousness. There is no sinner, at the very instant they become a believer and have this righteousness bestowed upon them, who does not become equal to Abraham, Isaac, Jacob, David, the patriarchs, prophets, angels, and martyrs. There is a great difference between you and those glorious prophets, saints, and martyrs we read about. There is a vast difference when you consider your blind mind, dull spirit, dead heart, and the multitude of strong lusts within you. Your heart may be dejected when you reflect on this. However, although there is a difference in terms of sanctification, in terms of the righteousness of justification, you are equal to Abraham, Isaac, Jacob, and any saint who has ever lived in the world. Your justification is equal to theirs. Certainly, if you knew this, if you believed it, it would seem impossible for you not to desire it with all your heart. You would have a deep hunger and thirst for such a righteousness.

Ninthly, this righteousness is continually presented by Jesus Christ at the right hand of the Father to please Him and ensure acceptance for those to whom it is applied. It is a special work of Jesus Christ's intercession at the right hand of the Father to present this perfect righteousness continually on behalf of those who belong to Him. And for you, though you are vile in this world, filled with sin, to have such a Mediator at the right hand of God the Father constantly presenting a perfect righteousness, so that it may be accepted on your behalf, as if He were saying, "Lord, although these poor creatures are full of unrighteousness, behold my perfect righteousness, which I perfectly obeyed. Accept that righteousness of mine." Isn't this a desirable object? Doesn't this call for strong desires, hunger, and thirst? Blessed are those who have such a righteousness to be clothed with.

Tenthly and finally, the acceptance that comes from this righteousness does not ebb and flow according to the variation in the gracious workings of our hearts. It remains constant forever. It's true that the Lord takes into account the different workings of our hearts, and in terms of the weakness of sanctification or the level of our progress, there may be a greater or lesser complacency in God's eyes, particularly in the manifestations of His complacency—since what is God's complacency but His self-revelation towards His creatures? The Lord is pleased with the righteousness of sanctification as well, as we will discuss later, just as He is pleased with this righteousness. However, although there may be different expressions of God's favor, and in some respects, we may say that the complacency of God's heart towards His servants may vary based on the difference in their graces in this life, in terms of acceptance for this righteousness, it always remains the same. There is always the same acceptance of this right-eousness, and there are no fluctuations in the acceptance of this righteousness for any believer. Oh, how blessed is this righteousness of Jesus Christ, and how desirable an object is it? Now you have heard the third aspect expounded: the workings of the heart in hungering and thirsting after it and the desirability of this righteousness.

The fourth aspect to discuss is the blessedness that accompanies hungering and thirsting for righteousness. Blessed are those who long for it, blessed are they.

Firstly, they come to understand the great mystery of godliness, the way in which God brings humanity to Himself. It is a truly blessed thing for the understanding to be enlightened and perceive the profound plan of God's redemptive work. Most people in the world believe there is only one way for God to reconcile with humanity: sinners must repent, feel remorse, and put an end to their sinful ways. However, those who hunger and thirst for righteousness are illuminated by a different heavenly light. The divine light shines upon them, enabling them to comprehend the deep counsels of God regarding His method of reconciling humanity to Himself. Blessed are those whose eyes have been opened, blessed are your eyes for seeing these things, blessed are those who hunger and thirst because of the enlightenment they have received.

Secondly, they are blessed in the present because their hearts are captivated by something of utmost importance. Nothing in all of God's works or in the concerns of mankind and creation holds greater weight than what I am speaking of—the righteousness of the Son of God applied through faith. For most of you, what captures your hearts? It is food, drink, indulgence, merry-making, companionship, and satisfying your lusts. There is no blessedness in these pursuits. But to have a heart that was once consumed by vanity and folly now captivated by a matter of infinite weight and consequence like righteousness—blessed is that heart.

Thirdly, blessed are they because now is the time when the righteousness of Christ is offered to sinners. And blessed are those who, through the work of God, are led into the way that brings them to receive the righteousness of His Son. In this time, as God offers the righteousness of His Son to sinners, imagine if your life had ended before you recognized the excellence of Christ's righteousness and before you developed strong desires for it. You would not have been blessed. But you are blessed because you are alive during this time when

God offers His Son's righteousness to sinners. You see your need for it, your heart yearns for it, and you are now on the path that God takes those whom He intends to bestow His Son's righteousness upon. Although you may not fully comprehend that it has been made yours, you are blessed because you are on the path that God uses to bring those whom He plans to bless forever through His Son's righteousness. Not long ago, you were pursuing folly and vanity, giving no thought to these matters. But now God has brought you this far. Blessed are you.

Fourthly, blessed are you who hunger and thirst so ardently for this righteousness, for it is a good sign that faith has already begun its work in your soul. Your intense longing for Jesus Christ provides evidence that the seed of faith has been sown in your heart. Otherwise, you would not cling so fervently to Christ. The longing of your soul for Him, an unwavering desire that nothing in the world can diminish, demonstrates that He is already present, stirring your soul to seek Him with great fervor.

Fifthly, and above all, blessed are those who hunger and thirst for righteousness, for they shall be filled. This means:

First, all fears and doubts will eventually be removed. Although you have some encouraging hopes, they are mixed with many uncertainties. Yet, you will be satisfied regarding them.

Second, all accusations of Satan will be answered. Satan may clamor against you, but this righteousness will appear in such beauty and glory that it will silence him.

Third, you will be filled. In other words, you will experience the benefits of this righteousness as if you yourself had satisfied and obeyed. Consider this: you will receive the fruit and benefit of this righteousness as if you had satisfied the Law and obeyed it. If it were possible for a creature to satisfy God's justice and fulfill the Law, tremendous rewards would be expected. You will receive as much as if you had borne the punishment your sins deserved. Moreover, greater benefits will come from what Christ has accomplished than if you had fulfilled them yourself. If it were God's way that to be saved, one must endure fiery punishment for thousands of years and perfectly obey His Law, you would consider it a blessed thing to have completed such a task. But now you must understand that if you had done so and God had reconciled with you, you could not expect the same love and acceptance from God as you can upon receiving the satisfaction achieved by Christ's perfect righteousness. Therefore, you will be filled, as you will receive more than if you had accomplished it yourself.

Fourthly, you will come to know that when God sent His Son to work such a righteousness, He had you in mind. In His eternal counsels, God determined that His Son should come into the world and work this glorious and eternal righteousness for the benefit of your soul and others. Won't this fill you?

Fifthly, Christ will one day present you before His Father, shining brightly in this righteousness. This is the desirability I previously spoke of, and now I mention it to illustrate how those who hunger and thirst for righteousness will be filled.

Lastly, you will eternally enjoy all the fruits of this righteousness. This will fill you completely, as you partake in the benefits and consequences of such a righteousness. Blessed are those who hunger and thirst for this righteousness, for they shall be filled. Thus, we have explored this second branch—the hungering and thirsting for the righteousness of the Lord Jesus Christ.

By way of application:

Firstly, the exposition we have just heard will serve as a rebuke to those who have never paid attention to or valued the righteousness we are discussing now. They have never felt any need for it and therefore have never hungered or thirsted after it. I fear that what I say today might sound like riddles to most people. I appeal to your consciences, in the name of God, when has He revealed the glory of this righteousness in its reality to your souls? When have your hearts been captivated by it? Can any private room or chamber testify to the fervent cries you have made to God, seeking your share in this righteousness? When have you experienced such stirrings in your soul for this righteousness? Lord, I am undone, I will perish forever! It would have been better for me to have never been born than to be without this righteousness of Your Son. I appeal to you, when has there ever been this kind of working in your hearts? Surely, if you are completely unfamiliar with these hungerings and thirstings for righteousness, you are not among those whom Christ pronounces blessed. You have hungerings and thirstings for other things that cannot benefit you. Here is an object that should raise the desires of a rational creature. Indeed, this is something that should whet your appetite.

Secondly, let what has been said ignite and sharpen your appetites for this righteousness. Say, "O Lord, today You have presented before me, through Your word, a glorious mystery of religion—a righteousness of Your Son—that I either did not know or paid little attention to before. Lord, I see that my happiness depends on it. I am eternally secure if I possess it. It doesn't matter much what happens to me in the world, what becomes of my reputation or wealth, as long as I have this righteousness to clothe me. I will be eternally fulfilled. Oh, may the heavens hear the cries of souls this evening who long for this righteousness! Or, even if some of you only wonder about the meaning of all this upon hearing it, let there be, at the very least, this result from what has been spoken: spend time alone with God, entreating Him to help you understand what has been said. Surely, it is one of the great mysteries of godliness. You will be ruined forever if you do not grasp it. Therefore, at the very least, cry out to God that He may reveal this to you. This will be a good step towards stirring up your appetite for this righteousness. There are two or three things that may serve to ignite our appetites.

First, consider that you are dealing with a righteous God. We have a remarkable Scripture in Romans 10:3, which states, "For they being ignorant of God's righteousness, and going about to establish their own righteousness, have not submitted themselves unto the righteousness of God." Note that they are ignorant of God's righteousness and therefore seek to establish their own. They have not submitted themselves to the righteousness of God. It is as if the Holy Spirit is saying, if they truly knew God's righteousness, they would never be satisfied with their own righteousness. But being ignorant of God's righteousness, they strive to establish their own. Oh, that God would cause a revelation of His infinite righteousness to your soul tonight! This would truly make you hunger and thirst for it.

Secondly, consider this: the Lord is resolute that His justice must be satisfied. No soul will ever be saved without justice being satisfied for that soul. This is God's determination. Understanding this truth and affirming it as a definite conclusion will greatly stir your heart to seek after this righteousness. God is a God of infinite righteousness, and it is certain that no soul will be saved without God being honoured in His infinite justice as much as in His infinite mercy. So what will become of humanity? If it were not for this satisfaction, they would all perish. This is why all the angels who sinned against God perish eternally—because there is no righteousness for them, no means of satisfying their sin. The same fate would await humanity if God did not determine to have His justice honoured either on them or on a substitute.

Thirdly, know that even Abraham, Isaac, or Jacob, the most righteous and glorious individuals to have ever lived, would be in great trouble without this righteousness. Yes, we can boldly say, woe to Abraham, Isaac, Jacob, and all the prophets and apostles if it were not for this righteousness. If these things are indeed true, then we must earnestly pursue the righteousness mentioned here.

# SERMON XVII

## Comforts to those that hunger

Blessed are those who hunger and thirst for righteousness, for
they shall be filled. Matthew 5:6

F or those who genuinely have their hearts stirred after this righteousness,
I have various words of comfort and consolation. There are many poor
souls who, in the awareness and burden of their sins, hunger and thirst for
the righteousness of Jesus Christ. Their thoughts and hearts are consumed by
nothing more than the righteousness of Jesus Christ, desiring it to be applied to
them through faith and made their own for their comfort. To such individuals,
I will briefly speak words of comfort and encouragement.

Firstly, if your heart truly thirsts after the righteousness of Christ that you
hear preached in the Gospel, and you bless those who are able to make it their
own, know that your thirst and Christ's thirst are the same. Christ longs for
souls as much as souls long for Him. It brings as much satisfaction to Jesus
Christ to see His righteousness applied to souls for their redemption as it does
to any soul to have the righteousness of Christ applied to them for their salvation. No soul can be more content in the assurance that Christ's righteousness
belongs to them than Christ Himself is in having His righteousness applied

to souls who hunger and thirst after it, as mentioned in the text. As evidence, consider this Scripture from Isaiah 53:10: "Yet it pleased the Lord to bruise Him; He has put Him to grief. When You make His soul an offering for sin, He shall see His seed, He shall prolong His days, and the pleasure of the Lord shall prosper in His hand. He shall see the labor of His soul, and be satisfied. By His knowledge My righteous Servant shall justify many, for He shall bear their iniquities." Take note that He shall see the labor of His soul and be satisfied. What is the labor of Christ's soul? It is the desire that after bearing the burden of the Father's wrath, souls would be given to Him and freed from sin through His sufferings. This is the labor of Christ's soul. If your soul is travailing after the righteousness of Jesus Christ, you are, as it were, in labor, longing for it to be delivered. Know that the soul of Christ is laboring just as much to redeem sinners as sinners are laboring to be redeemed. And according to the text, He shall see the labor of His soul and be satisfied. There is nothing in the world that can satisfy the soul of Christ more than having poor sinners come to Him and partake in His righteousness. For by His knowledge, His righteous servant shall justify many, and that will satisfy His soul. It is as if the Holy Spirit is saying that after all that Jesus Christ has suffered for souls, when any soul comes and believes in Him, the Lord Jesus will apply His righteousness to them and justify them. This is what will satisfy His soul. Therefore, this is a great source of help and comfort to those who hunger and thirst after the righteousness of Jesus Christ. You see the hunger of Christ, the travail of His soul, and what will satisfy Him. Surely, if this brings such satisfaction to His soul—justifying sinners—then you can find encouragement in this. When your soul is in travail and you long for this righteousness above all else in the world, and nothing can satisfy you except that, you will, in due time, see the travail of your soul and be satisfied.

Secondly, the greatest purpose that God has in the entire world, to bring glory to Himself, is accomplished by honoring the righteousness of His Son through its application to sinful souls for their redemption. Among all the things that God has done or will do in the world, the greatest purpose for bringing glory to Himself is that the righteousness of His Son may be magnified through the process of delivering souls from the guilt of their sins and presenting them as righteous before the Father. The Lord takes pleasure in no work as He does in this work. This is the masterpiece of God, the glory of God. Now, consider this: if this is the work in which God delights above all else and His purpose is to glorify Himself by magnifying the righteousness of His Son through its fruits—delivering sinful and guilty souls—then who will God honor and glorify if not those souls whose hearts He has stirred to seek after this righteousness, longing for it above all else? This is the very thing that God's heart desires to honor Himself with above all things, and it is the very thing that God has put into my heart to desire above all things. And I believe, truly I am sure, if I know anything about my heart, that if God would bear witness to my soul once that this righteousness of His Son is mine, I would dedicate myself forever to honoring Him. Even if I had a thousand lives, they would all be spent for the glory of His name. Surely, God's heart and your heart align closely in this matter. Therefore, find comfort and encouragement in your hungering and thirsting after this righteousness.

Thirdly, nothing is offered more freely than the righteousness of Christ. Among all the mercies that God bestows upon sinners, the mercies of Jesus Christ are given most freely. Many mercies were granted by God during the time of the law based on legal obedience. However, Jesus Christ and His righteousness have never been given to any soul except freely, purely by His grace. He is the gift of God. Alongside this freedom, there is an invitation for souls to come and receive it. You, who thirst after this righteousness as the water of life, consider the invitation in Revelation 22:17: "And the Spirit and the bride say, 'Come!' And let him who hears say, 'Come!' And let him who thirsts come. Whoever desires, let him take the water of life freely." You thirst for this righteousness as the water of life that would bring life to your soul. Now, pay attention to the invitation presented here. The Spirit, the Bride (referring to the Church), they all say, "Come!" Let everyone who hears also say, "Come!" And let everyone who thirsts come. Here, four times in one verse, the call is made to come. Furthermore, it states, "Whoever desires, let him take the water of life freely." There is nothing more freely given than this water of life. God does not sell it to anyone; whoever receives it, receives it freely. This is how God dispenses this great mercy: to whomever He has given it or will give it, it must be given freely. No previous unrighteousness can hinder it. If it could, then it would not be given freely. No unworthiness can hinder it either. So, why shouldn't I have my portion in it, just like anyone else? Why shouldn't I be blessed by it like anyone else? It's true, I am vile, I am an unrighteous wretch, I am unworthy, but the Lord gives this water of life freely, as stated in Isaiah 55:1.

Fourthly, I will add another consideration for your further comfort: nothing gives any soul the right to apply the righteousness of Jesus Christ except the free offer and the soul's belief, the soul's casting itself upon it. There is nothing prior to that which gives any right to this righteousness of Christ. You might say, "I could apply it, believe it, and cast myself upon it, but I fear I have no right to it." Now, this is an absolute truth, as certain as any we have in the Gospel: nothing grants any soul a right to Jesus Christ except believing in Him, venturing the soul upon His perfect and glorious righteousness. It is this act that gives a right to the soul. Therefore, do not fear, but come, you hungry and thirsting soul after this righteousness. Open your mouth and your heart wide, that you may be filled. Cast your soul upon this righteousness. Venture your soul and your eternal state. That is the best and quickest way to experience its comfort.

For those who hunger and thirst after this righteousness, I offer these cautions:

The first caution I will give you is to be careful, those of you seeking to have your souls justified through this righteousness, not to satisfy yourselves with any righteousness inferior to this, with any lesser righteousness. The devil will be ready to deceive you here, and he prevails with many. When their sins weigh heavily on their consciences, and they realize they stand guilty before the great God, just as those bound to eternal death, and they hear that salvation can only be found in Christ, they seek after Christ. Now, the devil seeks to deceive them with some other righteousness besides this. Oh, be cautious that nothing satisfies you except this righteousness. It is true that, through God's mercy, I have abandoned many sinful ways, and I find in my heart that I would not commit any known sin against conscience, even in secret, for all the world. This is good, but do not rest in this alone. Know that there is a righteousness beyond this. Do not think that this is sufficient to satisfy your conscience, that you have reached this point. No, nothing will satisfy my conscience except the application of the blood of Christ and His righteousness to my soul.

Secondly, be cautious not to be satisfied and contented with mere comfort. It may happen that you experience powerful flashes of comfort; during prayer, you might have such moments of comfort and joy that surpass anything you have ever experienced. Some have had such experiences, only to find that they amount to nothing in the end. Therefore, do not find satisfaction in that alone. Instead, ask yourself this: Is this the fruit of Christ's righteousness? Do I possess the righteousness of Christ? Do I feel the Holy Spirit's work drawing my soul to Christ and enabling me to rest upon His righteousness? If so, the Holy Spirit is indeed a comforter to me as a result of this. That is good. If your comfort arises as a fruit of your faith, casting yourself upon the righteousness of Jesus Christ, then it is genuine. Otherwise, your comfort may only serve to please and satisfy you temporarily, diverting your pursuit of this righteousness. Remember, this righteousness is the only thing that will sustain you and enable you to stand in peace before the Judgment Seat of God.

A third caution is this: In your quest for this righteousness of Christ, be cautious not to reason with flesh and blood. Avoid carnal reasoning and arguments that question how it is possible for someone as vile, wretched, and ungodly as you to receive such love and regard from God, to the extent that He would send His Son to be cursed, to die, and to work out a perfect righteousness to clothe your soul with. You may have heard of the glory of this righteousness, but how can it be that your soul could partake in it? Such reasoning engages with flesh and blood. In your pursuit of this righteousness, let such reasoning be swallowed up, and elevate faith alone. If faith is not tested in this crucial matter, it will achieve nothing. If reason interferes, it will spoil everything. For this righteousness is beyond all reason—it is infinitely supernatural. As Luther said, reason is the greatest enemy to faith. It is a profound mystery of godliness that even the angels desire to explore and marvel at. Therefore, as Christians, we must almost close the eye of reason and exercise faith in it. Faith alone can bring peace to your soul.

Fourthly, above all else, be extremely cautious not to misuse and pervert the grace of God. Beware of wantonness. You have heard the righteousness of the Son of God expounded—the glorious properties, the excellence, and desirability of it. It is something that very few hearts can endure. We know from experience that when men and women catch a glimpse of the righteousness of Christ, they often draw wicked and vile conclusions from it. They say, "Why do we need to seek anything further? Christ has done it all." Consequently, they become lax in their conduct. Guard against wantonness. Our society is marked by great licentiousness. I genuinely believe that if there has ever been a time since Christ when the grace of God has been perverted, it is these past four or five years. However, I find it recorded in the history of Germany that when Luther first began preaching Jesus Christ, there were individuals in his time who abused what he preached in the same manner. When the Gospel began to shine through Luther's ministry, men with weak and blinded eyes were unable to bear the glorious light that God caused to shine. They grossly misused it. Even Luther himself was greatly perplexed and troubled by those who abused the doctrine of free grace and justification by the righteousness of Christ. As we see, weak and corrupted spirits are inclined to misuse it. Above all sins, this sin goes most against the heart of God. God detests it. It is described in the Epistle of Jude as a dreadful mark of those who are destined for condemnation—those who pervert the grace of God. The Lord expects that everyone who comes to know this grace will fall down on their faces, adore, and magnify Him for it. They should spend their days in adoration and magnification, rather than using it as a means to indulge in sin, to nurture unrighteousness and licentiousness. Sadly, we find that since the time when people began speaking most about Free Grace and the Righteousness of Christ, their conduct has become even more licentious than before. Such abominable wickedness is detested by the Spirit of God. If there were any sign that a man or woman is unlikely to have any part or portion in this righteousness, the most probable sign would be turning this rich and glorious grace of God into wantonness. That concludes the discussion on hungering after the righteousness of Jesus Christ.

Now, let us proceed to the next point: hungering and thirsting after the righteousness of sanctification, or inherent righteousness. I will present the method in the same manner as before.

First, what is this righteousness that we are currently discussing? Secondly, what constitutes true hunger and thirst of the soul for this righteousness? Thirdly, what makes this righteousness desirable? Fourthly, why are those who hunger and thirst after it blessed? Fifthly, those who hunger and thirst after it shall also be satisfied with this righteousness. Lastly, the application of all these points.

Regarding the first point, you may wonder, "What is this righteousness that you are speaking of?"

It is the gracious disposition that God works in the soul through the Holy Spirit or the principle of holiness that God instills within the soul through the Holy Spirit. This enables the soul to direct its actions towards God as its supreme good, as if in a straight line. Therefore, it is called righteousness. It is also referred to as holiness or grace at times because it is freely given by God. When a soul that was once dead in sin receives the Holy Spirit's breath and is infused with gracious principles that empower it to act and work towards God as the ultimate end and the highest good, it experiences righteousness in the heart—this inherent righteousness. When you receive this work of the Holy Spirit and find these active and working principles within you, causing your soul to strive towards God as the ultimate end, and no obstacle between God and your soul can hinder these gracious workings, your soul does not take a detour but perseveres through all difficulties. That is acting in a straight line, going through all kinds of challenges in order to work yourself towards God. This is righteousness in the heart—inherent righteousness. When you have received this work of the Holy Spirit, you will find such active and working principles within you that elevate your soul towards God as the ultimate end. Whatever stands between God and your soul, your soul will persistently work through it, never ceasing until it overcomes it and reaches God, thus attaining the joy of experiencing Him as your God.

Or, put another way, it is the aligning and acting of the heart according to the right standard—the standard of righteousness set forth in the Word. This is the righteousness we are discussing.

Or, to elaborate further, it is an imprint of God's righteousness upon the soul, enabling the soul to act according to His measure, just as God Himself acts.

According to His measure, you may ask, how is that? To act as God acts means to love oneself as the highest end of all things, and to love all other things in relation to oneself, and to work for oneself as the ultimate end of all actions, ordering all other things in a way that leads to the attainment of oneself as the ultimate end. Likewise, a soul that bears the impression of this righteousness is enabled to work for God as the ultimate end, loving God for Himself and loving all things in relation to God. It acts for God as the highest end and orders all its actions in relation to God as the ultimate end. Thus, the soul acts in accordance with its measure and proportion, just as God Himself does. God makes Himself the ultimate end, and the soul makes God the ultimate end too. Just as God loves Himself as the highest good and loves all things in relation to Himself, the soul does the same. God works towards Himself and arranges all things in a way that allows Him to enjoy Himself as the ultimate end. The righteous soul does likewise, working towards God and arranging all things in a way that allows it to enjoy all things in relation to God as the ultimate end. This is the righteousness we are discussing. Blessed are those who hunger and thirst after this righteousness. Oh, how I wish it were so for me, says this hungering and thirsting soul. I feel an abundance of corruption within me that prevents me from acting towards God. I am convinced that the Lord is worthy—the infinitely glorious first being of all things. He deserves all praise and honour from all His creatures. I was created for Him so that I might live for Him. How happy would I be if I could make Him my highest end and if my heart could be detached from all other things and solely enjoy Him as my portion, and if I could act and work for Him, making His will the rule of my life. That would bring me true happiness. Oh, how I long for this to be the state of my soul.

Now, regarding the second point, understand that this hungering and thirsting stems firstly from the realization of the great good inherent in this righteousness. The soul recognizes that it would be a most blessed creature if it were empowered to act in this manner—to work in such a way towards God. If I could feel the Holy Spirit working in my heart, causing my heart to strive after the Lord.

Secondly, it thirsts after this righteousness for itself, in a spiritual manner. Not only because I am convinced in my conscience that I cannot go to Heaven or that I must go to Hell if I lack it, but because I see the inherent loveliness and excellence in righteousness itself. Therefore, I long for it because of its own surpassing excellence. An hypocrite may desire to overcome their sins and be empowered to perform their duties, but note this: their desire arises for the sake of peace of mind. They desire these things because they cannot have peace without them. It is not because of any excellence that they see in righteousness itself, but merely to pacify their conscience. However, this blessed hunger and thirst we are speaking of desires righteousness for itself. It is my righteousness. What could be better for my soul than to live for God as the ultimate end, to have my heart working towards God, and to make His will my own? What could be better for my soul than this?

Thirdly, this hungering and thirsting is limitless. By that, I mean the soul never sets a limit on how much holiness it desires. It seeks to possess holiness to the highest degree possible for any creature. Even if the Lord enables such a soul to overcome some corruptions and walk towards God in a more gracious manner than before, it still desires more and more. Its desires expand continually. On the other hand, a hypocrite may desire to overcome certain corruptions or perform certain duties, but they desire only as much as they believe will serve their purpose of avoiding perceived dangers. This is clear evidence that they do not desire righteousness for its own sake. For example, imagine two men desiring knowledge. One is sent to university, but only to please his father, so he desires knowledge for that reason. Or consider another person who desires knowledge for personal gain or advancement. That is their end. Once they achieve enough to attain their goal, they are satisfied. In contrast, a person who desires knowledge for its own sake sees the inherent excellence in knowledge itself. They realize that it elevates a rational being. They are never content, but continually yearn for more and more knowledge. They pursue it until their dying day, regardless of whether they receive recognition or employment. Their love for knowledge drives them because they love knowledge for its own sake. Similarly, a person who desires grace for some subordinate end is content with acquiring enough grace to serve that purpose. But anyone who desires righteousness for its own sake is never satisfied and constantly desires more and more grace as long as they live. This is the third aspect of this desire.

Fourthly, it is a ruling desire. All other desires are ordered and guided by the desire for the advancement of grace and righteousness. The soul declares, "Let my desire for the promotion of grace and righteousness rule and guide these desires." Therefore, as long as my other desires contribute to this primary desire for righteousness, I will nurture and pursue them. However, if I find that any desire in my soul towards anything else hinders my great desire for righteousness, rather than furthering it, I will forsake that desire. I will oppose it and even consider it a blessing if God thwarts that desire. This is the true desire for righteousness—when it becomes the ruling desire. It governs the soul, acting as the chief desire, and no desire can be nurtured within the soul unless it serves in some way this great desire of the soul—to hunger and thirst after righteousness.

Fifthly, the desires of the soul in hungering and thirsting after righteousness are accompanied by pain. As was mentioned earlier in relation to hungering and thirsting for the righteousness of Christ, there is pain involved. Just as natural hunger is accompanied by pain, so is this spiritual hunger and thirst. The guilt of sin is painful to the soul. Likewise, the unruly corruptions of the heart are grievous to it. When have you ever heard of Paul crying out due to his sufferings? He did not lament when he was buffeted or imprisoned. He even sang while in stocks. But when he felt his corruptions stirring within him and sensed the lack of some degree of righteousness, he let out a dreadful cry and exclaimed, "Wretched man that I am! Who will deliver me from this body of death? How can I gain power over these corruptions and be empowered to walk after God? Oh, if only I could have this, then I would be a happy man!" Therefore, you see that this hungering and thirsting after righteousness follows mourning. Blessed are those who mourn, and then blessed are those who hunger and thirst after righteousness. That means those who are first affected by mourning for the corruptions of their hearts, and upon experiencing this mourning, they subsequently develop this hunger and thirst for righteousness.

Sixthly, these desires must also be fervent. They are not mere wishes or idle thoughts but powerful and intense desires. One of our theologians said that the desires of a hypocrite are feeble, but the sincere desires of the soul are so strong that they can even cause the soul to faint. We see such expressions in Psalm 119:5, where David says, "Oh, that my ways were directed to keep Your statutes." David already had some measure of grace to guide him, but he longed for more. "Oh, that my ways were directed to keep Your statutes," he cried out. It's as if he said, "Lord, You know everything, and You know there is nothing in the world that would bring greater contentment to my soul than to have my heart directed towards keeping Your statutes. Even though I am a king and have great satisfaction in the world, this is the very thing that makes me sigh and send my desires heavenward." Similarly, in verse 10, he says, "With my whole heart I have sought You; Oh, let me not wander from Your commandments." He regarded wandering from God's commandments as the greatest evil that could befall him in this world. If God were to leave him to himself, he would surely go astray. So he pleads, "Lord, let me feel the powerful work of Your grace in my heart so that I may not wander from Your commandments." And in verse 20, he exclaims, "My soul breaks for the longing that it has unto Your judgments at all times." David's soul was shattered. There was never a man who desired anything in this world with greater intensity. What more powerful expressions can there be than these? And in verse 131, he says, "I opened my mouth and panted, for I longed for Your commandments." When we put all these together—the longing for directed ways, the whole-hearted seeking after God, the dread of wandering from His commandments, the soul breaking with longing for His judgments, and the panting for His commandments—we see the earnest desires of a gracious heart for righteousness.

Seventhly, these desires are also diligent. They are not idle desires like those of most people in the world who merely wish for grace, saying, "God, give me grace, and when You give it to me, I will do better." They do not go beyond that. But let me ask you, how much effort, how much striving is evident in your spirit? How much diligence, how much work does your soul put into pursuing grace? Therefore, consider this scripture in Psalm 63:1 and 8. The psalmist says, "My soul thirsts for You; my flesh longs for You." But notice what follows in verse 8: "My soul follows hard after You," says David. That is the fruit of genuine desires. If you have a desire to obtain grace, to attain righteousness, if you truly thirst for it, then this will follow: your heart will diligently pursue God through the use of all means that He is pleased to provide. If there are any ordinances of God that can further the work of your grace, you will desire them. And if there are any pains to be endured, if ordinary means are insufficient, you will be willing to engage in extraordinary measures. Suppose there is a corruption that you complain of, and ordinary means cannot conquer it. Even if it means mortifying the body, suppressing the flesh, or any other form of self-denial, you are resolved. If power against corruption can be obtained, you will pursue it. You are willing to do or suffer the most difficult things in the world to see these desires fulfilled.

Eighthly, these desires are enduring. They will persist and never be quiet until the thing is accomplished. In Psalm 119:20, previously mentioned, it says, "My soul breaks for the longing that it has unto Your judgments." Mark the phrase "at all times." Some of you may have experienced such soul-breakings and intense desires during good moods. You could pray mightily and cry out fervently to God for grace during those times. Perhaps it was when you were on your sickbed, afraid of death, or when you were stirred by a sermon. You returned home and manifested your desires to heaven, pleading with the Lord to help you, cleanse your heart, and give you grace. But is it true at all times? At other times, you are far from such intense pursuit of righteousness. However, it was different for David. His soul broke for the longing for God's judgments at all times. By "judgments," we mean His statutes, His commandments, His revealed will. David desired to have a heart in conformity to God's will as revealed in His Word. Similarly, in Psalm 143:6, he says, "My soul thirsts after You as a thirsty land." You know how a thirsty land opens wide, longing for water, and it never closes until it receives showers. That's how David describes it. "Lord, I am like a thirsty land. I feel a gaping in my heart, a longing for showers of Your grace. And until they come, my heart will remain open, just like a thirsty land." Thus, you have seen the kind of enduring desires that the soul has for this righteousness, as well as for the other aspects.

Now, I should proceed to expound on the great desirability of this righteousness. But all I will do for now is to urge you to reflect on what has been presented to you regarding the description of the hungering and thirsting soul's desire for sanctification. I believe that not one of you has been without some kind of desire for grace, although you may have had little understanding of what it truly meant. But now, in the presence of God, can you say, "Lord, You have worked such desires in my soul. To some extent, I can testify that it was not due to ignorance but to the enlightenment of Christ's Spirit. I was an ignorant and foolish soul not long ago, but the light of Your Spirit entered me and revealed to me the excellence of Your righteousness, the blessedness of living for You. And, Lord, You know that my desires for righteousness are for its own sake. No degree of righteousness can satisfy me until I reach heaven. I want more and more. Lord, You know that all my desires are ordered and guided by this great desire of my soul for righteousness, second only to my desires for the righteousness of Your Son. And, Lord, You know how painful it is for me to lack it. There is nothing in the world more burdensome to me than the body of death that I carry with me. If You were to ask me from heaven what I desire, I would answer, 'Lord, grant me the righteousness of Your Son for my justification, and grant me the righteousness of Your Spirit for my sanctification, to overcome my corruptions and enable me to live for Your praise.' And, Lord, You know that these desires have been fervent, not just temporary flashes, but consistent and settled. And they have been diligent. You know the efforts my soul has exerted and is still willing to exert, if only I could overcome these corruptions and be enabled to walk with You in holiness and righteousness. I am willing to endure any pain. And, Lord, this has been year after year. I am resolved that it will continue, by Your grace, even until my dying day. So, even if I perish, I would perish crying to You for the righteousness of Your Son and the righteousness of sanctification for my heart. Lord, this is what You have worked in my soul." Now, if you can make such an appeal to God, blessed are you. Blessed are those who hunger and thirst after righteousness in this manner. However, even though the mere mention of these things may stir some desires for the ways of God and righteousness in your hearts, the main objective is to present to you the beauty and excellence of righteousness and to comfort and encourage your soul in the pursuit of it.

# SERMON XVIII

## The Excellence of Sanctification's Righteousness

"Blessed are those who hunger and thirst for righteousness, for they shall be filled." - Matthew 5:6

The third aspect presented in the exploration of this significant and weighty subject of sanctification's righteousness, or inherent righteousness, is its excellence. What is it about this righteousness that causes a soul to hunger and thirst for it? Many things that people hunger and thirst for are nothing more than vanity, not worth the expenditure of our thoughts, let alone our spirits. Surely, Christ would never declare them blessed, those who spend their time and thoughts on vanity. However, there is great excellence in this righteousness, enabling the soul to glorify and honor God as the infinite first being of all things. The excellence of this righteousness lies in the following:

First, this righteousness is the proper disposition of the soul. Just as the health of the body depends on its proper and sound constitution, when the body is healthy, it can taste and savor the sweetness of things, and it can function and perform its duties in the place God has set it. However, if a person's body is afflicted with sickness and weakness, they cannot work, enjoy anything, or find contentment in what they possess. That's why a person desires health above all external blessings. What good is wealth and a great estate to a rich person if they lack good health? What good is it to have honors, promotions, friends, and all the pleasures this world can offer if one cannot derive enjoyment from these things? Sin, on the other hand, is the ailment of the soul. It robs the soul of its taste and diminishes the excellence of everything it enjoys. Therefore, Scripture often compares sin to the most repugnant things. When grace enters the heart, it overcomes all the soul's ill humors, bringing health to the spirit. It enables the soul to be healthy and whole in the service of God.

Secondly, this righteousness is a spark of the divine nature. As mentioned in 2 Peter 1:4, "by which have been given to us exceedingly great and precious promises, that through these you may be partakers of the divine nature." Grace and righteousness are one and the same. They are nothing less than a glimmer of the divine nature found in God Himself. When the soul comprehends this, how can it not long for it? It perceives greater glory and worth in the tiniest spark of this excellence than in all the world's glory presented in the most captivating and beautiful display. Through this righteousness, the soul comes to live even as God Himself does. Isn't that truly desirable?

Thirdly, it is the very image of God in the soul, and an image represents something in its chief excellence. Just as an image or portrait of a person does not depict their legs and feet, which are the inferior parts, but rather their countenance, their face—the image of a person is represented by their face, which is their glory or their head. Likewise, God's image in us is this righteousness, inherent grace. All creatures bear the footprints of God, and in every creature in the world, we can perceive these footprints to some extent. However, they do not bear God's image. If a person were to walk on the sand of the sea, only footprints would remain, not the image of the person. We couldn't say, "There is the image of that person," once they had gone. We would only see their footprints. Similarly, all the manifestations of God in the world, in creation and providence, reveal His footprints, indicating that God has been there. All creation displays the footprints of the Most High. However, when we behold a saint, we witness the glory of God. There, we behold the face of God. In Genesis 1, where the council was called, "Let us make man," how did they fashion man? After their footprints? No. But after their own image. Now, grace is the restoration of this glorious image. We must recognize that due to the fall, this excellent aspect of God's image was defaced and marred. There was darkness and deformity upon this glorious excellence. However, grace renews this image once again. The soul represents God in a vibrant manner. The image of a person is more vividly seen in their child than in a piece of wood. It is possible to depict it with such excellence and accuracy that it closely resembles the person, but it is still not as true to the person's image as their child is. Grace in the heart is the lively representation of God's image. God may see Himself there as a father sees himself in the face of his child. God cannot see Himself so clearly in all the world as in a saint. If God were to ask, "Where can I behold My image?" and looked to acts of providence, He might see His footprints; if He observed works of creation, He might perceive His power and wisdom. However, surely when He looks into the heart of a saint, there He sees His image most gloriously. Therefore, grace is an excellent thing. Its prototype was found in Christ without measure. He received this grace without measure, and from His fullness, we receive grace upon grace.

Fourthly, the excellence of this righteousness is evident in that it is the very life of God Himself. While a man may see His image, he cannot see His life. However, grace is God's life. We find a hint of this in Ephesians 4:18: "Having their understanding darkened, being alienated from the life of God." This implies that when the soul possesses this righteousness, it begins to live the same life as God—His very nature. The soul, acting as God acts, lives the life of God. When a creature acts as God does, pursues the same goals as God, and aligns its actions with His purpose, that is the life of God. God's life consists of willing Himself as the highest good, acting towards an ultimate end, and ordering all endeavors to align with that end. This is the excellency of God. And a saint comes to live the life of God by making God the supreme good, the ultimate end of all actions, and directing all designs towards this end. Thus, the excellency of this life of sanctification lies in the fact that, to some extent, every saint attains this end. How desirable, then, is this righteousness that enables the soul to live the life it must live here and throughout eternity?

Fifthly, it is the very glory of God in the soul of man. The soul not only lives the life of God but becomes the very glory of God. Romans 3:23 states that all have sinned and come short of the glory of God, or as it is in the original text, have been deprived of the glory of God. We are now deprived of the righteousness in which Adam was originally created. Adam existed in a glorious state in Paradise, and in that condition, he was the glory of God as the most excellent creature God made. However, through sin, he defaced that excellence. Yet, when this righteousness is renewed in the soul, God's glory enters the soul. People desire glory in the world. What are the thoughts and desires of almost every person focused on if not things that may elevate their own honor and self-importance? How desirable, then, should God's glory be to us? It shines in the souls of the saints. To have a principle that enables us to manifest this glory according to the measure of grace received is truly excellent. A wretched individual reaches such a height of excellence as to display the glory of the eternal God. It is not merely God shining upon the soul; it is God shining in the soul, revealing the radiance of righteousness to the entire world. This is a great mystery of the excellence of this righteousness. It not only shines from God upon the soul but also shines in the soul, revealing the brilliance of righteousness to the world.

Sixthly, by this righteousness, the glory of God is upheld in the world. This righteousness upholds God's honor. What glory would God have in the world if everyone were as unrighteous as some? You might think that the saints are of little worth. Let me tell you, it is for their sake that the world continues to exist. If God received no more honor from some than He does from most of you, what would become of you? The world continues not for your sake; it is not worthy of these excellent ones. Instead, God continues their existence to receive glory from them. God says, "I have created a world and filled it with a variety of creatures, but among all the works of My hands, none give Me the glory that My saints do." God instills in some individuals a principle by which they give Him the glory of their very being. Is this not a most excellent and desirable thing? For a creature to be able to fulfill the purpose for which it was created?

Seventhly, by this righteousness, all natural and civil righteousness is elevated to a more glorious condition than ever before. There is no action that a person can perform that holds any worth beyond the presence of this righteousness. In their natural state, people act based on natural principles. However, when grace enters the heart—this inherent righteousness—the soul acts on inward principles and transforms those actions into righteous ones. A gracious heart engages in its calling and pursuits in a spiritual manner. Carnal hearts are carnal even in spiritual matters, whereas gracious hearts are spiritual even in natural matters.

Eighthly, upon receiving this righteousness, every action, as far as this righteousness is present, surpasses the value of heaven and earth. You, who are saints, cherish your roles, cherish your duties. Luther, who praised faith and righteousness as much as anyone, had a saying: every good work that springs from faith is more precious to God than heaven and earth. Heaven and earth display God's glory passively, while these actions display it actively. An action performed for the glory of God in an active manner exhibits His glory more prominently than the entire world.

Ninthly, the excellence of this righteousness lies in the fact that it lifts the heart above all creatures and enjoyments, carrying the soul beyond them all. Before righteousness enters the heart, it remains beneath the creature, a slave to every whim. When the creature beckons, the heart obeys instantly. But this righteousness lifts the soul above them all. Now, the soul considers only God to be higher than itself. The soul acknowledges no supreme authority except God alone and submits to Him alone. The soul recognizes its own worth and excellence, understanding that no creature is fit or worthy to have communion with it. It is solely a companion for God Himself. If God desires its submission, it will obey anything He commands. However, its submission is only in relation to Him. Thus, the good of the creature does not lie in anything the creature can provide, nor does harm come from anything the creature can do. The good of the creature lies solely in God Himself. The soul is now infinitely expanded and can find satisfaction in nothing but God. Only a God can fulfill the soul's longings. Whereas before it was content with every desire and filthy vanity, now it seeks only real enjoyments—those that are capable of satisfying the soul.

Tenthly, the excellence of this righteousness is found in its principle of union and communion with God Himself. The soul enters into a relationship and close union with the Father. When God first made man, He not only gave him a body and a soul but also provided a means for him to enjoy communion with Him. This is the essence of man's happiness—to be capable of communing with God. However, this happiness was lost. Through the fall, man became a stranger to God. Yet, when God converts the soul, this communion is restored. At the initial work of conversion, the soul draws near to God, who was previously distant. "He who is joined to the Lord is one spirit." Now, the soul becomes fit for communion with such a great good. No creature is suitable for communion with God except angels and humans. Communion requires a harmony of lives between those who partake in it. Communion cannot exist where there is incongruity in the manner of living. Just as a man cannot commune with beasts because they do not share the same life, and beasts cannot commune with plants because they live contrasting lives, a natural man cannot commune with God because he does not live the same life as God. However, a saint comes to enjoy communion with the Lord by virtue of this righteousness. Previously, you wandered from God and pursued vanity without ever experiencing communion with Him. Communion with God was a trivial matter to you. You had heard of it and could discuss it, but it held no value for you. You did not appreciate it. But now, the soul enjoys something more precious than a thousand worlds. The more righteousness the soul possesses, the deeper its communion with God becomes. This is why the soul hungers and thirsts for more righteousness—for the more it enjoys God, the sweeter it becomes.

Eleventhly, this righteousness sanctifies all our actions to God and imparts worth to them. Before, our actions were not accepted and were regarded as filthy and polluted. To the pure, all things are pure, but to the defiled and polluted, all things are filthy. Thus, God saw them as such. To sanctify something means to set it apart for God. It is grace that sanctifies the soul. Whereas the soul was previously engaged in common uses, it is now set apart for God. Just as the vessels of the temple were sanctified and set apart for holy use, a godly person is separated for God, taken out of the world, and engaged in holy services. In Psalm 4:5, the soul is not only set apart for God by an act of God upon the soul, which has occurred from all eternity, but it is also sanctified by grace. Something is placed within the soul that enables it to set itself apart for God. As a result, it grows in grace and is able to sanctify all that it enjoys. It knows how to use all things for the glory of God. Whereas the world once had use of the soul, the soul now declares, "I am set apart for lofty purposes, for the glory of the God from whom I receive my being."

Twelfthly, this helps the soul to overcome the greatest evil in the world. Sin is the greatest evil, and one who is truly enlightened would rather suffer anything than be overcome by the slightest sin. A gracious heart looks upon the smallest sin with more indignation than any suffering. Only the Holy Spirit can overcome sin; it is the Spirit alone that can subdue iniquity. The soul possesses a principle within itself that overcomes sin and continues to do so until the work is perfected. Therefore, a gracious heart not only overcomes sin with the help of the Spirit but also from an inward principle that works against anything contrary to God.

Thirteenthly, its excellence lies in the fact that Jesus Christ achieves the purpose of His death through it. Surely, that in which Jesus Christ accomplishes the purpose of His death must be very precious. It is a part of the reason the Father sent Jesus Christ into the world: that we, being delivered from the hand of our enemies, might serve Him without fear in holiness and righteousness all the days of our lives (Luke 1:74). Christ came into the world to have a people to serve Him, to redeem a chosen generation. Who are they? They must certainly be a special people to have such a Redeemer. Man had lost all his holiness and righteousness that he had from the beginning and was covered in filth and misery. However, God's love for righteousness was so great that He said to Christ, "My Son, you must go into the world to restore righteousness. Such is My love for righteousness that you must go, even though you are the beloved of My soul." Christ responded, "Father, I am willing to go, and even if it costs Me My life to procure righteousness and righteous ones as subjects for Your mercy to triumph in, I am willing to die." How excellent, then, is the righteousness in which Christ achieves His end in dying!

Fourteenthly, this righteousness is the only thing, second only to the righteousness of Christ, that will be of value at death and judgment. When the world fails and their hearts tremble within them, all their civil righteousness, formality, and foolish pomp in the world—those things on which they placed their hope, the rock of their confidence and their support—will all crumble beneath them. However, next to the righteousness of Christ, this righteousness will sustain and comfort you. It will hold your head above water. Oh, how desirable it is! "O that we had oil in our lamps and grace in our hearts." When the foolish virgins saw the glory possessed by the wise virgins, they realized their folly in neglecting their own preparations and cried out, "Oh, that we had grace, oh, that we had oil in our lamps." Certainly, that which will be of such excellence then is no less valuable now.

Fifteenthly, this righteousness is an immortal seed. Once the soul is sealed in righteousness, it remains righteous forever. Even the smallest seed of it endures to eternity. The lastingness of a thing adds value to it. If you possess this righteousness, you have something that all the devils in hell cannot overcome. They may assault, trouble, and disturb your peace, but they can never undermine this righteousness. They can never undo you in that which is your righteousness, your happiness. This, too, is another excellence of this righteousness.

Lastly, this righteousness is nothing less than the beginning of heaven. In that golden chain in Romans, sanctification is not mentioned. Sanctification is heaven begun. Calling, justification, and glorification are mentioned, but sanctification is not. Therefore, sanctification is heaven itself, not just the way to heaven. Certainly, this is highly desirable. So, when we put all these things together, we can understand the meaning of the Scripture in Proverbs 12:26: "The righteous is more excellent than his neighbor." The righteous person is more excellent because:

- He is a healthy man.

- He possesses the divine nature.

- He bears the image of God.

- He lives the life of God.

- He partakes in exceeding great and precious promises.

- His sins are pardoned.

- He is accepted by the Father.

In all these ways, the righteous person is more excellent than his neighbor. It may be that his neighbor is a wealthy man, his landlord, his boss, or the most prominent person in the parish. But even if he is poor, if he is godly, he is better than his neighbor. Even if his neighbor is a lord or a prince, no matter how great he may be, the righteous person is more excellent than him. For you who hunger and thirst after this righteousness, behold the glorious object upon which your thirst is fixed.

Abundant comfort flows from this point to those who can prove themselves to be hungerers and thirsters. We see some excellence in it, and we desire more. If you say so and desire to have more, then know:

First, your hungerings are better than all the world's fillings. Your desires are better than all the cravings of those consumed by worldly pursuits. The worldly person says, "Who will show us any good?" But you say, "Lord, lift up the light of Your countenance upon me. Clothe my soul with righteousness. Bring me to a state where I can boldly stand at the throne of Your grace." Know that your hungerings are better than the world's fillings.

Secondly, your desires are better than all common gifts. The greatest talents and natural endowments possessed by the most glorious hypocrite in the world are nothing compared to your hungerings. Many can pray excellently and speak at length, and you may think, if only you had their gifts and abilities, how happy you would be. But your hungerings are better than those outward expressions. Those are just common workings, lacking distinguishing characteristics. However, your hungerings and thirstings for this righteousness are the breathings of the Spirit of God, the special workings of the Spirit.

Thirdly, this is the thing that has brought comfort to the most precious saints in the world, those who now rest in the bosom of the Father. They have found comfort in these hungerings and thirstings. Perhaps you cannot see the full manifestation of it or have full assurance of it yet, but they hungered and thirsted for God to lift up the light of His countenance upon them. Consider that chosen Scripture and meditate upon it as your portion. See how Nehemiah expressed himself: "O Lord, let Your ear be attentive to the prayer of Your servant and to the prayer of Your servants who desire to fear Your name." It is as if he said, "Lord, You know that even though we have many weaknesses, the desires of our souls are to fear You." Find comfort in this Scripture when you cannot find the righteousness you desire. When you have sad and dejected thoughts within you, thinking that God may reject you, use this Scripture: "Lord, You know that the desires of our souls are to fear Your name. Let me have this, and I am happy. Though corruption prevails over me, this spark is alive in me, for which I bless Your name. I desire to fear You." And Christ says in the text, "Blessed are they that hunger and thirst after righteousness." It is worth noting that He does not say, "Blessed is he who does this and that." No, He says, "Blessed is he who hungers and thirsts after righteousness." Although those who do these things are blessed, this is said to comfort the weak. "Blessed are they who desire to hunger and thirst after righteousness." Blessed are they who recognize their need for it and, in the midst of that, desire to fear God. This Scripture belongs to you. Find comfort in it as your portion, but be sure that your desires are sincere.

# SERMON XIX

## Those who hunger are blessed in the present

"Blessed are those who hunger and thirst for righteousness, for they shall be filled." - Matthew 5:6

There are two remaining aspects of blessedness to be explained before we fully apply it. They are blessed because they are enlightened to see true excellence. They are blessed compared to others who see no higher excellence than satisfying their physical desires. They are blessed because God has opened their eyes to perceive the surpassing excellence of righteousness and to understand its significance. Those whose eyes have been opened by God, and whose minds have been enlightened to comprehend the beauty, excellence, and glory of righteousness, consider it the greatest blessing under heaven, second only to beholding the righteousness of Jesus Christ, which God has revealed to them.

Secondly, they are blessed because they possess a magnanimous spirit. The Lord has bestowed upon them a spirit of magnanimity that surpasses that of others. People's desires reflect their spirits. A person with a lowly and base spirit limits their desires to lowly and base things. For example, some people, if they had enough money to drink with their friends, would not seek anything higher for a blessed life. On the other hand, someone with a greater spirit aspires to honors, advancements, and greater things. Their desires are commensurate with the magnitude of what their spirits pursue. Now, those whose spirits desire righteousness—first, the righteousness of Jesus Christ, and then the righteousness that is the divine nature, the image of God, the life of God—will not be satisfied with anything less. The world and carnal pleasures cannot satisfy them; only the righteousness of God can. This is a testament to a truly magnanimous spirit. Alexander desired great things and aspired to conquer the world, wishing he had more worlds to conquer. Why? Because he had a great spirit, and his desires were equally great. Similarly, a true, holy, and gracious Christian possesses a great spirit and desires great things. The world cannot sanctify the spirit of a Christian; righteousness is required.

Thirdly, this desire for righteousness is the seed of God, or rather, it is the fruit of righteousness already present in the soul. Thus, they are blessed. No soul can hunger and thirst for righteousness in this way without already possessing righteousness. There is righteousness within the soul because every entity desires what is suitable to its nature. What makes an ox desire grass, a fish desire water, or a bird desire grain? It is because these things are suited to their respective natures. Similarly, when there is a desire for righteousness, there is a suitability between righteousness and the soul. Therefore, righteousness has already begun in the soul. A soul that is suited to righteousness undoubtedly possesses the principles of righteousness, and for this reason, they are blessed.

Fourthly, those who hunger and thirst, even if they do not experience the righteousness they desire, are still blessed because in the covenant of grace, God accepts the will as if it were the deed. They have righteousness manifested by their desire, indicating that they have some principles of righteousness within them. Thus, they are within the covenant of grace, which grants them the privilege of having their will accepted as if it were the deed. It is important to consider this privilege—understanding how the acceptance of the will as the deed comes about. This is a significant point. Those under the law do not possess such a privilege; the law demands perfect obedience or rejects everything. Therefore, ignorant and graceless individuals who lack Christ within them mistakenly believe that God will accept their desires, their will, as if it were the deed. However, this privilege belongs to those who are in the covenant of grace, and it is a gift obtained through Jesus Christ—the acceptance of the will as the deed. Now, those who exhibit this kind of hunger and thirst for the righteousness of grace, alongside their hunger and thirst for the righteousness of Christ as previously explained, may be assured that the blessing of the covenant of grace belongs to them, and God accepts their will as if it were the deed. This is a tremendous blessing as it supports the soul amidst all its weaknesses. Even in the absence of righteousness, I can find comfort in my fervent desires for righteousness, knowing that the blessing of the covenant of grace is mine. It is accepted as if I possess the very righteousness I ardently hunger and thirst for. This concludes the fourth aspect of blessedness.

Fifthly, a significant aspect to consider is that those who hunger and thirst for righteousness are blessed because their hunger and thirst quench sinful and base desires in the soul. There is no better way to mortify sinful desires than through gracious desires. The same principle applies to all other affections. The way to overcome base and sordid love in the soul is through love for God and love for Jesus Christ. Likewise, the way to conquer sinful joy is through the joy of the Holy Spirit. Therefore, the way to mortify base and sinful desires in the soul, which wander after countless vanities and follies in the world, leading to the destruction of many souls, is to redirect desires toward righteousness. Blessed are those who have their desires rightly oriented, turned away from vain and base things and focused on righteousness—the image of God, the life of God, and the principles of union and communion with God. In this regard, they are blessed, for these desires quench unlawful and wicked desires, regulating the soul.

Sixthly, those who hunger and thirst after righteousness find the ordinances of God and the initial workings of grace to be exceedingly delightful to the soul. How sweet is the word to a soul that hungers and thirsts for righteousness? How sweet are all the ordinances of God, which serve as conduits of grace, appointed by God Himself? Any influence of grace on such a soul is greatly cherished. When the Lord enters the soul during prayer or through His word, quickening it or granting it strength to resist sin and temptation, it brings immense sweetness to the soul. Blessed are those who possess this hunger, for it enhances the sweetness of all ordinances and the beginnings of grace's influence.

Blessed are the souls that hunger and thirst after righteousness, for they have the gracious invitation of the Lord and Christ to come and receive mercy. The Lord invites these souls to come to Him, just as in the Gospel when they said to the poor blind man, "Be of good comfort, He calls you." Similarly, I say to all who can affirm that their souls, though weak, possess this hunger and thirst for righteousness: be comforted, for the Lord calls you. You are invited to come. I will provide you with these Scriptures as an invitation. In Isaiah 55, a well-known passage, it is written, "Ho, everyone that thirsteth, come ye to the waters, and he that hath no money, come ye, buy and eat, yea, come, buy wine and milk without money and without price." The grace of God is compared to these excellent things, and it is proclaimed to all who hunger and thirst to come to the waters. These waters represent both the righteousness of Jesus Christ and the righteousness of sanctification. Additionally, in John 7:37, there is another invitation. It is said, "If any man thirst, let him come unto me and drink." Take note that Christ calls out to those who hunger and thirst. They may face discouragement, unable to find the righteousness they desire, but Christ calls them to come to Him. They are truly blessed to be invited by Christ Himself, calling out to them. Furthermore, in Revelation 22:17, a passage quoted concerning the righteousness of Christ, is an invitation to those who hunger and thirst for this righteousness.

Eighthly, they are blessed not only because they are invited but also because they have numerous promises. There are many promises for the soul that hungers and thirsts. Let me share a few with you. In Psalm 10:17, it is written, "Lord, thou hast heard the desire of the humble: thou wilt prepare their heart; thou wilt cause thine ear to hear." God hears the desires of the humble and prepares their hearts. He will cause His ear to hear. Then, in Psalm 22:26, it states, "The meek shall eat and be satisfied: they shall praise the Lord that seek him, your heart shall live forever." Those who seek the Lord—those who hunger and thirst for Him—are promised satisfaction and the ability to praise the Lord. Their hearts shall live forever. A principle of life has been initiated, and their hearts will endure eternally. Perhaps you think that due to the corruption within your hearts, you will eventually falter, perish, and come to nothing. However, those who hunger and thirst for righteousness shall praise the Lord and their hearts shall live forever. One day, you will praise God for these desires and this hunger. This is another promise. Moreover, in Isaiah 41:17, it is written, "When the poor and the needy seek water, and there is none, and their tongue faileth for thirst, I the Lord will hear them, I the God of Israel will not forsake them. I will open rivers in high places, and fountains in the midst of the valleys, I will make the wilderness a pool of water, and the dry land springs of water." Observe how God's heart is present in this promise to those who thirst. It is important to note that spiritual blessings are represented by these expressions of outward things. During the times of the Old Testament, especially, the Lord promised Gospel graces in external ways, using outward things to signify spiritual blessings. Lastly, I want to emphasize two aspects of this promise. First, notice how many times God expresses Himself by saying, "I will do this for you." In verse 17, it is written twice, "I the Lord will hear them, I the God of Israel will not forsake them." Then, in verse 18, "I will open rivers in high places, and I will make the wilderness a pool of water." In verse 19, it is written, "I will plant in the wilderness the cedar, and I will set in the desert the fir tree." Six times in just a few words of Scripture, God declares, "I will do it." It is as if He is saying, "Poor souls who hunger and thirst, you cannot fathom how it will be done. You find your hearts so wicked, corruption so prevalent, and may think it impossible to overcome. But I, I, I, I, I, I will do it." The second aspect to be highlighted is that the Lord removes objections that may discourage those who hunger and thirst. Some may question how they can obtain righteousness, especially if they live in a place where there are no means or a lack of effective ministry. Let not that discourage you, for God will open rivers in high places and fountains in the midst of valleys. He will make the wilderness a pool of water and the dry land springs of water. Even in the wilderness, God can bring forth springs of water that will refresh and satisfy your souls. Additionally, in Isaiah 44:3, it is written, "For I will pour water upon him that is thirsty, and floods upon the dry ground. I will pour my Spirit upon thy seed, and my blessing upon thine offspring." Here is an excellent promise, extended to both you and your descendants. It is a grave misconception and contrary to the covenant of grace to hold the belief that the children of believers, the godly, have no promise or are not in any sense in covenant with God, just like any other person. In addition to other promises, God promises to circumcise the hearts of believers and their children. In this verse, He promises to pour water upon the thirsty and floods upon the dry ground. He will pour His Spirit upon their seed and bless their offspring. Thus, even the descendants of those who hunger and thirst for righteousness are blessed. It is possible that the things you have been praying for your own soul may be granted to your seed after you. You will receive as much as is necessary for your salvation and satisfaction, but for the specific things you have been praying for, they may be granted to your future generations. Here is a promise that God will pour water upon the thirsty and floods upon the dry ground. However lightly a carnal heart may regard the promises of the Gospel, those who possess grace would not exchange their portion in these promises for a thousand worlds. They embrace such promises and consider them greater riches than the numerous bonds and bills possessed by a covetous person.

But the main thing in which they are blessed is in what Christ says: "They shall be satisfied." And we have many promises for this, apart from Christ's statement. In Proverbs 10:24, it is written: "The desire of the righteous shall be granted." In Psalm 145:19, there is another promise: that God will fulfill the desires of those who fear Him. And in Psalm 103:9, it is said: "He satisfies the longing soul and fills the hungry soul with goodness." They shall be satisfied, but how? First, all hungry souls in this world will find contentment in the ways of righteousness, to the extent that their hearts will never turn away from those paths, regardless of the temptations they face. Surely, this provides some satisfaction. There is a certain satisfaction in a soul that remains unwavering in a way that no temptation can draw it away. If a bee attaches itself to a flower and sucks honey from it, and cannot be removed from that flower, it surely finds sweetness and honey there. Similarly, even those who have only just begun to experience true grace, although they hunger for more, find enough satisfaction that they will never turn to unrighteousness again. They will never abandon the ways of God. You may be complaining, saying, "I have been desiring for many years, hoping to overcome certain corruptions and to serve God with greater freedom and cheerfulness, but I do not seem to make progress. I get little. Why then does temptation come? If you cannot achieve anything, if you strive, labor, desire, and pray, and obtain nothing, temptation says to give up and return to your former ways." God forbid! says the gracious soul. "I will never return to my former ways, for although I cannot do as much as I would like, I have a thousand times more peace and contentment than I ever had in my former ways, and that is some satisfaction."

Secondly, those who hunger and thirst after righteousness will experience the growth of grace within them. More and more grace will come to them. Perhaps they will not always be aware of it, but grace will continually sustain them, at least to uphold them if not to comfort them as much as they desire.

Thirdly, there will certainly come a time when all these hungry souls will be fully and sensibly satisfied. There is a time when you will never sin again, when you will no longer be troubled by your wretched heart—proud, stubborn, carnal, and distrustful. There is a time when you will serve God as much as you desire, as much as you long to serve Him. You will have as much grace as you desire to have. Surely, that is a blessed time, and it will satisfy the souls of those who possess grace. There is a time coming when you will serve God to the fullest. It is as if you will have your belly full. You are now a vessel of mercy and will be filled with the grace of God within you. The very thought that such a time is coming provides great satisfaction to the soul in the present. How much more satisfied will your soul be when that time arrives! Blessed are those who hunger and thirst after righteousness—they will be satisfied.

Now, for the application, here is a use of comfort and encouragement for those who hunger and thirst after righteousness. Be comforted in your hunger and thirst for righteousness—it is a sign of life. Just as a crying child seeks the breast, it is undoubtedly alive. "As newborn babes, desire the sincere milk of the word, that ye may grow thereby" (1 Peter 2:2). It is a sign that you are at least a newborn babe. That's what the Apostle says. "As newborn babes, desire the sincere milk of the word, that ye may grow thereby, if so be ye have tasted that the Lord is gracious." Here is evidence of a newborn babe. Why does your soul desire the word so much? Is it not to grow thereby? What does that mean? It means having more power over your corruptions and being more able to serve the Lord in holiness and righteousness all the days of your life. You are a newborn babe, and there is life.

Secondly, it is a good sign of a thriving Christian, not just a living Christian but a thriving one. As you know from experience with the body, when a person begins to have a good appetite for food, when they become hungry, we say that they are getting better. A person who develops an appetite and tastes their drink is beginning to thrive. The same goes for the soul. You may not have the growth that your soul desires, but do you have an appetite for food? Can you taste your drink? Can you taste the waters of life? Can you say, "These are sweet. I desire more. I am thirsty and long for more"? When you come to the word, you receive some milk to nourish you, and you hunger for more. This is an indication that you are in a thriving condition. It is a sign of the health and wholeness of your soul. You do not have the disorders and corruptions that others have. Other people whose souls are burdened with the lusts of the flesh and the desires of the world—the ambitions, honors, riches, and pleasures of it—they can go for a whole year without the word. They only attend out of habit. But a poor, hungry soul, after just one day in the word, longs for the next feeding. They cannot imagine going without a meal. That is a sign that such a soul is thriving. So be encouraged by this.

Thirdly, there is an infinite fountain of grace open for poor souls. You, who hunger and thirst after righteousness, there is an infinite fountain of grace, and there is an abundance of bread in your Father's house. You do not need to seek satisfaction with husks. There is enough bread. "My flesh is meat indeed, and my blood is drink indeed" (John 6:55). Jesus Christ is an infinite fountain of all grace. He is filled with the fullness of God, and He is filled in this way so that hungry and thirsty souls may be satisfied. That is why Christ is filled. "And of His fullness have all we received, and grace for grace" (John 1:16). There is grace corresponding to the grace of Christ, to be received from His fullness. Although it is true that there is emptiness in your own heart and in all ordinances, apart from Christ, there is a fountain of grace available to satisfy you—a boundless fountain that has been the source of satisfaction for hungry souls since the beginning of the world. It is open to you, and you may come for it as freely as any soul ever did—to take that which may satisfy your soul.

Fourthly, your desires and God's desires meet. There is nothing in the world that God is more willing to bestow than righteousness. The Lord is more willing and free to bestow the righteousness of His Son (as mentioned earlier) and the righteousness of His Spirit than to give a piece of bread. You may receive one from God as easily as the other, for His heart is more in one than in the other. You desire to overcome sin, to be able to walk before God in holiness and righteousness, and God desires the same thing. Your heart and God's heart meet as one.

Fifthly, your desires and God's desires coincide. There is nothing in the world that God bestows more freely than righteousness. The Lord is more willing and eager to bestow the righteousness of His Son (as mentioned earlier) and the righteousness of His Spirit than to provide a piece of bread. You may receive one from God as easily as the other because His heart is more inclined towards one than the other. You long to overcome sin and serve the Lord in holiness and righteousness, and God desires the same thing. Your heart and God's heart align in unity.

Sixthly, if God fills the voids in nature and hears the cries of ravens, will He not fill the emptiness of your soul? God has ordered things in nature in such a way that there can be no emptiness. Philosophers say that the world would sooner cease to exist than have the slightest emptiness, for it must be filled with something or other. Now, the Lord has appointed that there must be no vacuity in nature, and surely He will not allow a void in an immortal soul. He has something to fill that empty soul of yours for the time being. The Scripture tells us that the Lord blesses every living thing, so will He not satisfy the hunger of a raven and provide water for a crying raven? Will He not then satisfy an immortal soul that hungers for His own image, that desires to overcome sin and serve Him in holiness and righteousness? Certainly, the Lord will satisfy you.

Seventhly, the Lord commands us that if our enemy is hungry, we should give them food, and if they are thirsty, we should give them drink (Romans 12:20). This is God's charge to us poor creatures. If we, with our evil nature, know how to give good things to our children, how much more will our heavenly Father do so? Therefore, if you hunger and thirst after righteousness, God will not deny you. He will give you bread and drink to satisfy your soul. We are required to do this for our enemies, so the Lord will do it even more for a soul that desires above all else to be reconciled to Him.

Eighthly, take comfort in this—you who hunger and thirst. Your hunger and thirst make you praying Christians. They are powerful elements in prayer, and it is a great blessing to be a praying Christian, especially in these times. There are no praying Christians like those who hunger and thirst, who feel the lack of the righteousness of the Son of God and the Spirit of God. They are the mighty prayers in Israel. Many may pour out lengthy prayers, but a prayer that comes from a hungry and thirsty soul is worth a hundred of those prayers that come from recited words and memory.

Ninthly, know further that the ordinances of Jesus Christ are appointed for you. There will come a time when Jesus Christ will immediately satisfy your soul. Until that time, He has appointed His ordinances—His Word and Sacraments—to satisfy hungry and thirsty souls. Comfort yourself in this, O blessed Saviour. I hope to have full communion with You in the future, but for the present, You have not left me destitute. I will gratefully take what You have provided for now, expecting a more immediate satisfaction from You later. Now, as I have sought to encourage those who are hungry and thirsty, secondly, I desire to present some considerations to stimulate our appetites for these desires of righteousness.

You who have hungered and thirsted, be careful not to lose your appetite and eagerness. There was a time when you had a strong desire for righteousness. Do you still have it? Be cautious not to lose it. When you come home feeling unwell and have no appetite for food, your spouse and children around you start to worry, and you are troubled, saying, "I have lost my appetite for food." It is often a precursor to death, and it may also indicate the death of the soul. Do not lose your appetites but strive to revive them. These considerations will serve to invigorate your appetites for the righteousness we are speaking of. I address those I suppose to have grace. Do not think this way: "I hope God has worked some beginnings of grace, and that may suffice for me." No, hunger and thirst for more—Lord, more, more grace. You have started something, but I long for more.

First, consider that you do not know what work God may call you to before you die. Therefore, it is not fitting for Christians to settle for a little grace; they should desire much. You may be called to a great deal of work. A little grace will help you do a small amount of work, but abundant grace will enable you to accomplish much. These are times when God calls all His people to do much work. And it may be that you will live to see times when you will be called to do more work than ever before. Therefore, hunger for more—Lord, strengthen me with more grace, so that I may be empowered to do all the service that You will call me to.

Secondly, others who have started their religious profession more recently than you have surpassed you. Perhaps you have been a kind of professor for twenty or thirty years or more. Now, how many young ones have started after you? Although many of them fall into disputes and errors, some are truly gracious and godly. How much of Christ, of God, of heavenly qualities, of wisdom, of holiness, have they acquired in just a few years—more than you have gained in the past twenty or thirty years? Shouldn't you hunger and thirst for more?

Thirdly, by having more grace, you will be able to do more good for others. It is not enough to have grace merely to secure your place in heaven; it is also so that you may be useful in the sphere where God has placed you. Weak Christians may manage to sustain themselves in this world and make it to heaven with great effort, but strong Christians are beneficial to others and do a great deal of good. Oh, that I may have enough grace to do good to others!

Fourthly, consider the strong hunger and thirst you had in the past for worldly things. Lord, I remember that in former times my heart was carnal, and how strong my desires were for the world. My thoughts revolved around my business and how I could prosper and achieve success. Lord, You know that many times my soul was strongly drawn to base and sinful lusts. Shouldn't my soul now be equally strong in its desires for Your righteousness?

Fifthly, know that it is impossible for you to have a heaven on earth. All Christians may come to experience a heavenly condition in this world, filled with unspeakable and glorious joy through believing in the ways of godliness. However, weak grace cannot achieve this; it requires strength of grace. Through strong grace, the soul of a Christian can be in heaven while still on earth and commune with God, His angels, and saints as if they were already in heaven. This can be attained, so continue to hunger and thirst for further degrees of righteousness.

Sixthly, growing strong in grace is the only way to help you against temptations. If you have only a little grace, you are susceptible to temptations from every side, and the Devil is ready to deceive you in various ways. However, with the strength of grace, you can resist temptations. It is a great mercy in these dangerous times in which we live to resist temptations. Just as a weak and sickly person needs a staff to walk and stumbles at every stone, a weak Christian stumbles at every offense. But a person who has gained strength can walk steadily. Strong Christians can do it. That is why you find that Saint Peter, in 2 Peter 3:17-18, gives a rule for remaining steadfast: "Beloved, seeing ye know these things before, beware lest ye also, being led away with the error of the wicked, fall from your own stedfastness; but grow in grace..." In these times, when there is a deluge of errors in the world that ensnare young and weak individuals, causing them to fall from their own steadfastness, the way to prevent this is by growing in grace. Hunger for more, maintain your appetite, and let your prayers and efforts be directed toward increasing righteousness, so that you may remain steadfast.

Seventhly, by increasing in grace, you will have a more abundant entrance into heaven when you die. You will pass away with greater peace and experience a bountiful entry into the Kingdom of our Lord and Saviour Jesus Christ. It is not enough to have a little grace, even though it may lead you to heaven. With abundant grace, you can have an abundant entrance. In 2 Peter 1:5, the Apostle encourages us to add one virtue to another. If you have acquired one grace, then strive for and add more. In doing so, you will make your calling and election sure. You will never fall and will be aided against your doubts, fears, and the power that the Devil has over you. The way to combat these challenges is by adding one grace to another and continually growing in the ways of godliness. By doing so, an abundant entrance will be granted to you into the everlasting Kingdom of our Lord and Saviour Jesus Christ. It is as if the Apostle is saying, "The broad gates of heaven will swing open for you." Just as in great houses, the small gate is ordinarily opened, but when great men, earls, and princes come, the broad gates are thrown open. Likewise, God will admit to heaven those with little grace, but they must struggle and face many discouragements. However, those who possess abundant grace will receive an abundant entrance. Oh, you Christians who have any beginnings of grace, continue to hunger and thirst for more righteousness, for it will lead you to an abundant entrance into the everlasting Kingdom of our Lord and Saviour Jesus Christ.

# SERMON XX

## Rules to help souls in the pursuit of righteousness

"Blessed are they which do hunger and thirst after righteousness: for they shall be filled." - Matthew 5:6

There are three things remaining in the text.

First, I will present some rules to aid souls that are earnestly desiring righteousness but cannot seem to find it.

Secondly, I will discuss what can support souls in a state of hunger for righteousness, even when they feel they are not growing in righteousness themselves.

Thirdly, I will rebuke the lack of genuine hunger and thirst for righteousness.

Regarding the first point, if the Lord has brought your heart to hunger and thirst for righteousness, can you honestly say that this is your condition? If not, you have little to say. Even those with the weakest degree of grace should be able to affirm that they have a genuine hungering and thirsting desire. If this is indeed the case, then observe these rules in your pursuit, so that you do not go astray.

First, even if you do not possess the righteousness you desire, make sure to renounce all unrighteousness. While I am still on a journey of hungering and cannot find the righteousness I desire, I resolve, O Lord, to forever renounce unrighteousness. Though I may not have the ability to serve God with the fullness of spirit I long for, and I may not be experiencing the growth in grace as I desire, I will keep this commitment in my heart: I will not engage in anything that appears unrighteousness. I will have nothing to do with it. In Psalm 119:2-3, the Psalmist says, "Blessed are they that keep his testimonies, and that seek him with the whole heart. They also do no iniquity, they walk in his ways." Those who seek the Lord with their whole heart do not engage in iniquity. While seeking God with their whole heart, they renounce all iniquity. There should be no tolerance for any form of sin. Even if I cannot guide myself as I would and do what I should, I will at least have nothing to do with my former unrighteous ways. This is of great importance for those souls whom God is bringing close to Himself, who are seeking Him but do not yet feel they have found Him. They should renounce unrighteousness. Many men and women seek righteousness (or at least they believe they do), but in the meantime, they allow themselves to indulge in unrighteousness. They deceive themselves by thinking that God will accept their desire for righteousness, even though they give in to unrighteousness. Beware of falling into that trap.

Secondly, in your hunger and thirst for righteousness, express your desires before God on a regular basis. Freely express your desires in the presence of God when you are alone in secret. Tell God about all your longings for His righteousness and His ways. It is easy to tell others about your desires, but it is important to daily express your desires to God after His righteousness.

Thirdly, ensure that you hunger and thirst for His righteousness specifically. Do not satisfy yourself with the fact that you hunger and thirst for something related to godliness. Let your heart sincerely long and thirst for all His righteous ways. Hunger for every form of righteousness, and let your heart be fully dedicated to desiring and thirsting after all His ways and commandments. Do not allow any form of unrighteousness to find a place in your life. Hunger for righteousness in all its forms.

Fourthly, once you have expressed your desires to God and hungered for all righteousness, evaluate the outcome. Consider what has become of your desires. How long have you been hungering and thirsting for righteousness? When did God begin to stir your heart and open your conscience to desire righteousness? Reflect on whether this hunger has been present for as long as you can remember or for a significant period. Then question what has happened to your desires during all this time. What has become of the many prayers you have offered to God, asking for His grace to renew His image in your soul? Examine what has happened to your desires. Many men and women have a superficial form of prayer and wish that things were better for them, but they do not look back to their desires. They do not consider whether God has granted their desires or not. They do not evaluate whether they have gained more power over their corruptions or greater ability to serve God in righteousness. If they do experience progress, they have reason to praise and bless Him. If not, they have cause for humility. But who examines daily what becomes of their prayers for grace? Who makes it a matter of praise or humiliation based on whether God grants or denies their desires?

Fifthly, make sure to manifest your desires by using all means available. Follow this rule and pay attention to the following detail: if one means does not work, try others. If ordinary means do not suffice, resort to extraordinary means. But in using these means, focus on righteousness. For instance, you might say, "I have good desires, and I also use means. I pray, I listen to God's word, I read, and I engage in discussions with godly people." But when you engage in all these activities, is it truly righteousness that your soul pursues and longs for? Can you honestly say that in your prayers, you seek to gain further righteousness and growth in righteousness? Do you find satisfaction in your prayers only when you have made progress in overcoming your corruptions that day? And when you listen to the Word, do you long for God to speak to your heart, enabling you to gain power over your corruptions, become strengthened in His ways, and experience increased grace, wisdom, humility, fear of His name, and spiritual-mindedness? Do you desire to receive all these blessings through His Word? For you, a good sermon is one in which God speaks to your heart, furthering righteousness within you. If you attend a sermon and do not encounter God there, furthering the work of His grace in your heart, regardless of how good the sermon may be for others, it is not beneficial to you. Because you do not experience the advancement of God's grace in your heart to a greater degree. How many times do we attend sermon after sermon without considering the necessity of approaching them with a panting desire for righteousness?

Moreover, I will provide you with a scripture to demonstrate that it is not enough to hunger and thirst for righteousness if you do not express it through the use of means. In Psalm 107:9, there is a gracious promise from God to those who genuinely long for righteousness. It says, "He satisfieth the longing soul, and filleth the hungry soul with goodness." The phrase "longing soul" in your books is translated as the "running soul" in Hebrew. It signifies a soul that diligently seeks from one means to another. If one thing does not suffice, it pursues another. Its desires must be satisfied, or it feels it cannot live. Therefore, a longing soul is one that actively pursues God from one means to another, never finding rest until it encounters Him and enjoys His ways of righteousness, as desired. Mark 7:24-25 provides an excellent scripture to show that when the heart is set on something, it leaves no means unattempted. It speaks of Christ who went to the borders of Tyre and Sidon, entered a house, and wanted no one to know. But He could not be hidden because a certain woman, whose young daughter had an unclean spirit, sought Him out. The passage implies that the poor woman, being deeply affected by her daughter's misery and believing that Christ could help her, resolved to find Him even if He was hidden. Thus, it is similar here. If the Lord withdraws Himself from the soul in one means, a soul that is aware of its need for righteousness will pursue God through one means after another. It will never be at rest until it meets with God and experiences Him in the ways of righteousness, in accordance with its desires. This is the fifth rule: let your hungering and thirsting manifest in the use of all means available.

Sixthly, in your hunger and thirst, be careful not to rest in your desires. Do not think that having desires is enough, saying, "I have desires, God has placed desires in me, and that's sufficient. Why do I need anything more?" Although it is true that there are many encouragements for those with genuine desires, it is equally true that when desires are genuine, the soul will not be satisfied with desires alone. I have desires, but it is the actual fulfillment of those desires that I seek. We read in Proverbs 13:12 that deferred hope makes the heart sick, but when the desire is fulfilled, it becomes a tree of life. Hope deferred means when the soul desires something and it does not come. But when the desire is fulfilled, that is the tree of life. Therefore, a soul that is rightly affected will not rest in desires alone. It will not think, "God has begun to work some desires in me, and I hope that's grace. Even the slightest degree of grace will be enough to bring me to heaven." No, I have desires, but nothing will satisfy my soul until I obtain what I desire.

Seventhly, exercise faith in Jesus Christ for righteousness. That is the way to have your desires satisfied. You do use means, and yes, I dare not do otherwise. My conscience compels me to pray, read, hear, and use all the means I can. But still, I do not find my desire satisfied. Therefore, here is another rule: in the use of means, look beyond the means and be careful not to rely solely on them or on your desires. Instead, look up to Jesus Christ, from whose fullness the hearts of the saints receive grace upon grace. The Father has placed fullness in His Son. All righteousness is in Jesus Christ. There is all grace, righteousness, and holiness in Christ beyond measure. Now, the way to attain righteousness is not merely through prayer, hearing, and using means, but by having faith in Christ. Look upon Him as a fountain filled with all grace, so that the souls of those who hunger and thirst may, by acting upon Him, draw grace from Him and be satisfied. Christ is the tree of life, and all grace comes into the soul from Him. I truly believe that many people remain in great spiritual bondage during their hungering and thirsting, laboring for grace, because they do not look beyond the means. They do not look upon Christ as the fountain of all grace and do not exercise their faith in Him. They mistakenly believe that they must have righteousness before coming to Jesus Christ. Now, that is a mistake. You must come to Christ so that you may have righteousness, for all righteousness is in Him. The truth is, there is no saving righteousness apart from union with Jesus Christ. It comes from communion with Him and from the indwelling of the Spirit of Christ in the heart. Therefore, the first action should be to go to Christ for this righteousness. Actively exercise your faith in Christ, strive to see Him as the one who possesses all the treasures of grace from the Father, intended to be communicated to the souls of those who will be saved. This is the way to have the desires of your soul satisfied. You may say that you have been struggling and laboring, and nothing comes. Try this means, try this way: act your faith upon Jesus Christ for righteousness. You may fear that you will presume, but never fear presuming when you act upon Christ for righteousness. There is a fear of presuming when you only believe in Christ to save your soul and deliver you from Hell. But when you act upon Him for righteousness, there is no fear there. When your soul desires righteousness and you realize that Christ is appointed by the Father to be the conduit of all grace, and you are called to entrust your soul to Him so that you may receive the work of His Spirit for the subduing of your corruptions and for enabling you to live righteously before God in this world, do not fear presuming in this case. Presumptuous hypocrites believe in Christ solely to be saved from Hell, but they do not value the righteousness of Christ greatly. They seek the Kingdom of Heaven for deliverance from pain and torment, but they do not pay much attention to seeking the Kingdom of Heaven and its righteousness. It is not that which will nourish their souls. But when you have a hungry soul after righteousness and you come to Christ to embrace Him, know that His flesh is true food and His blood is true drink, both for justification and sanctification as well.

Eighthly, if you find in your hungering and thirsting after righteousness that you have not yet obtained your desire, make this resolution within yourself: if my desire cannot be satisfied in this, I will never allow my desires to wander after other things until I find satisfaction here. Keep your heart in this resolution, and it will maintain your soul in a state where righteousness will come. Many men and women have good desires stirred in them for a time, but they vanish away because their desires remain unfulfilled, causing them to redirect their desires towards other things. But when the heart reaches the point where it says, "O Lord, my desires are so set on the renewing of Your image, on righteousness, that if I do not find satisfaction here, I will not find satisfaction in anything else," it becomes of great importance. It is crucial for you to strive to continually keep your appetite focused on righteousness. Be cautious of things that will diminish your appetite for righteousness. There are three things that will take away the appetite, both in the body and in the soul.

Firstly, a man loses his appetite either due to something that obstructs his stomach, such as certain humours that have accumulated and hindered it, or

Secondly, due to excess wind that fills his stomach, causing him to lose his appetite for food, or

Thirdly, due to lack of exercise, because he does not move or take action. This also applies to the spiritual appetites of people for righteousness. These three factors can diminish their appetites.

First, when corrupt influences and ill dispositions have entered their hearts, defiling their souls. Many individuals in their youth used to have strong appetites for righteousness. They would eagerly turn to the Word of God and pray with great fervor, as if they could tear open the heavens. However, now we see no such passion in them. Fearful influences have entered their hearts, tarnishing their souls.

Secondly, some frivolous influences can also dampen their appetites. By this, I mean when their hearts indulge in worldly pleasures. There are many who have made enthusiastic professions of faith and have seemed to have great hunger and thirst for righteousness. The ordinances of Christ were once precious to them. However, now they are wholly focused on worldly matters and surrender themselves to the pleasures of the flesh. They value the company that brings them the most carnal satisfaction. Such influences have filled their stomachs with empty desires, thereby diminishing their appetite for spiritual matters.

Thirdly, appetite can wane due to lack of exercise. Many Christians become dull, heavy, and sluggish. They may abstain from the prevailing sins of the time and avoid indulging their fleshly desires, yet they grow listless and negligent. There is no fervency in their hearts for God. However, if you wish to keep your heart warm, it is not enough to engage in prayer merely out of convention. Instead, pray until your heart becomes warm again. It is similar to a person who lacks appetite going out into the fresh air, which may have some effect. But if their appetite is severely diminished, they will not just take a short walk but continue walking until they feel warm. Then they return home with a hearty appetite. Likewise, let Christians engage in spiritual exercises abundantly to maintain their appetites for spiritual things.

Ninthly, do not let your desire for more righteousness make you forget what you already have. Look to it. If God has been pleased to give you any measure of power over your corruptions, any ability to serve Him, take note of it. Bless God for it. Just because you don't have everything you desire, don't say that you have none at all. Don't devalue God's grace and think that it's all counterfeit just because it doesn't meet your desired degree. It's like if someone gave a relative several pieces of gold to start their trade, and they said, "What has he given me? These are just a few counters." A relative would feel wronged by such a response. The same is true for many souls seeking righteousness. The Lord has already given you the graces of His Spirit, which are as valuable as gold, so that you can prepare for Heaven. Even if you don't have as much as you would like, be careful not to diminish its worth. Instead, bless God for every little thing, every good impulse, every good inclination. Bless God for them and expect more. Just as poor individuals who were on the verge of starvation would be grateful for a piece of bread and bless God for it, instead of scorning it and saying, "Will this satisfy our hunger?"—for if they did, you wouldn't give them any more—so it is with the soul. If God gives you anything, bless Him for it and say, "Lord, I find this sweet. I find the beginnings of Your grace's work sweet to my soul. Oh, that I had more!"

Tenthly, another rule to follow in this hungering and thirsting for righteousness is to be careful not to seek this righteousness for your justification. This rule is of great importance. As you have heard before, the righteousness of Christ alone justifies the soul before God. However, this righteousness of sanctification enables us to serve God according to His way. Yet, it is not the righteousness by which I can stand before His tribunal on the great day. There is a significant mistake here. Many poor souls desire more grace, but why? Because they believe that through their grace, they will be able to stand before God and be accepted for eternal life. They think, "If I were able to overcome my corruptions and fulfill my duties more, then I would be able to look upon God's face with comfort and joy." However, you are mistaken in this belief. It's true that the work of His Spirit is a comforting evidence of God's love for your soul. God loves and takes delight in that. But never think that you can present your own righteousness to God for justification. Therefore, hunger and thirst after this righteousness, but understand that it is the righteousness of your Son, Lord, by which I expect to be justified. However, I desire this grace to be in my heart not for my justification, but for my sanctification.

Eleventhly, in your hungering after this righteousness, let your soul be willing to endure all discouragements and trample down all difficulties and hindrances that come your way. When you are hungering after righteousness, you may encounter more temptations than ever before, more stirring of corruption than ever before. You must anticipate this and be prepared. Those who have experienced this work of God in their hearts can testify that when they began to strive and labour after righteousness, they faced stronger temptations and more stirring of corruption. However, this did not discourage them. They overcame it, just like the poor woman in Matthew 15:22. A woman from Canaan came from the same region and cried out to Him, saying, "Have mercy on me, O Lord, Son of David! My daughter is severely demon-possessed." But He answered her not a word. And His disciples came and urged Him, saying, "Send her away, for she cries out after us." But He answered and said, "I was not sent except to the lost sheep of the house of Israel." Then she came and worshipped Him, saying, "Lord, help me!" But He answered and said, "It is not good to take the children's bread and throw it to the little dogs." And she said, "Yes, Lord, yet even the little dogs eat the crumbs which fall from their masters' table." This is a remarkable Scripture in the Book of God, demonstrating that when the heart is set on something, it will trample upon all discouragements. Note that this poor woman faced numerous discouragements at that time while seeking Christ.

Firstly, the woman comes and seeks Christ, crying out, "Have mercy on me, O Lord," but He does not respond. When you are hungering and praying to God for grace, if God does not answer you immediately, you may become disheartened. This woman cried out, and Christ did not answer her, yet it did not discourage her. So, do not let it discourage you either if Christ does not respond right away when you seek Him.

Secondly, the disciples came and urged Christ, "Send her away, for she cries out after us." The disciples spoke rudely. Many poor souls seeking Christ have friends who come and discourage them, behaving churlishly towards them. This may hinder you as well. However, if your desires are genuine, it should not discourage you. It did not discourage this poor woman.

Thirdly, Christ responded, "I am not sent but to the lost sheep of the house of Israel." Christ expressed that He had no obligation towards this woman, as she was not part of the house of Israel. This was a discouraging answer. When Jesus Christ said that He was sent only to the lost sheep of Israel, what was this poor woman to do? It is the same for many in their pursuit of grace. They may think, "Maybe I do not belong to God's chosen ones, not part of that small number for whom Christ was sent." Though Christ said this to her, it did not discourage her. Instead, she worshipped Him and said, "Lord, help me." She did not dwell on Christ's response but persisted in her strong desire, asking the Lord for help.

Fourthly, Christ answered, "It is not good to take the children's bread and cast it to dogs." Here is another discouragement. Christ referred to her as a dog and the food as meant for children. If God were to speak to you in this way, as you may sometimes think, that He rejects you like a dog when you cry out for sustenance in the form of righteousness, this might discourage you. Christ told the woman that she was a dog, and one might have thought this would have discouraged her. However, it did not. She responded, "Yes, Lord, yet even the dogs eat the crumbs which fall from their masters' table." She acknowledged her unworthiness but requested even a crumb for a dog. Upon this response, Christ heard her, and she was satisfied. This was the result of a significant work of the Spirit of God in this woman's heart. So, in your desire for righteousness, do the same. Even in the face of discouragement, persevere, and you will eventually find satisfaction. Many have had promising beginnings but have been deterred by discouragement. Therefore, strive to overcome obstacles as best as you can. An illustrative story can be found in the Book of Kings. During a severe famine in Samaria, the prophet prophesied that the price of grain would significantly decrease the next day. The captain expressed doubt, saying that even if God were to open the windows of heaven, it would not be possible. However, the prophet assured him that he would witness it but not partake in it. When the time came, the people sought the grain so desperately to satisfy their hunger that they trampled the captain, who was second to the king, to the ground. This was due to their earnest desire for sustenance. Similarly, a soul that is famished for righteousness will trample over anything in its path and be willing to part with anything to further the grace of God within it. This is akin to the poor people in Egypt who lacked grain and were famished. They brought their money to Joseph to buy grain, then their livestock, and eventually, they sold their lands and possessions to satisfy their hunger. Finally, they sold themselves as bond-slaves to Pharaoh, all to obtain grain and alleviate their hunger. Nothing stood in their way as long as their hunger was satisfied. This illustrates how the soul will overcome any obstacle and be willing to part with anything to advance the grace of God within. And that concludes the rules to be observed in our hungering and thirsting after righteousness.

The next thing is to show what can sustain the hearts of those who hunger and thirst for righteousness but do not see themselves growing righteous.

Firstly, consider that even the slightest degree of grace is as true and certain an earnest of eternal life as the greatest degree. Some may misuse this concept from the Word, but do not let that cause you to forfeit your portion. If your soul experiences such a longing for righteousness, even if you do not possess the righteousness you desire, take comfort in knowing that the smallest measure of true grace, the tiniest seed (which must exist in a soul that possesses such a desire), is as genuine and secure an earnest of eternal life as the greatest measure. I do not say this so that you may settle for any degree of grace, for it is base to say, "Why do I need more?" I speak to those whose hearts are upright and will not misuse this truth. It is called the earnest of the Spirit, and just as a person in a transaction can bind the deal with a small sum of money, such as twelve pence, as effectively as with twenty shillings, so it is here. Although it is true that where there is little grace, there cannot be as much honour to God as where there is abundant grace, the smallest measure of grace seals the deal with God for eternal life, making it as certain for you as if you possessed as much grace as Abraham, Isaac, and Jacob. Perhaps, because you have only a little, you may not fully recognize it or have assurance in your conscience, but it is as certain with God. You are just as certainly translated from death to life, even if you have the smallest degree of grace.

Secondly, where there are genuine desires, the Lord views your imperfections not as your own, but as the sin that dwells in you. This is what the Apostle meant when he said, "It is no longer I" when I express powerful desires for grace and encounter strong corruptions. It is no longer I, but sin that dwells in me. Therefore, to the soul strong in its desires for grace, even though many imperfections remain, the Lord does not view your imperfections as primarily yours, but as sin in you. There is a twofold self, as it were: a corrupt self and a self of grace. The Lord does not charge the remnants of sin in the soul that possesses sincere desires for His grace as heavily as He does with the corruptions in the ungodly. Scripture affirms that the Lord hates the workers of iniquity, but the sin within the souls of the ungodly makes them the objects of God's wrath and hatred. However, the remaining unrighteousness within the saints, though it is their sickness (for that is how the soul in this situation perceives the remaining corruptions within it), does not make their souls objects of God's wrath, but rather objects of His pity and compassion. Consider this distinction between the remaining sin in the saints and the corruptions in the ungodly. The unrighteousness that remains is the sickness of the soul, and the bowels of God's compassion are towards His sick children just as they are towards His strong children. Let me present this to you: Suppose you have a child who is weak but eager to do whatever you ask of him. This child has entered a room and the door has been shut behind him, so he believes no one can see him. Perhaps you look through a keyhole and observe what the child is doing. He is crying and lamenting, saying, "Oh, how wayward I am! I wish I could please my father and mother more. How little I am capable of doing for them. I long to show greater obedience and walk before them in a manner that is never undutiful again. That would be the happiness of my life if I were never undutiful to my father and mother again." Imagine if you were to witness your child bemoaning himself because he cannot improve and desiring to live in a more obedient manner. Would not your heart ache for such a child? You know the child does not believe you can see him, but by chance, you catch a glimpse. Would not your heart yearn for him then? Know that God is a compassionate Father. Why do you possess such compassion for your children? Is it not a drop from the infinite compassion found in God? When you are alone and lamenting that you cannot live more honourably for God, if you could, you would consider your life happy. Know that God hears all this. God looks upon you and observes it all. Surely, God will not cast away someone who has a heart that hungers and thirsts after what is acceptable to Him. The Scripture compares Christ to a shepherd and believers to sheep. He says, "My sheep hear My voice." This expression derives from the practice of shepherds in certain countries, where sheep are accustomed to responding to the voice of their shepherd. When the shepherd calls, the sheep follow him (similar to calling a dog). Suppose when the shepherd arrives, a large portion of the flock responds and follows the shepherd's call, but there are one or two sheep entangled in thorns. They struggle and strive to break free but find themselves unable. They recognize the shepherd's voice and desire to follow him, but they realize they cannot. Thus, they begin bleating and crying after the shepherd until he takes notice of them. When the shepherd arrives at the spot and sees the poor sheep laboring to follow him, will he not have compassion for this sheep and untangle it from the thorns? This is the situation of poor, weak Christians who find themselves entangled in the thorns of some corruption or ensnared by a heart ailment. Christ calls to the soul, and the soul recognizes His voice, loving Him and desiring to follow Him. The soul tugs and strives, but it has become trapped. Yet, Christ hears the voice of this sheep and comes to its aid.

He observes how it longs to follow Him and pities this poor sheep. Eventually, He rescues it from the thorns and cares for it as much as He does for any other sheep. If this is your condition, even if grace has not yet arrived, you can find comfort in your desire and derive comfort from this very passage: "Blessed are those who hunger and thirst for righteousness, for they shall be satisfied."

# SERMON XXI

## Considerations to support the hearts of those who hunger for righteousness but lack growth in righteousness

"Blessed are those who hunger and thirst for righteousness, for they shall be filled." - Matthew 5:6

The fourth thing to support souls seeking after grace through means but unable to find that they have obtained it is this: Consider that conquering the will of a sinner is a significant work of God upon the soul, and it is a work that God accepts. When God conquers the will, the major work is done. The will is the central driving force of the soul, and when it turns, all the lesser wheels and components of the soul also move. The great difficulty in bringing a soul to eternal life lies in conquering the will. The inferior affections are easily influenced and compelled to obey once the will is overcome. The understanding can be compelled to acknowledge the truth when it is revealed, and the affections will embrace and obey the truth when the will is surrendered to it. However, the will presents the greatest hindrance. The challenge lies in gaining control of the will and bringing it into submission to God. It is a greater work for the will to be conquered and surrendered to God than for a person to accomplish what God requires. God values the gaining of the will's obedience more than the ability to perform the desired actions. We might think that if we could only perform the desired actions, we would be happy and accepted. But take comfort in knowing that God accepts the will, along with the desire to obey Him, as if you were able to do the deeds to the fullest extent of your desire. In 2 Corinthians 8:10, the Apostle commends the believers not only for their willingness to act but also for their eagerness to do so a year ago. He praises their willingness to fulfill God's will even before they had the ability to do it. The will was present long before they had the ability. The Apostle commends them more for having the will to obey God's mind than for merely doing it to the best of their ability. You hunger for God, desiring communion with Him. You want to serve and honor Him to the utmost. You would consider it a great privilege if the Lord enabled you to pray and sanctify His name like other saints. However, you cannot achieve what you desire. Know that God is as honored by your willing heart as if you were able to fully accomplish your desires. This is more significant than if you could do the deeds. Hypocrites can perform any external act of obedience, yet their wills are never brought into obedience to the truth. Therefore, let this be a great source of support for our souls when we find our wills brought into submission. Even if we lack the power to act, we are weak and have many failings, and we cannot do what we desire—we wish to be more obedient, to pray better—know that God has the better part of us. He has obtained the best part of us, which is what He values the most. Consider the gaining of your will as the most valuable part and value it more than any other service you are capable of. Many people think the will is insignificant but would perform better if they could. They do not understand the significance of changing the will. It is the most difficult work of all—gaining control of the will of a sinful soul and bringing it into obedience to the truth.

Fifthly, know for your further comfort that where there is even the slightest degree of grace, there will be growth. Where true seed is sown, God's blessing is upon it. God, who has begun His good work, will bring it to completion in His appointed time. God never initiates a work and leaves it unfinished. He always perfects His own works. Just as God is perfect in Himself, whatever work He undertakes on the soul, He completes perfectly. Although grace may be weak and feeble at first, know that God will continue to perfect the work He has begun. When you find yourself desiring good and longing for righteousness but unable to do as you wish—when your desires surpass your ability—reason this way: God is making you see the vanity of your own heart, the easiness with which you thought you could overcome corruption and the insignificance of standing against temptation. Hereby, you are convinced of your own folly and vanity. Be at peace and submit to God's dealings in this matter. Do not interpret God's dealings as intending harm. Instead of harboring harsh and negative interpretations of God's dealings, we should use such dispensations for our good. Conclude that the Lord, by keeping you low and in a sad condition, intends to elevate you to higher glory and prepare you for greater comfort. He keeps you low and in a sad condition to keep your heart aware of its former vanity and to reveal the excellence of His grace. Therefore, do not conclude that God has forsaken you or that you will never obtain the righteousness of Jesus Christ simply because you cannot find that you have obtained it upon seeking. No, reason this way: God intends to humble me, not to abandon me.

In conclusion, consider for your support when, after a long time of seeking through means, you do not find that God reveals Himself to you and satisfies you with the assurance of grace and the righteousness of Jesus Christ. Consider this: God intends for the work of righteousness to appear in your humbling and abasement rather than giving you power over your corruptions. It is God's design in this matter, and you should interpret His dealings with you in that way. God has various ways of working His grace, and in keeping you humble and low, grace is exercised. You should say, "Is this God's will, to keep me in darkness and uncertainty about my condition, so that I may walk cautiously? It is good that the Lord's will be done." You should believe in God in this condition as much as if you had tangible apprehensions of your interest in righteousness. Sometimes we expect righteousness to bring us joy, growth, and comfort. When it works in that way, we have good hope, and we think our peace with God is secured. But if God chooses to work it in self-abasement, humbling the soul and causing spiritual dejection, it is still a manifestation of the truth of righteousness in the heart, as valid as the highest raptures and elevations of joy. Therefore, find peace in this understanding. It is a mercy that the work of God is upon you in any way. There was a time when we did not care for anything of God, when our hearts were turned against Him, and we focused on worldly things. But now the Lord has started His work. Even if it is still in the stage of humiliation and downward growth, bless God for it, and know that you can never be thankful enough for this mercy. When the work of grace operates in self-abasement, it is as certain evidence of the truth of righteousness in you as the greatest elevations and raptures of joy. This concludes the second point in the first use.

Now, there is only one more thing remaining: to rebuke and reprove those who do not hunger and thirst after righteousness in this way. Many will say, "This is an excellent point, and blessed be God, we do hunger and thirst after righteousness. Although we can do little, we can claim that our desires are good." But beware of deceiving yourselves with these desires, for many desire but their desires will never lead to any good. I have already explained the desires that demonstrate a soul truly hungering and thirsting after righteousness. Now, I will add some reproof by discussing false desires.

First, those who see no excellence in grace should be reproved, as they do not truly desire it. How can you claim to desire something you see no value in? Are there not many among you who, like those in Job 14:21, say to God, "Depart from us, for we do not desire the knowledge of Your Law"? Such people are wicked, but you may argue, "Surely, none of us are so vile and wicked as to dare to bid the Almighty depart from us." Although few may say it explicitly, many secretly hold this sentiment in their hearts. What do your statements mean, then? Are they not to the effect of questioning the need for so many means, so much preaching, and such reformation? Can we not follow the old ways we were taught? These new ways are unfamiliar to us, and we have never heard such talk about government, worship, and the strictness of the ways to Heaven as you tell us. Can we not do as others do and still be saved? In the past, attending to the Word was seen as dishonorable, and those who did so were ridiculed and labeled as Puritans. But now, it is seen as dishonorable not to come to the Word. Oh, how things have changed among people! Yet, for most, the preaching of the Word seems dull and uninspiring. They prefer the fullness of worldly things, saying, "Let us have all the creature comforts. Let righteousness go wherever it pleases." There is a dog-like appetite in people for the things of the world; they always crave more. Just like a dog, even if you give it as much as you can, it still desires more. Similarly, people long for the things of the world, and their appetites continually yearn for them.

But you may argue, "We pray to God, go to church, hear the Word. What more should we do? We live peacefully and morally, and we harm no one. Surely, this will lead us to Heaven." Such individuals believe they possess enough righteousness and see no need for the glorious and excellent righteousness of Jesus Christ. However, those who truly understand righteousness desire it more and more. They are never satisfied with any righteousness other than that, and they are not content with any degree of righteousness they have attained.

Second, let's address the matter more directly. The second group to be reproved are those who content themselves with desires and believe that once they have desires, their work is complete, and they need not go any further. They acknowledge that having desires is commendable, but beware—your desires may be false. Many desire, but their desires are cold and lackluster, offering them no benefit. Therefore, false desires can be identified by certain characteristics.

Firstly, desires are false when they are satisfied with ignorant desires. Has God enlightened your heart to see the excellence of grace, that it is more valuable than rubies and worth more than the Gold of Ophir? Has God revealed to you the need for grace and your desperate condition without righteousness? If not, then your desires are false. Many have a false appetite, like sick people who think they could eat food, but when it is brought to them, they cannot consume it because their stomachs fail them. Similarly, some desire righteousness and see its worth, but when God, through the preaching of His Word, presents grace to them, they have no interest. How often has God moved you by His Spirit, and you have refused to listen? Although you claim to desire with all your soul, when God offers it to you, you have no desire. If your desires were genuine, they would be constant. But your desires are not sincere; they are a false appetite because they are not unwavering.

Secondly, false desires are those that content themselves with foolish desires. It is when people desire the end but not the means. They want to be happy but are unwilling to use the means that lead to happiness. Would we not consider a person foolish if they desired food, saying, "Oh, I wish I had something to eat, bread or meat," but made no effort to obtain it? They would not seek it or make any effort to acquire it. Similarly, some desire grace but do not make use of all the means or ask God to bless the means for their spiritual progress. Can you honestly say that, in the presence of God, you have used every means prescribed in His Word to attain what you desire? Have you missed no opportunity to engage in the means that can advance you towards your goal? If you can truly say this, then you can find comfort knowing your desires are sincere. But if your desires are great, yet your efforts are lacking and you do not make use of all the means available, do not delude yourself—your desires are not genuine.

Thirdly, false desires are those that are absurd. They desire grace but continue to live in a manner that is completely contrary to grace, inconsistent with it. They want grace and righteousness, yet they also desire their lusts. They desire righteousness but take pleasure in unrighteousness. How can you claim to desire righteousness in such a case? You may argue, "Is there not some unrighteousness in even the best? Don't they have weaknesses and sin like others, especially those who make great professions?" Although there may be unrighteousness in the best, they do not take pleasure in unrighteousness. Taking pleasure in unrighteousness cannot coexist with a genuine desire for righteousness. Therefore, desires that are so absurd as to desire grace but also desire that which is inconsistent with grace are not genuine.

Fourthly, false desires are satisfied with weak and feeble desires. These desires remain as mere wishes and daydreams. Individuals could wish for grace, righteousness, and deliverance from future wrath. However, they are not resolute enough to say, "I must have it or I will perish." Such wishes do not lead to any growth. A person who desires grace for its own sake is determined—they must have it. It is like a hungry person who is on the brink of starvation, saying, "Give me bread, or I will die. Give me food, or I will perish." In the same way, the soul cries out, "Give me grace, let me have Christ, or I am eternally lost. What good is it to have abundance in this world but lack grace?" Such feeble desires are like little sprigs that emerge from the body or root of a tree. They do not bear fruit but harm the tree by drawing sap from the root and hindering fruit-bearing. Similarly, desires and wishes like these will never satisfy God, nor will they ever satisfy your own conscience.

Fifthly, false desires are conditional desires. These desires are based on conditions. They want grace and holiness, but only to the extent that it aligns with their own ends and designs. They want to preserve their wealth, freedom, comfort, and reputation in the world. They will accept righteousness as long as it does not interfere with their goals. They like the ways of holiness only if it suits their purposes. But if desires were genuine, they would be resolute, saying, "Let me have grace on any terms. Grace alone can make me happy. Whatever happens to me, let me have grace. Even if I perish or endure great hardship, as long as I have grace, it will make up for everything. I am willing to let go of anything if I can have grace, for it will bring me true happiness."

Sixthly, when men's desires are fleeting and inconsistent desires, they only desire in certain moods and moments of conscience when they are overwhelmed by the terrors of God. But such desires are hypocritical. They desire grace merely to serve their own needs, to silence their conscience, not out of a genuine appreciation for grace. They do not see the excellence of grace that would cause them to desire it, but rather seek it for the relief of their troubled conscience and to quiet their restless spirits.

Seventhly, when their desires are lazy desires, those desires are false. They are unwilling to make efforts to obtain what they desire. The Scripture is striking and, indeed, terrifying in Proverbs 21:25: "The desire of the slothful kills him, for his hands refuse to labour." I fear that this verse may prove to be truly dreadful for many. Their desires, though directed towards what is good, remain stagnant, and they trust in them, thinking they have the work of grace in their hearts when, in truth, it is not so. They deceive themselves in this crucial matter. In Proverbs 13:4, the sluggard's soul desires but gains nothing. They desire what is good, yet have nothing. They are like the women mentioned by the Apostle in Timothy, always learning but never coming to the knowledge of the truth. They have lazy desires that do not prompt them to action. Many will one day bear the weight of these neglected and overlooked matters upon their consciences.

But you may ask, "What should we do? We do what we can. We cannot do more. We do our best." It is well if you truly do so. Let me present two or three things for your consideration. Beware of the danger in making this plea.

First, you claim to do what you can. Will it be proven true in the end? Can you enter the presence of God and honestly say, "Lord, I have done everything in my power. I have utilized all means to attain grace, and I cannot find it. I do not know of any other means to employ. Lord, I have done what I can"? Go into the presence of God and examine your hearts honestly. See if you have truly done your utmost. Can you say that when you wake up in the morning, you arise with a spiritual heart? Do you go to prayer to seek God for yourself and your family? Yet, even then, you cannot find your heart as you desire. You pray for the Lord to keep your heart close to Him, and after prayer, you watch over your heart, thoughts, words, and actions, ensuring they are holy and aligned with the rule. Can you say that you have done this? Can you say it to God? Perhaps you can say it to others and easily convince them, but can you tell God that you have done so from morning until evening? How delightful your life would be if you were truly earnest in this pursuit! How peacefully you would sleep at night after diligently guarding your own heart! Despite your weaknesses and failings, you could find solace in knowing that your heart has been sincere. Many never think of God throughout their lives. Do you do what you can when you never consider God? They use this plea, saying, "What can we do without the grace of God?" Yet, be aware that God gives you some common grace that would enable you to do more than you currently do, but you do not exert the strength that common grace offers. Beware of making this plea, as God may hold you accountable.

Secondly, suppose God were to hold you to your word, to this plea, and say, "Sinner, do you dare to gamble your eternal destiny on this plea? You claim to do what you can, and if I cannot convince you that you could do more, I will concede that you have done what you can. But if you have not done what you can, you will fail, and your eternal fate will rest upon this plea. Do you have the audacity to stand by such a plea in times of sickness? You realize you could have done more, and you cry out, 'I could have done more. I could have had greater communion with God, a closer relationship with the saints.' Now, what your conscience tells you in sickness, you could have done in health, and you can do it, as sickness does not grant any power to act but awakens individuals to realize what they were capable of. When people approach their sickbeds or face death, they recognize that they could have done more for God and lived in greater holiness during their time of health."

Thirdly, to convince you that you are not doing what you can, consider this: What do you think a damned soul in hell would do if God commanded them to go and make the most of their time? Based on their use of that time, they would either return to hell or come to heaven. Do you believe such a person would neglect any opportunity? Do you think they would not act? The torments of hell do not provide people with newfound strength, but they convince them that they could have done more. I could mention many more points, but these should be enough to convince you that you are not doing what you can. Therefore, we are to be reproved if we make this plea. But blessed are those who hunger and thirst after righteousness, for they shall be filled. And thus, I have completed the longest of the Beatitudes, which contained the most material.

Verse 7: Blessed are the merciful, for they shall receive mercy.

In this Beatitude, we witness a beautiful connection with the preceding verse: "Blessed are those who hunger and thirst for righteousness, for they shall be satisfied." And now, "Blessed are the merciful." You desire mercy, says Christ, and that is a compelling argument for you. You long to partake in mercy, but do you also desire righteousness? Do you yearn for a share in the righteousness of Jesus Christ and for God's mercy to pardon your sins? And are you merciful? Nothing fills the soul with more mercy than the realization that our sins are forgiven through the righteousness of Jesus Christ. This understanding stirs compassion within us. There are many reasons that may urge a person towards kindness and pity, but none is more persuasive for the soul to embrace mercy than knowing that it has received mercy through the righteousness of Jesus Christ. Those who are acquainted with the righteousness of Christ and the righteousness of inherent grace desire others to experience the mercy of God as they have. If you hunger and thirst for righteousness and show mercy, then you are blessed, for the merciful shall receive mercy.

But who is this merciful person? What kind of individual is he? In general, mercy can be described as follows: It is a grace from God by which the soul genuinely grieves over the miseries of others and earnestly desires to help and relieve them according to its ability. Mercy has misery as its object. Just as an envious person envies the prosperity of others, I, as a merciful person, have compassion and pity for the misery of others. For my part, I thank God for my comfortable circumstances, for I lack nothing and have everything my heart desires. However, the saints around me are in distress. Oh, how I wish I could assist those who are suffering! The miseries of others evoke sensitivity and compassion in the hearts of the merciful saints.

Now, you may ask, what distinguishes the mercy of a truly gracious person from the mercy of others, such as the Papists and the Heathens who also display mercy and compassion? In the general description of mercy I provided, I mentioned that it is a grace of God's Spirit that compels a person's mercy towards those in distress.

# SERMON XXII

## The Various Workings of Mercy in the Heart

"Blessed are the merciful, for they shall obtain mercy." - Matthew 5:7

Our task now is to reveal: First, the various workings of mercy in the heart. Secondly, the motives for it. Thirdly, the object of mercy. Fourthly, the gracious manner in which mercy operates. Then, we shall consider the promise made to the merciful, that they shall receive mercy.

Regarding the various workings of mercy in the heart, they are as follows:

1. The initial act of mercy, upon noticing the miseries of others, is to grieve for them. Compassion arises towards those in distress. A merciful person does not disregard or despise the sufferings of others. They do not believe that the miseries of others do not concern them. Instead, they perceive these miseries as personally relevant. Their hearts are deeply moved by the sufferings of others.

2. From this compassion springs a fervent desire to alleviate their suffering. "Oh, if only I knew how to relieve and assist those who are in any

form of distress, be it physical or spiritual!"

3. The heart becomes deeply concerned with finding ways to offer help. It not only wishes and desires to assist but also engages in thoughtful contemplation. The merciful person reflects upon how they can be of help to those in misery. Proverbs 14:22 beautifully captures this: "Mercy and truth shall be to them that devise good." Here, we find a description of the merciful person and the promise of mercy to them. They actively devise good and continuously ponder ways in which they can be instrumental in aiding those in dire circumstances. While a covetous person contemplates how to benefit themselves or make a profitable deal, a merciful person contemplates how they can distribute and do good. This represents the third act of mercy—an earnest and thoughtful consideration.

4. A timely application of mercy follows. The merciful person does not keep their mercy confined to their thoughts alone. Instead, they employ all that they possess for the benefit of those in misery. Whether they possess wealth, talents, friends, physical strength, or even if they are poor and destitute with nothing but their prayers, they find a way to utilize all that they have to assist those in need. A merciful person does not view the good things given to them by God solely for their own enjoyment but as resources to be employed for the public good as much as possible. This constitutes the fourth aspect—an attentive and purposeful implementation.

5. The act of mercy includes being willing to give abundantly for the sake of others. The merciful person is prepared to part with much of what they possess for the betterment of others. They are willing to lend a hand or provide assistance, but most importantly, they are willing to relinquish their possessions. They recognize that their possessions are their own, yet they view them as stewards rather than personal treasures. Consequently, if they perceive that the Lord or their fellow human beings require their possessions, they willingly part with them, guided by the desire to bring glory to God and do good. This exem-

plifies the fifth quality—a readiness to give generously.

6. The merciful person is also inclined to forgive those who have offended them. They possess great compassion in this regard. Even if they witness ingratitude or unworthiness in those who need their mercy, they still extend mercy and overlook their shortcomings.

7. Mercy tempers justice temporarily. While it does not obstruct justice from eventually receiving its due recognition, mercy intercedes when justice is on the verge of striking its blow. In such instances, mercy, like the mercy of God, pleads, "Lord, spare, spare a little longer." Just as the angel intervened when Abraham raised the knife to sacrifice Isaac, divine mercy pauses justice from fully exerting its power. Similarly, human mercy restrains justice and strives to find alternative solutions where the offender can be spared without compromising justice. It seeks to moderate the consequences of justice to the greatest extent possible.

8. Lastly, mercy impels one to place oneself in the same condition as those who are in distress, whether it be poverty, pain, or any other kind of suffering. Mercy urges one to empathize and identify with the suffering of others. Though they may enjoy comfort and abundance, merciful individuals recognize that these blessings hold little value as long as others endure hardship. They ponder how they would feel if they were in the same predicament and strive to treat others as they would want to be treated. Thus, they embody true mercy. This marks the final quality—a willingness to stand alongside the suffering.

These are the various workings of merciful hearts.

Secondly, when mercy is a product of God's grace and not merely a natural inclination found in unregenerate individuals, mercy arises from gracious motives. When the heart acts mercifully in a gracious manner, it is driven by these motives and sustains its compassionate actions.

Firstly, the soul perceives God as the God of mercy and recognizes the excellence of mercy in God Himself. The vitality of mercy in God touches the depths of His compassion towards His suffering creatures. Thus, if I am a child of God, why should I not also be moved to compassion? Why should there not be a resemblance between myself and the God I profess to be my Father?

Secondly, I myself am in constant need of mercy. I depend on mercy for my daily sustenance, for it is mercy that upholds me and keeps me from the depths of hell. It is mercy that provides for me. Therefore, if I require such mercy to survive, why should I not show mercy towards others?

Thirdly, I not only need mercy, but I have received mercy. The Lord has shown mercy to me—mercy towards my body, mercy towards my soul. I have experienced preemptive mercy, delivering mercy, healing mercy, comforting mercy, and saving mercies of all kinds in times of distress. I have cried out, and the Lord has shown pity and come to my aid. Now, having received such abundant mercy, it is only fitting that I extend mercy towards my brethren.

Fourthly, when the mercy of God stems from grace, it arises from contemplating the mercy of God in Christ. It is not merely recognizing that God is merciful and has shown mercy in general providence, but it involves looking at the mercy of God in Christ—the tender mercies of God in Christ. While a person in a natural state may come to acknowledge and know that God is merciful, a merciful person who perceives God's mercy towards them in Jesus Christ demonstrates genuine mercy. Through Christ, the concentrated beams of God's mercy converge like a burning glass, warming the heart. Just as scattered sunlight brings light, glory, and warmth, the beams of God's mercy in general providence can warm people's hearts and evoke natural compassion. However, when our mercy arises from contemplating the mercy of God in Jesus Christ—a burning glass of mercy—it profoundly warms and enlarges the heart of a merciful person. This represents true mercy, surpassing that of a natural person.

Fifthly, the consideration of my unworthiness also plays a role. I have received mercy, not just ordinary mercy, but mercy in Christ, despite my unworthiness. Why has God made a distinction between me and others? What has caused such disparity that one person is poor while I possess a comfortable estate? Some of you may have arrived in the city with barely anything and have witnessed how God has elevated you to a position of wealth. If the grace of mercy is at work within you, the contemplation of your unworthiness, that God has made a distinction out of free grace and not due to anything in yourselves, greatly expands your capacity for mercy.

Sixthly, further consideration is given to the relationship between those in misery and God. Even if it is a creature, it still bears some relation to God. Every creature, even a brute animal, is a creation of God and thus has a connection to Him as the work of His hands. However, if it is a human being, especially a Christian, or even more so, a saint, the relationship to God is much more significant. For those who are merciful in a gracious manner, this relationship and the individual's state of misery become powerful motivators, moving them with a compassion that surpasses natural pity.

Seventhly, the recognition that through acts of mercy, I will bring honour to God drives me to engage in such compassionate actions. It is not merely about helping those in distress or gaining a good reputation; it is about honouring God through the exercise of mercy. This is what compels my heart.

Lastly, there is an inherent love for the exercise of mercy itself and love for those in misery, regardless of whether they are strangers. This love works within a merciful heart, inspiring them to act with compassion. These are the motives that set a merciful person in motion on the path of mercy.

Regarding the object of mercy, a brief word is necessary (as it was hinted at in the discussion of the relationship between a thing and God). We are called to show mercy.

Firstly, a good person shows mercy even to their beast. Look at your animal and consider that there is not much difference between you and it. You are made from the same material, and God could have made you the vilest creature, like a toad. Therefore, God expects that you treat His creatures, in which He has an interest, with mercy and not cruelty.

Secondly, we are called to show mercy to all of humanity. If you cannot give to a specific individual, at least give to humanity as a whole. Do not allow them to perish, except in certain cases where Scripture dictates that others should perish if they persist obstinately in wickedness. For instance, Scripture states that those who refuse to work should not eat. Or, in the realm of justice, God wills that wicked people perish in their sin. However, apart from those circumstances, unless it is a matter of justice, we should have compassion for wicked individuals when the hand of God brings misery upon them. It is true that a time will come when the saints will be so consumed with love for God that they will no longer feel compassion towards wicked people. They will have no form of compassion for them in the future when it is fully revealed that they are reprobates, and it will be eternally glorious for God to withdraw all mercy from them. But in the present world, we should have pity on them because, although they are presently wicked, we do not know if they may ultimately belong to God and be vessels of His mercy. Even the most wicked blasphemer or morally depraved individual may be set apart by God to be a vessel of mercy, to the glory of His free grace. Therefore, since we do not yet know otherwise, mercy should be extended towards them, with compassion for their souls and bodies.

Thirdly, we are to be especially merciful to those in terms of their souls. Many individuals possess compassionate hearts towards others when they see them in poverty, destitution, and on the brink of starvation. However, some of these compassionate individuals show no concern for the souls of others. True mercy extends towards the soul first and then towards the body.

Fourthly, the object of mercy is such that the less guilt someone has in their misery, the more they should be pitied. For example, when someone falls into misery solely due to God's intervention and not because of their own wickedness, great mercy should be shown to them. I admit that even if people fall into misery due to their own wickedness, they must not be left to perish, except in cases where legal proceedings and justice demand it. However, if their misery is solely caused by the hand of God and not their own wrongdoing, much mercy should be extended to them. For instance, if their estate is swept away by a providential event like a fire or the actions of wicked individuals, and it is not their fault, and they have lived conscientiously, they deserve abundant mercy.

But above all, while we are to do good to everyone, our mercy should be particularly shown to the household of faith, to fellow believers, as God shows the most mercy to them. However, it is sufficient to mention the objects of mercy.

Regarding the gracious manner of showing mercy to those in misery, mercy must possess certain qualities.

Firstly, I must never be so merciful as to go against any principles of justice. There must be a harmonious relationship between the two. Note how they are interconnected. Blessed are those who hunger and thirst for righteousness, which includes not only the righteousness of Christ but also righteousness between individuals. Blessed are the merciful. We must be merciful while still upholding righteousness. Grace involves a blessed blend of the two. Although one vice may be contrary to another, one grace is never contrary to another. Justice and mercy are never opposed to one another. They can coexist in a gracious mixture. I can be a merciful person and still hunger for righteousness to prevail in the world. This should be the primary consideration in the gracious manner of showing mercy.

Secondly, I must be merciful in such a way that it does not harm those to whom I intend to show mercy, or harm others through them. For example, showing mercy to someone in a manner that hardens them in their evil ways is not a gracious act; it is foolish compassion. Similarly, showing mercy to one person in a way that harms others is not righteous. Many times, mercy may be shown to one individual but result in cruelty towards many others. In Psalm 112:5, the Holy Spirit describes a merciful person as one who guides their affairs with discretion. They demonstrate wisdom in their acts of mercy, considering the poor and guiding their affairs with prudence.

Thirdly, in the exercise of mercy, there must be simplicity of heart. Romans 12:8 states, "He who gives, let him do it with simplicity." You may wonder about the meaning of this.

Firstly, I must not have any hidden or selfish motives in my giving. I must do it sincerely and without any ulterior motives. Many people are charitable and perform good deeds, but they have hidden motives that serve their own interests.

Secondly, sincerity means not showing partiality in the way I extend mercy. God expects me to show mercy to one person more than another according to reason, but not to be merciful in a partial manner. This means that even if others are equally in need of my mercy and deserve it just as much, I should not let my personal biases determine the course of my mercy. Doing so would be lacking in sincerity.

Lastly, when we show mercy, we must offer it up to God for acceptance through Jesus Christ. We should present our mercy in Jesus Christ so that it may be accepted by God. We can see a wonderful example of this in Nehemiah, one of the most merciful men mentioned in scripture. Yet, he pleads to be accepted in mercy for the failings he had in showing that mercy. In the text, it says, "Blessed are the merciful, for they shall obtain mercy." They will receive mercy for the shortcomings they may have in their acts of mercy. Therefore, we can see who this merciful person is.

Now, let's explore why this merciful person is blessed. In Proverbs 22:9, it says, "He who has a bountiful eye will be blessed, for he gives of his bread to the poor." Allow me to explain the blessedness of this merciful person in these specific aspects.

Firstly, when God wants to describe a truly godly person, He calls them a merciful person. In Psalm 32:6, it is mentioned that "every one that is godly" will pray to God. In the original text, they are referred to as "kind men." Godly men are often denoted by their kindness. Therefore, wherever we encounter the terms "godly" and "saints" in the Old Testament, they are synonymous with merciful individuals. This indicates that mercy is an essential aspect of godliness. Similarly, in James 3:17, it is mentioned that wisdom from above is "full of mercy and good fruits." Mercy is thus a significant component of righteousness and sanctification.

Secondly, the merciful person is blessed because they possess a quality that is close to God's heart and reveals His excellence and glory. Nothing in a saint is closer to God than the disposition of mercy. God takes pride in His mercy, exalting Himself through it. He is known as the merciful God. In Exodus 25, the mercy seat is elevated above everything else so that it may be seen. Scripture states that God delights in mercy. Therefore, a person who displays a merciful disposition, which is dear to God, is undoubtedly blessed.

Thirdly, the merciful person is blessed because they are recipients of numerous precious promises. While it is impossible to mention all these promises, there are several passages that highlight the blessedness of the merciful person. Proverbs 11:25 states that the generous soul will be made fat, and the one who waters others will also be watered. Psalm 112:9 describes the one who disperses and gives to the poor, stating that their righteousness endures forever, and their horn shall be exalted with honor. In 2 Corinthians 9:8, it is declared that God is able to make all grace abound toward the merciful, providing them with sufficiency in all things so that they may abound in every good work. These passages demonstrate the abundance of blessings that await the merciful person.

Fourthly, the merciful person is blessed because they receive the blessings and prayers of those in misery whom they have helped. The blessings of the poor are upon the merciful person. Their prayers are heard, and they are praised by the widows whose hearts sing for joy due to their generosity. Job 29:13 states, "The blessing of him who was ready to perish came upon me, and I caused the widow's heart to sing for joy." The merciful person is esteemed by those they have aided, who bless God for sending such a person to assist them in their distress. In the text, it is mentioned that they shall obtain mercy, which is a unique privilege. Even if we had no other scriptural encouragement for this duty, the promise of obtaining mercy alone should suffice. We may fear that by showing mercy, we may end up in need ourselves, becoming impoverished. However, in Proverbs 11:25, it is stated, "The generous soul will be made fat." This expression may seem paradoxical, as we often believe that one becomes fat by being stingy. Yet, Scripture assures us that the generous person will be enriched. Showing mercy results in not only receiving mercy but also having our own needs abundantly supplied.

Fifthly, all the good we possess originates from God's mercy. There is no goodness that we enjoy in any creature that does not stem from God's mercy. God says, "You have a merciful disposition. Are you merciful? Do you do good to others? Do you have compassion for those in distress? Are you in need yourself? Here is My mercy to help you, here is My mercy to pardon you." It is noteworthy that God works in those whom He intends to save so that they become like Him. They undergo a transformation that aligns them with God's will in all things. For example, those whom God has elected for glory will choose Him in due time. Those whom God intends to justify through Jesus Christ will justify Him and His ways. Those whom God has separated for future glory will be separated from the world in the present. And those whom God intends to show mercy to will possess merciful dispositions. If God has given you a merciful heart, you can be assured that God will show mercy to you in the end. Therefore, blessed are the merciful, for they will obtain mercy. They will receive forgiveness for their sins and be blessed in their souls. This promise is fruitful and blessed, for we all need mercy in our distress. None of us who enjoy the comforts of this world are exempt from the need for mercy. When we find ourselves in a condition where we require mercy, we can be sure that God will extend His mercy to us because He has instilled merciful dispositions within us towards those in misery.

Sixthly, in this very aspect, you have a powerful encouragement and help for your faith. Mercy is your own disposition, so you can rely on God's mercy without presuming. When you, with a merciful and loving disposition, extend your kindness to the saints in their distress, it is not presumptuous for you to rely on God's mercy in your own difficulties. When you are about to believe, what stumbling block lies in your way? A poor soul might ask, "Can a wretched creature like me receive mercy from God? Will the Lord ever look upon me?" Lord, you may answer as follows: "You have instilled in me a disposition to show mercy to those in misery. If there is but a single drop of mercy in me to extend compassion to others, is there not an infinite ocean of mercy in you, Lord? Is it not much easier for you to show mercy to me when, through that small drop of mercy within me, you have already touched my heart with mercy towards others?" This perspective serves as a powerful aid against temptations and discouragements when embracing God's mercy. The mercy we possess is merely a drop from the fountain that is in God. Our mercy, if it is genuine and spiritual (as described earlier), is an effect and fruit of the mercy that resides in God Himself. Lord, it is easier for you to show mercy to my soul than for me to show pity to those in misery. Lord, the misery in others demands more from us to alleviate, compared to your Majesty relieving us. Lord, in showing mercy, you lose nothing, for your mercy is infinite, and you lose nothing. On the other hand, when we show mercy, we give something of ourselves, even though it is what we receive from God. Therefore, it is easier for God to show mercy.

Lastly, consider that nothing keeps people in bondage and the terrors of conscience for sin longer than their unyielding disposition towards those in misery. Therefore, blessed are those who are merciful and possess a gentle disposition, for this will be a means to alleviate the inward throbs and terrors of conscience. We often draw conclusions such as, "Surely the Lord will never be merciful to me. How can God show mercy to such a wretch as I am? I am so stubborn and hard-hearted that I cannot show mercy or forgive those in misery. How then can the Lord forgive me, who has wronged Him more than anyone has wronged me, and yet I cannot forgive them or let go of those wrongs?" But you, with a merciful heart, may think as follows: "Lord, must I have a heart to forgive seven times, yes, seventy times seven? And Lord, can't You do much more for me? Must I forgive my brother seventy times seven times in a day if he offends me? Can't You forgive much more? This is a great help to faith and prayer, that the Lord would show mercy to us in our difficulties and provide help in times of trouble." Psalm 112:6-7 states, "Surely he shall not be moved forever. The righteous will be in everlasting remembrance. He shall not be afraid of evil tidings; his heart is steadfast, trusting in the Lord." Whatever circumstances may arise, the merciful person will not fear them. The days may be dark and troubles may loom large, but the merciful person will not be afraid. Evil tidings will not frighten the merciful person. There is a famous passage in Isaiah 58:7-8 that describes the manner of fasting, both negatively and positively. It shows what they did in their false humiliations and then proceeds to say that if they do certain things, "Then your light shall break forth like the morning, your healing shall spring forth speedily, and your righteousness shall go before you; the glory of the Lord shall be your rear guard. Then you shall call, and the Lord will answer; you shall cry, and He will say, 'Here I am.'" God will respond, saying, "Listen, a merciful person cries out! There is someone in distress calling out to Me. I must come down and listen to this person's request. I must go and see what the matter is. A merciful person is crying out." God will say, "Here I am. Call upon Me. What do you need?" It is a merciful person who cries out, and God will respond, saying, "Here I am." Verse 10 states, "Then your light shall dawn in the darkness, and your darkness shall be as the noonday." Verse 11 continues, "The Lord will guide you continually, and satisfy your soul in drought, and strengthen your bones; you shall be like a watered garden, and like a spring of water, whose waters do not fail." If you complain about spiritual deadness and barrenness, the reason may be that you have a harsh and cruel disposition. However, the merciful can go to God and plead their case, saying, "Lord, I showed mercy to my brethren in their distress, and my mercy was in obedience to Your command. Therefore, Lord, hear me."

To make an application of this point:

First, there is an abundance of comfort for those who possess merciful spirits. Whoever you are, wherever you may be (although I fear there are but few, like gleanings after the vintage, scattered even in large assemblies), listen to your consolation. Has the Lord stirred your hearts to empathize with the sorrows of the saints abroad, even while you have plenty at home? Have you experienced bondage alongside them, and have your own comforts lost some of their sweetness because the Church and the people of God have been in such dire straits? If this is the case, take comfort.

Firstly, you excel in what is God's excellence, and this is a great virtue. It is the best service you can render. You may complain about your inability to pray, feeling disquieted and burdened by your spiritual deadness, dullness, and lack of inclination. But if you have a merciful heart, know that it is most pleasing to God. In Micah 6:4-5, the people ask, "With what shall I come before the Lord, and bow myself before the High God? Shall I come before Him with burnt offerings, with calves a year old? Will the Lord be pleased with thousands of rams, ten thousand rivers of oil? Shall I give my firstborn for my transgression, the fruit of my body for the sin of my soul?" God responds, saying, "No, I do not require any of these offerings. I only require you to do justice and love mercy." Therefore, you can boldly approach God with these qualities. Perhaps you cannot bring rivers of oil or eloquently express yourself, but if you bring a heart that loves mercy, you possess something that God delights in.

Secondly, having a merciful heart is a sure sign of your election unto mercy. Colossians 3:12 states, "Therefore, as the elect of God, holy and beloved, put on tender mercies." God enables you to have the means to help those in distress. It is more important to have a heart that shows mercy than to have the resources to do so. It is a greater mercy for God to make you willing to show mercy than if you possessed wealth but lacked the willingness to show mercy. Therefore, where do you place your riches? Do you consider it wealth to have control over the world and hold positions of power? If this is your happiness, be aware that you have little evidence of your soul's election. But if you are truly filled with grace, you will say, "Lord, I thank You for my possessions, talents, and riches, but more than anything, I bless You for giving me a compassionate heart to pity those in distress. I am grateful that You have granted me a heart to show mercy to the miserable. I also thank You that I can serve You better with my wealth compared to those who lack such resources. I value my estate because it allows me to be more serviceable to God than others. This is a clear sign of true grace."

Thirdly, you can expect an expanded heart in prayer with comfort. Many times, you complain about your constricted and lifeless heart. Could the cause of this be your cruelty towards others? When you face affliction, the Lord will remember your desire to pray better. In James 2:13, it is written, "For judgment is without mercy to the one who has shown no mercy. Mercy triumphs over judgment." Although you may have read this Scripture many times, perhaps you have not fully understood its meaning, or it has been misinterpreted. Many believe this Scripture refers to God's mercy prevailing over the judgment of the law and condemnation. However, I understand it differently. When judgments are executed upon a kingdom or families, the mercy shown to the afflicted will cry out, and the Lord will hear the cries of mercy during times of judgment. The mercy they extended to others will plead on their behalf. Regardless of the judgments that may come, that soul can confidently say that the Lord intends mercy for them. The merciful person will be delivered. Even if there is a storm in the land and misery abounds, the Lord will remember that person's acts of mercy towards the afflicted. The merciful person can rejoice amidst judgment, as they are above judgment. The Lord has revealed Himself to them by instilling a merciful disposition, and thus, they need not fear judgment. Their mercy will speak for them, preventing judgment from taking hold. Therefore, blessed are the merciful, for they shall obtain mercy. In times of trouble, the merciful person will triumph and boast over judgment. Judgment will not prevail because their acts of mercy will be remembered in their time of distress.

# SERMON XXIII

## Comforts to those that are of merciful spirits

"Blessed are the merciful, for they shall receive mercy." - Matthew 5:7

K now that this is a significant proof that you truly hunger and thirst for righteousness. Therefore, Christ joins it with the statement, "Blessed are those who hunger and thirst for righteousness, for they shall be filled." Blessed are the merciful, for they shall receive mercy. You may think that your heart desires righteousness, and God knows that you can appeal to Him, testifying that you indeed hunger and thirst for righteousness. But at times, you may doubt the genuineness of your hunger and thirst. Here is a rule: Do you possess a merciful heart towards others? While you hunger for God's righteousness, does your soul also desire the well-being of others? Do you seek to do them good, both physically and spiritually? This is evidence of the truthfulness of your hunger for righteousness. However, if you take pleasure in having a desire for righteousness while harboring a cruel and unmerciful heart towards others, your hunger for righteousness is flawed. These two qualities are intertwined and cannot be separated. Blessed are those who hunger and thirst for righteousness;

blessed are the merciful. Unmerciful individuals do not genuinely desire grace. This paves the way for addressing the second part of the application. Whatever encouragement could be further discussed, we shall incorporate it into the exhortation.

Therefore, secondly, there is a reprimand for unmerciful individuals, those whose hearts remain unaffected by the miseries of others and have no concern for their well-being as long as they find contentment for themselves. Some of you may regard this topic as a common and merely moral point. I do not know what weight you assign to it, but I have found, and you may also find it if you examine the Scriptures, that mercy is not only emphasized in the Old Testament but also in the New. Christ places significant importance on mercy, second only to faith itself. Consider these three key aspects: faith, mercy towards others, and unity among believers. These are the three fundamental aspects that the Gospel emphasizes the most. I know of no other point that is as extensively covered in Scripture as mercy, and this particularly in the context of the Gospel. Many religious professors underestimate the significance of mercy, viewing it as an ordinary matter. As a result, they lack the conscientiousness to exercise this grace as they should. However, if you understood the Scriptures, you would recognize that Christ places great value on mercy. "Blessed are the merciful." Therefore, be aware that:

Firstly, an unmerciful heart is wretched and vile. You who care only for yourselves, as long as your tables are filled, your backs are clothed, your houses are furnished, and your children are provided for, regardless of the plight of others—what distinguishes you from them? What makes your flesh superior to theirs, justifying your indifference to their welfare? Oh, wretched and vile heart! Why are you more important than others? It does not matter what happens to them. Such an attitude should be directed towards you. Some people, upon gaining more than others, not only fail to extend their souls to assist others but also regard them with contempt, despising the poor, as mentioned in Proverbs 14:21. They hold those beneath them in disdain, those in a lower social standing or less fortunate condition. "He who despises his neighbor sins, but blessed is he who has mercy on the poor." Beware of such a disposition; God does not look favorably upon it. Moreover, there are those who spend their resources on their own desires rather than on the necessities of the poor. They have more than others and could use their abundance to bless the less fortunate, but instead, they squander it on their own lusts—for the gratification of their appetites or indulging in excess. They are unwilling to freely donate even a small sum for good causes and helping others. They lavish pounds on their unclean and immoral desires, while neglecting the needs of others. They have no conscience when there are numerous divine commands to show mercy and when the excellence of mercy is repeatedly emphasized, declaring the blessedness of the merciful individual. As for you, who possess more than others but allocate it solely to satisfy your lusts, you are an unwise soul. How foolishly you employ your wealth! You could use it in a way that would cause hundreds to bless God because of you. Instead, you use it to accumulate guilt upon your soul. And there are others who, although they may give something, do so begrudgingly, only parting with what is forced from them. There is no freedom, no joy in their acts of charity towards others. If anything is given, they consider it a loss. It is gone. But whatever is consumed by their own appetites or spent on personal vanity—whether in sports, entertainment, or excessive drinking—that is not seen as wasted. They do not appreciate the significance of their distribution to others, viewing it as a squandering. This is an indication of a carnal heart that does not understand the ways of God. If you truly comprehended what is written in Scripture, you would consider the portion of your estate given with a merciful heart for the relief of others as the most valuable part of your wealth. Likewise, there are those who plan to give something to the poor or others upon their death, but during their lifetime, they selfishly live only for themselves. They cannot trust God for anything, and as for promises such as those found in Scripture, they are of no importance to them. These individuals may regard them as mere empty words. I shall address these individuals, those with callous and unkind hearts towards others, those who are entirely self-centered.

Firstly, it is certain that you do not know God, regardless of what you may say about religion. If you possess an unmerciful heart towards others, you are a man or woman who does not know God. I will present this Scripture as evidence: "There is no truth or mercy or knowledge of God in the land" (Hosea 4:1). No mercy and no knowledge of God are mentioned together. Certainly, where there is knowledge of God, there will be mercy. As the Psalmist says, "The dark places of the earth are full of the haunts of cruelty." In dark souls that lack knowledge of God, acts of cruelty abound. You can conclude that anyone with a cruel disposition, a hard-hearted disposition, a stingy and selfish disposition, simply does not know God. If they understood who God is and the abundance of mercy He possesses, if they recognized His delight in mercy and His glory in bestowing goodness upon His creatures, it would be impossible for their hearts to be so ungenerous.

Secondly, God has a significant contention against you. You may argue that you are not obligated to help specific individuals and that there is no evil in not wronging others. However, your lack of mercy is sufficient to provoke the Lord's contention against your soul. In the aforementioned verse, Hosea 4:1, it is written, "The Lord has a contention with the inhabitants of the land because there is no truth or mercy or knowledge of God in the land." God contends with that land, that family, that person who lacks mercy. Can you withstand God's contention?

Thirdly, know that your disposition is entirely contrary to that of God. Therefore, it is a despicable one. No disposition is more opposed to God's disposition than a cruel, harsh, and hard-hearted one. God is mercy itself. Your heavenly Father is merciful. As we discussed earlier, God is the God of mercy. Therefore, your heart possesses a disposition that stands in direct opposition to God. There is a vast difference and opposition between the disposition of God's heart and the disposition of your heart.

Fourthly, a curse rests upon your heart. Undoubtedly, a hard heart is cursed. There are dreadful diseases in the depths of the soul, where the heart is hard, corrupted, devoid of compassion. There is a curse upon such a spirit. No curse could be greater than a hardened heart that is devoid of the fear of God and refuses to do good to others.

Fifthly, there is a curse upon everything you possess. An unmerciful person has no sanctified use of their possessions. You keep your estates and believe they are entirely your own. You may say, "Can't I do whatever I please with what belongs to me? Can't I eat, drink, and indulge myself with my own possessions?" However, your unmercifulness defiles and curses everything you own. In Luke 11:41, there is a peculiar statement: "But give as alms those things that are within, and behold, everything is clean for you." It's an unusual expression, suggesting that without this act of mercy, nothing is clean to a person. Those who do not share what they have but keep everything to themselves find that nothing they possess is clean. In other words, nothing is sanctified; everything is defiled and cursed. Consider the context: in verse 39, the Pharisees were preoccupied with external cleanliness. The Lord told them, "Now you Pharisees cleanse the outside of the cup and of the dish, but inside you are full of greed and wickedness." They were meticulous about cleaning cups, dishes, and other external objects. They focused on ceremonial cleanliness and their own form of superstitious purification. Instead, Christ says, "But give as alms those things that are within, and behold, everything is clean for you." Therefore, if you have been blessed with wealth beyond others, if you have more than what is necessary and can afford some moderate enjoyment, use the remainder to alleviate the suffering of those in need. This is the proper use of the possessions that God has entrusted to you. By doing so, everything in your possession will be sanctified. However, if you possess a base, miserly, and self-centered disposition, keeping everything for yourself, for the sake of pomp, luxury, and personal pleasure, then nothing is clean to you. No matter how grand and splendid your possessions may appear in your house, they are all defiled and cursed. Thus, it is an evil thing to possess an unmerciful heart towards others.

Sixthly, be aware that the suffering of others continually cries out against you. While you are comfortably situated in your home, free from pain, hunger, and trouble, many fatherless children, widows, and Saints who are in dire circumstances cry out to heaven on account of you. They seem to say, "Lord, you have granted such and such individuals great wealth, yet here we are without bread. This suffering is caused by those who have more than enough but are entirely self-centered, preoccupied with satisfying their own desires."

Seventhly, know that not only carnal individuals but also many who profess religious faith are guilty of this. Many of them have callous and cruel hearts. They believe that attending sermons, praying in their families, and perhaps abstaining from worldly defilements are sufficient to please God. They value the ordinances of worship and ceremonial purity. While it is good to focus on these aspects, if you neglect the work of mercy towards those in need while engaging in these practices, all your religious acts are like filth and refuse in the sight of God. God does not care for any acts of religion when an unmerciful heart is present, no matter how diligent you may be in attending sermons, praying, fasting, or participating in any other religious ordinances. Let me provide you with a couple of noteworthy Scriptures to support this. The first is found in James 1:27: "Religion that is pure and undefiled before God the Father is this: to visit orphans and widows in their affliction, and to keep oneself unstained from the world." Here, the Apostle clearly states that pure and undefiled religion consists of visiting orphans and widows in their affliction. If this passage were from the Old Testament, some might argue that it pertains to the legalistic aspects of religion. However, here in the New Testament, the Apostle emphasizes that pure religion encompasses these actions. Those who desire to keep themselves unstained from the world, to be free from defilements in worship, and to have a purer form of religion should pay attention to their involvement in acts of mercy. This is the epitome of pure religion and undefiled before God. We need more individuals who embody this kind of purity, Puritans who genuinely practice mercy and compassion towards others. Another remarkable Scripture that supports this idea is found in Isaiah 58. If you read the various expressions in that chapter, you will find verse 3 to be quite full of meaning. It states, "'Why have we fasted, and you see it not? Why have we humbled ourselves, and you take no knowledge of it?' Behold, in the day of your fast you seek your own pleasure and oppress all your workers." It would be better if we never engaged in such fasts, where the purpose is to pursue personal pleasure and engage in strife and contention. Then, in verse 5, the passage questions whether such a fast is pleasing to the Lord: "Is such the fast that I choose, a day for a person to humble himself? Is it to bow down his head like a reed, and to spread sackcloth and ashes under him? Will you call this a fast, and a day acceptable to the Lord?" Instead, verse 6 provides a clear answer: "Is not this the fast that I choose: to loose the bonds of wickedness, to undo the straps of the yoke, to let the oppressed go free, and to break every yoke?" Moreover, it includes feeding the hungry, providing shelter for the homeless, clothing the naked, and not neglecting your own flesh and blood. We are to regard everyone, even strangers, as our own flesh and blood. Only then will "your light break forth like the dawn." Therefore, in times of fasting, let us focus on this aspect. This is the fast that God requires. Fasting and alms should go hand in hand. The more we fast, the more merciful we should be towards others. Otherwise, our fasting is worthless. Though there are more Scriptures to support this, these two are particularly relevant. They demonstrate that where there is no mercy, everything is rejected. Even our prayers are rejected. Zechariah 7:6 states, "When you fasted and mourned in the fifth month and in the seventh, for these seventy years, was it for me that you fasted?" In verse 10, the Lord speaks, saying, "Execute true justice, show mercy and compassion to one another." You only had yourselves in mind when you fasted and prayed.

Eighthly, if you possess an unmerciful heart, your prayers are not only unaccepted but also act as witnesses against you. When you come before God to pray for mercy, while remaining unmerciful yourself, the Lord will bring your prayers as witnesses against you. He will say, "Behold, here is a cruel, hard-hearted wretch. When given the opportunity, they will exploit others to the fullest extent, allowing them to perish and suffer without any concern. Yet they come to me seeking mercy." Know that during your prayers, the Lord will remember all your cruelty and hardness of heart towards others. This is the evil consequence of your lack of mercy.

Ninthly, you can expect that God will harden others against you. Tenthly, know that this sin of cruelty and hardness of heart towards others is worse than a heathenish sin. Josephus, in his fifteenth book of Antiquities, chapter twelve, tells a notable story about Herod, whom you can read about in the Scriptures. Herod Agrippa, the one who was killed by worms, Josephus speaks of him during a time of widespread famine and calamity. Herod melted all the gold and silver in his possession, even the exquisitely crafted pieces, to make money. He spared nothing for the sake of fashion and craftsmanship. With the proceeds, he bought corn and distributed it to the poor, providing them with work as well. He also gave a significant portion to strangers. Moreover, because the famine was so severe that people didn't even have seed to sow their fields, he not only provided bread but also seed for the next year's harvest. Thus, even wicked Herod, whom we condemn, demonstrated such mercy to those in misery.

But here, it must be acknowledged that the blessed ones are those who are merciful. Indeed, they are blessed if their mercy is graciously extended as an act of faith, offered in the name of Christ. However, Herod's example was primarily an outward display of mercy. Despite being ungodly and reprobate, he showed remarkable compassion towards those in need.

The eleventh point is that the Lord declares unmercifulness as the sin of Sodom and Gomorrah. One of the great charges against Sodom was their lack of mercy. In Ezekiel 16:49, the Lord accuses Sodom of its vile and enormous sins, stating, "Behold, this was the guilt of your sister Sodom: she and her daughters had pride, excess of food, and prosperous ease, but did not aid the poor and needy." This sin was one of the reasons why Sodom was destroyed by fire and brimstone from heaven. Therefore, unmercifulness is undoubtedly a greater evil than we realize. The evil of being unmerciful is worse than we can imagine. Therefore, I beseech you to examine yourselves and be humbled before the Lord for this sin. Every individual with a substantial estate has reason to examine their conscience. You may say to the Lord, "You know that much of my wealth has been wasted on vanity and my own desires. Yet, when it comes to a good cause, I hesitate to give even a small amount, while hundreds of pounds are spent purely on my will and desires." Be humbled for this sin, for the Lord sees it differently than you do. This sin may be the reason God completely forsakes you in times of distress.

But the main point is an exhortation. Since Christ pronounces the merciful as blessed, let us embrace this grace of mercy. Oh, how we need more merciful individuals in these times of crying out for mercy! Sadly, this is also the worst time for hardness of heart and cruelty. Surely, anyone who amasses wealth through base means in these times can expect a curse upon that wealth more than ever before. Therefore, this Scripture is timely. May the Lord imprint it upon your hearts, so that you may depart with it written within you: "Blessed are the merciful, for they shall receive mercy." There have never been such objects of mercy. Many have endured woeful extremities, even for the sake of God, and other saints of God cry out for mercy. We have received mercy ourselves; it is a time of God's mercy toward us. We hear of mercy every day, almost every week. One mercy follows another. This town surrenders, that army is utterly defeated and plundered. We were afraid we would fall into the hands of cruel, bloodthirsty soldiers, but the Lord has delivered us from them. He has magnified His mercy in keeping England and this city alive, preserving our families and our estates to the extent that they have been preserved. It is a time of mercy. The depths of God's mercy are so vast, so tender towards us, that it calls for us to show mercy to our brethren. Let us look around and see nothing but mercy. There are places where they see nothing but signs of God's displeasure, justice, wrath, and misery. But wherever we look, we see mercy.

Even now, as we gather here, we can see one another as objects of God's mercy, having the liberty to exercise and join together in calling upon God, in praying to Him. What mercy is this? And since these times, hasn't God been merciful to your souls, revealing His Gospel and the glorious aspects of eternal life to you? When you return home, what can you see but mercy? Look at your spouse; there's mercy. Look at your children; there's mercy. Look at your table; there's mercy. Look at your servants; there's mercy. Look at your bed; there's mercy. Look at everything in your house; mercy is written upon it. Look at your own body; there's mercy. Take the Bible and read about God's eternal plans for your eternal well-being; there's mercy. A family can kneel down and thank God for preserving and providing all the outward comforts they need. There is nothing but mercy around us. In the midst of such mercy, how can we be unmerciful? All these mercies cry out to you, calling for mercy towards others.

Furthermore, consider the beauty and excellence of mercy. Chrysostom made a remark about mercy, stating that it is more excellent than the ability to raise the dead. Even if God were to grant someone the power to raise the dead, having a heart that is merciful towards those in misery would still be a greater good. We need not rely solely on Chrysostom; the Scriptures themselves contain profound expressions regarding the excellence of mercy. These expressions should cause us to wonder how anyone professing godliness can lack compassion towards those in need. Scripture presents six notable expressions regarding the excellence of this grace.

The first is that it is called the administration of service, the service of God (2 Corinthians 9:12). Many people cling to their traditional liturgy and find it hard that it has been taken away from them. Here, however, you have a liturgy that you can keep, one that is accepted by both God and men. Embrace this liturgy—the works of mercy. It is called God's liturgy, whereas you used to call the liturgy Divine service. Here is a Divine service that you can offer to God. All of you who possess wealth can engage in this Divine service. You may complain to one another, saying, "If only we could have our Divine service back." Well, now you can have it every day, and it will be even more acceptable to God than before—abundantly so. Therefore, since it is gone, make up for it by engaging in this ministry, this liturgy, as the word originally meant.

The second commendation of this grace is that it demonstrates the professed subjection of individuals to the Gospel. Until one's heart becomes merciful towards others, they have not fully submitted themselves in a professing manner to the Gospel. You cannot truly demonstrate a professed subjection to the Gospel until your heart is filled with mercy towards your brethren. This is clearly stated in the same Scripture, 2 Corinthians 9:13, where the relief and mercy towards others are referred to as the professed subjection to the Gospel. Therefore, if you desire to manifest a professing subjection to the Gospel, proclaim that the Gospel has been mercifully revealed to you by the Lord, causing your hearts to turn away from worldly things and extend mercy to those in need. In doing so, you manifest your professing subjection to God's Gospel.

Thirdly, it is called the exceeding grace of God (2 Corinthians 9:14). The Apostle was deeply moved by the fact that God enlarged their hearts in mercy towards others. He referred to it as the exceeding grace of God, surpassing ordinary grace.

The fourth commendation is that it is called the unspeakable gift (2 Corinthians 9:15). The Apostle declares it as the unspeakable gift of God. When God grants you a heart to be merciful to others, you give to them that which God has given you. This is truly an unspeakable gift from God.

The fifth expression from Scripture is this: it is called a sweet smell (Philippians 4:18). If you want your houses to smell sweet, you can achieve it through acts of mercy. It is the best perfume in the world. Even the wealthy use incense to perfume their houses, but if you want your home to smell sweet, perfume it with works of mercy. When you show mercy to others, you have perfumed your houses, your bodies, and your souls. It creates a sweet smell that is pleasing to God.

The sixth expression is that it is an acceptable and pleasing sacrifice to God. There are three aspects to consider. If you want to offer a sacrifice to God, the work of mercy is both a sacrifice and one that is acceptable and pleasing to Him. In 2 Corinthians 9:14, it is referred to as a sacrifice that is acceptable and received by God. So, when you perform acts of mercy, you are offering a sacrifice. The altar on which this sacrifice is offered is the person in misery. In Hebrews 13:16, there is a similar expression stating that acts of mercy are a sacrifice that pleases God. Therefore, when you die, what will bring you more comfort: the realization that you spent so much in a tavern or that you relieved the needs of numerous poor people? Will you reflect on how much you spent on your own desires or on a whore, or will you rejoice that you were a means by which many poor and distressed individuals blessed God because of your acts of mercy? Isn't it better to leave behind a sweet memorial of works of mercy than material possessions? Your acts of mercy will serve as a testimony before God on the day of judgment (Luke 16:9). They won't merit salvation, as the Papists teach, but they will testify on your behalf. As the learned Chemnitius explained, when rich individuals fail and become sick or die, there may be ministers of God who were once poor scholars and were helped by them. These ministers will testify and say, "Lord, I was a poor youth, and if this person hadn't shown mercy and provided me with an education, I would have spent my days in poverty. Through Your mercy, You have made me an instrument of good in Your Church, and this person was a great means of it through their generosity and mercy." This testimony will speak well of them on the day of judgment. Similarly, a poor family may testify, "If it hadn't been for this person, we would have perished and starved. Lord, have mercy on this individual who showed us mercy." Therefore, make friends through your unrighteous wealth, the riches that are often used in unrighteous ways, to sustain people's lusts. The more friends you make in this manner, the Lord will accept you, and you will be received into everlasting habitations. This will be an incredible reward for your acts of mercy. While you may be preoccupied with making your house grand and splendid, consider the possibility of obtaining everlasting habitations. Those who show mercy in a gracious manner have this promise.

Now, let's address some objections that hinder the work of mercy.

Some may say, "I am poor and insignificant." Scripture reveals that even poor people should be merciful. Though you may be able to do very little, do something. Remember the story of the widow's mite, which was accepted more than all the treasures of the rich (2 Corinthians 8:1). The churches in Macedonia, despite their great trials and deep poverty, abounded in generosity.

Others may claim that their wealth is uncertain and that they need to reserve something for themselves. Ecclesiastes 11:1 provides excellent guidance in this regard: "Cast your bread upon the waters, for you will find it after many days." Give to others, even if your wealth is uncertain. The Holy Spirit uses your concerns about uncertain times as an argument in favor of mercy. When troubles come, give even more abundantly, knowing that the works of mercy will bear fruit. Just as the clouds gather rain from the earth and then pour it down, don't keep your wealth to yourself. Instead, pour it out onto the poor, who are in great need. You have accumulated wealth through various means, and now that you are rich, empty yourself for the sake of those who lie upon the earth. When a tree falls, it falls in the direction it leaned while standing. Similarly, the direction your heart inclines will determine your actions. If you are abundant in mercy and good works, that is the direction in which you will fall. So, be found lying in that direction on the day of judgment, in proportion to the state of your heart and your works.

You might argue that you lack suitable objects for your acts of mercy. Ecclesiastes 11:4 provides an answer to this covetousness: "He who observes the wind will not sow, and he who regards the clouds will not reap." If a farmer constantly watches the wind and clouds, afraid that the weather will not be favorable, they will never be able to sow or reap. Likewise, the Holy Spirit advises against scrutinizing the need for mercy and the suitability of the recipient. You might think, "I may give to some who are good and some who are not, and I don't know if any good will come from what I give." But in Ecclesiastes 11:5, the Holy Spirit reminds us that just as we don't know how the spirit moves or how bones grow in the womb, we don't fully understand the works of God, who orchestrates everything. Therefore, do not be discouraged by the apparent lack of results. There are hidden ways in which God's providence works for His purposes and your good. So, continue to do all the good you can. In Ecclesiastes 11:6, it further advises: "In the morning sow your seed, and in the evening withhold not your hand, for you do not know which will prosper, this or that, or whether both alike will be good." Even if you see no immediate results, your acts of mercy may bear fruit in ways you cannot comprehend.

Finally, Hebrews 13:14-16 offers significant insight. It reminds us that we have no permanent city in this world and that we seek one to come. While we have no permanence, we can offer the sacrifice of praise to God continually, which is the fruit of our lips, giving thanks to His name. But in addition to praise, we should not forget to do good and share, for such sacrifices are pleasing to God.

But I may become destitute if I give. Look at Proverbs 28:27: "He who gives to the poor will not lack." Do you dare trust God for your soul's salvation based on His promise, but not trust Him for your body and material possessions? There is no surer path to need than having an unmerciful disposition towards others. The text states that he who gives to the poor will not lack, but he who hides his eyes will face many curses. If you fear scarcity, why not engage God's promise that you will not lack? Scripture provides a way for God to be bound to you: "He who gives to the poor shall not want."

You may argue that your deeds of kindness will be quickly forgotten. No matter how many good things you do, they are soon forgotten. Refer to Hebrews 6:10. Perhaps you have done many good things in secret, which indicates that you do them in faith, fearing they will be forgotten. But fear not, for God is not unjust to forget your work and labor of love shown toward His name, in that you have ministered to the saints and continue to do so. Notice how God engages Himself. Why should God take note of our actions? We can only do what we have received from God. Yet, God binds Himself in this way. It is as if He says, "Are you a merciful person? Do you do good in your community? I would be an unrighteous God if I forget you." God is not unrighteous to forget your labor of love and your work in ministering to the saints. Serve the saints, and God will not forget your labor of love. He is not unrighteous to do so. It is unrighteous of people to forget what you do for them, but God will not be unrighteous to forget your labor of love in ministering to the saints.

You may argue that very few people act in this way and that you do as much as others. Consider Philippians 4:15: "Now you Philippians know also that in the beginning of the gospel, when I departed from Macedonia, no church shared with me concerning giving and receiving but you only." This was a commendation for the Philippians. Despite Paul being such an instrument of God's glory, no church supported his needs except the Philippians. This is a high commendation. If God has given you a merciful heart more than others, do you not consider it a great mercy and blessing? Being rich in good works is greater than being rich in money. This will add to your commendation and bring comfort to you on the day of Christ. Therefore, beware of vain reasoning in your hearts against acts of mercy. Whenever you are called upon to perform acts of mercy, be cautious of those reasonings in your heart that oppose it. Let your vain reasonings be silenced. In Deuteronomy 15:7-8, it is stated: "If there is among you a poor man of your brethren, within any of the gates in your land which the Lord your God is giving you, you shall not harden your heart nor shut your hand from your poor brother. But you shall open your hand wide to him and willingly lend him sufficient for his need, whatever he needs." Then in verse 9, it warns: "Beware that there is not a wicked thought in your heart, saying, 'The seventh year, the year of release, is at hand,' and your eye be evil against your poor brother and you give him nothing, and he cries out to the Lord against you, and it becomes sin among you." Beware of wicked thoughts arising in your heart, objecting against acts of mercy. All objections against acts of mercy stem from wickedness in people's hearts. Scripture consistently charges us to help our poor brethren and to guard against objections to acts of mercy. Remember, "Blessed are the merciful, for they shall obtain mercy."

# SERMON XXIV

## Motives to show mercy

Blessed are the merciful, for they shall receive mercy. - Matthew 5:7

T he commendation of this grace of mercy has been abundant. Consider it further. God shows you more mercy than others so that you may do good to others. Why would God have some poor and some rich if not to crown patience in some and mercy in others? In 2 Corinthians 1:4, the Apostle speaks of spiritual mercy, comforting us in all our tribulations. Why? So that we may be able to comfort those who are in trouble with the same comfort we ourselves receive from God. This is the purpose of God's comfort in our tribulations—to help deliver others. The same applies to outward afflictions. If God has comforted your soul, brought you out of distress, answered your doubts, and delivered you from fears, then when you see others facing dreadful temptations, know that God requires you to show them mercy. He has comforted you and delivered you so that you can help deliver them. The same goes for bodily distress. Some of you were poor in the past, and the Lord helped you and blessed you with wealth. Whether you were poor or not, God has given you abundance, not just for yourself but so that you can comfort those in need. It is part of God's purpose in making distinctions between individuals.

Another motive to consider is the great relief it brings to those in affliction. Even though you may be in affliction, straits, or deep poverty, know that the Lord has taken care of you. He has given His Spirit's grace to His saints to be merciful to the afflicted. The Lord weighs upon them and charges them to exercise the grace of mercy. Surely the Lord takes care of you, and though you lack, He has endowed His saints with the grace of mercy to help you in your misery. Do not discourage those in distress, preventing them from crying out to God, thinking that He has made such a difference between you and them and that no one cares for them. When they see your compassion and mercy, they will acknowledge God's goodness, realizing that the Lord has cared for them and has secretly commanded you to pity and help them. Therefore, be merciful.

Furthermore, by showing works of mercy, even those of you in moderate circumstances can receive a reward as great as the most eminent saints of God. In Matthew 10:41, Christ says, "He who receives a prophet in the name of a prophet shall receive a prophet's reward, and he who receives a righteous man in the name of a righteous man shall receive a righteous man's reward." Show mercy to the righteous, and you can receive the same reward.

Those of you who are poor may say, "We can do little for God. We are weak and can be employed in only small services for God." But here is a way for you to receive the reward of God's prophets and the most eminent saints—by showing works of mercy to them.

To impress these things upon your hearts, fully internalize the principle that it is better to give than to receive. These are the words of Christ. It may be challenging to instill this principle in the hearts of many who believe that everything they bestow in acts of mercy is lost. No, he who gives to the poor lends to the Lord, and the Lord will repay. It is far better than anything else one may enjoy. Consider the saying of an ancient, "How much more glorious is it to do good to many than to live sumptuously."

Secondly, if you want these things to resonate, remember the times when you yourself needed mercy. When you see an object of mercy, think, "Have I never been miserable myself? Have I never been in need of mercy? Have I never experienced the necessity of mercy?" And it may be that I am well now, with everything going well for me, but what if I soon become an object of mercy? What if all comfort and support are taken away, and I find myself in dire circumstances? Then I would truly value mercy. Is mercy good for you then and not now? Make these times real to you. People who are healthy, peaceful, and prosperous carry on as if there will never be a change. But the mere thought of your own change and the sad condition you could soon be in should strongly compel you to show mercy to others.

Lastly, let your eyes affect your heart. Do not turn away from those in need; instead, look upon them. Lamentations 3:51 says, "My eye affects my heart." Looking upon those in misery is a powerful means to stir the heart. Those of you who enjoy all comforts, look upon the lamentable objects in the world and the city. Look into the hospitals among wounded soldiers and the desperately poor. Let your eyes move your heart to show mercy. For blessed are the merciful; they shall receive mercy.

We now move on from this point of mercy and proceed to the sixth rule of happiness that Christ presents.

Verse 8: Blessed are the pure in heart, for they shall see God.

There is a good connection between these two. Some people are willing to do good works and be beneficial to others while having unclean and guilty consciences themselves. They think that by doing so, they can silence their consciences. Many, I believe, silence their consciences with such things. However, Christ says, "Do not deceive yourselves. Blessed are the merciful; they shall receive mercy." But He adds this as well, "Blessed are the pure in heart." Purity of heart is necessary, not just mercy. Many acts of mercy can be done by those who are unclean and wicked at heart. Therefore, ensure that your hearts are clean and pure.

Blessed are those who have pure hearts.

Christ establishes this as the rule of blessedness, in opposition to the Pharisees' perspective. They believed that blessedness relied on external purity and ritualistic washing. However, Christ emphasizes the importance of looking inward to the heart. Blessed are those who possess purity in their hearts. Let us consider the meaning of this purity.

Firstly, purity of heart involves cleansing the heart from the guilt of sin through faith. It is being washed with the blood of Jesus Christ. Acts 15:9 states,

"And he made no distinction between us and them, having cleansed their hearts by faith." This scripture is often interpreted as referring to the work of sanctification that occurs through faith. However, upon closer examination of the context, it seems to refer to the purity that comes through faith in justification. It speaks of the Gentiles, who were considered unclean by the Jews. But the Apostle affirms that God has taken away their uncleanness and purified their hearts through faith. By believing in Jesus Christ, the Gentiles are accepted by the Lord as children of Abraham. Through faith, their hearts are purified, and they are regarded as clean before God. We are all naturally impure, and simply forsaking gross sins or living a better life does not make the heart pure before God. It is only through the cleansing of the soul with the blood of Jesus Christ that true purity is attained. The moment the soul believes in Jesus Christ, it is washed from the guilt of sin and stands before the Lord as pure as a newborn child, but even more so, for original corruption is cleansed, and the soul is purified from all the filthy and abominable sinful ways that defile it. This initial purification must occur; otherwise, all other forms of purity are meaningless.

Secondly, a pure heart is one that is guided by pure principles. The Scripture speaks of those with corrupt minds and, conversely, those with pure minds. There is much impurity in the thoughts of individuals, in the higher chambers of the soul, so to speak. When the soul acts from corrupt principles and holds unworthy perceptions of God and godly matters, it operates with base and corrupted notions. However, when the soul is purified, these corrupt principles are eradicated, and it acquires pure principles and a proper understanding of God, the ways of God, the covenant of grace, and the path of a Christian. The soul possesses correct apprehensions of everything that promotes holiness. Therefore, impurity arises from erroneous thinking and corrupt notions.

Thirdly, a pure heart is one that has expelled the love for every known sin and refuses to engage with it, no matter how insignificant. It is a heart that has renounced every known sinful way. Although impurities may remain, a pure heart can genuinely appeal to God, declaring that it hates and abominates every known form of sin. This is referred to as purity of heart in the language of the Gospel. If individuals were rewarded according to the law, this may not be considered purity. However, in the Gospel, a heart that sincerely renounces known sin and can appeal to God, acknowledging its abhorrence towards sin, is deemed pure. Reflect on your own conscience to determine if this is the case. The blessing is attached to this purity, and the opposite is what renders the soul subject to God's curse.

Fourthly, a pure heart is one that aligns with the holiness of God. It corresponds to God's holy nature and His law. This alignment constitutes purity.

Fifthly, purity of heart involves having right and consecrated ends, dedicating oneself to God's service, making Him the ultimate purpose of all things, and pursuing righteous aims in all actions. This purity is an emulation of God's holiness. God is a holy God, and holiness implies consecration, dedicating oneself to a specific end. God consecrates Himself to Himself as the ultimate end. He is His own ultimate end, and the excellence of His nature propels Him to work towards Himself as the ultimate goal. He wills everything according to this end, in accordance with His infinite excellence. This is God's purity. A pure heart is consecrated to God, making Him the ultimate end of all things and acting as God does. It has right ends and aims for God in all actions. The heart can genuinely appeal to God, saying, "Lord, You who search and examine all hearts, test my heart. I am willing for my heart to be open to the world regarding certain matters." This is a pure heart.

Sixthly, a pure heart works towards good ends with simplicity and straightforwardness. It is not enough to have good intentions while employing devious methods and mixing human cunning. Many individuals pride themselves on having general intentions aligned with God's purposes, but they employ cunning and devious strategies that stem from their own corrupt nature, thereby tainting their actions. True purity entails pursuing good ends while attaining them with the simplicity and straightforwardness of the Gospel. While craftiness and strategies may be suitable in worldly matters, they have no place in matters concerning Christ. A pure heart carries out all its endeavors with the plainness and simplicity of the Gospel.

Lastly, a pure heart aligns with every profession and duty undertaken. When individuals profess their faith in God and His ways, their hearts must correspond to their profession. A pure heart matches the profession made and the services rendered. Impurity and uncleanness in the hearts of hypocrites arise when their profession is great and glorious, but their hearts do not align with it. Therefore, when individuals make a profession of faith and engage in service, their hearts must genuinely correspond to their actions. This is purity. If all these qualities are present, blessedness follows.

However, it must be acknowledged that finding such purity in anyone is a challenge. Proverbs 20:9 states, "Who can say, 'I have made my heart pure; I am clean from my sin'?" In response, it is said that Christ speaks in a Gospel manner. Purity of heart, which is deemed acceptable, can still coexist with remaining impurities. Yet, alongside these dispositions, two factors must be considered.

Firstly, there must be a genuine effort to identify the remaining corruptions within the heart. Individuals should willingly search and discover all the corruptions, including the secret wanderings and turnings of the heart. The Lord knows that if He were to ask from Heaven, individuals would desire to know the depths of their hearts. This willingness to search for and understand one's corruptions is crucial.

Secondly, there should be sincere mourning over every remnant of impurity. When the heart identifies any corruption, it mourns over it, recognizing it as the evil and disorder within. It is noteworthy that the more peace one experiences through assurance of being cleansed by the blood of Christ, the greater the mourning and lamentation for any remaining impurities. Ezekiel 36:25 speaks to this phenomenon, "I will sprinkle clean water on you, and you shall be clean from all your uncleannesses, and from all your idols I will cleanse you." A new heart will be given, and individuals will remember their own evil ways and loathe themselves for their iniquities and abominations. God considers them cleansed when they genuinely loathe themselves for their sins and abominations. Those who loathe themselves the most for their iniquities and abominations are those who have been most cleansed of them. This Scripture highlights the danger of individuals inappropriately magnifying free grace to the point of foolishness and licentiousness, failing to recognize the remaining evils in their hearts. They mistakenly believe that they are cleansed by the blood and the Spirit of Christ. However, the text promises that when the Lord cleanses His people, they will loathe themselves for all their abominations and evils.

Though there is evil remaining, still one who has true purity watches over themselves to prevent occasions of evil as much as possible. And fourthly, such a person loves the strictest rule. I find much impurity in my heart, but God knows the strictest rule I aim at, and my heart is most aligned with those who grow the most in godliness.

Fifthly and lastly, my soul longs for perfection. I hope there is a time coming when all my defilement shall be done away with. For now, my soul is washed and perfected in terms of justification. And I look forward to a time when it shall be perfect in terms of sanctification. Oh, that that time were come! Certainly, here is a pure heart. So do not say, "Where is the pure heart? Who can make their heart pure? Are there any who are pure?"

The next thing is to explain the excellence of a clean heart. First, a pure heart shows its excellence as the fruit of the blood of Christ and the work of the Holy Spirit. Those two Scriptures you had, from Revelation 1 and Ezekiel 36, clarify this. It is washed with the blood of Christ and cleansed by the Holy Spirit. Surely, the fruit of the blood of Christ is purity. When the blood of Christ and the Holy Spirit, like water, are poured out upon the soul, they work gloriously to bring about cleanliness and purity.

Secondly, this purity of heart is the cause of soundness of spirit. It helps against disturbances so that even though there are outward occasions to disturb the heart, when the heart is clean within, it will not be disturbed as others are. It is similar to the body. If a person's body is dirty and they catch a slight cold, they will quickly become sick. Any external factor that disrupts their regular routine will reveal the filthiness of their body. They may attribute it to the cold they caught, but in reality, it is the impurity of their body that causes the illness. A dirty body is susceptible to diseases on any occasion. But a person with a clean body, free from the impurities that affect others, can endure cold or heat and face any external situation while remaining healthy and sound. This is due to the cleanliness within their body. Likewise, with the heart, impure hearts are greatly disturbed by any temptation to evil. A multitude of filth appears in their hearts when tempted. They attribute it to the temptation, but if there hadn't been much impurity in their hearts, the temptation would never have prevailed. Jesus said, "The Devil comes and he finds nothing in me." Take, for example, the passion of anger. Many of you may seem to live fair and pleasant lives, but if someone angers you and you lose your temper, a great deal of filthiness and baseness is revealed. You may say it was the person who angered you and provoked you, but the truth is that the anger and filthiness were already present in your heart. The temptation merely stirred them up. A pure-hearted person, one whose corruptions have been mortified, who is cleansed from pride and self-love, can remain meek and composed even when wronged. They can entrust their cause to God and express their grievances to Him. Blessed are the pure in heart, for they have sound and whole spirits and are not easily disturbed like other people. Consequently, they have sound hearts.

Thirdly, the pure in heart have much peace of conscience. They are able to look upon the face of God with peace and joy. When God reveals Himself through His great works in the world, their consciences speak peace to them, and they rejoice that they have to deal with such a holy God. All of this stems from the cleanliness in their hearts. In Job 11:14-15, it is said, "If iniquity be in thine hand, put it far away and let not wickedness dwell in thy Tabernacles. What then? For then shalt thou lift up thy face without spot, yea, thou shalt be steadfast and shall not fear." Notice that it speaks of having clean hands and putting iniquity far from oneself. When we not only remove iniquity from our actions but also from our hearts, when wickedness is far from both our Tabernacles and our hearts, then we are able to lift up our faces without blemish, remain steadfast, and fear nothing, regardless of any evil tidings. We can look upon the face of God, lift up our countenances, and not fear. When a person has guilt in their heart and an impure conscience, facing God's presence becomes terrifying, and horror threatens to overwhelm them. The presence of God is dreadful to an impure heart. Blessed are the pure in heart, for they shall see God. The presence of God brings joy to them, but not to others. In Psalm 51:7-8, David, having defiled his heart, began to perceive God's presence as terrible. He cried out, "Wash me thoroughly from mine iniquities and cleanse me from my sin." And later, "Make me to hear joy and gladness." He recognized that he had polluted his soul with sin, and the voice of joy and gladness had departed from his heart. His bones were burdened with the weight of his sin. But he pleaded with the Lord to cleanse him, and then the voice of joy and gladness would return to his soul. Can any of you, whose consciences are impure and reveal the base uncleanness in your hearts and ways, rejoice? Do you have gladness in your countenances and ways? Surely, you do not know God. You do not know Him, for if you knew the God you have to deal with, you could never have joy in your hearts until the Lord had cleansed you. It is a sign that the grace of God is in the heart of a person when they have dealt with their sin, and nothing in the world can bring joy and gladness to their hearts until the Lord has cleansed them. Therefore, blessed are the pure in heart. There are many excellencies in this purity of heart.

Fourthly, blessed are the pure in heart because they are fit to serve God's purposes in the ways of the Gospel. There are no individuals suitable for God's design and ways in the Gospel except those with clean hearts. God does not delight in using cunning and crafty individuals who employ sinful craftiness. It is true that the Lord requires us to be wise as serpents and innocent as doves when we live among wicked people. But I speak of cunning and craftiness in dealing with God. He takes no pleasure in using such methods. However, those with sincere, upright, and genuine hearts are suitable to serve God's purposes in the ways of the Gospel. As in Psalm 24:3-4, "Who shall ascend into the hill of the Lord? Or who shall stand in his holy place? He that hath clean hands and a pure heart, who hath not lifted up his soul unto vanity, nor sworn deceitfully." Such a person shall receive blessings from the Lord and righteousness from the God of their salvation. Who is the person who shall ascend to the hill of God, whom God will receive into His Church, and who is fit to bring honor to God in His Church? It is the one with clean hands and a pure heart, one who has not lifted up their soul to vanity. This is a particular impurity in people's hearts when they elevate their souls to vanity, mixing their own ulterior motives with any services they are engaged in. However, the one who does not lift up their soul to vanity, who looks at God with a single eye, is the one who shall ascend to God's holy hill. This is the generation of those who seek the Lord. The blessing of God shall be upon such individuals.

Fifthly, another point to consider is that the pure in heart are recipients of numerous gracious and blessed promises. Blessed are the pure in heart, for they are under many blessed promises. In Psalm 18:26, it is written, "With the pure thou wilt show thyself pure." And in Psalm 73:1, it says, "Truly God is good to Israel, even to such as are of a clean heart." It is as if to say, regardless of the world's ways, God is truly good to Israel, to those who possess clean hearts. A clean heart is invaluable. Therefore, continue on, those whose hearts the Lord has begun to cleanse, and strive to make them cleaner and cleaner, and keep them clean. You who are holy, remain holy. Regard it as your riches, regard it as worth more than the entire world to have a clean heart. There may be someone who possesses greater wealth and is more esteemed in the world, but the more people engage in worldly vanities, the more their hearts become defiled. The Lord has limited me in material possessions, but blessed be His name, my heart is, to some extent, cleaner than others'. There are those who possess greater talents than I do, but often, excellent abilities are accompanied by very impure hearts. Although I cannot do what they can, my conscience testifies to me that my heart is clean. Whenever I engage in prayer, I can enter into the presence of God with a clean heart. This should bring you comfort in the absence of any worldly comforts. It will protect you from the defilements of the times in which you live. In Psalm 119:1, it is stated, "Blessed are the undefiled in the way, they walk in the law of the Lord." It is a blessed thing to be undefiled in our way, to live in the world and maintain our purity, unblemished by the world's contaminations, and to keep our hearts clean. There are very few among us who have achieved this. When we reflect upon the past times in which we lived, times filled with great temptations towards evil, where is the man or woman who does not have cause to lament the defilements of their conscience and heart due to the pollutions of the era in which they existed? We have soiled ourselves with superstitious vanities in the past, and it is not only our actions that have become defiled, but even our consciences. It would be just for the Lord if we were never to see the promised land He is leading His people to, because we have stained ourselves with the superstitious vanities of the times in which we lived. How fortunate is the individual who lived in those former times, when there were so many pollutions, and yet managed to keep themselves undefiled in their way! I may have lost more than others, but I preserved the cleanliness of my heart and conscience, and this is what brings comfort to my soul. Blessed are those who achieve this; the blessing of God is upon them and will certainly manifest in a glorious manner.

# SERMON XXV

## Wherein a pure heart is Blessed

"Blessed are those with pure hearts, for they shall see God." - Matthew 5:8

We began discussing this sixth rule of blessedness in our previous session and will now continue. It is indeed a blessed thing to possess spiritual cleanliness in the soul of a person, a pure heart. It is blessed for several reasons.

Firstly, if we consider the excellence of a person's soul, the more excellent something is, the more valuable it is to keep it clean and free from defilements. For instance, if you have a piece of coarse cloth, you may not be as concerned about keeping it clean compared to fine lawn or cambric. A stain on the latter is more significant than on a piece of sackcloth. Similarly, the excellence of a person's soul surpasses all other creatures created by God, except for angels. Therefore, maintaining the purity of one's soul, keeping it unstained and free from filth, is an excellent pursuit.

Secondly, a pure heart allows a person to savor and appreciate the word of God, relishing spiritual and heavenly truths. Those who possess clean hearts are blessed because when they hear the pure word of God, their hearts truly relish and savor it. Just as a clean stomach relishes and savors wholesome food, those with clean hearts relish the pure truths of God. Conversely, when individuals have defiled hearts, even the most wholesome and blessed truths of God become tasteless to them. They lack the ability to appreciate and savor these truths due to the uncleanness of their hearts. Some of you may remember a time when you could better relish and savor spiritual things. Examine your hearts and you will discover that it is because of the defilement of your hearts. Perhaps you have defiled your consciences through sin against conscience or live in some secret sinful habit. It is no wonder that you can no longer appreciate and savor the word as you once did.

Thirdly, a clean heart enables a person to draw near to God in all acts of worship and enhances the value of their offerings. In James 4:8, it is written, "Draw near to God, and he will draw near to you. Cleanse your hands, you sinners, and purify your hearts, you double-minded." By purifying their hearts, individuals become capable of drawing near to God. Those with unclean hearts dare not approach God, and even if they try, their consciences cannot draw near to Him. They may enter their closets to pray, urged by their consciences, but they cannot draw near to God because their hearts are unclean. Therefore, purify your hearts and strive for cleansed hearts. Only then will your heart leap in God's presence, drawing near to Him. This purity also enhances all the services we offer to God. In Malachi 3:3, there is a prophecy that when Christ comes, He will purify the sons of Levi, refining them like gold and silver, so they may offer the Lord an offering in righteousness. You may offer many things to God, make numerous prayers, and assume that God will save you based on your good prayers. However, any offering presented with an impure heart is defiled and repulsive to the Lord. True offerings of righteousness arise when the Lord has purified the heart. In Proverbs 21:8, Solomon says, "As for the pure, his work is right." Although the way of a man may be perverse and strange, the work of the pure is right. When the Lord cleanses the heart, even with its weaknesses, the work is right in God's eyes. In 2 Timothy 2:21, it is stated, "If a man therefore purge himself from these, he shall be a vessel unto honor, sanctified and meet for the Master's use, and prepared unto every good work." A purged vessel is sanctified, suitable for the Master's use, and prepared for every good work. On the other hand, those with unclean spirits resemble filthy vessels, unsuitable to be presented in the Master's presence. Hence, when St. Paul speaks of the service he rendered to God, he affirms it was with a pure conscience (2 Timothy 1:3). He thanks God, whom he serves with a pure conscience, as if in the presence of God. Blessed are the pure in heart, for they are fit to draw near to God, fit for every work assigned by God, and their purity enhances all the services they offer to Him.

Fourthly, a person with a pure heart leads a convincing life before others. Grace's beauty and excellence become evident in the conduct of those who keep a clean heart before God. Proverbs 22:11 states, "He that loveth pureness of heart, for the grace of his lips the king shall be his friend." Oh, that God would fulfill this promise, making the king a friend to Puritans! In the past, among all men in England, those known as Puritans, many of whom sought to worship God in purity, were considered the most despised in the land. However, there is a promise that the one who loves purity of heart, for the grace of his lips, the king shall be his friend. God has the power to make the king a friend to those who love purity of heart. The purity of their hearts will guide their conduct in such a way that the king's conscience will be convinced they are upright men. Others who have surrounded the king may have flattered and deceived him, leading him into evil ways that have caused much harm in the kingdom, resulting in the oppression and shedding of blood for thousands. Yet, the king will observe that these individuals walk uprightly, consistent with their principles. He will recognize their integrity in every aspect and declare, "I will be their friend." Let us pray that God fulfills this promise. Certainly, a clean conversation arising from a pure heart is a powerful means of conviction. It is not merely professing purity more than others but walking consistently and displaying the beauty and excellence of a clean heart in one's conduct. This will convince anyone in the world. People may speak ill of them, accusing them of hypocrisy, but let the world speak as the world does, according to its own understanding of matters concerning religion. You, on the other hand, continue walking in the ways of holiness with constancy, maintaining consistency in all aspects of your conduct, demonstrating the purity of your heart. Eventually, their consciences will acknowledge that your ways are better than theirs. Even those who have criticized you will recognize your honorability. Purity of heart is a mighty convincing force when it shines through one's life and conduct.

Fifthly, blessed are the pure, for all things are pure to them. Titus 1:15 says, "Unto the pure all things are pure, but unto them that are defiled and unbelieving is nothing pure; but even their mind and conscience is defiled." If God has sanctified your heart and you strive to sanctify His name in all your ways, know that all things are sanctified to you. This single statement is worth a kingdom, worth the world. The fact that all things should be made pure to those who are clean is a promise from the Lord. It means you have a sanctified and pure use of everything when you labor to keep your heart clean before the Lord.

Sixthly, those with clean hearts will endure and never become apostates. While individuals may make great professions and ultimately become apostates, someone with a clean heart who walks sincerely before God will persevere. It is like gold; genuine gold will not be consumed in the fire, unlike something merely gilded with gold that contains more dross. Such a gilded item will be consumed when exposed to fire, but pure gold will withstand it. Similarly, when the Lord subjects His people to afflictions, casting them into the fiery furnace, those who only make a profession of being His people and have outward holiness will be consumed. However, those with clean hearts will endure through their trials, remaining faithful until the end.

Lastly, purity of heart yields fruitfulness in the ways of holiness. Those who keep their hearts and consciences clean will thrive and grow in holiness. In John 15:2, Jesus speaks of the vine, saying, "Every branch in me that beareth not fruit he taketh away: and every branch that beareth fruit, he purgeth it, that it may bring forth more fruit." If any impurity has entered your heart, the Lord, through afflictions or other means, will purge your heart. This purification will result in you bearing much fruit. It is similar to children who are filled with ill humors; they do not thrive and grow. However, if you administer something to purge those ill humors, they will soon thrive and grow significantly. The same applies to many of you who do not thrive in the ways of religion, who do not grow in godliness, and fail to bear fruit to God's glory. It is because much impurity and filth have entered your hearts. If the Lord would graciously cleanse you through the renewal of the Spirit, washing in the blood of Christ, and the work of repentance, you would grow in godliness and bear much fruit to the glory of God. Oh, blessed are the pure in heart.

And therefore, my brethren, this point may bring comfort to those whose consciences testify that although there are many weaknesses, their hearts do not align with the evils of the times. It is one thing for evil to be present, but another to be mixed with it. There may be dross, but it does not mingle with the heart. If your conscience affirms this, you can find great comfort in this point. Even though some sin remains, the purity of heart can bring peace to your spirits, even in the awareness of many sins upon you.

In Isaiah 1:16, it is written, "Wash yourselves; make yourselves clean; remove the evil of your deeds from before my eyes; cease to do evil." Then in verse 18, it says, "Come now, let us reason together, says the Lord: though your sins are like scarlet, they shall be as white as snow; though they are red like crimson, they shall become like wool." When sins are washed away and one becomes clean, they are as white as snow, as wool. And now the Lord will reason with the soul. You may reason with God, and He will reason with you when you have cleansed yourself and made yourself clean. Even if there have been sins as scarlet and crimson, when your heart does not mix with these sins, when you can renew the acts of faith and repentance, and when you can appeal to God regarding your sincerity and efforts to walk with Him in the purity you are capable of, it is not the greatness of your sins that your conscience tells you are due to weakness, sins you do not entertain or find suitable. The Lord will reason the case with you, and you may reason the case with Him. Blessed are the pure in heart. So, strive to keep your hearts clean and pure. Therefore, be vigilant over your hearts daily. Be careful not to let soil and filth enter your hearts, and cleanse them daily through the renewed work of faith and repentance. Although a Christian may keep their hearts from being stained by the gross sins of the world, dust will accumulate within every day. Oh, strive to keep your hearts bright. Some of you love cleanliness in everything, in the furniture of your houses, your stools, tables, linen, in everything. You will not be satisfied until there is not a speck of dirt on them. But if they become even slightly soiled, you are displeased. Look at your hearts in the same way. The Lord loves, so to speak, a neat Christian who daily cleanses their heart anew. Especially if you have been overcome by sin and brought greater defilement to your heart, do not linger in that sin. Never find rest and peace with your soul until you have washed away that sin in the blood of Christ, until you have peace in your conscience concerning that sin. I fear some of you may have consciences that tell you that you have persisted in some sins for a long time. Take heed not to remain in any sin but cleanse immediately.

And lastly, because I would now address the promise... Oh, how far are most of us from this purity of heart, and what infinite cause there is for shame and embarrassment among many of us. The Lord knows, and our consciences know, that there is wretched uncleanness and filthiness in many of our hearts. Oh, the defiled consciences that many men and women have in this place! You may be clean in your bodies, in your garments, in your clean linen. But oh, the filthy, disgusting souls within you! God sees your souls as filthy as a carcass lying in a ditch. How can you come into the presence of God as you do—boldly, presumptuously—when you are conscious of such filthiness? Men and women with corrupt consciences, who have committed many acts of injustice, who have defiled their consciences for many years, yet they continue in it and have never made any restitution. As long as you hold onto anything that is not yours and have not restored it, all this time your conscience has been rotting and becoming more corrupt. As long as you persist in that sin without making restitution, if God enables you in any way... And then the consciences of men are impure, burdened with an abundance of sin. If God were to command conscience to speak, it would say, "Lord, this sin was committed against my counsel and advice, and I warned them against it, yet despite that, they committed this sin and others." And then there is the impurity of our hearts. Oh, what a filthy sty of uncleanness is found in the thoughts of many men and women! Within the thoughts of their minds lies the most abominable filth, and one would wonder how an infinitely holy God could bear to look upon such filthy creatures and not come forth in wrath against them. Even the best among us can find much uncleanness in our thoughts. Sometimes, when you have been in the presence of God in prayer, how have you defiled yourself with impure thoughts? How have you entered God's presence with a soul smeared with filth and come out with a soul defiled by abominable thoughts? And then there is the uncleanness of your will, affections, and desires. What desires have you had for sin, defiling your soul? The faculties of men and women's souls are as filthy as any cage of unclean birds. If you truly understood the infinite purity of God's nature, the holiness of His Law, and the reality of your own heart, you would abhor yourself. Some of you thank God that you have good hearts, but it is because God is not known, the holiness of His Law is not known, and your own hearts are not known. If you knew these three things, you would indeed have cause to abhor yourself. Let me ask you this: sometimes, when you have been brought to your sickbed, when you have realized that you have to deal with God, have you not had misgivings? When you have been about to enter the presence of the infinitely holy God, have not your consciences reproved you for your uncleanness? Have not your consciences told you, "How can you stand in the presence of this holy God?" We read in the Prophet Isaiah that, although he was a holy man, a man with much purity and cleanliness, even when he caught a glimpse of God, the angels cried out, "Holy, holy, holy is the Lord of hosts!" And Isaiah responded, "Woe is me! For I am lost; for I am a man of unclean lips." (And certainly, if he had unclean lips, he saw further uncleanness in his heart.) "For my eyes have seen the King, the Lord of hosts." The sight of God caused him to cry out in anguish, realizing he was lost. If, then, God were to bring you to deal directly with Him, oh, the terror your conscience would bring upon you. Those uncleannesses in your heart, though they may not trouble you now, may trouble you one day. It is like a chimney that is very dirty; if fire enters it, it creates a flame that is hard to extinguish. Similarly, when afflictions befall men and women with sooty, filthy hearts, those afflictions are likely to burn most intensely. I appeal to your consciences in this matter. Suppose God were to say, "Well, the whole congregation and everyone in the world shall know the uncleanness in each of your hearts. They shall know every impure thought you have ever had, every impure desire, every secret impurity in your hearts. It shall be known to the city and to the whole world." Would that not trouble you? To think that God would expose your innermost being? The infinite God knows all; His piercing eye sees through and through. All the uncleanness of your hearts is before Him as clearly as any actions you have ever done... And consider this, especially those of you who profess holiness and purity, yet God and your consciences tell you that you live in secret haunts of wickedness. Some servants, perhaps false to their masters and governors, guilty of secret impurity, may try to cover their uncleanness by showing great fervor in prayer and in attending worship services. Who would suspect them of falsehood or impurity? The same goes for others. This is an abominable thing—to have an unclean heart and think to conceal it by making a profession of religion. You take the name of God in vain in a dreadful manner. Know that the wickedness of your heart will be exposed. It is just for God to leave you to the wickedness of your heart, to break forth into outward, actual sins. This is the curse of God upon hypocrites: they maintain much secret wickedness in their hearts for a long time, and the saints think well of them because of their profession. But this is God's curse upon them: the Lord leaves them to the filthiness of their hearts and allows them to break out into scandalous sins, becoming a reproach that will never be blotted out... But we have now finished with this part of the text. We come to the other part.

For they shall see God.

The world might say about those who are pure, strict, and conscientious, and who refuse to go against their consciences, that they are ignorant and foolish, especially women. Even though they may be considered simple and ignorant in worldly matters, they will see God, they will know God. Their knowledge may be limited in other areas, but the promise is that they will see God, they will know Him. Those who strive for purity and refuse to defile themselves like others are often subject to mistreatment in the world. The people of the world may outsmart them with their cunning ways. Even though the worldly people may surpass them in cunning, those who have sincere and straightforward hearts find comfort in this: even if they lack the craftiness and shrewdness to provide for themselves in the world, they have the blessing of God upon them—they will see His face. They shall see God.

To see Him does not mean seeing God with physical eyes, for no one has ever seen God in that way. God is invisible, and we must not think of Him as having a physical form or shape like humans or other creatures. He is a spiritual and infinite being and cannot be seen with physical eyes. However, to see God means to know Him through the eyes of understanding and to experience His presence. Seeing God is used in Scripture to denote knowing and experiencing God. They shall see God in this world, and the cleaner their hearts become, the more they will perceive God. They shall see Him in glory in the future. Just as a clear glass reflects the brightness of the sun more than a dirty or cloudy glass, when the hearts of people are pure, God's glory shines upon them, and there is a reflection of His glory in their hearts. They shall see God, as Augustine said, "O most sweet light of minds that are cleansed." He referred to God as the most sweet light of cleansed minds. Before we consider the main promise of seeing God, there are a few important points to note.

First, the clarity or impurity of one's spirit determines their understanding of God and spiritual matters. It follows from the statement, "Blessed are the pure in heart, for they shall see God." I mean that a person's understanding of God and spiritual things corresponds to the cleanliness or impurity of their spirit. If someone has a pure spirit, they will gain a deeper understanding of spiritual matters. Conversely, if their hearts are unclean, their spirits will struggle to grasp spiritual truths. In Proverbs 9:10, it is said, "The fear of the Lord is the beginning of wisdom." Those who have pure hearts and fear the Lord gain true understanding. They possess an excellent understanding of heavenly matters and the things of God. True understanding can only be attained through knowledge of the holy. No one can claim to have understanding without knowledge of the holy. When a person's heart is clean, their sight becomes clear. In Daniel 9:13, we find a notable scripture that highlights how the understanding of God's truth depends on the cleanliness of our hearts. It says, "That we might turn from our iniquities and understand your truth." In other words, as long as we continue in our iniquities and defile our souls with sin, we will be unable to understand God's truth. But when we turn away from our iniquities, our understanding becomes clear, and we come to know God and His truth in a way we never did before. In Daniel 12:10, it is written, "Many shall be purified and made white, and refined, but the wicked shall act wickedly. And none of the wicked shall understand, but those who are wise shall understand." When God purifies the heart, He grants understanding of His ways. On the other hand, the wicked, with their impure hearts, cannot understand God's mind and His ways. The understanding of a person is influenced by the condition of their will and affections. The state of the will and affections leaves an imprint on the understanding, just as the stomach affects the eyes in certain diseases. If no foul vapors ascend to the eyes, they remain clear and able to see. But in some diseases, when vapors rise to the eyes, they become affected and see according to those vapors. Similarly, if a person's heart is clean, they see the truths of God clearly. However, if the heart is unclean, it hinders the understanding from focusing on God and His truth. The unclean heart turns the understanding away and prevents it from contemplating God, instead diverting it to things that align with the impurity of the heart. It is no wonder that those with unclean spirits fail to understand the things of God when their hearts obstruct the understanding from being enlightened and convinced. Conversely, when presented with a temptation that corresponds to the impurity of their hearts, they latch onto it, and their corrupted will and affections cause the understanding to be completely absorbed in it, thinking of nothing else but what serves to support and maintain their sinful state.

Second, the will has great influence over the understanding. The will can direct the understanding to focus on one task or another, to turn away from one object or another. If a person's will and affections are clean, the will directs the understanding to meditate on God and spiritual matters, to fix its gaze on spiritual things. However, if the heart is unclean, the will turns away the understanding, preventing it from contemplating God and His things. Such objects are unsuitable for an unclean heart. Even if God Himself were to present Himself before a person with an unclean heart, the heart would not allow the understanding to dwell on God. Instead, it would turn away from God to something that aligns with the impurity of the heart. Therefore, it is no wonder that they do not understand the things of God when their unclean spirits prevent the understanding from functioning in a way that could illuminate and convict them. Conversely, if there is any temptation presented that suits the impurity of their hearts, they immediately latch onto it, and their corrupt will and affections cause the understanding to be entirely occupied with it, thinking of nothing else but what supports and justifies their filthy and sinful ways.

Third, the Lord takes no pleasure in revealing Himself to someone with an unclean heart. If a person's conscience or heart is defiled and immersed in filth, the Lord does not delight in revealing Himself to such an individual. The Lord sees that such a person will reject the truth. He asks Himself, "Why should I reveal myself to an unclean heart that will distort every truth presented to it?" As a result, in righteous judgment, the Lord allows them to be given over to those things that will harden their hearts in their impurity. There is a dreadfully severe scripture in Ezekiel 14:4 that speaks of God's reluctance to reveal Himself to people with unclean spirits. It says, "Therefore speak to them and say, 'Thus says the Lord God: "Everyone of the house of Israel who sets up his idols in his heart, and puts before him what causes him to stumble into iniquity, and then comes to the prophet, I the Lord will answer him who comes, according to the multitude of his idols."' " It is a terrifying scripture indeed. If anyone, even a prophet, comes to you with idols in their heart, maintaining secret evils, and insisting on indulging in certain sinful ways, no matter what is said to them, they will receive only what will harden them in their sin. "He that is filthy, let him be filthy still." When they hear the word, they will only gather what their corrupt heart can use to harden themselves in sin.

This stark difference in people's perceptions can be seen when they were living in impurity before God cleansed them. A person who lived in impure ways might have come to hear the word a hundred times, listening to attributes of God and the mysteries of Jesus Christ, and the glorious things of the kingdom of God. Yet, they never saw any excellence in these things. They did not grasp the fear of God or have any profound understanding. They could live for many years in enmity against God without being troubled. But when God purifies their hearts through His Spirit, their perspective changes. Now, when they hear the word and listen to sermons about the glory of God, they see God in a different light. They no longer simply hear attributes of God but feel a deep reverence for His glory. They wonder why the whole world does not fear God. They realize they could live for many years in enmity against Him, and they would not want to return to that state even for a thousand worlds. They see how dreadful it is to spend even a moment in enmity with God. Why is this so? They hear the same truths as before, but now their eyes are opened. When they hear about Jesus Christ, their hearts rejoice at the richness of God's grace in Him. It is not something new they hear; rather, their hearts are cleansed, and their eyes are opened. There is a significant difference in the way they perceive things after God has cleansed their hearts compared to before. This highlights the root cause of the widespread ignorance in the world. It is not because the things of God are difficult to understand or because people lack the means to understand them. It is because of the impurity of their hearts. It is no wonder that people live under the means of grace, hearing sermons, yet fail to comprehend the true meaning of Jesus Christ, as their hearts are so filthy and unclean. In 2 Timothy 3:7, the apostle speaks of women who are always learning but never able to come to the knowledge of the truth. This can also be applied to men who are burdened with sins and led astray by various lusts. They are continually learning but unable to grasp the truth. Why? Because they are led astray by lusts and burdened by sins. When individuals have impurity in their hearts and are burdened by corruption in their spirits, it is no surprise that they fail to come to the knowledge of the truth. Therefore, do not think that your ignorance can excuse you, saying, "I act according to my knowledge, and not everyone can attain the same level of understanding as others. I am a weak and simple person, incapable of comprehending things as others do." Oh, it is not so much a lack of intellectual capacity as it is the impurity of your heart. The foul vapors that arise from your corrupt heart darken the light of truth, preventing it from shining into your understanding.

# SERMON XXVI

## The uncleaness of heart cause of error

"Blessed are the pure in heart, for they will see God." - Matthew 5:8

The reason why there are such errors among us about God and His ways is due to the impurity of people's hearts. Let's observe two types of individuals: first, those who were once religious professors but have strayed, becoming worldly, indulgent, and driven by their carnal desires, resulting in the adoption of peculiar opinions; second, young ones with profane and impure hearts. As soon as their consciences begin to stir within them, they make a superficial profession of religion, yet their hearts remain full of lust, never emptied or humbled for their sins. Moreover, the Devil has found a way to dissuade people, claiming that true repentance is merely legalistic, hindering their relationship with Jesus Christ rather than enhancing it. Consequently, they adopt a religious facade without undergoing genuine works of humility. Consequently, their hearts remain as impure as ever, leading to distorted thoughts about God, Christ, the Covenant of Grace, and eternal matters. Their hearts have never been cleansed. I want to highlight that those who fall into numerous vile and damnable errors can be categorized into two groups: firstly, individuals who were once zealous professors but have begun to indulge in worldly, sensual, and vain behavior; secondly, young ones who assume the religious profession without truly understanding the gravity of sin. Such individuals fail to truly see God. Their hearts are so corrupted and vile that they cannot perceive God as He truly is, nor can they appreciate the true beauty and excellence of godly things. Let me provide you with a couple of Scriptures to demonstrate how errors arise from the lusts of people's hearts rather than mere intellectual mistakes. In 2 Timothy 3:5, 8, it is stated that those who have a form of godliness but deny its power resist the truth. They have corrupt minds and are disqualified concerning the faith, similar to Jannes and Jambres who opposed Moses. The passage advises turning away from individuals who have a superficial form of godliness but deny its transformative power. The apostle emphasizes that there is no point in engaging with such men. He describes their dispositions as those who resist the truth, possess corrupt minds, and are disqualified concerning the faith. Another Scripture, 2 Peter 2:18, speaks of false teachers who allure people through their fleshly desires and wantonness by using grandiose words of vanity. They target those who had previously escaped from error but are still entangled in it. The passage is highly relevant to our times. In verse 19, it states that while these false teachers promise liberty, they themselves are servants of corruption. They are known for their inflated and impressive language that amuses people. These words may seem profound, but they are empty and devoid of substance. They are like a balloon filled with air that bursts upon examination, revealing their vanity and emptiness. When you hear them preach, you may have cause for suspicion when they use elaborate language that appears to contain great ideas. However, upon closer examination, you will find that their words are mere vanity and emptiness. They entice people through their words that align with their fleshly desires. The power of their speech lies in its appeal to people's lusts rather than the evidence of truth. All their methods are driven by lusts and much wantonness. They target those who had genuinely escaped from error, emphasizing their true escape. Thus, it is evident that these errors arise when individuals are led astray, being promised freedom and liberation from various forms of bondage, while the false teachers themselves are slaves to corruption. Therefore, the prevalence of errors in our times stems from the impurity of people's hearts, leading to a departure from the truth. The best way to protect ourselves from the errors of the times is to maintain clean hearts. Purify your hearts, walk uprightly before God, and the Spirit of God will guide you into all truth. When you need to understand God or His mind in any matter, it is crucial to prioritize the cleansing of your hearts. Otherwise, you will make mistakes when seeking counsel regarding the mind of God. If you truly desire to know the mind of God, it is not enough to claim willingness; you must actively seek it. Furthermore, when you inquire, you must be willing to accept truths that may contradict your own desires. If you are reluctant for God's mind to deviate from your preconceived notions, it indicates impurity in your heart. Additionally, when you seek God's mind, a principle within your spirit may strongly influence your heart in a different direction, making it challenging to convince you of God's mind if it opposes your personal biases. Moreover, you may be unwilling to thoroughly examine anything that is presented to you if you fear it may contradict your beliefs. You are reluctant to scrutinize it and instead desire to find objections against it. All these tendencies arise from the impurity of the heart. Therefore, it is just for God to withhold His blessings from those individuals, preventing them from seeing God and understanding His ways. Beware of these tendencies. Approach God with plain and open hearts, regardless of your previous thoughts, justifications, or personal ends. Allow God to reveal His truth, and be ready to yield to it with a pure and straightforward heart. However, if God sees that you have cunning hearts and ulterior motives, seeking to intertwine your ends with His, it is just for Him to blind you, preventing you from seeing Him in any aspect of His ways. The way to know the mind of God is to cleanse your hearts. Many claim to desire knowledge of God's mind, saying they would do anything that aligns with His will. However, examine your heart. Can you willingly surrender your own ends, counsels, and ways, regardless of what they were? Are you willing to embrace any evidence of truth, no matter how contrary it may be to your own thoughts and desires? If so, then it is likely that you will come to know God's mind. But if you claim to desire knowledge of God's mind while your heart is corrupt and opposed to Him and His mind, never expect to attain it. Only a pure heart can yield to His mind, even if it contradicts your previous beliefs. Yes, blessed are those with pure hearts, for they will see God.

Firstly, it's not a matter of willingness; they simply don't know how to handle it, so they must inquire. And secondly, when they do inquire, they are reluctant to accept the truth. They are unwilling for God's mind to align with a path that contradicts their own desires. They would rather have God's mind conform to their own than allow their hearts to align with the mind of God. This reveals impurity in their hearts. Thirdly, when they seek to understand God's mind, there is a principle within their spirits that turns their hearts and firmly directs them in another direction. Consequently, it becomes challenging to convince such individuals of God's mind if it opposes the bias of their hearts. And fourthly, they are unwilling to thoroughly examine anything presented to them. When faced with something that might challenge their beliefs, they avert their thoughts, reluctant to examine it. They eagerly look for objections and are determined to find anything to discredit it. All of this stems from the impurity of their hearts. It is only just that God withholds His blessings from them, preventing them from seeing Him and understanding His ways. Take heed of this. Approach with humble and open hearts, regardless of one's previous thoughts, justifications, or personal agendas. Let God reveal His truth, and I am ready to yield to it with a pure and sincere heart. However, when God sees people with cunning hearts, ulterior motives, and their own ends in mind, when they try to intertwine their desires with His, it is only just for Him to prevent them from seeing Him in any aspect of His ways. They shall remain blinded. The key to understanding the mind of God is to purify your hearts. Many claim to desire knowledge of God's mind, saying they would do anything in accordance with His will. Now, examine your hearts. Can you willingly surrender your own ends, plans, and ways, regardless of your previous inclinations? Will you embrace any evidence of truth, even if it contradicts your own thoughts and desires? If so, then it is likely that you will come to know God's mind. However, if you claim to desire knowledge of God's mind while your heart is corrupt and opposed to God and His mind, never expect to attain it. Only a pure heart can yield to His mind, even if it contradicts what it previously held. Yes, blessed are those with clean hearts, for they will see God. That concludes this point.

Take note that the sight of God does not depend on the natural understanding of individuals, but rather on the cleanliness of their hearts.

Many humble Christians wonder how they can truly know God and comprehend the mysteries revealed in His Word. They feel incapable of reaching such heights. But take comfort, for if your heart is clean, free from wicked desires and lusts, there is a promise for you: you shall see God. The sight of God does not rely on human intellect, but on the purity of the heart. Even when the great scholars of the world remain blind to Him, unable to see God in a saving manner, He will reveal Himself to your soul if you possess a clean and pure heart. The sight of God is made possible through the revelation brought by Jesus Christ, the great Prophet of His Church. He can instruct those of weak understanding as easily as those of great intellect. God delights in making Himself known to those who have a pure heart and a genuine desire to know Him and embrace His truth. The Lord takes pleasure in revealing Himself to such individuals.

Now, let us come to the main point: blessed are the pure in heart, for they shall see God. This means that the sight of God is the ultimate blessing for humanity. The sight of God encompasses understanding His nature, His plans, His ways, and His will, all of which are relevant to our eternal enjoyment of Him. To illustrate this, consider the story of Eudoxine, a philosopher who desired to behold the sun with full clarity. He was willing to endure being burned if only he could approach and observe its nature and movements. He believed that such knowledge held immense value. If knowledge of a mere creature holds such excellence, imagine the magnificence of knowing God Himself, of beholding His divine nature. This desire is evident in Philip's plea to Jesus in the 14th chapter of the Gospel of John. Philip said, "Lord, show us the Father, and it will be enough for us." If only we could see God, our hearts would be content, regardless of our own fate. Likewise, Moses expressed a fervent desire to see God's glory in Exodus 33:18. He pleaded, "Please show me your glory." Oh, the sight of God is truly a blessed thing! It is the sight of the infinite and glorious source of all things, the very fount of all goodness. How immensely blessed it is to behold such magnificence! People flock to see those who have been great instruments of good in the world. The presence of Alexander the Great or contemporary figures such as the King of Sweden or Sir Thomas Fairfax garners much attention. Yet, the sight of the first being, the cause of all good, surpasses any earthly spectacle. It is a sight that only the rational creature, with its capacity for understanding, can experience. The rational creature is not satisfied merely by observing what pleases the senses in the present moment. Instead, it constantly seeks the cause of its existence. The understanding of a rational creature ascends from effect to cause, continuously probing deeper until it reaches the supreme cause, the highest source of all things. Thus, individuals shall see God. This is humanity's blessedness.

To see God means to comprehend His essence, His plans, and His will concerning our eternal state. Furthermore, those who see God shall perceive Him as their God, possessing a personal connection to all the goodness, excellence, and glory they witness in Him. They will perceive it as their own, as having a share in it. Consider the difference between a stranger looking upon a king sitting on his throne and a queen or the king's eldest son doing the same. The stranger observes the king's glorious display with awe, but the queen or the king's heir views that glory as their own. It reflects upon them. They possess a sense of ownership. This is how the promise should be understood. Those who see God behold His excellency, glory, majesty, and greatness as their own. It becomes their happiness. They shall see God.

God reveals Himself and fulfills this promise in various ways, including immediate revelations to the soul. The soul of a human being can have an immediate connection with the infinite being of God, despite its finite nature. Just as the soul of Jesus Christ, being both God and man, had a union with the divine nature despite its finiteness, so can the finite soul of a human being have a close connection with God's essence. The soul is capable of a more immediate revelation of God than we can express or conceive. Although the fullness of this revelation shall be experienced in the future, even now in the world, we can taste a portion of the glory that awaits us in heaven. We can experience a union and communion with God that is a glimpse of what is to come. We can even have a foretaste of the beatific vision, where our souls intimately encounter the essence of God. However, we lack the ability to fully describe such experiences. Just as a person's eye can see everything except itself, the soul can act upon God without fully comprehending the manner in which it does so. Those who have undergone the purification of their hearts will testify that they see God in a manner different from before. Their testimonies may not adequately capture the extent of their perception, but they can affirm, "We were blind, but now we see. We see God in a way we never have before."

Moreover, in addition to this more immediate revelation of God to the soul, those who are pure in heart also perceive God in His works. They behold the greatness of God in the reflection of His glory in the creation. When they look at the heavens, the earth, and the seas, they see God in a new and profound way. Oh, the magnificent glory of God that is evident in the rising of the sun, the moon, and the stars, as well as in the vastness of the seas and the body of the earth! Perhaps, after the sermon on such days, many of you will take a stroll in the fields. But what do you see? You see the green grass, other people walking about, and trees. Yet, what do you see of God here? If your purpose is solely to contemplate God as He reveals Himself through His works, then it becomes a different matter. A spiritual heart, when it gazes upon God's works, transcends the mere physical creation and immediately directs its gaze towards God Himself. It looks up to heaven and sees the God of heaven, the God of the earth, and the God who forms and sustains all things. It sees the glory of its God in all the creatures. Indeed, when a person with a purified heart contemplates the works of God, they do not merely see land beyond their own; rather, they perceive that they cannot see more land than what belongs to their Father.

Although God's brilliance shines through His works, it is even more clearly revealed in His Word. It is a sign of a spiritual person when they see more of God's glory in the Scriptures than in all the great works that have ever been done in the world. Suppose the Lord were to take a man or a woman and show them all the countries in the world, even taking them to heaven and revealing the sun, moon, and stars, enabling them to understand their motions, showing them the seas and the ebb and flow of the tides, and granting them knowledge of the nature of plants and the mysteries of arts and sciences. Yet, after all that, when they come to read the Word, they would say, "I have seen the limits of all earthly perfections, but Your Word is exceedingly broad. In Your Word, I see more than I do in the entire book of nature. A few lines of Your Word reveal more to me than all the wonders of nature combined." This indeed is a testament to the purity of heart. A pure heart approaches the Word not as they would any other book but sees the wisdom, purity, and authority of God within it. The Word is not a sealed book to such a soul but an open one. They also see God in all

His ordinances; they are the means by which God is perceived. This includes the ministry of the Word, the sacraments, and all other ordinances. God enters the soul through these means, and the soul views them as instruments through which God is revealed. Additionally, they see God in the saints. In the saints, they behold the image of God, the reflection of God in His creation. However, in the saints, they witness the vivid image of God, just as the image of the father is seen in the child. Although those of the world may see little of God in the saints, once their eyes are opened and their hearts are purified, they cannot look upon any godly men or women without perceiving the abundant glory of God in them. This is what makes them cherish fellowship with the saints, for they see so much of God in them. Furthermore, they see God in their own spirits more than ever before. Their spirits were once shrouded in darkness, but now, having been sanctified, the presence of God dwells within them. They perceive God within their own hearts.

Above all, those who are pure in heart see God in the face of Jesus Christ. It is in Him that they behold the glory of God. The Scriptures speak of Christ in the Book of Hebrews as the exact imprint of God's nature, the radiance of His glory. There is no such description of all the angels in heaven or all the men in the world. True, humanity was created in the image of God, but Christ is described as the radiance of God's glory and the exact imprint of His nature. Therefore, Christ Himself declares that no one can know the Father except through Him. He says, "No one comes to the Father except through me. If you had known me, you would have known my Father also. From now on you do know Him and have seen Him." Knowledge of the Father is only possible through Jesus Christ, through understanding who He is. No one knows the Father except the Son, and those to whom the Son reveals Him. In Christ, all the treasures of wisdom and knowledge are hidden, and in Him dwells the fullness of the Godhead bodily. This is an extraordinary declaration, one that no human being could utter, nor even an angel. The words "In Him dwells the fullness of the Godhead bodily" would not have been fitting on the lips of any man or angel. But in Christ, the glory of God is revealed. To make a comparison with lesser things, consider that you cannot directly gaze at the sun in all its brilliance as it exists in the firmament. Yet, when the sun shines upon the water, you can observe its radiance. In the same way, while our eyes in this world are unable to directly behold the essence of God or adequately express it, we can come closest to beholding God in Jesus Christ. It is in Jesus Christ, as God-man, that we can perceive a great portion of God's glory and even catch a glimpse of His face. This is why it is stated in the Gospel that we behold God with an unveiled face. The apostle Paul, in distinguishing the new covenant from the old, notes that our understanding of God was limited during the time of the Law. In the old testament, there is an expression that says, "No man can see God and live." However, in the new testament, we find the expression that says, "We all, with unveiled face, beholding as in a mirror the glory of the Lord." This distinction emphasizes that we can now behold the glory of God with an unveiled face, no longer requiring a veil like Moses did. We see the glory of God through the Word, the ordinances, the saints, and our own spirits. Yet, the brightest mirror of all is Jesus Christ. Thus, it is declared in 2 Corinthians 4:6 that God, who commanded light to shine out of darkness, has shone in our hearts to give the light of the knowledge of the glory of God in the face of Jesus Christ. God, who once commanded light to shine out of darkness, has now shone in our hearts, enlightening not only our minds but also our hearts. This light shines to give us the knowledge of God and the light that reveals the glory of God. Consider these gradations: God has shone in our hearts to give knowledge, to give the light of knowledge, to give the light of knowledge of the glory of God. All of this is achieved through the face of Jesus Christ. Oh, how blessed are those with a pure heart who come to see God in the face of Jesus Christ! It is a mystery that can only be understood by those who experience it. Those who see God in Christ understand the profound significance of such a sight and would not trade it for anything in the world. However, it is impossible for them to fully express it to others. Blessed are they who truly see God in this way. Seeing the light is a glorious thing, as Solomon says. Imagine if God had created us with only four senses—hearing, smelling, feeling, and tasting—and then, in our time, decided to add a fifth sense, sight. How glorious would that be for us? Similarly, consider a man who has spent his entire life in a dark dungeon, never having seen light. If, one day, he were released from that dungeon and beheld the radiant sun, it would be an indescribably glorious experience for him. Likewise, if animals, which possess only the sense of sight, were granted understanding to comprehend things, what a wondrous transformation it would be for them!

Yet, when God grants us a spiritual sight of Himself, the change is even greater and surpasses all other glories. It is far more blessed than giving sight to a person who has never experienced it or endowing reason to animals. To see God is a blessed thing, and Scripture describes it to us in various ways.

First of all, it is the result of the Covenant of Grace, although some may disregard its significance due to their lack of understanding. Just as animals are unaffected by the absence of reason because they are unaware of its meaning, or as a person with all four senses would not comprehend the concept of a fifth sense, the world remains unaffected by the absence of the sight of God because they have no knowledge of it. However, the Scriptures establish it as a fruit of the Covenant of Grace. In Jeremiah, the Lord states, "They shall teach no more every man his neighbour, and every man his brother, saying, Know the Lord; for they shall all know me, from the least of them unto the greatest of them, saith the Lord; for I will forgive their iniquity, and will remember their sin no more." It is both a fruit of the Covenant of Grace and a result of the forgiveness of sins, which is the special mercy of the Covenant. The reason why many of you do not know God is that your iniquities have not been forgiven, and God still remembers your sins. You are not in a covenant relationship with God. When God brings you into covenant with Himself and forgives your sins, He enables you to know Him.

Secondly, God revealing Himself is a great expression of love—God's love for the soul, manifested through His self-revelation. In John 14:21, Jesus says, "He that hath my commandments and keepeth them, he it is that loveth me; and he that loveth me shall be loved of my Father, and I will love him, and will manifest myself to him." Christ revealing Himself to the soul is an act of His love and the love of the Father.

Thirdly, it is the blessedness of the glorious Church to see God. When the Lord raises His Church to the highest state of glory, one of the special blessings will be the sight of God. Revelation 22:4 states, "And they shall see his face." Many aspects are mentioned to convey the excellence and glory of the Church, but this is the most significant—seeing God's face. In comparison to what will be in the future, we currently see very little or nothing at all. We only see the back parts of God. However, there will come a time when the Church will enjoy a great measure of God's presence, even in this world. The previous chapter indicates that this will happen when the kings of the earth bring their glory to the Church. They will not bring their glory to heaven, but the Church will see the face of God.

Fourthly, seeing God is the beginning of life, and even the beginning of eternal life. "This is life eternal, that they might know thee the only true God, and Jesus Christ, whom thou hast sent into the world." One does not truly live until they come to know God. Those in the world are like lifeless bodies, but when they come to know God, they begin to truly live—the life of eternity. Oh, blessed are they!

Fifthly, it is the glory of heaven for the saints to see God. 1 John 3:2 says, "Beloved, now are we the sons of God, and it doth not yet appear what we shall be: but we know that, when he shall appear, we shall be like him; for we shall see him as he is." Although I do not speak of the present moment, I mention this verse to emphasize the blessedness of seeing God. It is the expression used by the Holy Spirit to describe the blessedness of the saints in heaven. "We shall be like him, for we shall see him as he is." This will be our happiness when we reach heaven—seeing God.

Sixthly, the angels also find great happiness in seeing the face of God, not just the saints. In Matthew 18:10, when describing the happiness of angels, it is written, "In heaven their angels do always behold the face of my Father which is in heaven." Here, Christ warns against offending the little ones because their angels always behold the face of His Father.

Seventhly, and I shall add further, it is the happiness—even for Christ Himself—to see the Father. We find this in John 10:15: "As the Father knoweth me, even so know I the Father." Christ emphasizes His excellence by declaring that the Father knows Him and He knows the Father. Jesus Christ takes pride in knowing the Father. He promises this happiness to the pure in heart—that they too will see God.

But why is it considered such a blessed thing? There are various reasons, and I will mention a couple now. First, it is a blessed thing to see God because it perfects human understanding. God has given humanity an intellect capable of comprehending all that is true, all truth in general. Therefore, the understanding cannot be perfected until it apprehends the fundamental truth.

Secondly, it brings infinite satisfaction to the understanding. The two are inseparable; perfection necessitates satisfaction and rest. Imagine if all the beautiful things in the world were combined into one object—that would be a remarkable sight. Now, consider that all beauty, excellence, and glory in all creatures are found in God. When the soul beholds God, it sees all things that are excellent, resulting in a kind of infinite satisfaction. As David says in Psalm 17:15, "As for me, I will behold thy face in righteousness: I shall be satisfied, when I awake, with thy likeness." This psalm was likely composed by David when he was driven from Saul's court. He implies that though he cannot behold the face of the king due to his negative reputation, he will behold God's face in righteousness, and upon awakening, he will be satisfied with God's likeness. It provides infinite satisfaction to the human mind. Many of you seek satisfaction in base and carnal desires. You find satisfaction in being well-dressed, indulging in food and drink, and engaging in impure and debased activities. But what is the comparison between the satisfaction of the soul in the sight of an infinite God and the satisfaction of a soul in base, carnal desires? Blessed are those who see God; they will be satisfied. In Psalm 36, the psalmist speaks of the sight of God, even in His house. He exclaims, "How excellent is thy lovingkindness, O God! Therefore the children of men put their trust under the shadow of thy wings. They shall be abundantly satisfied with the fatness of thy house; and thou shalt make them drink of the river of thy pleasures. For with thee is the fountain of life: in thy light shall we see light." This is the source of satisfaction, the river of pleasure, and the fountain of all that is good. "In thy light shall we see light." The light of God will shine upon the souls of the pure in heart, enabling them to see God, who is the source of all life. Oh, the soul's yearning for God!

Thirdly, Scripture declares that the sight of God is the very source of all grace in the soul, as it allows the soul to partake in the divine nature and be transformed into the image of God. In 2 Peter 1:2, it is written, "Grace and peace be multiplied unto you through the knowledge of God, and of Jesus our Lord." All grace and peace come through the knowledge of God and Jesus our Lord. According to His divine power, He has given us all things that pertain to life and godliness through the knowledge of Him who called us. The knowledge of God is a wellspring of good for the soul. Through this knowledge, we receive exceedingly great and precious promises, enabling us to partake in the divine nature and escape the corruption that is in the world through lust. All of this is achieved through the knowledge of God. In 2 Corinthians 3:18, it says, "But we all, with open face beholding as in a glass the glory of the Lord, are changed into the same image from glory to glory." Beholding the glory of the Lord transforms the soul into His likeness, to the extent possible. What enables the saints in heaven to be so similar to God? It is their sight of Him. As the Holy Spirit proclaims, "We shall be like him, for we shall see him as he is." Thus, the sight of God in heaven, as He truly is, transforms the souls of the saints, making them like God. They perfectly bear the image of God, seeing Him perfectly. The more a soul sees God in this world, the more it is transformed into His image. Oh, blessed are those who see God, for by seeing Him, they are transformed into His likeness. Is it not a blessed thing for a creature to be elevated to such excellence, to become like God Himself? This transformation comes through the knowledge of God. If only people would fall in love with the sight of God, they would discover a superior excellence for mankind beyond indulging in carnal desires. Alas, poor creature! While you satisfy your flesh, what do you truly see? You see your money, your possessions, and lavish feasts. But what is this sight compared to the sight of God? You possess an impure and unclean heart, and therefore, you believe there is nothing better than beholding these things. But blessed are the pure in heart, for they shall see God.

# SERMON XXVII

## Wherein the sight of God appear to be such a happy thing

Blessed are those with pure hearts, for they will have the privilege of seeing God.  Matthew 5:8

Seeing God is a truly blessed experience. It awakens and activates the virtues within the saints. When God is presented before the soul, it draws out and stimulates every grace they possess. This happens because God is a suitable object for the soul. Just as an impure heart is inclined towards unclean things, the sight of God before a pure soul ignites holiness, glory, and excellence. It has an infinite power to animate and invigorate all the virtues of the saints, making them vibrant and alive.

Furthermore, seeing God enables the soul to worship Him as the true God. Those who are ignorant of God worship what they do not know. However, when the soul beholds God, even in this world, the name of God is sanctified within the soul, and true worship is rendered in a holy manner.

The sight of God diminishes the glory of worldly pleasures and diverts the heart from seeking comfort in earthly things. Once the soul sees the comfort of God, the allure of worldly pleasures that were once admired fades into insignificance. One glimpse of God's glory has the power to overshadow the entire world, just as the light of a candle diminishes when the sun rises. When God revealed His glory to Abraham, it led him to leave behind his country, his kindred, and all worldly possessions. The appearance of the God of Glory redirected Abraham's heart. Similarly, if God were to shine even a single beam of His glory upon someone, it would redirect their heart away from any strong lust or attachment. Only God Himself would be sanctified in their sight. How blessed are those who have seen God!

Moreover, seeing God strengthens the soul to endure all hardships and triumph over every difficulty. You may complain about the hardships of suffering and the troubles encountered in the ways of God. However, if God were to appear to your soul, it would immediately fortify you against all difficulties. The sufferings endured for His sake would seem insignificant. Consider the example of Moses in Hebrews 11:27. By faith, he left Egypt without fearing the wrath of the king. How did he endure? By seeing the Invisible One. Moses saw the God of Glory, and that vision propelled him to leave behind all the glory and privileges of Egypt. Despite the numerous challenges he faced, including leading thousands of people through the Red Sea, Moses remained undeterred by fear. He never regretted his decision, for he saw the Invisible God. Therefore, those easily discouraged in the ways of God have never truly seen God. The sight of God empowers the soul to overcome all difficulties. To see God is to encounter the One with whom you have to deal. It is a sight that humbles Saul and stops him on his path of opposition. Likewise, it emboldens and encourages the heart of a saint on their journey when they realize they are dealing with the Lord Himself. Oh, how blessed are the pure in heart, for they shall see God!

Indeed, seeing God minimizes the significance of all afflictions and enables the soul to navigate any obstacles with ease. You may perceive suffering as challenging, and troubles may obstruct your path in God's ways. However, the appearance of God to your soul would instantly strengthen you, making those difficulties insignificant in your eyes. In the Book of Matthew 18:10, it is written, "Take heed that ye despise not one of these little ones: for I say unto you, That in heaven their angels do always behold the face of my Father which is in heaven." The repetition of the word "heaven" emphasizes that it is the place where God's face is seen. In comparison, what we have now is merely a glimpse of

God's back. Heaven is the throne of God, and there the saints will behold God upon His glorious throne. The sight of God in heaven surpasses any sight we have of Him in this world. We currently walk by faith and not by sight, and our sight of God is through His works, His Word, and His Son. While we behold the glory of God through His wisdom, power, and goodness reflected in His creation, it is still an indirect sight. In heaven, we will see Him face to face. Just as you eagerly desire to see the face of a skilled craftsman whose work you admire, God has fashioned this world, the work of His hands. Yet, in heaven, you will not see God through His works but will have an immediate vision of Him. Here, we come to know what God is not rather than what He is. We describe Him by negations, such as infinite, incomprehensible, eternal, and immutable. But in heaven, we shall see Him as He is, not only what He is not but what He truly is.

This promise speaks of the future sight of God. It refers to the sight of God in heaven. We sometimes believe that God has revealed much of Himself through His great works, His Word, and His Son. However, there is still much more to know about God than we currently comprehend. No one can see God and live; there is a sight of God that cannot coexist with this earthly life. In heaven, we will see God. There, God will manifest Himself with even greater beauty and glory than we have experienced thus far. The promise in Psalm 102:16 states, "When the Lord shall build up Zion, he shall appear in his glory." God will reveal Himself in His magnificent splendor, adorned in His glorious robes. Just as noble men and princes wear their finest attire on their wedding day, God will display His glory when He builds up Zion, the delight of His soul. Blessed are those who will see God in all His heavenly beauty and glory. However, the sight of God here in this world is by that sight that we commune with Him. We cannot have true communion with God without seeing Him. Many saints can testify from their own experience that they would not trade a single sight they have had of God in their interactions with Him for the world. They know it is blessed, blessed here, but even more blessed in the hereafter. They shall see God.

This promise primarily pertains to the future sight of God. We often think that God has revealed much of Himself through His great works, His Word, and His Son. However, there is still much more to know about God than we currently comprehend. No one can see God and live; there is a sight of God that cannot coexist with this earthly life. They shall see God in heaven. There,

God will manifest Himself with even greater beauty and glory than we have experienced thus far. The promise in Psalm 102:16 states, "When the Lord shall build up Zion, he shall appear in his glory." God will reveal Himself in His magnificent splendor, adorned in His glorious robes. Just as noble men and princes wear their finest attire on their wedding day, God will display His glory when He builds up Zion, the delight of His soul. Blessed are those who will see God in all His heavenly beauty and glory. However, the sight of God here in this world is by that sight that we commune with Him. We cannot have true communion with God without seeing Him. Many saints can testify from their own experience that they would not trade a single sight they have had of God in their interactions with Him for the world. They know it is blessed, blessed here, but even more blessed in the hereafter. They shall see God.

The sight of God in heaven will be more immediate than it is now. It will not be a sight mediated through various means and reflections, as it is currently. Instead, it will be an immediate union with the very essence and being of God, allowing for a direct vision of His essence. This is evident from various Scriptures, such as 1 Corinthians 13, where it is mentioned that we currently see God as through a glass dimly, but then we shall see Him face to face and know Him fully. Our current sight of God is mediated through something else, but in heaven, we will see Him directly, without any intervening medium. We will see His essence. It may seem impossible for a finite creature to comprehend the knowledge of the infinite God, but Scripture reveals that even a finite creature like Jesus Christ, who is both God and man, can possess knowledge of God's very being. This suggests that the nature of humanity is capable of a mode of revelation and union with God that surpasses what reason alone can comprehend. In heaven, the saints will be filled with God's presence and behold Him within themselves. Just as the fullness of the Godhead dwelt bodily in Christ, so spiritually, the saints will experience the fullness of the Godhead. This is described in Colossians 2:9. The fullness of the Godhead dwelt bodily in Christ, and spiritually, it will be present in the saints. Certainly, Christ sees God, perceiving His very being and essence, as the fullness of the Godhead dwells bodily in Him. Similarly, the saints who have the fullness of the Godhead dwelling spiritually in them will see God. They will behold Him immediately, not as one sees a color but as one sees light. Light is first present in our eyes, and from that, we perceive colors. Similarly, God's very being will be the primary focus of the soul's vision. Currently, we see God through His effects, perceiving His glory through His wisdom, power, and goodness manifested in creation. But in heaven, we will see Him directly, as a workman is seen in person rather than through their works. We shall not see God through His effects but will have an immediate vision of Him. In this world, we know more about what God is not than what He is. Our descriptions of Him often consist of negations. However, in heaven, we shall see Him as He truly is.

And we will also see God in the unity of His nature. Here, we perceive God in various aspects, but we cannot fully comprehend that God's excellence is singular. When we seek to know and see God here, we do so through the different manifestations of His attributes: His power, wisdom, holiness, goodness, faithfulness, eternity, simplicity, and infiniteness. These attributes are distinct, but they are all part of the one infinite excellence of God. They are diverse ways in which God's singular excellence is revealed. It is like looking at the sun through different colored glasses. The same sunlight passing through a blue glass appears blue, through a green glass it appears green, and through a red glass it appears red. However, the sun itself remains unchanged. Similarly, the excellency of God works in various ways, appearing diverse to us, yet He is one great excellency composed of many excellencies. Blessed are the pure in heart, for they shall see God in the unity of His being.

We will also come to understand the great mystery of the Trinity. We will comprehend how there are three Persons but one God. We currently perceive these things through faith, but then we will perceive them through sight.

We will see God in His eminence, infinitely above all creatures. In heaven, we will see Him as He truly is. We will witness everything He does and continues to do for all eternity. The saints will see God, not only His existence but also His ongoing work. Consider that in less than six thousand years, the Lord has displayed His glory in His works. Wouldn't it be a blessed thing for anyone to have been with God and witnessed everything He has done from the beginning of the world until today? But surely, even after this world comes to an end, God will remain everlasting, and the saints will remain with Him forever. They will be there to see what God will do for all eternity because God will continue working forever. After these six thousand years, God will still be working, and it is likely that He has only just begun. He will continue to work on greater and more glorious things throughout eternity. Imagine a creature being granted the opportunity to live with God, not only to see who God is but also to witness His heart, counsels, will, and ways, and to see what God will be doing for all eternity. This must surely be a blessed sight.

This sight of God will not require any kind of discourse or effort, as it does now. We will see everything at once, without any fatigue or difficulty. Currently, we often need to exert ourselves to move from one thing to another. But then, it will be intuitive, just as the eye takes in an object in an instant. We will effortlessly take in the object of God's presence. We will see Him fully, as our understanding will be elevated to look upon the face of God without any weariness. Just as our eyes cannot look directly at the sun without damaging our sight, our current ability to behold the face of God is limited. However, in heaven, our souls will be raised to such strength that we will be able to gaze upon the face of God forever, without growing weary. In this world, we often catch glimpses of God, fleeting moments of His glory. How sweet it would be if those glimpses were not so brief. But in heaven, we will have the constant shining of God's glory upon us. Oh, blessed are the pure in heart, for they shall see God. Some say that Christ connects the sight of God with purity of heart because Scripture tells us that the heart is purified by faith. When the soul believes and is purified by faith, it willingly surrenders its reason and allows faith to transcend reason. As faith believes what the soul cannot see, it will be rewarded by God, who will grant the sight of all that faith has believed. Now, you have the glorious revelation of God and the mysteries of salvation, which are beyond your reason's understanding. Yet, by faith, you believe them even though you cannot fully comprehend them. In the future, God will enable you to see fully what you now believe. You will have complete insight into the reasons behind the mysteries of the Gospel and the things of God that you currently perceive through faith. Oh, it is good for us to be willing now to let our reason be swallowed up by faith, for God will reveal all things to us in the future through sight, in ways that a rational soul can comprehend. We shall see God.

One further circumstance will enhance the blessedness of seeing God. We will see Him when He fully reveals Himself to us, making Him an even more delightful and satisfying object. It will be like seeing a creature with inherent beauty, such as a tulip, but with the added fragrance of a violet, possessing the sweetness of all the world's aromas combined. Similarly, the saints will see God, and it will be a wondrous delight because, along with the glorious excellence they will witness, there will be a divine fragrance emanating from God, as He pours Himself out to their souls. Many things could be said about this matter, and there are elaborate notions written about it, but it may not be fitting or beneficial to further explain or acquaint you with such notions. I will instead make some application of this excellent point.

"Blessed are those with pure hearts, for they will see God.

Firstly, if seeing God is such a blessedness and it is promised to those with pure hearts, then consider, those of you living in impurity and filthiness, think about what you are losing because of your sin and what you are likely to lose. This promise is for the pure in heart. But don't your consciences trouble you and tell you that there is woeful impurity in your hearts, vile uncleanness, which reflects in your lives and actions? So, what do you lose because of this? You lose the glorious sight of God. You live in this world without seeing God, and as a result, you will never behold His face for your good. Certainly, your lusts will cost you dearly. If a person is so attached to their lusts that they must give up their sight in order to keep them, it is like the story Ambrose tells of Philotimus, who suffered from a disease due to drinking and impurity. Physicians warned him that if he did not change his ways, he would lose his eyesight. Upon hearing this, his heart was so fixated on his lusts that he said, "Farewell, sight." It was as if he were saying, "I would rather lose my sight than give up my lusts." Oh Lord, how many such desperate individuals are among us today? If any such person exists, may the Lord of Heaven rebuke them and speak to their hearts. This is your condition; you are fixated on your lusts. So, what do you think about this glimpse of heavenly excellence, the sight of God? Will you part with your lusts or lose your sight? What will your answer be before God today when you hear that the sight of God is linked to purity of heart? And as the Apostle says in the well-known passage in Hebrews, "Without holiness, no one will see God." So, if you continue in any known sinful way, if your heart is still set on any beloved lust, and if you cannot be swayed from it, then your resolution is desperate. Farewell, pleasant sight! Farewell, the sight of God Himself! I would rather please my eyes and the desires of my heart than partake in the blessed and glorious sight of God. Oh, your lusts will cost you dearly. Therefore, consider how people live in this world without God. They have no sight of God. You may speak about God, but there is undoubtedly a sight of God that cannot coexist with the love of any sin. Though we cannot precisely express the difference between the sight of God one person has in this life compared to another, Scripture is clear that whoever continues in the path of sin does not truly know God (1 John 2:4). When someone claims to know God but does not keep His commandments, they are a liar, and the truth is not in them. It is as if the Holy Spirit is saying, 'The sight of God contains so much that it is impossible for it to coexist with a life of sin.'

Secondly, if seeing God is such a blessedness, how wretched are those who take no delight in seeing Him and would rather not see Him than see Him? This is the cursed disposition of many hearts, and indeed, it is the disposition of all who have guilty consciences. I mean all men and women with guilty consciences are led to this state through the guilt they bear. They would rather not see God than see Him. Oh, what a terrible state you find yourself in! Miserable creature, what is there in your lusts that can outweigh the loss of seeing God and bring you to a point where you desire never to behold His face? You do not consider it a misery to not see God, but rather a happiness. It is truly a cursed disposition. You would consider a child desperately wicked if they were to say to their father or mother, 'I wish I would never see your face.' Yet, every ungodly person says this. 'Oh, that I might never see Your face.' You might argue that nobody would say such a thing, but indeed, it is the language of your actions. We read in Job 21:14 about the description of the wicked, 'Therefore they say to God, "Depart from us, for we do not desire the knowledge of Your ways." ' Although we may not hear people utter these words, I do not think Job actually heard people say this. It was the language of their actions. They said to God, 'Depart from us, for we do not desire the knowledge of Your ways.' The sight of God, in fact, engages the soul in duty. The truth is, for a person to have a sight of God and still resolve to continue in their sin, these two things are incompatible with each other. Therefore, wicked individuals would rather abandon holiness than see God.

Thirdly, how miserable are those who will consider the sight of God as their greatest misery, a curse, and something dreadful? Certainly, their sin has brought them to a wretched state. Yet, this is the state of impure hearts and guilty consciences. Among all the sights in the world, the sight of God will trouble them the most and be the most dreadful. They will see God, but they will see Him as a terror to their souls. Their sight of God will become their curse and misery. They will see God as an enemy, beholding His infinite holy face and, through it, realizing how much God detests them. When you come to see how holy God is, you will also see how infinitely He hates you. You will perceive what an enemy He is and will be to you for all eternity. We read in Revelation 6:16-17 about the kings and mighty men of the earth crying out to the mountains and rocks, asking them to fall upon them and hide them from the sight of the Lamb. Similarly, on the day of judgment, when God appears in His glory, they will see the infinite God they have dealt with and the infinite power that will be exerted to their misery. They will witness His infinite justice upon them, and the strokes of it will be upon them forever. This will be so dreadful that they would rather have hills and mountains fall upon them than behold the sight of God. Oh, you poor creatures, what misery have you brought upon yourselves! On that day, when the saints look upon the face of God and rejoice in the revelation of His glory, going to meet this God who appears in His glory, you will be standing there trembling and shaking before the great God. You will realize that He is the infinite God you have sinned against and rebelled against, the infinite God who comes in all His glory to avenge Himself upon you for all eternity. This will be your condition if you have an impure heart. It is the pure in heart who will see God with comfort. If I were to mention only one thing to reveal the evil of an impure heart and to cause you to be restless until you have your hearts cleansed in the blood of Christ and purified by His Spirit, I would say this: your impurity will make God's presence dreadful to you. Currently, you defile yourselves with impure thoughts, covetous thoughts. Secretly, you defile your hearts with injustice and ill-gotten gain, thinking you can obtain for yourselves in that way. Thus, your souls become defiled. No wonder worldlings and impure individuals have such poor and low thoughts of God. They defile their souls to the extent that they cannot see God. Strive to keep yourselves clean.

And you who, through God's mercy, have had your consciences and souls purified, keep your souls pure and continue to strive for more and more purity. Do it for this reason: the more pure you become, the more you will see God.

Isn't it comforting to see the face of God? Light is comforting (Ecclesiastes 11:7), so how much more comforting is it to see God? Therefore, cleanse your souls more and more. Also, make use of this privilege of your eyesight; use it. Jesus Christ promises that you will see God, and if this is the blessing promised to you, then make use of it, set your eyes upon God while you live in this world, and make it your work to contemplate on God. Many, even Christians, live as if there were no blessing in seeing God. But if there is such a blessing, then why aren't your thoughts more focused on God? Every time you see God in His creation, you should gaze upon the glory of God and say, 'This is my God.' When you look into His Word, participate in His ordinances, and worship Him, why don't you fix your heart and eyes upon Him? A Christian who fixes their eyes upon God becomes a truly glorious Christian. If we would converse with God and fix our eyes upon Him, we would experience tremendous growth in holiness. Just as purity of heart makes us fit to see God, the sight of God will make us more and more pure in heart every day. So, before you close your eyes at night, you may have a sight of God, and when you open your eyes in the morning, you may have a sight of God that fills your heart with joy. Thus, you can live comfortably regardless of the state of the world. If you keep yourself in the sight of God, live above the world. God sets you before His eyes; you should set God before yours. By doing so, you shall also die comfortably. While we live in the flesh, we cannot have the full sight of God, but a Christian can die comfortably. Think this way when you are about to die: 'I am going to the place where I will come to know, just as I am known. I will know God perfectly and understand all the mysteries of the Gospel perfectly.' This will make death comfortable for the saints as they depart from this world. Therefore, rejoice in this blessing from Christ and exercise your faith in it. Let it occupy your thoughts: Blessed are the pure in heart, for they will see God."

# SERMON XXVIII

## The Order of this Beatitude

"Blessed are those who promote peace, for they will be called the children of God." - Matthew 5:9

W e recently concluded our discussion on the sixth Beatitude, which promises the vision of God to the pure in heart. Now we turn to the seventh Beatitude: "Blessed are those who promote peace, for they will be called the children of God." It is interesting to note the placement of this Beatitude—it is the seventh in order. In Proverbs 6, we find a list of seven things that the Lord hates, and the seventh item mentioned is "one who sows discord among brethren." In contrast to God's hatred, the seventh blessing pronounced is upon the peace-makers. It follows logically from the previous Beatitude, "Blessed are the pure in heart," as the impurity in people's hearts leads to discord in the world. If there were more holiness, there would be more peace. Indeed, peace and holiness are intertwined. Hebrews teaches that without holiness, no one can see God. The Epistle also joins purity of heart and peace-making together. A pure mind and heart contribute to peace. In James 3:17, we see a similar connection with wisdom: "But the wisdom that is from above is first pure, then peaceable." Likewise, in this Beatitude, purity of heart precedes peace-making.

Corruption in people's hearts causes disturbances and divisions. James 4:1 asks, "Where do wars and fights come from among you? Do they not come from your desires for pleasure that war in your members?" If we were to ask ourselves where conflicts and divisions originate, our tendency might be to blame specific groups or parties. However, the Apostle's answer is different—he attributes wars and fights to the lusts within our hearts. Wars and divisions between nations, in communities, and even within the Church are a result of the lusts in people's hearts. Discord in families, cities, and within individuals all stems from the lusts within our hearts. Saul, before his moral decline, had a peaceful disposition. But once corruption entered his heart and conscience, he became cruel and perverse. Those who keep themselves pure, with clean hearts and consciences, are peaceable and capable of making peace with others. On the other hand, corrupt hearts cause disturbances, divisions, and impurity. Wicked individuals, filled with sin, are bound to be troublemakers. Isaiah 57:20 describes the wicked as a troubled sea that cannot rest, casting up mire and dirt. God declares that there is no peace for the wicked. The fruits of the flesh, as listed in Galatians 5:20, include hatred, variance, emulations, wrath, strife, seditions, heresies, envying, murders, drunkenness, and revilings. All these spring from the flesh. Therefore, it is clear that the pure in heart, who will see God, are also peace-makers. It is a common perception that those who strive to live conscientiously are blamed for causing trouble. Yet, those who walk according to God's appointed rule, seeking light and refusing to deviate, regardless of personal interests or peace, are considered troublemakers. In the past, those labeled as Puritans were considered troublemakers of the state. However, Christ deems them the best at making peace—first, the pure in heart, then the peace-makers. Jeremiah, too, experienced being branded as troublesome in Jeremiah 15:10: "Woe is me, my mother, that you have borne me, a man of strife and a man of contention to the whole earth." Though Jeremiah pleads his innocence, stating that he walked with a pure conscience before all, everyone regarded him as a troublemaker. This is the distorted judgment of wicked people. The same occurred in the early days of Christianity, where Christians were accused of turning the world upside down. Whenever trouble arose, the blame was immediately placed on Christians. Today, those who are accused of causing trouble and disturbances are often the ones who walk closely and strictly with God, according to the rule of His Word, striving to maintain purity and cleanness. Yet, these are the peace-makers and the children of God. Despite what the world may think, these individuals sustain the world. The Lord will eventually vindicate those who walk closely and strictly with Him. However, let us focus on the subject of this Beatitude—those who promote peace.

The peace-makers.

The term "peace-makers" is generally understood by interpreters as those who either maintain peace or actively work towards establishing it. It is indeed a blessed thing to have a peaceful heart within oneself, to cultivate peace in one's own soul. A contrary disposition—one that is stubborn and perverse—is cursed. But a peaceable, gentle, and quiet disposition is blessed. Moreover, it is even more blessed to be an instrument in bringing about peace in the places where we live and among those with whom we interact. In the present times, there is a great need for peace-makers.

Firstly, there are those who strive to make peace between humans and God. When Christ says, "Blessed are the peace-makers," we must understand it primarily in a spiritual sense, although we should not exclude other aspects. Blessed are those who, having experienced the blessedness of peace themselves and having obtained peace with God, earnestly desire to bring others into reconciliation with Him. When a husband has experienced God's transformative work in purifying his heart through faith and has tasted the sweetness of peace with God, he desires to see his wife's soul reconciled to God as well. Likewise, a wife who has found peace with God and has a purified heart through faith desires to see her husband's heart turned to God. The same applies to brothers, kin, neighbors, and others. Those who have known the peace of God will do everything possible to bring their brothers and sisters into peace with God. They will share their own experiences and warn them about their current condition. They will explain how they themselves were once enemies of God and how they abhorred their previous state. They will exhort others to consider their ways and the enmity in their hearts toward the blessed and eternal God. They will teach them what God's Word reveals about the glorious work of reconciling sinners to Himself. Such peace-makers will plead, pray, and instruct others to be at peace with God. Blessed is the person who, in a gracious manner, labors to draw others into peace with God and whom God blesses in these endeavors. They can thank

God that they have been instrumental in reducing enmity towards God by even a single enemy. They may rejoice knowing that, through their efforts, they have blessed the world. It is indeed a blessed thing to labor for the reconciliation of souls with God.

Consider the immense evil from which you deliver the souls of your brothers and the great good you bring to their lives. The souls of your brothers will bless you if you are instrumental in making peace between them and God. When you lie on your deathbed, passing into the infinite ocean of eternity, you will bless God that you ever knew such peace-makers. Even in heaven, you will continue to bless God for knowing them. Is it not a blessed thing to labor to draw others into peace with God?

The work of the ministry is a blessed and honourable calling. How beautiful are the feet of those who bring the glad tidings of peace! People should regard it as such. The first duty of a minister when entering a new place is to proclaim peace. As Paul says, "To us is committed the word of reconciliation." This is our great mission, the work that God has appointed some individuals to undertake. God sends them to those who are currently enemies of Him but in whom He has thoughts of peace. He commands them to bring the message of peace, to reveal His desire for reconciliation, and to show people the way to be reconciled to Him. They are to strive with all their might, even to the point of giving their lives, to bring others into peace with God. Such labor is worth more than a thousand lives if it leads to peace between souls and God. Ministers must be diligent in this work, for it is a cursed thing to be negligent in such a great work. When the ministry has succeeded in making peace, the word has accomplished its purpose. Ministers should be careful and faithful in their work, knowing that if they win even one soul to peace with God, that soul will bless them forever. Ministers deserve the blessing and prayers of those whose lives they have touched.

Indeed, blessed are the peace-makers in all these senses.

And if so, oh, how blessed is that great peace-maker Jesus Christ, who is designated by the Father to reconcile man with Him. All human beings have fallen from God in Adam and are in a state of enmity against Him, that's certain. Neither the angels in heaven nor the creatures on earth can reconcile even a single sinful soul with God; it is a task too great for any creature. However, Jesus

Christ, the wisdom of the Father, the second person, looks upon the wretched and miserable state of humanity and realizes that if left to themselves, they are all doomed to eternal enmity with God, and God would become their eternal enemy. Therefore, He steps in and mediates between wretched man and God, as appointed by the Father, to make peace. He stands as the great Mediator of the second Covenant. His heart is so dedicated to the task of making peace between man and God that He is willing to lay down His life for it. Colossians 1:20 states, "And having made peace through the blood of His cross." Indeed, Jesus Christ's heart is so committed to being a peace-maker between the world and God that He willingly sheds His blood and even becomes a curse. Consider, you children of men, the vast distance that existed between God and you, and how Christ—both God and man—had to intervene to make peace between you and God. He shed His blood and became a curse to accomplish this great work of God. This, my brethren, is the great mystery of godliness. We should spend our days in admiration, standing, wondering, and blessing our Saviour, the great peace-maker. If it were not for Him, we would all be eternal enemies of God. Let our souls bless Jesus Christ, and the greater the curse upon Him in this work, the more let our souls bless Him. This work will be the eternal exercise of angels and saints, offering blessings, honor, praise, worship, and service to Him who sits upon the Throne and to the Lamb forevermore, for He has redeemed us by His blood, as stated in Revelation 5. Those who have experienced the blessing of peace with God know how to bless God for Jesus Christ. To all of you who sometimes bless God for outward peace, abundance, and comfort in this world, I appeal to your consciences with this question: When did you spend time in your closets, admiring the glory of God in the great work of the mediation of Jesus Christ, who makes peace between your souls and God? When did your hearts truly focus on this great work above all else in the world, and when were your spirits lifted in admiration, worship, and praise of God and Jesus Christ, the great peace-maker? Bless and magnify and praise the name of God and bless His Son, who is God blessed forever, for this great work of making peace between your souls and God. It would be a good indication that Christ has been a peace-maker for your souls if you have been deeply affected by it. However, if the work of Christ in making peace between man and God means nothing more to you than mere hearing, and the great mystery of godliness in the Gospel passes lightly away when you hear it without your hearts being moved, it is much to be feared, nay, it can be concluded with certainty that peace has not been made between your souls and God to this day. We do not know what His blood may accomplish or its subsequent effects, but it has not yet had this gracious effect on you. Now we turn to the second matter.

Blessed are the peace-makers.

Peace-makers between man and man are blessed. I confess that I had intended to speak very briefly about this matter at this time, and not from this Scripture. I have preached many sermons on the subject of heart divisions, covering almost every necessary aspect of it— the evil of divisions, the causes of them, and the means to heal them. Therefore, I thought to pass over this topic briefly. However, since there are many who have either not heard or have no current use for those previous sermons, and because of the necessity of the topic, I shall speak a little about peace-making between man and man.

Engaging in this work is especially delightful, particularly in these times. To meddle with the subject of peace between man and man is one of the most challenging tasks for any minister, especially during such times. It is difficult because people's hearts are impure, filled with filth and uncleanness, and how does one go about making peace with them? It is difficult because hardly anyone can bring themselves to acknowledge that they are in any way responsible for the lack of peace among others. If all the people in England were gathered together, and you were to go from one person to another asking if they were contributing to the divisions in the country, they would vehemently deny it. Each person would disavow any involvement. They would cast blame upon each other, with neither side willing to yield. All cry for peace, and many times, even those who cry out for it are the main obstacles to achieving it. They cry for peace in a manner that hinders it when they speak about it. It is very difficult to address this matter because a person cannot discern how to approach it practically without offending one side or the other. Some form of concession is necessary for peace to exist between two conflicting parties. The Spaniards have a proverb: "Stone and mortar make a wall," because one yields, but two hard things do not. Since it is so challenging for anyone to yield, it is equally difficult to meddle in the subject of peace. Moreover, it is even more difficult now than ever because those who are the greatest contributors to division and conflict all claim the National

Covenant as justification for their parties and the promotion and maintenance of disunity. It is reminiscent of the situation with the Sacrament, which God ordained to be a means of unity in the churches. It is called the Communion because it is intended to unite the churches. However, due to human corruption, nothing has caused as much disunity as the Sacrament. Similarly, although the Covenant was undoubtedly intended for unity, through human corruption, if precautions are not taken, it may lead to even greater divisions. To approach parties in conflict and division requires great care in one's conduct. Indeed, considering it initially, I was almost discouraged from speaking about it due to the current disposition of people's hearts toward peace. The Prophet Hosea states in Hosea 7:7 that the people were as hot as an oven. It means that the people were so committed to their own ways and courses that whatever the Prophet said to them was in vain. It was as if he threw a few sticks into a red-hot oven, and they were instantly devoured and reduced to ashes. As if to say, all my words have no effect on them, and they do not respond to anything I say, just like a little straw that is cast into a hot oven. Truly, my brethren, are not people's hearts similarly heated in their divisions? Some are resolute and seemingly set on fire at this time, so that what is said to them is instantly devoured and comes to nothing. It is as unprofitable at this time as anything else, though nothing is more necessary. Although it may be so unprofitable, because there is so much blessedness in it, I shall address the topic a little. It is a blessed thing to be a peace-maker. Certainly, those who handle it well demonstrate a gracious disposition of heart and are therefore blessed. It indicates a very gracious, holy, and spiritual disposition of heart to be a peace-maker between man and man, provided it is done in a spiritual manner and for spiritual purposes. A person who wishes to meddle in matters of peace among others must first ensure that their own relationship with God is well. They must possess a peaceable disposition themselves. If someone of a froward or turbulent disposition were to speak of peace and denounce divisions, everyone would be ready to challenge them. They must exhibit much self-denial, not considering themselves or their own party in any way, but aiming purely for God's glory and the public good. Therefore, it is evidence of much grace in the heart, and thus the person is blessed. They are blessed when they handle matters wisely, prudently, and graciously.

And then blessed, because by this means, they shall prevent an abundance of evil. Oh, the woeful evils that result from disputes and divisions—national divisions, sea divisions, church divisions, family divisions, personal divisions, divisions between neighbours, and the like. I had intended to speak briefly about each of them. Oh, the abundance of sin committed during times of division. In former times, there were many great sins committed among the people of God, but I firmly believe that in no thirty-year period since the Gospel was known in England has there been as much sin among godly people as in these past three years. God's people have defiled themselves with sinful dispositions more in these last three years than in any thirty-year period since the Gospel was known in England. It is like a family where more sin can be committed in one hour of brawls, contentions, and strife than in another family in an entire year. I truly believe that sometimes in certain individuals, a single person, in a fit of passion and contention, can commit more sin in one hour than they would in a whole quarter of a year. That hour may accumulate more guilt than all the sins they commit in that quarter of a year combined. I fear that many of you may have experienced this personally. Just as we read of Moses, who, in a fit of anger, broke the two tablets when he came down from the mountain, although his anger was holy and for God's sake. Likewise, many men and women, in the grip of sinful anger, break all ten commandments at once. Oh, the abundance of sin committed through divisions! The Apostle James says in James 3:16, "For where envying and strife is, there is confusion and every evil work." Oh, my brethren, it is this abundance of sin that causes the devil to agitate our divisions because he sees the vast amount of sin that is committed— the reviling, the hatred, the brawling, the sinful thoughts, plotting, contriving, and counseling, the wicked words and actions. People only strive to harm one another as much as they possibly can. The devil looks at the sin and aims for that. It is not so much the division itself that the devil is concerned about, but the sin that accompanies it. Austin used a simile that I have found helpful: when a fowler wants to catch birds, he sets his net on the other side of the hedge and throws stones into the hedge. He doesn't expect to kill the bird with the stones, but rather to cause a disturbance and make the bird fly out, hoping to catch it in the net on the other side of the hedge. That is his aim. Similarly, when the devil stirs up divisions and strife, he tempts people to throw stones at each other, provoking strife and creating a great commotion. But what the devil aims for is the net on the other side of the hedge. He knows that this will be the cause of an abundance of sin—bitterness of spirit, wrath, wicked words, wicked actions. And thus, he catches poor souls. When you are tempted to a fit of passion, know that the devil expects a great deal of sin to follow. Now blessed are the peace-makers, for they are the means to prevent an abundance of sin. That is a most blessed thing. What greater blessing can a person have than to be an instrument in preventing sin? It is a blessed thing to prevent even one sin, but to be an instrument in preventing so much sin must undoubtedly be blessed. Blessed are the peace-makers, for they are also instrumental in bringing about an abundance of good. All things flourish where there is peace—spiritual things flourish, and little things grow to great heights. Oh, blessed are the peace-makers! They are the cause of much good. To demonstrate both the evil of its absence and the goodness of peace would require a lengthy discussion, but I have covered those topics elsewhere and will not mention them now. Blessed are the peace-makers, for they are instrumental for God in a work that He greatly delights in. When you read the Scriptures, you will find no duty more emphasised, backed by arguments, motives, and persuasions, and no duty that has stronger exhortations than peace. Read the Epistles to the Philippians, Ephesians, Colossians, Romans, and Corinthians, and you will consistently find that peace is what the Holy Spirit most persuades men to pursue. Even Christ Himself, the great peace-maker, is concerned not only with peace between God and us but also between man and man. He takes pride in this title. Other great captains used to boast of the places where they engaged in wars, like Scipio Africanus. But Christ derives His name from peace. He was prefigured by Solomon, the Prince of Peace. He came into the world during a time of peace, and the angels sang a song of peace, "Glory to God on high, peace on earth." His ministers were appointed to go and preach peace. His kingdom consists of righteousness and peace. His blessing is a blessing of peace. When He rose again, He spoke peace. His legacy is a legacy of peace: "My peace I leave with you." And the apostolic benediction is still "grace and peace." Therefore, we can conclude easily that there is nothing God's heart desires more than to see peace. Blessed, then, are the peace-makers, for they are instrumental in something that brings the Lord much glory. Certainly, they shall also be blessed by many. Just as when David had an unpeaceable disposition towards Nabal and intended to harm him, but when Abigail came and, through her wisdom and peaceable spirit, calmed David's anger, bringing him to a state of peace and tranquillity, David immediately blessed God for Abigail and blessed Abigail herself. He said, "Blessed be thou, which hast kept me this day from coming to shed blood, and from avenging myself with mine own hand" (1 Samuel 25:33). If people do not have wicked and vile hearts, when their corruption is stirred, and they have bitter thoughts and desperate resolutions, if God sends a person of peace to them—someone who approaches them with a calm and peaceable spirit, persuades them with scripture, and quells their boiling emotions, cooling their passionate hearts and dampening their desperate resolutions—then, if they are not desperately wicked, they will see cause to bless God for it. They will say, "Well, blessed be God who sent such a person to prevent me. I now see that I would have done something I would have later regretted." Blessed are the peace-makers, for they shall be called the children of God.

# SERMON XXIX

## Blessed are Those Who Promote Peace Between People

Blessed are the peacemakers, for they shall be called the children
of God. - Matthew 5:9

It is a truly blessed thing to be an instrument of peace between man and
man. I recall the story of Moses in Exodus 2:13-14, where he involved himself in a quarrelsome situation with the intention of making peace. The Holy
Spirit later records this in the New Testament as a significant commendation of
Moses. "And when he went out the second day, behold, two Hebrew men were
fighting, and he said to the one who did the wrong, 'Why are you striking your
companion?'"

Now, Moses could have lived a comfortable life at the court, enjoying all the
pleasures it had to offer. Why did he choose to intervene in the disputes among
his fellow Hebrews? In Acts 7:26, among the great commendations of Moses, it
is written, "And the next day he appeared to two of them as they were fighting
and tried to reconcile them, saying, 'Men, you are brothers. Why do you wrong
each other?'" The Holy Spirit does not forget that Moses was not content with
merely living at the court and indulging in worldly delights. Instead, he took

an active interest in resolving conflicts among his brethren, doing everything possible to reconcile them. The Holy Spirit remembers this act in later ages. Thus, we must reflect on the matter of making and maintaining peace between individuals.

It is important to note that the blessing does not come upon those who are at peace with sin or seek to make peace with the sins and corruptions of others. Instead, the blessing is bestowed upon peacemakers who foster harmony among brethren and neighbors. While we should strive to be at peace with all people to the best of our ability, we must never attempt to be at peace with sin. Even though God desires to reconcile the world to Himself, He will never reconcile with sin. God and sin can never be reconciled. Not even Christ's actions, though not intended to reconcile God and sin, could accomplish such a reconciliation. God will always remain an eternal enemy of sin, and that is His glory. Therefore, when we strive to make peace, we must not seek peace with the corruptions and sins of others. We should not love peace to the extent of accepting it while it is entwined with the filth of guilt and sin. We must not flatter and appease the corruptions of others. There is no blessedness in doing so; it brings a curse upon us. However, although we should never be at peace with the sins of others, we can exercise forbearance towards sinners. When we confront their sins, we must do so using the weapons appointed by God. The magistrate has a role in opposing sin, as does the church. There may be a tendency for people to display more turbulence in opposing the faults and corruptions of others than what God allows. Yet, the focus here is on peace between one person and another.

Therefore, I shall first present some general rules for peace between individuals, followed by more specific rules for family peace and neighborly peace. I must confess that I initially intended to discuss peace within the church and the commonwealth as well, but I will explain later why we will not address those topics now.

First, we should never resort to violence unless it is absolutely necessary. If our goals can be achieved through means other than violence, we should always explore those options. When we witness disorderly conduct or actions contrary to our expectations, we should first consider whether there are any means to rectify the situation before resorting to violence. Violence should always be the last resort. However, this is not the approach adopted by most people. When something displeases them about someone, they immediately respond with hostility. Their first instinct is to employ violence as a means to restore order. Yet, this is not the attitude of a child of God. Blessed are the peacemakers, for they shall be called the children of God. As I will explain later, this means they shall be like God. The Lord Himself does not delight in grieving His creatures. Scripture declares that He does not take pleasure in the death of a sinner; He does not willingly inflict punishment. Therefore, we should be like our Father. If there are alternative means available to us besides violence, we should exhaust those options before engaging in violent actions.

Second, if violence becomes inevitable, it should be limited to what is strictly necessary. When I mention the extent of violence, I am referring to both the subject against whom it is directed and the violence itself. The violence should not extend beyond what is necessary, and wherever possible, it should be tempered with gentleness and love, if there is hope for reconciliation through such means. Violence should not be employed recklessly. In terms of the subject against whom the violence is directed, it is essential to ensure that when someone displeases us, we confront that person directly regarding the specific matter in which they have transgressed. It is a common occurrence for neighbors to become angry with an individual within a family and, as a result, harbor animosity towards the entire household. This type of behavior causes significant division. The same applies to towns, churches, and commonwealths. However, these rules pertain to peace in a general sense.

Thirdly, if you desire peace in the world, you must be prepared to accept that it may come at a cost. Everyone claims to desire peace. As Augustine commented on the Psalms, when the topic of peace is raised, all of humanity expresses their immediate desire for it. With one voice, they say, "I desire it, I wish for it, I want it, I love it." Everyone longs for peace, but they are unwilling to pay the price for it. What does this mean? Well, they want peace, but they want everyone else to conform to their own opinions. They want to have free reign to do whatever they please without anyone opposing them. But when the heart is devoted to peace and is influenced by Christ to be a peacemaker, that person is so determined to pursue peace that they are willing to pay a high price for it, except when it comes to sin. The truth is, peace is never too costly unless sin is involved. We often say that we can buy gold at too high a price, and the same applies to peace. If we betray our consciences or compromise the truth for the sake of peace, it is too high a price to pay. But we should be willing to sacrifice what belongs to us and not to God, especially when it concerns public peace. If every man and woman firmly resolved, saying, "As long as I live, wherever God places me, I will strive to bring peace where I reside, and I am willing to pay any price to achieve it," and if they were willing to pursue any means of peace that is not sinful, then we would see the glory of God, the advancement of the common good, and the welfare of our brothers' souls. For where there are conflicts and disputes, there is an abundance of sin, as I have experienced. Now, when I have the opportunity to prevent sin and do good, I am determined, no matter the cost, not to be negligent in promoting this. This resolution must be present in every person, to be willing to pay a high price for peace, for peace is a precious commodity that is not obtained through mere desires or by pointing fingers at each other. So, I ask those who cry out for peace, what has it cost you?

The fourth rule for fostering peace is that every man and woman should consider it the most honourable thing to yield first. The wicked principle that exists in the hearts of people, which suggests that it is disgraceful to be the first to yield, is what causes disturbance in the world and in all societies. But if people were guided by the principle that the one who begins to yield in the face of a breach is the most honourable, it would greatly contribute to peace. Believe me, it is so. Just as it is a great part of God's honour to initiate reconciliation with us, as Scripture states, "God was in Christ reconciling the world to Himself," and God was in Christ even from eternity. If God had not taken the initiative with us, we would have resisted Him for all eternity. Mankind would have remained an eternal enemy of God if God had not first sought reconciliation. Now, if it is God's honour to initiate reconciliation with us, then it is the honour of His creature to initiate reconciliation with fellow creatures. You may say, "Let him come to me and yield, for I am superior to him, or he has wronged me, and the inferior ought to yield." But if God had taken that approach with you and said, "Let the creature yield, for he is inferior, and let any creature who has been unjust and wronged Me yield," what would have become of you? If you desire to be called a child of God, then be a peacemaker like God. Initiate the work of reconciliation. If another person initiates it, you have lost the honour of doing so and a significant part of the reward. It is not praiseworthy when another person starts to make peace, and then you join in. Even my base nature can do that. But if, for the sake of peace, you can yield to someone inferior to you and be the first to seek peace, that is truly honourable in the eyes of God and man. This is the fourth rule.

Fifthly, address breaches early. When there is a breach between you and another person, whether it is within a state, church, neighborhood, or family, take immediate action to mend the breach. Do not allow it to escalate before attempting to resolve it. Scripture compares contention and strife to the breach of waters. When there is a breach, you cannot simply stand and watch, thinking that you will stop it later. No, you must act promptly. You never know what the consequences may be. Great breaches often arise from small beginnings, and addressing the issue early on can prevent immense evils that later become irreparable. This is another rule for peace.

Sixthly, if you find it difficult to achieve peace, persevere. Pursue peace and try various approaches. Do not be satisfied with saying, "Well, God knows I desire peace, and I have made some feeble attempts." Have your efforts resulted in the desired outcome? If not, go on and try again. Explore different possibilities. Whatever a person's heart is set on, they will exhaust all possibilities to achieve it. If your heart is set on peace, even if you face setbacks the first and second time, you will continue to persevere. The Scripture instructs us to pursue peace and follow after it. Consider my text: "Blessed are the peace-makers," it does not say, "Blessed are the peace-wishers." Some individuals possess good intentions and claim, "I wish there were peace," and perhaps they make some feeble attempts. But has their work achieved peace? They should not rest until they have accomplished it. If there are any means left untried, explore those options.

Seventhly, if, after exhausting all means, you still cannot achieve peace because some individuals persist in their contentious spirits, then observe this rule: Determine to conduct yourself in a convincing manner before them. They may have troublesome spirits, and every word you speak seems to provoke them. Nevertheless, resolve to behave in a convincing and upright manner, even if it causes you trouble. However, break off with this resolution: "I will do my best to convince them through a consistent display of goodness, holiness, justice, and righteousness. Perhaps, by doing so, I can heap coals of fire upon their heads and soften their hearts. I am determined that, regardless of the evil they do to me, I will do good to them." As Calvin once said of Luther, who had a passionate and fiery temperament, "Let Luther call me a devil, let him call me whatever he likes, I will still acknowledge Luther as a precious servant of God, whom God uses as an instrument for great good." That is a peacemaking spirit. This is the way to make peace when all other means have been exhausted and people's spirits cannot be pacified. Walk before them in a convincing and consistent manner, even if it takes months, or even years. Your conduct will eventually prevail upon their hearts more than any other means you attempted to make peace between you and them. In truth, in these times, the people of God are facing as many trials in this regard as in any other age. I wish God would impress this one thing I am speaking of upon their hearts. There are so many clamors, outcries, and reports among us that one wonders how so much dust has been raised. It is astonishing to see the bitterness and madness that has taken hold of individuals who once seemed to be godly and religious. But the best course of action is to wait upon the Lord, follow His ways strictly and without offense, commit your cause to God, and in due time, all these clamors and disputes will fade away, coming to nothing. Your light will shine brightly, and God will incline the hearts of others toward you. They will be convinced and say, "Truly, this person is a child of God. Let us observe their conduct and ways. The Spirit of God is evident in everything they do." This is our way: to walk in a convincing and consistent manner, especially when we cannot bring peace to others by any other means.

Lastly, engage in fervent prayer. Pray for the peace of Jerusalem, pray for peace in the kingdom, cities, churches, neighborhoods, and families. Devote much time to prayer for peace. This is a powerful spiritual aid. I could provide scriptural references for each of these points, but the topic is so extensive, and I have previously spoken about it. Therefore, I will only mention the main aspects. Many of you lament the troubles of the times and the contentions among people, the bitterness of spirits. But I appeal to your consciences today, in the name of God, and ask: How much time have you spent privately pouring out your hearts to God, complaining to Him in secret, just between you and Him? Perhaps some individuals may pray with others and mention the contentions, but it is done with a spirit of contention. However, when you are alone, have you fervently prayed to God, earnestly pleading with Him to find means of reconciliation? "O Lord, we cannot see how people can be reconciled. Their hearts are so far apart. But You, who know how to reconcile heaven and earth, surely You know how to reconcile people with one another." Pray fervently for this, and know that your prayers will eventually return to your own bosom. This concludes the general points.

Now, let's discuss the specifics. For peace within families, observe the following rules.

Firstly, pay attention to the temperaments of the individuals in your family. Husbands should consider the temperament of their wives and indulge them accordingly. Likewise, wives should consider the temperament of their husbands. Parents should consider the temperament of their children, and masters should consider the temperament of their servants. Everyone should observe the temperaments of one another, even fellow servants, as it greatly contributes to family peace.

Secondly, be mindful of the appropriate times to discuss matters within the family. Do not engage in hasty debates at any given moment. Husbands should refrain from debating with their wives when they are upset, and the same goes for wives. Instead, exercise restraint. If a wife desires a peaceful life and complains about certain misconduct in her husband, I appeal to her: What do you do when your husband misbehaves? Do you immediately react and engage in arguments with him while he is angry? Instead, wait for the most suitable time, when he is most receptive, to discuss the unjust actions. Present it to him in a loving manner. Husbands should follow the same principle with their wives. If something has been done incorrectly, wait for the most opportune moment to address it in a manner that is more likely to be received positively. This greatly contributes to peace within the family.

Thirdly, if anyone is angry with another family member for a specific reason, they should be cautious not to become angry with them for everything just because of one mistake. It is often observed that if something is amiss in a family, a contentious spirit causes individuals to become angry with everything and everyone in the family. Wisdom should guide you to recognize that just because one thing upsets you, it does not mean that everything else is displeasing. Other actions might be done just as well as they were when you were pleased. You are presently displeased with one thing, so confine your displeasure to that particular matter. Do not allow bitterness to overflow. This is a common ailment that physicians observe in the body when gall spills over and does not remain in its proper place. Likewise, when something displeases you, do not let your heart become angry and bitter towards everything. It is a major cause of strife within a family.

Fourthly, superiors should desire obedience out of love rather than fear, and inferiors should obey out of love rather than fear or necessity. The cause of disturbance within families lies in servants and children only obeying out of fear or when compelled by necessity. They do not genuinely care about obedience. Meanwhile, governors treat their children and servants as if their love does not matter at all; they only care about having their will obeyed. If you adopt such principles within your family, it will undoubtedly cause great turmoil. However, if the superiors desire and strive for obedience out of love rather than fear, and if the inferiors obey and serve out of love for their superiors rather than out of necessity, peace will abound in the family.

Fifthly, remember that when there is a need to oppose others within the family due to wrongdoing, show the most love during that time. Demonstrate your greatest love to them, especially then, so they may be convinced that you genuinely intend their good. As the proverb goes, "Let a man love me and beat me." If you find it necessary to express displeasure within your family, make sure that your concern is to exhibit love. The individuals you express displeasure towards should be convinced that even during those moments, you still love them. This approach significantly reduces bitterness. Otherwise, if you oppose them out of bitterness, even if the cause for opposition is just, bitterness will only breed more bitterness. Instead of subduing their faults, you will only provoke them further. However, if you oppose them in a way that reproves them or, if necessary, punishes them, while making it evident that you have their best interests at heart and mean them no harm, it will greatly affect their spirits and promote peace within the family. A quiet habitation is a great blessing upon a family. It is desirable for peace and tranquility to prevail from morning to night, from the beginning of the week to the end, and from the start of the year to its conclusion. Everyone should know their duties, with governors performing theirs and children and servants fulfilling theirs, resulting in a quiet habitation.

Now, let's turn our attention to neighbors. Anyone involved in neighborly matters must possess great self-denial, wisdom, love, and meekness when dealing with others. The following rules are to be observed for peace between neighbors.

Firstly, do not harbor ill feelings towards a neighbor solely based on hearsay. Much strife and commotion arise between neighbors, but often, upon examination, there is no substance to the conflict—it was merely a figment of the imagination. It is similar to false alarms in the military; there is no truth to it, and as soon as they discuss it, they shake hands and become friends. Be cautious not to entertain grudges based solely on hearsay. Consider that the peace between you and your neighbor is precious, and you are reluctant to lose its benefits and sweetness over nothing. Therefore, inquire whether the hearsay is true or not. If necessary, approach your neighbor directly to clarify, rather than fostering resentment that may lead to contention. This is the first rule.

Secondly, be careful not to be stubborn in your judgment regarding your own cause. Be willing to listen to those who are not personally involved in the matter. Above all, be cautious about forming judgments while in a state of anger. Although people tend to be resolute in their judgments when angry, the truth is that their ability to judge is weakest when anger arises. During such times, do not rely on your own judgment. When anger takes hold, judgment dissipates. People have the feeblest judgments when consumed by anger, yet they become most resolute in their judgments at that time. This is the second rule. If you desire peace among neighbors, do not be overly insistent on your own judgments regarding your own cause, particularly in moments of anger. Instead, take a step back, reflect, and pray over it.

Thirdly, before engaging in disputes with a neighbor, pray first. Pray to God for guidance in the matter. Say, "Here is a situation that is likely to cause great disturbance. Lord, guide me. Lord, help me. Direct me in this, that I may not do anything dishonorable to Your great name, nor anything contrary to Your will." I appeal to your consciences on this matter. Those of you who have dealt with neighbors, I appeal to your consciences. Can you honestly say that whenever you had a falling out with a neighbor, you first sought God's guidance and asked Him to teach you how to conduct yourself in the situation, resolving to act according to the directions granted through His Word and Spirit? Surely, contentious and unpeaceable individuals seldom pray and commit their causes to God. Consequently, God leaves them to themselves, bringing much trouble not only to themselves but also to others.

Fourthly, do not bring a matter into the public eye before exhausting private means of reconciliation. Regardless of any offense between neighbors, the following rule must be observed: First, employ private means to address the issue. Christians are specifically instructed that if a brother offends them, they should address the fault privately. If the offender persists in their wrongdoing, then take two or three witnesses in private. Only after these attempts should the matter be brought to the church. Therefore, private means should be exhausted before making any faults or weaknesses of our brothers public. However, if the offense is public in nature, then public means may be employed without further delay. But if the matter is private, refrain from publicizing it until you have tried to resolve it privately.

The fifth means of peace is this: Make an effort to engage one another in acts of love. Consider it a great benefit when God provides an opportunity for you to engage with your neighbor. We should actively pursue peace. When individuals are engaged with one another, they are less likely to break the peace. Conversely, when they live as strangers to one another, even small matters can lead to peace being shattered.

Sixthly, another rule to promote peace is this: If my benefit clashes with my neighbour's convenience or interests, I should consider it an affliction for myself. Although I may have a lawful right to pursue my own interests, if it leads to contention with my brother, I should view it as a great affliction for myself. While God does not forbid us from seeking our rights, if we see that obtaining them will cause affliction to our brothers, we should regard it as our own affliction.

Seventhly, take delight in doing good yourself and rejoice in witnessing others doing good. This is the path to peace. When a spirit of envy prevails in people's hearts, it undermines peace. One person envies another, seeing them acquire more than themselves or receiving greater recognition and honor. When envy takes hold, contention arises. However, when individuals strive to do good in their appointed positions and genuinely rejoice in the good that others accomplish as instruments of God, they can appeal to God, saying, "Lord, you know the joy it brings to my heart to hear or see how You use others as instruments of good, just as You use me." This attitude is pleasing to God.

Eighthly, the final suggestion I propose is that there should be regular gatherings among neighbours to maintain peace and reconcile any breaches of peace. This is especially important for those in leadership positions within towns and communities. These meetings should take place in their own homes, as it is most honorable, safe, and fitting. Meeting in one's own residence is likely to be more beneficial. People in parishes and towns should gather at their own homes rather than in taverns. While meeting in taverns is not inherently wrong, it is more honorable for town leaders to convene in their own dwellings. Meeting in one's own home is an expression of love, unlike meeting in a tavern. Additionally, it is less risky. Even though there may be no ill intentions when going to a tavern, there is a greater temptation present. Although sometimes only a small amount is consumed, on other occasions, excess may occur. Thus, matters of peace and love may become entangled with excessive eating, drinking, and indulging the flesh. This hinders the pursuit of good and can result in disputes among those partaking in liberal use of alcohol. Therefore, although meeting in taverns is not inherently evil, you are aware of the Apostle's instruction: "Finally, brothers and sisters, whatever is true, whatever is noble, whatever is right, whatever is pure, whatever is lovely, whatever is admirable—if anything is excellent or praiseworthy—think about such things." Certainly, those who act as instruments of peace bring about great good and are blessings to their communities. Many will thank God for them. If only a few influential individuals in a parish or town were to commit to this approach, what abundance of good could they achieve? They should not say, "I have my own affairs to attend to, what do I have to do with them?" I must confess, this resembles the language of Cain when God inquired about his brother Abel, and Cain replied, "Am I my brother's keeper?" Let no one say, "Am I my brother's keeper?" It is your responsibility if you want to prove yourself to be a child of God. Just as God considers reconciling the world to Himself the greatest work, so you, in positions of influence, should consider it your own work to reconcile differences within your parishes. Do not allow matters to escalate into bitterness, violence, and rage. What good is accomplished then? Many times, during meetings, everything may be progressing well, with unanimous agreement for the advancement of the Gospel and the benefit of the community where God has placed you. However, a single resentful word can ignite a fire, wasting the opportunity for great glory that could have been given to God. Do you value your own passion, pride, and honor more than public service for God, the church, or the commonwealth? If so, you do not belong to God. A child of God would prioritize God's cause over personal matters. Therefore, blessed are the peacemakers, whether in families, parishes, churches, or the commonwealth. I admit that I had many thoughts about these topics that I intended to address. However, considering the present circumstances and the state of people's spirits, I cannot satisfy my conscience by deeming it an opportune time to discuss anything. Addressing the matter of making peace would necessitate touching upon our differences and the desires of both sides. Currently, people's spirits are so unsettled that I am convinced anything said would be like throwing stubble into an oven. Therefore, I prefer to refrain and entrust the cause to God, praying for Him to bring peace among us.

# SERMON XXX

## The Difference between Independency and Presbytery

"Blessed are the peacemakers, for they shall be called the children of God." - Matthew 5:9

You know that I have not yet consider any matters of controversy among you. But please allow me to briefly address that great controversy known as Independency and Presbytery. I will first explain where the main difference lies, as many individuals have passionate and opposing views. However, if you were to ask these individuals if they truly understand the controversy and its essence, they would be unable to provide a clear explanation. Some might say that Independents advocate for the absence of any form of government and a general tolerance for all things. They believe this is the crux of the difference. Yet, due to this misunderstanding, they are led astray and engage in actions that they would not otherwise if they were properly informed. I have no doubt that many who are fervent in their support of either side are godly, holy, and righteous individuals. They act according to their conscience, believing that they are serving God faithfully through their strong opposition. Thus, in a few words, let me present the main aspects of Independency and Presbytery that hinder peace among us.

The primary distinction lies in the fact that those referred to as Independents firmly believe that there can be no power or authority in the Church except that which is established by Christ. They assert that only those who are appointed by Christ can hold positions of leadership within the Church. While some hold this view, others go even further, stating that not only should the appointment of Church officers be made by Christ, but the scope of their authority should also be determined by Him. Just as in a commonwealth, where courts and jurisdiction exist solely by the authority of the supreme judiciary, the jurisdiction within the Church is determined by the authority of the supreme Jesus Christ. Christ appoints not only the offices but also delineates the extent of their authority. However, this is merely an illustration to facilitate understanding.

Now, regarding the controversy: Those known as Independents believe that the ruling power of ministers, who are appointed by Christ to feed the people through preaching and administering sacraments, extends only as far as their pastoral power allows. In other words, their authority to govern and rule over people in Christ's name is limited to the pastoral charge entrusted to them for the purpose of preaching and administering sacraments. The extent of their authority to rule is determined by the boundaries set by Christ for their pastoral ministry.

On the other hand, those known as Presbyters believe that a minister's authority can extend further. Although a minister may have a pastoral charge limited to one congregation, they believe that by joining with others, their ruling power can extend to hundreds or thousands of congregations that they have never seen before. They argue that their pastoral charge, concerning preaching and administering sacraments, only extends ordinarily to one congregation. Now, regarding whether the ruling power of any minister extends beyond their pastoral power for preaching and administering sacraments, whether they have authority to govern others collectively rather than merely feed them through Word and Sacraments, this is where the controversy primarily lies. I do not intend to advocate for either side, but merely seek peace.

If the controversy lies here, I appeal to your consciences. Are you so certain, so convinced of one side that you can vehemently oppose the other? Is one side so evident and clear to you that you would take it upon yourself, as you would answer to Christ, to employ the full force of civil authority to compel the adherence of one side or the other? I mention this regarding both sides, as it would be a great evil for those who profess Independency to force those who profess Presbytery to adopt their beliefs and practices. Likewise, it would not be pleasing to Jesus Christ if one side were to use civil means to coerce the other, as it would not lead to peace.

But now, if you insist, saying, "We will force them to do so," it is true that you can physically restrain people from drifting apart by chaining them together. But will that bring peace to the Church of Christ in terms of their hearts?

I have observed another factor that greatly contributes to the disruption of peace: the misunderstanding of the concept of schism. People mistakenly believe that because the word is mentioned in the Covenant, they are obligated to vehemently oppose anything that truly constitutes schism. They are willing to sacrifice peace for this, regardless of the consequences. However, let us carefully consider this: Is it considered schism if a member of a Church, acknowledging it as a true Church, decides to join others? Are they automatically deemed schismatics?

To avoid unnecessary disruption of peace, allow me to clarify. Imagine that there are genuinely pious and conscientious individuals within a Church. However, there are certain practices in the Church that they believe are not in line with the mind of Christ. Despite prayer and seeking God's guidance, they cannot reconcile these practices with their conscience. They testify before God, with their own consciences bearing witness, that they would gladly join such a Church in all aspects of God's worship, except in those specific practices that would go against their conscience. They make every effort to inform themselves, humbly approaching the elders and seeking guidance to resolve their doubts. Yet, even after receiving explanations, they find themselves unable to agree. In such cases, what would you have these individuals do? Suppose there are a hundred of them who are unable to partake in communion. Should they immediately sever ties with the congregation? No, they should wait and see if God will reveal His will to them. After exhausting all means and still remaining unconvinced, should these individuals live without participating in the sacraments for the rest of their lives? Has Christ so bound a member of a congregation that if they cannot join a Church without sinning, they must never join any other? Such a claim requires clear justification if anyone were to assert it.

Now, suppose these individuals humbly request the liberty to join together and participate in the ordinances of Christ. They hold the same foundational beliefs as this Church, and they consider its members as brethren. They are willing to join in worship and other aspects of their faith. However, due to their conscientious objections, they cannot partake in certain practices. Should they be left without access to these ordinances for the rest of their lives? If these individuals demonstrate godliness in their lives and peacefully follow the revealed will of God as far as they understand it, do you truly believe that this constitutes the schism mentioned in Scripture, the schism that we should oppose? Is this what people are opposing today when they speak of schism?

Allow me to present a different scenario. During the time of the Bishops, there were individuals known as Non-Conformists, who were considered pious men. They could not conform to certain practices, such as kneeling during the sacraments or accepting the authority of Prelates. As a result, they were labeled schismatics by the Bishops. Now, many of our brethren in Scotland who resided in England at that time, and even many of the most godly ministers in the kingdom, believed that those who could not partake in the sacraments due to their objections to kneeling and the use of the cross were in error. I believe this is still the prevailing belief today.

However, if the State had granted these Non-Conformists the freedom to gather and partake in the sacraments without these practices, would they still be considered schismatics? Suppose the State had allowed all the Scottish brethren living in London to meet in specific locations in the city where they could observe the sacraments without those ceremonies and without recognizing the authority of Bishops. Would they be schismatics under these circumstances?

You may argue that if the State allowed it, then they would not be schismatics. However, consider this: Schism is a sin against the Church. If something is deemed schism before the State allows it, it will remain a sin even after the State permits it. The nature of the act does not change based on the approval or disapproval of the State. I am confident that almost all of you, who are godly individuals, would have considered it a great mercy if the Non-Conformists had received such favor from the State. If they had been granted the liberty to gather in designated places as long as they remained orthodox in their beliefs and led godly and peaceful lives, I believe none of you would have labeled them schismatics. So, if there are other godly individuals in the kingdom whose consciences are troubled by certain practices, yet remain orthodox in the fundamentals of the faith, desire fellowship, and are willing to participate in the ordinances of Christ in a manner consistent with their conscience, why are they accused of schism? Why is it considered a breach of the Covenant that must not be tolerated? There lies the mistake. If there were a proper understanding, there could be ways for brethren to live together in unity, fear God, and walk peaceably with one another. However, I will say no more on this topic, and it is unlikely that you will hear me speak further on such matters, unless there is a compelling reason to do so. Therefore, let us proceed to the promise.

"Blessed are the peacemakers, for they will be called the children of God."

This promise of being called the children of God should surely encourage everyone to strive for peace. When spoken by Christ, it holds great significance. The question arises: Why are peacemakers called the children of God? And why is this promise specifically attached to peacemaking?

Peacemakers are referred to as children of God because in their work of fostering peace, they resemble God Himself. They engage in a task that is deeply aligned with God's heart, one that He holds dear from all eternity. No other work can compare. Reconciling the world to Himself is a matter that lies closest to God's heart. Therefore, those who engage in peacemaking show themselves to be of the same spirit as God. Consequently, they are deemed the children of God. Just as those who resemble the Devil are referred to as children of the Devil, those who resemble God are children of God.

Moreover, being the children of God empowers peacemakers to actively contribute to peace. They draw inspiration from their Father, who is a God of peace. Their deep satisfaction in experiencing the Fatherly love of God and enjoying the blessed privileges of being His children leads them to possess peaceable dispositions. Nothing cultivates a peaceable disposition more than finding inner contentment. For instance, imagine a merchant who hears about a prosperous ship returning from the Indies, carrying a significant investment in which he is involved. Although he may encounter unpleasant circumstances at home, his children may be difficult, and his wife may be in a bad mood, his inner satisfaction shields him from becoming easily angered. His joy in the news he received about his fortune allows him to tolerate numerous issues within his family during that time. Conversely, if the same merchant experiences setbacks and hears distressing news abroad, his discontentment spills over into his home, making him irritable towards everyone. This happens due to a lack of inner contentment within his spirit. Undoubtedly, the absence of inner satisfaction and guilt within individuals' hearts is a significant cause of quarrels and conflicts. However, those who are the children of God, who acknowledge God as their Father and enjoy the precious privileges bestowed upon them, find immense satisfaction within themselves. Regardless of how the world behaves, since the world will always be the world, and wicked people will always be wicked, they are not disturbed. They may pray for and lament over the world, but they refuse to let it disrupt their peace. They declare, "O my soul, return to your rest, for I find satisfaction in it." Consequently, they exhibit peaceable dispositions towards others. Therefore, this promise is attached to peacemakers— they will be called the children of God and will truly be regarded as such.

Moreover, being called the children of God signifies a higher degree of blessing. It is a great privilege to be a child of God, irrespective of whether the world considers one a child of the Devil or even calls one a Devil. For instance, John Huss, on his way to martyrdom, had pictures of Devils placed on his coat as if he had emerged from hell, but he was still a Son of God. Similarly, Christ Himself was not always called the child of God; instead, He was referred to as Beelzebub and the Prince of Devils. However, being called the children of God implies an additional blessing. It means having the promise from Christ that not only are they the children of God, but also that others will recognize and acknowledge this truth within their hearts and consciences. The power of peacemaking lies in its ability to convince others. It possesses such beauty and excellence that even wicked individuals are compelled in their consciences to believe that these peacemakers are undoubtedly the children of God. They discern the Spirit of God at work within them. This confirms that peacemaking has an undeniable convincing power. In fact, if we were to ask every person in England why they hinder peace, not a single individual would admit to it, even though many are undoubtedly guilty. Conversely, making peace is highly admired. Even individuals with stubborn and self-centered spirits, who struggle to cultivate peace within themselves, appreciate it when they witness peace in others, particularly in matters that do not directly concern them. They are willing to endure personal suffering for the sake of peace and the prevention of sin, allowing the glory of God to prevail. They themselves suffer in order to advance this peace. When individuals with obstinate and selfish dispositions observe this in others, it provokes different thoughts within them. Their conscience tells them that if someone angers them, they will retaliate and demand submission, with the other person having to make the first move. However, they also observe others who, despite being wronged, are willing to endure and suffer for the sake of peace. They do so out of love for peace and to reconcile neighbours and fellow human beings. Certainly, such individuals are children of peace. Each time I encounter such people, they remind me of the God of peace, Jesus Christ, the Prince of peace, and the gentle, dove-like Holy Spirit. Without a doubt, they are the children of God. This is the essence of the promise—others will be convinced of their identity as the children of God.

Therefore, being a child of God is a blessed state. This brings us to the first point: being a child of God is a great and blessed thing.

The second point emphasizes that it is not only a blessing to be a child of God but also a tremendous mercy to live in a way that convinces the consciences of others, compelling them to acknowledge us as the children of God. These are the two points to consider.

For the exploration of the blessedness of being a child of God, this point would naturally be extensive if approached in a simple manner. However, I shall refrain from doing so. There is no need for me to cite specific scriptures to you. Consider the profound love that the Father has bestowed upon us by calling us the Sons of God. This is indeed the love of God, that we are called the Sons of God. Furthermore, this is the fruit of election. In Ephesians 1:5, it states, "Having predestinated us unto the adoption of children by Jesus Christ to himself, according to the good pleasure of his will." We must contemplate what predestination entails. It aims specifically at the adoption of children as the primary objective. This is the blessing God seeks when He beholds humanity. He discerns those He intends to pass over and leave to the course of justice, but He also recognizes those who are pleasing in His eyes. These individuals are made so by God's design. They are set apart for adoption as His children, and He becomes their Father for eternity. Initially, I intended to consider this aspect as the opening of the discussion on the blessedness of being a child of God.

First, let us grasp the mystery of godliness in this matter. It is a profound mystery because those who were once children of wrath and disobedience are now transformed into the children of God. There is not a single child of God, except for the only Son, Jesus Christ, who was not a child of wrath before becoming a child of God in actuality. Every man and woman who is now a child of God was undoubtedly a child of wrath previously. It is a mystery revealed solely in Scripture, not something that can be known through natural enlightenment. This reveals the blessedness of mankind—to become children of God despite once being children of wrath, disobedience, and enemies of God.

Secondly, the mystery of godliness lies in the fact that although they are adopted children, they are also born again through regeneration. This is a gospel mystery. In Scripture, we are referred to as adopted children. Among humans, it is not possible for the same person to be both adopted and begotten—a child by adoption and a child by natural birth from the same individual. However, in this case, it is different. All the children of God are both children by adoption and children by regeneration. They are not begotten in the same manner as the second person of the Trinity, who is the Son of the Father, or as the God-man who was conceived by the Holy Spirit. Yet, through the work of the Holy Spirit, which is the next most glorious work after these, children are regenerated unto God by an imperishable seed of the Word. They are begotten unto God. Nevertheless, despite this dual identity, they remain children by adoption. Adoption occurs when a person, without any children of their own, takes in and acknowledges another as their child or heir. Similarly, as those who were not children by nature, God, through His incomparable grace, adopts us. The fact that He adopts and regenerates us is a profound gospel mystery within this context.

Thirdly, the great mystery lies in the fact that they become children of God through their union with Jesus Christ, the only Son of God. Their sonship is attained through their union with Jesus Christ, the eternal Son of God. They become children of God in a more elevated manner than through mere creation. Their sonship surpasses that of the angels. Although Scripture refers to angels as the sons of God, the saints are children of God in a higher sense. The angels are not children of God through their union with the eternal Son of God, becoming one with Him and partaking in the glorious radiance of His sonship. Therefore, every believer, every godly peacemaker, becomes a child of God through their union with the eternal Son of God. They bask in the radiance and glory of His sonship. This sonship exceeds that which Adam and the angels possessed. By faith, we are made the sons of God.

Fourthly, another mystery lies in the fact that all the children of God are heirs. Every single one of them is an heir, unlike in human families where only one child typically inherits. However, with the children of God, each one is an heir. Sons and daughters alike, they are all heirs. This is the glory of the saints, as the scripture declares, "If sons, then heirs" (Romans 8:17). It does not specify that this applies only to firstborn sons. No, if they are sons, they are heirs. This is affirmed in Romans 8:17.

Fifthly, there is a fifth mystery, even more profound than the others. It is not just that each one of them is an heir, but they are also joint heirs with Jesus Christ. To be joint heirs with one another is a great blessing, but to be joint heirs with Jesus Christ is an extraordinary blessing. Consider this: whatever inheritance Jesus Christ, the eternal Son of God, possesses, to the extent that any believer is capable of enjoying its benefits, they too possess and will possess alongside Jesus Christ. Romans 8 reinforces this point: "And if children, then heirs; heirs of God, and joint-heirs with Christ." Perhaps believers may not have any earthly possessions, not a single piece of land, but they are heirs of God. They may not inherit the property of a nobleman or prince, but they are heirs of God. Moreover, they are joint heirs with Christ. There are two aspects to this.

Firstly, they have a share in all the inheritance of Christ. Regardless of their current earthly status, whether they are the poorest youth, man, woman, or maid, if God reconciles them to Himself, they possess an interest in all the glory, blessedness, and excellence found in Jesus Christ. They partake in everything that God the Father will do for Jesus Christ. Hence, in John 17:23, Christ speaks to His Father, saying, "And hast loved them, as thou hast loved me." There is abundant blessedness in receiving the same love from God the Father that Jesus Christ receives. Thus, they are joint heirs with Christ. That is the first aspect.

Secondly, they are as certain of their salvation and glory as it is certain that Jesus Christ will be eternally happy. This certainty arises because they are joint heirs with Jesus Christ. When individuals are joint heirs, the rights of one are as certain as the rights of the other. If someone is a co-purchaser with another, their rights to a piece of land or a house are equally valid. Although Jesus Christ is their elder brother, He is also referred to as an everlasting Father. They are joint co-purchasers. In fact, being a joint heir is more significant than being a co-purchaser, as the right of inheritance is superior and nobler than the right of purchase. In certain cases, it may also be more certain. Thus, the saints possess all the good that Jesus Christ possesses, and they can be as certain of it as Christ Himself. Christ will be disinherited before a believer, for a believer is a joint heir with Jesus Christ. How blessed, then, are the peacemakers! They are the children of God, children of God in a glorious mystical manner. They are such children that they are joint heirs with Jesus Christ, possessing an interest in His glory. They cannot be disinherited any more than Jesus Christ Himself can be. I shall provide you with a scripture that offers the utmost comfort to the saints. Christ unites Himself and them in their relationship with His Father. In John 10:17, towards the end, He says, "I ascend unto my Father, and your Father; and to my God, and your God." This scripture is almost as comforting as any other in the Book of God. To ascend to the Father who is Jesus Christ's Father and our Father—to have the same God who is Jesus Christ's God and our God—how indescribably consoling that is! The same God who is the God of Jesus Christ is my God, and the same Father who is the Father of Jesus Christ is my Father. Oh, blessed are the peacemakers! They shall be called the children of God.

# SERMON XXXI

## The Mystery of Godliness in Adoption

"Blessed are the peacemakers, for they shall be called the children of God." -Matthew 5:10

Indeed, they are heirs of everything, the entire inheritance. Among humans, the more one possesses, the less others have. If a father, even a wealthy one, gives a large portion to one child, the younger ones receive less. Or if the father decides to divide his inheritance, one may receive a lot while the other receives only a little. However, among the children of God's inheritance, it is not so. No child of God receives less because another has more. Each one inherits everything in God, in Christ, in heaven. It is the inheritance of every child of God in one way or another, for the benefit of all.

Sixthly, another aspect to consider is that in Christ, there are far greater privileges for the child of God than in former times. This is one of the mysteries of the Gospel. It is true, "Is not Ephraim my dear son?" The saints in earlier times were children of God, but in the time of the Gospel, they have far higher privileges and prerogatives than before. This is a part of the mystery of the Gospel. Formerly, God had children in their non-age, under tutelage. Even the most eminent saints were like children in their non-age, and they did not come into their inheritance. But we, in comparison to those who have reached maturity, are like children. This is clearly explained in Galatians 4. "Now I say, That the heir, as long as he is a child, differeth nothing from a servant, though he be lord of all; but is under tutors and governors until the time appointed of the father. Even so we, when we were children, were in bondage under the elements of the world. But when the fullness of the time was come, God sent forth his Son, made of a woman, made under the law, to redeem them that were under the law, that we might receive the adoption of sons." So it seems that until Christ came, the adoption of sons was not possible. Why were the saints not children before Christ came? In terms of how God treated them, they were not considered children. They were not sons in the sense of being mature and able to enjoy their inheritance. However, they were sons in the same way that the sons of kings, when they are young children, have tutors and governors who treat them like other children of ordinary people. God did not reveal much to them about the excellence of their inheritance at that time. Just as noble men and princes entertain their children with trinkets, rattles, and toys, not revealing their future possessions until the children reach maturity, so it was with the saints. In comparison to the ordinances of the Gospel and the privileges of the Gospel, what the people had under the Law were like rattles, trinkets, and toys given to amuse children. That is why the Holy Spirit refers to even those ordinances as beggarly rudiments. But now, through Christ, we have been redeemed so that we may receive the adoption of sons and come to enjoy a significant portion of our inheritance. It is a special part of the children's inheritance to have the Gospel clearly revealed to them and to receive the blessings and privileges of the Gospel. We will discuss this in more detail shortly. Thus, we have explored the mystery of godliness in our adoption.

And the benefits of being children, or the privileges that we have by being children, are very great and numerous. I remember Luther in his commentary on Galatians 4:7 saying, "If we only knew what this privilege was, all the riches of all the kingdoms in the world would be as filthy dung to us." That's his expression. The greater the pomp and glory of the world, the more we would despise it if we truly understood the excellence of this privilege of being children. There are great privileges in it. In 1 John 12, it says, "To as many as received him, to them gave he power to become the Sons of God." He gave them authoritative power to become the Sons of God, so they may claim it and assert it. They have a kind of authority and privilege in becoming the Sons of God.

Now the first privilege of a child of God is this: great honor is bestowed upon them. Just as the dignity of the Father determines the honor and dignity of the child, if the father is a yeoman, so is the child regarded. If the father is a gentleman, so is the child. If the father is a duke, prince, or monarch, the child is honored according to the father's honor. Being a child of God must necessarily be honorable. The children of great men on earth are honored, but the children of the infinite God must have honor surpassing them by virtue of their birthright. The reflection of the Father's honor shines upon them. It's what David expressed in 1 Samuel 18:22. When some came to discuss marrying Saul's daughter, David asked, "Seemeth it to you a light thing to be a king's son-in-law, seeing that I am a poor man and lightly esteemed?" Now, Saul was a wicked man, and it was only a son-in-law relationship. If that was considered such a great honor and privilege, how much more is this?

Secondly, the second privilege of the children of God is that they are freed from all kinds of bondage. They are freed from a spirit of bondage and from all forms of bondage. They are no longer bond-slaves as every person is by nature. You know what Christ said, "Do the children pay tribute or strangers? The children of the kingdom are free." They are not in the same servitude as others. They are not even servants in the traditional sense. They are at a higher level than servants. Although being a servant of God is a great privilege, they go beyond that. In Galatians 4:7, it says, "Wherefore thou art no more a servant but a Son." They go beyond the position of a servant in the house of God. Moses had the great honor of being called "Moses, my servant," but the least believer in the time of the Gospel possesses a greater privilege: they are a Son. There is no longer a spirit of servility but a freer spirit in the child of God. In Romans 8:14-15, it says, "For as many as are led by the Spirit of God, they are the Sons of God. For ye have not received the spirit of bondage again to fear, but ye have received the spirit of adoption, whereby we cry, Abba, Father." I will speak more about the spirit of adoption later. But for now, I only want to demonstrate their privilege in being delivered from the spirit of bondage. They no longer serve God in a mercenary way as before, nor do they serve out of a slavish fear. Even the godly people among the Jews, as stated in Hebrews 2:15, were subject to bondage throughout their lifetime due to the fear of death. There was a spirit of bondage and fear in the hearts of God's people in earlier times. Now, God expects His children to serve Him from a different motive—out of a principle of love, as befits children. We will discuss this further when we address the duties of children as they are the children of God. Indeed, they were also under the bondage of a more burdensome form of worship—the bondage of the Law. But now, the children of God are freed from that. They are free from the bondage of sin and the bondage of the Law. That is the second privilege—they are free from bondage.

Thirdly, the third privilege is the complete fatherly love with which they are embraced. God, who is the infinite, glorious, first being, embraces them with complete fatherly love. All the love that has ever existed in any parent towards their children is like a single drop in the infinite ocean of fatherly love that God has for His people. Those of you who are fathers or mothers know what the love of a parent towards their children means. If you are godly, when you experience that natural affection and love for your children who are born from your body, you should strengthen your faith by considering this: If I, as a parent, have such affection and love for my children, how much more affection and love does God the Father have for His children? Why does God take on the title of Father if not to provide a foundation for the faith of His people to look up to Him and witness His love? His love is as complete as the love of all parents in the world combined towards their children. Yet, even the natural affections of all the most loving and tender-hearted parents in the world, if united in one parent, would still pale in comparison to the love of God the Father towards His saints. That is the third privilege.

Fourthly, the fourth privilege of the children of God is their rightful claim to the creatures, which is restored to them by virtue of being children. The Jews were deprived of a great part of the comfort of the creatures, but now the children of God have their rightful claim restored, renewed, strengthened, and increased. Their right to all comforts in all creatures is affirmed. It is true that Adam had a right to the creatures initially, but through sin, he lost it. Therefore, all mankind lost their right to the creatures.

You may ask, "Are wicked people then usurpers when they make use of the creatures? Do they have no right?"

I admit that this has been taught at times—that though they have a right before men, they have no right before God, and they are usurpers. However, there may be a misunderstanding in that view. While it is true that we have lost all our rights, that must be acknowledged, if God, through a free donation, grants them the right, gives the creatures back to wicked people, gives the earth to the children of men, we cannot say that they are usurpers if they have received it as a free gift from God during His season of bounty and patience towards the wicked. But still, they do not have the same right that the children of God have. Their right is merely by donation, whereas the right of the child of God is partly by purchase and partly by inheritance. They have a claiming right, whereby they can boldly and in a holy manner assert their ownership of all good things from all creatures that they need, as their own. A wicked person may have many comfortable things in the world for their immediate sustenance, and I dare not say that they are usurpers if they obtain them lawfully. For in His bounty and patience, God does give these things to wicked people. We say, "What is freer than a gift?" However, no wicked person in the world can claim these things and say, "Lord, these are mine, they are my inheritance, my purchase." This is the privilege of the children of God. If a criminal, through their offense, has forfeited their estate and all rights to the good things in a kingdom, but if those in supreme power, in their benevolence, grant them some provisions for their last meal before execution, we cannot say they are usurpers. They have a right to it; it is given to them, even though they have forfeited everything. This is the difference in right between a child at their father's table and a criminal on the night before they go to the gallows. This is the distinction between the rights of the two before the Lord. Therefore, when you look at your possessions and see your houses furnished with good furniture, when you look at your tables and see them filled with abundant dishes, consider what right you have to all these things in relation to God. Is it merely the right of donation, as a criminal may receive to sustain them before execution, or is it the right of children? If you are children of God, you approach your tables as you would approach your father's table. It is the provision that your Father has made for you, and that is how you should regard it. This is the privilege of the children of God. Oh, how blessed it is to be a child of God then!

And then the sixth privilege of a child of God is this: they have free access to their Father's presence. They can come into their Father's presence at any time, and as long as they are recognized as children, they can come with comfort. God does not treat His children like David treated Absalom, saying, "Let him not see my face." No, God loves to have His children in His presence. It is part of the redemption through Jesus Christ that we can approach God's presence. We have access through Jesus Christ, and we can always come and stand before our Father. This is a great privilege that those who are children of God cherish.

Sixthly, by being children of God, they come to have the image of God renewed in them. A father communicates some of his nature to his child, but a father cannot communicate all the good things he desires to his child. A father with wisdom cannot transfer his wisdom to his child, and a father with holiness cannot pass on his holiness to his child. However, God can communicate whatever He pleases to His children. He shares His image with them, the very essence of His glory. The reason a father cannot share wisdom and holiness with his child is that he begets the child as a human being, not as a human being already possessing those qualities. But when God begets a child, if He begets a child for Himself, He must beget the child in a way that resembles Himself in some manner. God Himself is holy and infinitely wise. Holiness and wisdom are inherent to His being; they are not accidental attributes. Therefore, all who are children of God, having His image upon them, are like God in the very aspects that constitute His excellence—His holiness and wisdom. They share in the life of God. Every parent begets a child, and the parent makes the child partaker of their life. The very life of God primarily consists of His holiness and His act of directing everything towards Himself as the ultimate end.

Seventhly, a child of God has the Spirit of God communicated to them. We see this in the previous scriptures, Romans 8:14, 15, and 16. We are led by the Spirit, being Sons. We have received the Spirit of Adoption, by which we cry, "Abba, Father." In the mentioned passage, Galatians 4:6, it says, "Because you are Sons, God has sent forth the Spirit of His Son into your hearts, crying, 'Abba, Father.'" A learned man made an observation on this verse, saying that it does not state, "God has sent forth the Spirit of His Son into your minds to give you knowledge and understanding," but rather, "into your hearts, crying, 'Abba, Father.'" The Spirit of His Son, who now rules in the heart, God has sent into it. This is a great blessing from God—to receive His Spirit. This Spirit enlightens the mind, sanctifies the heart, reveals the deep counsels of God to the soul, and guides the soul on the path of eternal life. This is the privilege of all Sons—they share in the Holy Spirit. I recall in one of the Gospels, Jesus said, "How much more will your heavenly Father give good things to those who ask Him." Another version says, "How much more will your heavenly Father give the Spirit to those who ask." This signifies that the Spirit of God encompasses all good things. Oh, blessed are those who partake in the Spirit of God, who are not led and driven by their own spirits but by the Spirit of God.

Eighthly, the privilege of God's children is that they receive His protection. God, as their Father, provides for them and safeguards them. If any of your children are in danger, what do they do? They run to their father or mother and complain to their father. The father, to the best of his ability, protects his children. Therefore, there is a natural instinct in the children of God to seek refuge in their Father's protection. Indeed, a carnal heart, when wronged, can only resort to rage, frustration, and seeking revenge. But a child of God's response is to go and pour out their grievances to their Father, to tell God about all the wrongs done to them, all the slanderous accusations. They immediately go to their Father and lay their complaints before Him. There is a significant verse in Psalm 109:4, where David says, "For my love, they are my adversaries." What then? They are my adversaries, and God knows I only intend good for them. There is no bitterness or rage in my spirit towards them. Yet, they are driven by a wicked spirit. What then? But I pray. You have it written in your books, but I give myself to prayer. "But give myself" is added in another translation to complete the meaning. They are my adversaries, but am I an adversary to them in return? No. But I pray. They are my adversaries because of my love. But I know what to do. What will you do? I know what He will do. It's as if David is saying, "I will go to God and inform my Father about all of this. I will turn to prayer; that will be my help and refuge." This is the privilege of God's children—they have the protection of their Father. He will safeguard them from all the wrongs and injuries inflicted upon them.

Ninthly, lastly, they will have a kingdom. We are made kings and priests to the Father through Jesus Christ. So, my brothers and sisters, we can say about this matter of being children, of adoption, just as the Apostle did in Romans 8. After speaking about the benefits of both justification and adoption together, he concludes by saying, "What then shall we say to these things?" What shall we say after considering all this? These things are real, they are certain truths. What shall we say about these high prerogatives and privileges of the children of God? Oh, who would not be a peacemaker when they have such a blessing as this? But faith is required to make these things a reality to the soul.

Lastly, one thing I want to mention about their privileges is the compassion of God towards them as a Father. God has compassion on them in their sins and afflictions. In Psalm 103, it says, "As a Father pities his children, so the Lord pities those who fear Him." There is a well-known passage in Malachi 3:17, "And they shall be Mine, says the Lord of hosts, on the day that I make them My jewels; I will spare them as a man spares his only son who serves him." If you have a servant who displeases you, you can dismiss them, but you will not be so quick to turn away your child or disinherit them. A man with a father's affections will never disinherit his child, even if the child returns to him despite their faults. This is the state of God's children. If they were in any other relationship to God, they might be cast off. For example, a wife may be divorced by her husband and never be welcomed back, no matter how remorseful she is, if she commits adultery or impurity. In Jeremiah 3:1, it says, "They say, if a man puts away his wife, and she goes from him and becomes another man's, shall he return to her again? Shall not that land be greatly polluted?" She can never return to him. However, it is not the same with a child. A child can never be in such a disposition that they are incapable of receiving their Father's love. No other relationship can be so wholly lost that there remains no possibility of receiving the benefits of that relationship. But a child can never lose the capacity to receive some fatherly love as long as they live. Even if they are disobedient children, upon their return to the Father, even if they have been prodigal sons, some form of fatherly affection will be stirred. No parent in the world who possesses natural affection can completely withhold love from their child. If they were certain that their child's heart has changed, their affection would flow towards them. This is the relationship of a child—I emphasize that it can never be entirely lost, and there will always be the capacity to receive some Fatherly love. A servant may be expelled from service, making it impossible for them to be received back, and likewise, a wife. However, this is not the case with a child. This is their privilege.

But now, if you ask me what I should say about these things, well, I shall speak about these specific privileges. I have listed ten privileges, and I may mention nine or ten duties that follow from our being children.

Firstly, let us learn to conduct ourselves in a manner befitting the children of the Most High. We should demonstrate that we are of noble lineage, not possessing a base, vile, and sordid spirit. In Acts 17:11, it is said of the Bereans that they were more noble than those in Thessalonica. The word used implies that they were of better breeding, more noble. Oh, let all those who are children of God reveal their lineage through their holiness and gracious conduct before others. It is unbecoming for the children of royalty to be engaged in squalor or behave in a base manner. Instead, they should conduct themselves according to the status of their Father, as befits the children of God. Therefore, the children of the living God must carry themselves in a manner that is above the world, above the vanities of the world. They should view these things as too insignificant and lowly for them. It is exceedingly inappropriate for a child of God to have a downtrodden spirit due to a lack of worldly comforts, as if they were utterly ruined. Oh no.

Instead, live according to this standard. Regard your Father as the Lord of heaven and earth and understand that all power, goodness, excellence, and treasure that He possesses, you have a right to in some way or another. So, when affliction befalls you, do not allow your heart to sink immediately as if you were utterly destroyed. Remember your relationship—you are a child, and God protects you and is responsible for providing for you and doing you good. There is a significant statement in 2 Samuel 13:3 about Jonadab: "Now Amnon had a friend whose name was Jonadab the son of Shimeah, David's brother. And Jonadab was a very crafty man. And he said unto him, Why art thou, being the king's son, lean from day to day? wilt thou not tell me?" He noticed that Amnon's countenance was dejected, and he appeared sickly due to a sorrowful heart. So, he asked, "Why are you, a king's son, so dejected in spirits? Don't you have enough that belongs to you to comfort your heart as a king's son?" This should be the attitude of the children of the living God. If you believe that you are a child of God, that God has adopted you and set His heart upon you as a child, oh, why should a lack of a few external comforts depress you?

You may argue, "If I were a child of God, He would not let me lack these things." Oh, you are mistaken in this. God has other ways of expressing His fatherly love to you than through these external things. A sick and weak child might say the same, "If my father loved me, why wouldn't he give me such and such food?" But the child requires medicine. Don't you love your child when you give them medicine instead of what they cry for? If God is your Father and you are His child, will you not allow Him to nurture you as His child, just as you care for your own child? Indeed, let me say more to you than this: Even without outward comforts, you may experience the same fatherly love that Jesus Christ, His Son, had. Won't that suffice? You may say, "That will indeed suffice." Notice in John 17:26 how God's love worked towards Jesus Christ, His Son. Did He not allow Him to lack many external comforts in this world? There was a time when He hungered and needed bread. The Devil would have wanted Him to doubt His Father's care. Oh no, although the foxes have holes and the birds of the air have nests, He did not have a place to lay His head. You have a just as comfortable dwelling as Christ did. Christ was thirsty and had to ask a woman for a little water to drink. There are very few of you who face more dire circumstances in terms of worldly things than Christ did. Yet, do you not think that God the Father loved His Son? Won't that love suffice for you, the same love that Jesus Christ, the Son of God, had? Although you are a child, you are no less dear to God than Jesus Christ, the Son of God, was to the Father. Oh, therefore, raise your spirits in the absence of all outward comforts in this world, for you are a child and have an inheritance to come in the future.

Secondly, there must be reverence. "If I am a father, where is my honor?" says God. And if you call on the Father, who impartially judges according to each one's work, conduct yourselves throughout the time of your stay here in fear. It is true that we are children and thus freed from the bondage of the law. Nevertheless, we must still have reverence for the Father, walking before Him with filial respect.

Thirdly, if God is a Father, then there must be love for Him. Whatever you do, do it out of love. Do not be mercenary. A servant does not care to do anything beyond what they will be paid for. But a child does not think this way. They do what they do out of love. Oh, that we could offer all our obedience out of love for God, so that we need not argue by saying, "Must we necessarily do this or go to hell? Can no one be saved unless they strictly adhere to this?" It is a base spirit to argue in this manner. No, what suffices for a child is what pleases the Father. Let any minister of God expound on any point and show someone with a child-like disposition that it will please God, that it will be deemed acceptable by God, and, oh, a child will seek the pleasing and acceptable will of God. They do not fulfill their duty merely for wages. Most people, however, render their service solely for wages. Otherwise, what is the reason why, during times of prosperity, you are not as devoted to serving God as when you are lying on your sickbed or deathbed? Why do people on their sick and deathbeds cry out, "Oh, if only I could live, then I would serve God better. I would not live in sin as I have done before"? Why? It is because they fear going to hell. But if it were out of love, when I have the greatest prosperity of all, this would captivate my heart even more. Oh, then you will abound in service when you serve out of love.

Fourthly, and furthermore, you must be obedient to God. Love must be the motive, and in all your ways, you must be obedient children. In Ephesians 5:1, it says, "Be ye therefore followers of God, as dear children." A command of God should hold more weight for you than all else in the world. Let me provide you with an example used by the Holy Spirit to illustrate children's obedience to their parents—the obedience of the sons of the Rechabites, which the Holy Spirit records to honor them. In Jeremiah 35:5-6, it says, "And I set before the sons of the house of the Rechabites pots full of wine, and cups, and I said unto them, Drink ye wine. But they said, We will drink no wine: for Jonadab the son of Rechab our father commanded us, saying, Ye shall drink no wine, neither ye, nor your sons for ever." That was argument enough. This was a long time after the command, and although Jonadab had no authority to impose it on his sons, their obedience professed their duty to their father. Because their father commanded them, they would never drink wine, even if they were allowed to. Oh, the command of a father should have a strong hold on us if we profess ourselves to be children.

Fifthly, another duty is to trust in our Father and rely on Him. When the Father promises something, the child relies on Him. A child relies on their father for provisions and all necessary things. When a child desires something from their father, they don't need to present persuasive arguments; it's enough to call him "Father." The word "Father" holds enough persuasion to overcome all arguments. When a stranger wants something, they must provide reasons to obtain it. But a child doesn't need to because they are their father's child. And if a child has angered their father and the father is angry with them, the child still trusts in the father and relies on his fatherly love. There is no better way to obtain something from the father than to cast oneself upon his fatherly love. There is a significant difference between the confidence of a stranger and the confidence of a child, and a great difference between the confidence of one born again by the Spirit of God, the confidence of a child, and the confidence of a stranger. I'll provide you with a Scripture about the confidence of the children of God relying on their Father and His grace and mercy despite their offenses. In Isaiah 64:6-7, it says, "But we are all as an unclean thing, and all our righteousnesses are as filthy rags; and we all do fade as a leaf, and our iniquities, like the wind, have taken us away. And there is none that calleth upon thy name, that stirreth up himself to take hold of thee: for thou hast hid thy face from us, and hast consumed us, because of our iniquities." Then in verse 8, it says, "But now, O Lord, thou art our Father; we are the clay, and thou our potter; and we all are the work of thy hand." Even though we are all unclean and our righteousness is like filthy rags, and we fade away like a leaf, and there is none who calls upon God's name or stirs themselves up to take hold of Him, we are all wicked and vile, and God has consumed us, yet, O Lord, thou art our Father. This is the answer to everything. Thou art our Father, and she still relies on God as a Father. Oh, this title of Father is a mighty rock of faith, a strong foundation of faith for all the saints that God is their Father. Oh, then trust in Him, rely on Him for provision, for help. Wouldn't it be a great dishonor for any father if his children went to all the neighbors to beg for bread and said, "My father will not give it to me, and I will starve despite having a father"? This would be considered a great dishonor. Parents want their children to look to them for provision and leave them to provide for them. So, if you call God Father, let God alone provide for you, and rely on Him just as the heart of a child relies on parents for everything it needs. Therefore, even if you encounter great sufferings, continue to exercise faith in God as a Father. There is a promise to strengthen the faith of a child. In 2 Corinthians 6:18, it says, "And will be a Father unto you, and ye shall be my sons and daughters, saith the Lord Almighty." Notice that it is an exhortation to come out from false worship, to separate oneself, to touch no unclean thing, and God will receive you and be a Father to you, and you shall be His sons and daughters, saith the Lord Almighty. If we seek to worship God as a Father and separate ourselves from all false worship, we may suffer greatly, face opposition and hatred from others, and encounter difficulties in the world. Yet, says God, even if others cast you out, even if your own parents are against you, I will be a Father to you, and you shall be my sons and daughters, saith the Lord Almighty. I am the Lord Almighty, capable of doing good to you, able to help you and meet all your needs. Therefore, do not be afraid. Rely on Me, trust in Me, for I am your Father, says the Lord Almighty.

Again, if you are children, then delight in the presence of your Father. Make use of the spirit of adoption, come before your Father often. When you pray, do not approach it as a mere duty but go to prayer as children go to their father. Oh, God takes great delight in the spirit of adoption. I remember Luther's expression about it. He said that the word "Father" holds more elegance before God than Demosthenes or Cicero had in all their elegant orations. It pierces the heavens and fills them with its sound. Oh, make use of the spirit of adoption, love to be in the presence of your Father. Even if God, your Father, seems angry with you, do not leave His presence. A child with a childish disposition, not a base and sordid disposition, will not be cast out of the Father's presence. You can read in Psalm 51:11, even when God was angry with David, he pleaded, "Cast me not away from thy presence." It was as if he said, "Let me be in your presence, even if it means facing your frowning countenance." Cherish duty as your privilege, to be often in prayer before your Father. Those of you who pray as a mere task, who do not understand the meaning of the spirit of adoption, who do not experience your hearts leaping within you when you go to God in prayer, surely you should fear that you are not yet among the number of children.

Seventhly, if you are God's children, be zealous for Him. A child would be zealous for the honor of their father. Yes, a child would fight for their father even if the father is angry with them. A servant would not do the same for their master. I recall the story of Crassus' son. Once, when he saw his father in danger, he was unable to speak, but when he saw a soldier about to kill his father, his natural affection broke through the barriers of his speech, and he cried out, "Oh, spare Crassus!" He had never spoken before, yet when he saw his father in danger, his lips opened, and he cried out, "Oh, do not kill Crassus." It should be the same with you. Even if you have never spoken a word in your life, when you see your father dishonored, cry out, "Oh, spare the honor of God! Do nothing that dishonors God!" Even those of you with meek and quiet spirits, who are willing to endure anything concerning yourselves, when you see your father attacked, your spirits should boil within you. If you were truly children, you would act in this manner.

Eighthly, and you would imitate your Father. Be holy as your Heavenly Father is holy. Show forth the image of your Father. It is an honour for a child to resemble their father, and a father loves their child even more for it. I remember it was said of Theodosius' son, that good Emperor, that he would never die as long as his son lived. We say of certain individuals, "So-and-so will never die as long as this child is alive." This should apply to all the children of God. They should strive to display the virtues of the One who called them out of darkness into His marvelous light (1 Pet 2:9). They should conduct themselves in such a way that everyone who interacts with them is reminded of God. There should be the image of God in the child, so that whenever they are seen, people are reminded of God. I have heard from the Word how holy God is, and God and Jesus Christ possessed a meek and quiet spirit. I have heard much about God from His Word, and whenever I witness the holy conduct of someone, it reminds me of God. They are undoubtedly led by the Spirit of God, which is the evidence of being a child (Rom 8). If we are led by the Spirit of God, we are the sons of God. Among other things, in terms of peaceableness, be like your Father. If you want evidence that you are begotten from above, I say, show forth the gracious Spirit of God within you by loving peace. This way, you will not only be the children of God and have comfort in your own souls that you are the children of God, but you will also be called the children of God. And that's the next point, that this is a great blessing, not only to be the children of God, but to be called the children of God. And this is the duty of all those who are the children of God, to walk in such a way before others that they may be called God's children, so that the thoughts of others may be convinced and say, "Truly, these are the children of the living God."

Ninthly, let the children of God walk towards one another as children of the same Father. While it is true that the children of wild persons who have no education at all, but are rude, may fight with one another, and their parents might overlook it because they are rude and uncultured, if people of any rank and standing in the world who have received proper upbringing witness their children quarrelling and fighting in front of them, it would be extremely distressing to them. It is enough that the children of the world quarrel and fight among themselves; let those who profess God to be their Father, O let them not quarrel and fight in the presence of their Father. Certainly, the Spirit of God cannot bear it. But let us move on to what remains.

"They shall be called the children of God."

They shall not only be so, but be accounted as such in the world before others. That's the point.

Doctrine: It is a great blessing not only to be God's children but also to conduct ourselves in such a way that convinces all those with whom we live that we are the children of God, so that in their consciences, they shall acknowledge us as God's children and call us so. It was a great part of the glory of Christ himself, not only to be the Son of God, but to be declared as the Son of God (Rom 1:4). "And declared to be the Son of God with power, according to the spirit of holiness, by the resurrection from the dead." He was the Son of God, and that was glory. He was also declared to be the Son of God, which was a special part of His glory. Likewise, it is a great addition to our glory to be called the Son of God. Christ emphasized this, desiring the world to know that God had sent Him. He often spoke of it. Why was it not enough, O blessed Saviour, that you knew the Father had sent you, and the Father knew He had sent you? No, He wanted the world to know that the Father had sent Him. This is something the saints should value as a great blessing from God, that even the world should know the relationship they have with God, that they are the children of God. They shall be called so by walking in such a way that people are forced to acknowledge them as God's children. Through this,

First, a great deal of glory comes upon themselves, as they are honoured in the consciences of others.

Secondly, through this, their Father is glorified as their lives reveal to whom they belong. Moreover, their profession is glorified, and the mouths of wicked individuals are silenced. Their consciences are convicted. Much good is accomplished through this. Those who not only possess grace but also manifest it to convict others are of great use in the places where they live. Even the most wicked and vile would say, "If they were all like these individuals, then I could have good thoughts of them. Then we would not know what to say against them." They would be ready to listen to anything said when there is a conversation that is convincing. It will be a means to restrain their malice against others when they see that at least some walk in a manner that manifests nothing but the image of God. Oh, it is a great blessing to be someone who compels even wicked individuals to call them God's children. Therefore, let us

First, know that it is not enough to have grace in the heart and say, "What do I care for people, as long as I have a good conscience?" No, it is the duty of all to walk in such a way that they may be called the children of God. Therefore, it is not enough to have grace in the heart; it must also be evident.

Secondly, how vile are those who profess a close relationship with God, yet walk in such a way that nothing of God appears in them? Through their scandalous and wicked lives, they make people think that persecuting them is doing God a service. Especially in these times, when God's children should walk as children, they should be conscious of walking in a way that convinces the world. Woe to those who are offensive! Woe to those who are stumbling blocks, not only to themselves but also to all who are on the same path. The world is inclined toward offenses and delights in them. Therefore, God's children should strive to be even more inoffensive. We will discuss each of these points in more detail, as well as the main point if we ever reach verse 16: "Let your light so shine before men, that they may see your good works, and glorify your Father which is in heaven." For now, I only address this in relation to the text, particularly regarding peacemaking. Blessed are the peacemakers, for they shall be called the children of God. Peacemaking is a very convincing attribute. Therefore, those who hope to be children of God should demonstrate it by having peaceful and gentle dispositions. Some individuals, whom we hope belong to God, possess such rough and harsh natures that there is little evidence of God's Spirit within them. They display nothing but an evil, proud, perverse, and contentious spirit within their families and in all their interactions. This is unacceptable. Those who profess to belong to God should manifest themselves as His children in this regard, by being peaceable, meek, gentle, and loving. All you professors of religion, make conscience of this. It is often said of many religious individuals that they are proud and froward if crossed in any way. There is no quietness, humility, gentleness, meekness, patience, or love seen in them. Learn from the connection between peace-making and being called the children of God to take out this lesson today. As in many other things, you should manifest yourselves as God's children, especially in demonstrating a gentle, meek, patient, and loving spirit in your families and in the places where God has placed you. Furthermore, it is not only about having peaceable spirits, but about being peaceable in a way that manifests the Spirit of God within you. Some people naturally have a peaceable spirit because they cannot endure trouble and avoid troubling others. They live quietly among their neighbors, avoiding conflicts. However, this does not always come from a gracious disposition but from a dull and sluggish spirit.

Question: But you may ask, when is a person of such a peaceable disposition that they manifest themselves as a child of God in their peaceableness?

Answer: Firstly, when our peaceableness does not hinder our duty. A person may love peace but also love to fulfill their duty. They can be peaceable among people and still be active in the performance of their duty to God. They can actively engage in the cause of God and the public good while maintaining a peaceful approach. Some people think that the only way to be peaceable is to do nothing, allowing things to go whichever way they will. They avoid putting themselves in uncomfortable situations. While they may be commended as quiet and peaceable neighbors by some, God will never acknowledge them as His children based on this kind of peaceableness. The true peaceableness of a child of God lies in the ability to be active and diligent in fulfilling their duty while maintaining meekness, tranquility, and peacefulness. It is an excellent balance between a lifeless and sluggish spirit and a violent and furious spirit. Led by the Spirit of God, a person knows how to be active and diligent in their duty while carrying out their work with meekness, tranquility, and peacefulness. This is the true mark of a child of God.

Secondly, when a person has a peaceable disposition and aims more for God than their own tranquility. Some individuals have peaceable dispositions, but why? It is merely because they dislike trouble and desire peace. However, when a man or woman considers this, they realize that dishonor is brought upon

God and numerous sins are committed between brethren through disturbance, discontent, and unrest. Therefore, in order to prevent such great sin and honor God, I will deny myself even if it goes against my fleshly desires. I acknowledge that my flesh is inclined to seek revenge and make those who have wronged me aware of their wrongdoing. But in order to prevent sin and bring honor to the name of God, I will set aside my own interests, endure wrongs, walk peaceably with others, and strive for peace with them as well. This peaceable spirit demonstrates that I am a child of God who aims for God and denies myself. Some individuals would be peaceable if it serves their own purposes. However, I choose to be peaceable myself and make peace with others, even if I gain nothing from it. I consider it my good to be wrapped up in the glory of God, and thus I make peace because I do not want the name of God to suffer. This is the kind of peace-maker who shall be called a child of God.

Thirdly, such a peace-maker is like God Himself, as we find recorded in Scripture that making peace is attributed to God. It is as follows: Firstly, God is willing to be at peace with those who are unworthy. Secondly, even to those who have wronged Him. It is not enough to say that they have wronged me and they are unworthy; you should strive for peace with them. For God causes His sun to shine upon the unjust as well as the just, and we are commanded to love our enemies so that we may be declared as the children of God. Thirdly, God initiates the work of peace. If God had not begun the work of reconciliation between mankind and Himself, what would have become of us all? Now, those who desire to be such peace-makers as to evidence that they are children of God should not stand and say, "He has wronged me, let him yield first." No, if God had said that, what would have become of us? But God yields first. Oh, now you should be a child of God in this, to strive for peace as God does and initiate it first with them. Even if they do not fulfill their duty by initiating peace with you, you should still begin with them as a child of God ought to do, who desires to be like their Father.

Lastly, be a peace-maker who loves the peace that God loves and delights in. Your Father loves truth, but He loves truth, peace, and holiness together. Do not allow anything against holiness in the pursuit of peace. God does not want any of His children to commit any sin for the sake of peace, to save themselves or others from trouble. He does not want them to obtain peace through sin. It is true that one cannot buy peace at too high a price, except through sin. But committing any sin to gain personal peace or the peace of others, in that regard, you are buying gold at too high a cost. This is not the kind of peace-making that befits a child of God. Blessed are those who are peace-makers, for they shall be called the children of God. And that concludes our discussion of the ninth verse. Now, let us move on to the tenth.

"Blessed are those who are persecuted for righteousness' sake, for theirs is the kingdom of heaven." - Matthew 5:10

It's a peculiar kind of blessing, just like the others. Some of the other blessings may seem strange, like the first one: Blessed are the poor and those who mourn. It's unexpected that they should be considered blessed. And now, those who are persecuted. Isn't it equally surprising that they should be the most blessed people in the world? Christ begins with the poor and ends with the persecuted when revealing who the most blessed individuals are. My brethren, consider whether the wisdom of Christ aligns with the wisdom of the world or not. When describing a blessed person, would you start with the poor and end with the persecuted? Oh, the wisdom of Christ is not in accordance with the world's wisdom. His thoughts on blessedness differ from those of the world.

Secondly, it is remarkable that Christ needs to speak of the blessedness of those who are persecuted after mentioning the blessedness of the previous traits. What? Blessed are the peace-makers, and blessed are the persecuted. What connection is there between these two? Or what link can there be? For if a person has a peaceable disposition, who will harm them? Surely, they will escape persecution from everyone. Perhaps there are some individuals (though godly) who have a turbulent and hot-tempered nature, and they may be persecuted. But will the peace-makers be persecuted? Will those who, in the places where they live, cause no harm to others but instead strive to do all the good they can, be persecuted? Yes, indeed, even these, if they are godly, even these, if they are righteous, must not think they can escape. None who are truly godly and righteous, even if they have the most peaceful and peaceable dispositions in the world, must not assume they can evade persecution. Therefore, these two traits are linked. Yes, this blessedness that follows persecution is added to all the previous ones to indicate that a person can possess all the previous traits and yet be a persecuted individual. For example, a person can have a humble and impoverished spirit and still be persecuted. A person can have a mournful spirit, mourning for their own sins and the sins of others, and still be persecuted. A person can have a meek spirit and still be persecuted. A person can hunger and thirst for righteousness. A person can be merciful and still be persecuted. A person can have a pure heart, devoid of selfish motives, and still be persecuted. Yes, a person can be a peace-maker and still be persecuted. Such is the wickedness of the world and the vileness of human nature that nothing can prevent them from persecuting the saints, even if they possess impoverished, mournful, meek, pure, merciful, and peaceable hearts. This is the connection between these traits.

"Blessed are those who are persecuted"; the word translated as persecuted, δεδιωγμένοι, comes from διώκω, which means a hard and persistent following of something. It is used sometimes in a positive sense. The same word found here and in other Scriptures is used in a positive sense. For example, in 1 Thessalonians 5:15, "Follow that which is good," the Greek word used is the same. It also appears in Hebrews 12:14, "Follow peace," and in 1 Corinthians 14:1, "Follow after charity." Therefore, it means to pursue something so diligently that one does not stop until they achieve their desired outcome. The Apostle Paul uses it in this sense in Philippians 3:14: "I press towards the mark; I persecute the mark," indicating the zeal with which he pursued his goal. In an unfavorable sense, it means to follow something thoroughly. Now, if you want to understand what persecution is, it is simply this: an unwavering pursuit of harming and destroying someone. When individuals eagerly pursue an evil cause and relentlessly follow someone to harm them, refusing to cease until they achieve their intentions, they can be said to persecute these individuals. Persecution is not merely causing harm to someone; there is a distinction between wronging someone and persecuting them. They may wrong someone in a single act, or they may accidentally harm them. However, persecution involves continually following and relentlessly pursuing a person or woman, seeking to harm them. Oh, blessed are those who are persecuted, those whom the world's persecutors target and eagerly seek to harm. This is for righteousness' sake. It is not the punishment itself that makes a martyr; it is the cause. Those who are followed hard for their sins, their wickedness, those who suffer for evildoing, those who suffer for being evildoers, they are not blessed in this sense. God does not want them to suffer in that way; it is a part of God's curse upon them that as they do evil, they shall suffer evil. The blessed saints strive to avoid suffering for wrongdoing; they would rather endure all the evil in the world than commit the slightest transgression. There is a significant difference between these two scenarios.

"Blessed are those who are persecuted for righteousness' sake, for theirs is the kingdom of heaven."

If you observe, the same promise is made to those who suffer persecution as to those who are poor in spirit. Ambrose, commenting on this passage, says that one promise pertains to the soul's blessing. The poor in spirit will have their souls blessed forever in the kingdom of heaven. The other promise pertains to bodily afflictions, for those who suffer persecution. Even their bodies will go to heaven. But I believe this interpretation does not fully capture the meaning intended by the Holy Spirit here. I would interpret it differently. Those who are poor in spirit consider themselves unworthy of anything. They seem to be among the lowest ranks of all the saints of God. The poor in spirit feel dejected when confronted with their poverty. On the other hand, those who endure persecution belong to the highest ranks. The martyrs who suffer for Jesus Christ are glorious beings. Someone who feels dejected due to their own poverty may say, "I am a person of low spirits. I am unable to overcome my difficulties. I am unworthy for God to even look at or regard me." However, there are others with exceptional spirits who can endure any opposition. They can endure the confiscation of their possessions, imprisonment, reproach, and even shed their blood. Yes, they are truly blessed. Now, take note that the same promise is given to both the dejected, those who feel unworthy, and those who suffer martyrdom for Jesus Christ. A weak and impoverished Christian can achieve the same glory as the most glorious martyr ever did. Therefore, this same promise is attached to both.

Furthermore, this promise is given to those who are persecuted because those who endure persecution in this world have their names cast out as filth and vile. They are regarded as wicked and ungodly individuals. The laws of kingdoms and the ruling spirits are often against them. However, Christ tells his disciples not to be troubled, even though they suffer injustice in the kingdoms of the world and are condemned as evildoers, as if they were the troublemakers in their communities. "Be not troubled, for yours is the kingdom of heaven." As I recall, Luther said in another context, upon hearing the determinations against him in Nuremberg, "It is otherwise concluded in heaven than in Nuremberg." Likewise, those who are persecuted can find comfort in the fact that even though the kingdoms of the world stand against us, the kingdom of heaven belongs to us. There is another court where everything will be reexamined, and in that court, the enemy will be defeated.

Secondly, theirs is the kingdom of heaven. By enduring persecution in this world, even though you suffer the loss of your reputation, liberties, possessions, and perhaps even your life, do not be discouraged because the kingdom of heaven belongs to you. It is the path to that kingdom, which will compensate for everything. You will receive as much glory as the affliction you endured while suffering. It will be proportionate to your suffering. I recall a story about the Emperor Caligula. When Agrippa, who had previously suffered and been cast into prison for advocating on his behalf, came to the throne, one of the first things Caligula did was release Agrippa and present him with a golden chain that weighed as much as the iron chain he had worn in prison. Similarly, Christ says, "Yours is the kingdom of heaven." Consider the suffering you endure in this world, for your reward awaits in the kingdom of heaven. And this is the meaning behind this blessedness.

Now, there are three main points in this verse that I want to address.

First, it is essential to understand that all disciples of Christ, no matter how blameless their conduct in the world, must expect to face persecution, and that persecution will be for the sake of righteousness.

Secondly, even though they experience persecution, they are and will be blessed in their suffering. They should not be disheartened or troubled by their sufferings because, amidst it all, they are blessed and will continue to be blessed.

Thirdly, this is the great blessedness of the saints, and particularly of those who endure persecution: they will inherit the kingdom of heaven. The kingdom of heaven will be their reward.

I had intended to discuss the first point, but I see that I cannot proceed with it. Instead, I will only elaborate on a passage in Timothy: "All who desire to live a godly life in Christ Jesus will be persecuted." Pay attention to the phrase "all who desire to live godly."

You may argue that they can be godly but lack wisdom in their actions, and therefore bring suffering upon themselves. However, it is not about wisdom alone. It applies to all who are determined to live a godly life, regardless of the consequences. For example, someone in a household may start thinking, "My ways and the ways of this family are not good. I wish I could do better. But if I do, my master or mistress will hate me, and my friends will hate me. Therefore, I must be cautious about what I do." However, all who desire to live godly, even if they desire the love and acceptance of their master, mistress, and friends, know that whatever they suffer, they see it as the way of God. They are resolved to pursue this path.

Furthermore, all who desire to live godly understand the significance of the term "godliness" in English. It represents the nature and work of grace in the heart. It means living from a godly principle unto the glory of God. To live godly is to be determined that the guiding principles of one's life will not be of a carnal nature or based on worldly wisdom. Instead, they will be godly principles received from God. The aim is to live in a way that brings praise and honor to God. They have resolved not to live for themselves anymore, but for God. All who desire to live godly.

Those who content themselves with mere wishes will not face persecution. They may claim to have a good heart towards God and argue, "Why should I trouble myself with public displays in the world as long as I have a good heart towards God?" Such individuals may avoid persecution. However, for those who desire to live godly, that is, to manifest it in their lives and conduct, persecution is inevitable.

Lastly, all who desire to live godly in Christ Jesus must be prepared to face persecution. There is a kind of religious profession that people can have without undergoing any suffering. This refers to refraining from gross and notorious sins. This kind of godliness may be accepted in the world, but it is not in Christ Jesus. It does not manifest the power, life, and effectiveness of the Spirit of Christ. However, those who truly desire to live godly in Christ Jesus must expect to endure persecution. The more fervent and zealous they are, the more they should anticipate suffering. Individuals who maintain a moderate and cautious approach, avoiding suffering at all costs, are not exhibiting the zealous spirit of Christ. If they were truly zealous, they could not avoid persecution. All who desire to live godly in Christ Jesus must suffer persecution. This is a lesson Paul learned directly from Christ, even though he did not live during Christ's time. Christ appeared to him, and he received the Spirit of Christ. No doubt, Paul was familiar with this sermon of Christ, forewarning all disciples that they must expect persecution. As soon as Paul was converted, he was told that he would suffer great things for the sake of Jesus' name (Acts 9:16). Paul, a young convert, was informed right at the beginning of his journey with Christ about the great sufferings he would endure. The Lord Christ trains converts in this aspect from the very beginning. This is an important point for young followers of the faith to consider: all who desire to live godly in Christ Jesus must be prepared to face persecution.

# SERMON XXXXII

## Disciples of Christ Must Expect Persecution

"Blessed are they which are persecuted for Righteousness' sake,
for theirs is the kingdom of heaven." - Matthew 5:10

We briefly touched upon the first point towards the end of the previous discussion, so we didn't consider it too deeply. The first lesson Christ teaches anyone who comes to Him is this: "If any will be my Disciple, let him deny himself and take up his cross and follow me." (Matthew 16:24) As soon as Saul was converted, he was immediately told about the sufferings he would endure for the sake of Christ. (Acts 9:16) The Apostle Paul later affirmed that all who desire to live godly in Christ Jesus will suffer persecution. (2 Timothy 3:12) We spent some time examining the emphasis in each word of that text. Now, I will proceed to further elucidate the point through Scripture, examples, and reason, and then apply it.

In the Book of Joshua, we read about the Gebusites. As soon as they entered into a covenant with Joshua and the people of God, the surrounding kings rose up against them. They had been peaceful with their neighbors before, but once they entered into a covenant with Joshua, opposition arose. Likewise, although people may live peacefully in the world before God works in their hearts, if they surrender their lives to Jesus Christ and enter into a covenant with Him, they must expect persecution. The whole world will be against them. In Genesis 15:12-17, God informed Abraham about the sufferings his descendants would endure. After making a covenant with Abram, God caused him to fall into a deep sleep, symbolizing the afflictions his seed would experience in Egypt. This foreshadowed the sufferings of believers throughout history. The New Testament echoes this truth in Acts 14:22, where believers are exhorted to endure tribulations on their path to the kingdom of God. Tribulation is the lot of the godly. On the other hand, Job 21:13 may appeal to a worldly heart, as it speaks of spending days in wealth and suddenly descending to the grave. But for the godly, it is through many tribulations that they enter the kingdom of heaven. Peter, in 1 Peter 5:10, did not dare pray against all persecution for the saints. Instead, he acknowledged that suffering plays a role in perfecting, establishing, strengthening, and settling believers. Peter understood that those who profess the truth and strive for perfection must also endure hardships. When we examine the seven churches in the Book of Revelation (Revelation 2-3), we find that only two of them had relatively little mention of their suffering. The Church of Sardis was rebuked for having a name but being spiritually dead, and the Church of Laodicea was criticized for its lukewarmness. These two churches, which were the worst among the seven, suffered less. Those who have a mere appearance of life and those who are lukewarm may avoid persecution. It seems that the worse individuals are in their profession of religion, the more likely they are to escape suffering. Conversely, the more fervent and genuine their godliness, the more likely they are to endure persecution. Christians must expect persecution. In this sermon, Christ preached to His disciples, and they experienced the truth of His words. Scripture, as well as ecclesiastical accounts, testify to the fact that almost all the apostles suffered violent deaths, except for John, who was miraculously delivered from boiling oil but still faced banishment. Ecclesiastical accounts provide details about the other apostles' martyrdoms. Although there are slight discrepancies regarding the manner of their deaths, they all agree that the apostles suffered violent deaths. Peter was crucified upside down, Andrew was crucified by King Aegeas of Edessa, James the son of Zebedee was slain by Herod, and John was banished. Philip was crucified in Hierapolis, Bartholomew was beaten to death while preaching, Thomas was killed with a dart, Matthew was slain with a spear or sword, James the son of Alphaeus was thrown from the pinnacle of the Temple and then stoned, Lebbaeus was slain by King Agbarus of Edessa, Paul was beheaded in Rome under Nero, and Simon the Canaanite and Jude were killed in a riot. Matthias was stoned to death. Thus, the apostles experienced what Christ had foretold—that they would face persecution. Christ armed them in advance with His words, as He preached this Scripture to them. The apostles, who were closest to Him, were prepared for the persecution they would later endure, even to the point of death, with the exception of one.

If you were to ask me first, how it comes to pass that believers suffer persecution, I would say there are three reasons: firstly, because of the Devil; secondly, because of the nature of wicked people; and thirdly, because of the holy purposes that God has in the sufferings of His people.

Firstly, the Devil is the old Serpent, the Scorpion, the old Dragon. Satan, meaning adversary, is like a roaring lion seeking whom he may devour. The Devil intensely hates God, and therefore he hates everything that belongs to God or anything that reflects God in any way. The Devil's sin is one of malice, which is akin to the sin against the Holy Spirit. The sin against the Holy Spirit leads one to hate God and everything associated with Him, causing a desire to bring harm to others. I recall a story of a man who was believed to have committed the sin against the Holy Spirit. When asked if he wanted his wife and children to be saved, he responded, "There was a time when I wanted my wife and children to be saved, but now I wish that both they and the whole world were damned." This hatred stemmed from his enmity towards God, rather than towards his own family or the world. This is the nature of the sin against the Holy Spirit, although I believe it can be committed even without such explicit expressions of malice. The Devil, having committed a sin of the same nature, hates the image of God and despises anything that is related to God. If possible, he would prevent anyone from being saved. But if he cannot stop some from being saved, he is determined to make their salvation as difficult as possible. The Devil is called the Prince of this world, and he holds significant sway over it. The world is under his captivity, and he is known as the god of this world. Therefore, because the Devil despises God and His saints to such an extent, all saints must expect hardships.

Secondly, this poison of the old Serpent is absorbed by wicked and ungodly people. In Genesis 3:15, God speaks of putting enmity between the woman and the serpent, and between their offspring. There is a natural hostility between the godly and the wicked, an inherent antipathy. Antipathy is the most profound, secret, deadly, and ongoing form of opposition. Such an antipathy exists between the saints and the wicked. I have read about how the smell of spices can provoke a tiger into a rage. Similarly, the fragrance of God's grace in the lives of the saints can infuriate the wicked of the world. In the hearts of people, there is an opposition to godliness that surpasses all reason because it is driven by antipathy. Antipathy represents the opposition of one creature against another, for which no logical explanation can be given. It is akin to a lion being a fearsome creature that is not scared by the neighing of horses or the beating of drums or the rattling of spears but is terrified by the crowing of a cock. The same kind of unexplainable opposition exists between the wicked and the godly. Even if the godly live inoffensively, there will be opposition without any reasonable cause. Some people may feel faint at the sight of a particular dish without any rational explanation. Likewise, the wicked and the godly have an innate opposition. The Apostle Paul, reflecting on his persecutions of the saints, acknowledged that he was mad. He realized that there was an antipathy between the hearts of the wicked and the hearts of the godly. This antipathy cannot be cured in this world unless either God removes the saints from the wicked or the wicked from the saints. Just as there is a natural opposition between fire and water, there will always be an opposition between the godly and the wicked. In Psalm 19:9, it is written that the righteous are an abomination to the wicked, and the wicked are an abomination to the righteous.

But you may ask, even though the Devil and wicked people possess such vile natures that they hate the saints, does not God reign over all? Does not the Lord rule in the world? Yes, indeed He does, and there is cause for rejoicing. If it were not for God reigning by His almighty power, wicked people would never allow a single saint to exist in the world. As soon as any godliness begins to appear, fathers would not tolerate it in their children, nor would one neighbor tolerate it in another. It is God who restrains the rage of the Devil and wicked people. However, God allows His saints to undergo persecution, and He has many holy purposes in their suffering.

Firstly, He demonstrates His great power in enabling weak and vulnerable individuals to endure all the sufferings they encounter. I remember a heathen who observed Christians in the early days enduring great tortures and torments with courage and cheerfulness. He exclaimed, "Truly, the God of the Christians is a great God, a God who empowers His worshippers to endure such great sufferings with courage." God's tremendous power is evident in keeping the graces of the Spirit alive in the hearts of the saints amidst persecution.

Secondly, while God demonstrates His power, He also aims to exercise the grace within His people. Therefore, according to His holy will and counsel, He permits His saints to endure persecution, that their graces may be exercised. This includes the exercise of their love for Him. Scipio, a Roman general, once boasted about his soldiers, saying that if he ordered them to throw themselves off a tower, they would willingly sacrifice their lives simply out of respect for him. The Lord Jesus Christ could say the same. He has thousands upon thousands of saints who, if it is His will for them to pass through fire and water, suffer the loss of their possessions, liberties, or lives, would do it. The Lord takes great pleasure in the exercise of the graces of love, faith, patience, and humility. The Church has never been more fruitful than when it has been watered with its own blood. Like a rose cast into the still, the fragrance of the exercise of grace is more delightful than when it blooms beautifully on the bush. The exercise of grace is a greater good than the enjoyment of any worldly comfort. If only we were rightly grounded in this profound mystery of godliness! Do you consider the exercise of a grace to be a greater blessing than the enjoyment of the world or any earthly comfort? If so, then you are truly blessed. These truths have not been revealed to you by flesh and blood; rather, your heart is aligned with the heart of God, and you have been taught by heavenly instruction. Even if you suffer from the hand of God Himself, if it serves to exercise your graces, you are not at a loss. And even if you endure severe afflictions from the hands of men, if you find that these sufferings result in the manifestation of your graces, then you are truly blessed. This is God's purpose in permitting His people to undergo persecution.

And then there's a third purpose, which is important to consider. It is the discovery of the hearts of people. Without suffering for the sake of Christ, there would be little distinction between the hypocrite and the sincere believer. I recall reading about a heathen named Pamettrius who said to the Bishop of Rome, "Make me a bishop, and I will be a Christian." He desired the honor and prestige of being a bishop, thinking that would make him a Christian just like anyone else. If there were only prosperity in the profession of Christianity, how could the truth and sincerity of people's hearts be revealed? Fiery trials create a clear separation. Indeed, suffering helps us discover our own hearts. Before experiencing suffering, we are unaware of the impurities within us. But when suffering comes, we become aware of the dross in our hearts. It also reveals us to others. In Luke 2:35, when speaking of the sufferings that would follow the profession of the Gospel, it is said to the Virgin Mary that a sword would pierce her soul so that the thoughts of many hearts may be revealed. When hardships accompany the profession of the Gospel, acting as a piercing sword, the thoughts of many hearts are laid bare. God intends to expose the thoughts of people's hearts through persecution. Formal professors of faith are like withered leaves on a tree. When the storm comes, it becomes evident which leaves are withered and which ones are still connected to the life-giving root. If you hang heavy objects on a rotten branch, it will bend and break, exposing its true condition. Similarly, when persecution comes, it reveals who is genuine and who is not. It shows whether individuals follow Christ out of a sincere heart or out of self-interest. Just as a servant walking behind two gentlemen on the street could go unnoticed, it becomes apparent whom he serves when they reach a parting way. He will leave one and follow his true master. Likewise, some may seem to follow Christ but are actually pursuing their own selfish ends. As long as Christ and their own desires align, it is difficult to determine if they truly follow Christ or not. However, when Christ and their personal interests diverge, their true allegiances are revealed, and their affections become evident. The Lord takes great pleasure in uncovering the hearts of people in this world.

Fourthly, the Lord's aim is to conform His saints to the likeness of His Son, Jesus Christ. The Apostle Paul, in Philippians 3, declares that he considers all things as rubbish compared to the surpassing worth of knowing Christ. He not only desires to be found in Christ, clothed in His righteousness, but also to be conformed to His death. Who would not want to be conformed to the glory of Christ in heaven? However, being conformed to His death is another matter. It was said of Christ, "Ought he not to suffer these things and then enter into his glory?" Therefore, the Lord desires all His people, who are chosen before the foundation of the world, to be conformed to His Son. He wants all the members of Christ to share in His sufferings.

Fifthly and finally, the Lord allows His people to endure persecution as a righteous judgment against the wicked and ungodly of this world. It is a way of leaving them to their own base corruptions, causing them to stumble over the stumbling stone, and ultimately perish forever. I truly believe that the sufferings of godly people have been the cause of eternal destruction for countless individuals. There are many other holy purposes we could discuss regarding why God allows His saints to endure persecution, but I will not dwell on that point.

Now, in terms of practical application, let me address it briefly.

When you begin to embrace any religious profession, never expect to find rest in this world. Do not deceive yourself in matters of Christian faith. In Micah 2, it is stated, "Depart, for this is not your rest." Do not find satisfaction in earthly dwellings, financial gains, reputation, freedom, honor, or credit. Depart from them and set your heart on things above. You have been appointed to face persecution. Just as Paul said when he was advised not to go to Jerusalem out of fear of suffering, "I do not know what I will encounter in Jerusalem, but I know wherever I am, persecution, bonds, and afflictions await me." It is a fundamental and sure principle that wherever I am, I will face bonds and afflictions. Therefore, it is crucial for all of us to prepare in advance and store up treasures for such times. Do not assume that we will always enjoy peace and prosperity.

But you may wonder if this concern applies to us now. I must admit that I would not have deliberately chosen a text like this, but since it has come my way, let me say this: There may be much evil in our hearts of which we are unaware. Just as the prophet told Hazael what he would do, that he would commit great acts of cruelty, Hazael responded, "Am I a dog, that I would do such things?" Similarly, if we were told before attaining power that we would burden God's faithful servants and cause them to cry out to Heaven, we might consider it the most uncharitable thought. We might even feel like dogs if we were to do such things. However, we cannot deny that people are already doing such things, things they themselves would never have imagined doing before. Many who were once intimately acquainted with each other, sharing their innermost thoughts, praying and fasting together, shedding tears together, and groaning under previous persecutions, have now become harsh and cold towards brethren who were as dear to them as their own souls. These brethren have not become worse in their walk with God; their consciences testify that they are as close to God as ever. Yet, there has been a significant change in their spirits. We do not know the depths of evil in people's hearts, which is why we must always be prepared for persecution. There is no time so peaceful and serene that we do not need to prepare for suffering. Therefore, when you begin to embrace the Christian faith, reckon that persecutions will accompany you. In Acts 22, you can see how Paul anticipated suffering wherever he went. Hence, to prepare, I will not extensively consider the common advice for preparing and enduring suffering. Instead, I will offer a few words of guidance.

Firstly, when you profess faith, do not base it on hearsay or ulterior motives or to please others. When you enter the Christian profession, ensure you lay a solid foundation. Understand what you are building upon. It is not enough to be moved by the word of God and feel a temporary sense of joy. The stony ground experienced this but stumbled when troubles arose. Therefore, when you hear the word and are initially affected by it, do not assume the work is completed at once. Instead, strive for a deep foundation. The main foundation is to comprehend the way of the covenant of grace and be thoroughly informed about it. Additionally, humble your hearts before God so that the seed of His word can penetrate and take root. Those who have been made aware of the tremendous breach that sin has caused between God and their souls will not be greatly concerned about persecution. I recall Luther speaking about himself on numerous occasions. Although he faced persecution as much as anyone, he was well acquainted with spiritual troubles and the humility that comes from recognizing one's sinfulness. Consequently, he was not afraid of the Pope's threats. Likewise, we read about Paul, who knew he would face persecution for the sake of Christ as soon as he was converted. Yet, God had prepared Paul's heart. Paul recognized that he was chosen to be a vessel for bearing the name of Christ and, therefore, would experience hardships. How did God prepare his heart? He struck him down from his horse and caused him to cry out, "Lord, what do you want me to do?" This experience prepared Paul to endure anything for the sake of Christ. Thus, those who have truly understood the wretchedness and cursedness of their own selves will not regard suffering as a great burden. They may have suffered eternal torment in hell, being fuel for God's wrath to burn upon for all eternity. Therefore, what is it for them to be called upon to suffer for the name of Christ? This reflection alone has the power to prepare individuals for suffering and provide them with solace during their trials. When they consider, "What evils can men inflict upon me that compare to the torments I might have suffered from the wrath of God for my sin?" it diminishes the significance of any suffering endured for Christ's sake. Consequently, we must strive to be emptied of ourselves and conclude that it is better to lose everything for God than to enjoy all for ourselves. Imbibe this principle: there is greater value in the exercise of self-denial, which allows us to endure suffering, than in the enjoyment of worldly possessions.

There are many other means that could be mentioned, but I would like to move on to the main point: Blessed are those who suffer persecution for the sake of righteousness. If people suffer persecution for their wickedness, they are cursed. But when they endure persecution for righteousness, they are blessed.

You might ask, how many men suffer persecution for righteousness' sake? In my previous discussion, I touched on this point. Firstly, I will show you that not all sufferings for religious matters can be classified as persecution. Secondly, many individuals may be persecuted by others for the sake of righteousness without even realizing it. These are the two aspects I intended to address.

Regarding the first point, you may wonder to what extent men can suffer for matters of religion. When should suffering arise in religious matters?

In certain cases, men can suffer for matters of religion righteously, and it is just for those who impose the suffering. If men commit sins in religious matters that go against the light of nature and can be understood as sins by anyone who chooses to acknowledge it, then they may rightfully face consequences. I can provide you with a Scripture to support this: Job 31. It specifically addresses idolatry, and in that case, men may justly suffer. Verse 26 states, "If I beheld the sun when it shined, or the moon walking in brightness, and my heart hath been secretly enticed, or my mouth hath kissed my hand, this also were an iniquity to be punished by the judge." This Scripture cannot be explained away like some Old Testament passages concerning the kings of Judah. I admit that the strength of suffering during the time of the Law under the kings of Judah is not as compelling as other cases. There is a significant difference between them and current rulers. I have previously outlined the distinction between the people who lived under the Law's tutelage and the authority of the kings of Judah and present-day governors. However, Job was not under the Law's tutelage. The kings of Judah are regarded as types of Christ, and their rule was symbolic. On the other hand, the passage in Job does not pertain to any type but aligns with the light of nature and is approved by God. Therefore, worshipping the sun and moon, which can be recognized as idolatry by anyone through the light of nature, should be punished by the judge. Hence, there are some religious evils that can be addressed by men. Magistrates should not tolerate idolatry, which is clear and can be understood through the light of nature.

Can we go further?

Certainly, in other matters of lesser importance that are contrary to the common teachings of Christianity and clearly revealed, even those in positions of power and the general population can agree that if individuals remain ignorant of these matters, it is willful ignorance. Such things should not be tolerated. The same reason that justifies punishment by Christians for acts against the light of nature also applies to those who act against the common teachings of Christianity.

Furthermore, a magistrate can go so far that, due to the wicked behavior and insolent nature of individuals, they can take it upon themselves to act as though they will answer to Jesus Christ on the Last Day. They can clearly perceive that what is being displayed is sheer wantonness and stubbornness, not weakness and infirmity. To the extent that it is appropriate to counteract wantonness and stubbornness, the Lord has appointed external means, including outward punishment, as an ordinance. By nature, such punishment has an inherent efficacy. External elements possess an efficacy bestowed by the God of nature to counteract what appears to be outward stubbornness, wantonness, or rebellion. Thus, suffering may occur in matters of religion. Those who advocate for tolerating anything and everything, believing that the civil sword should resolve all controversies in religion, need to be cautious. If they are not careful, they may unwittingly subject the people of God to persecution.

The other two points I have discussed are sufficient to refute the great error that is being decried among us, which is the notion that men should endure everything without any form of governance. The Lord will judge those who have wronged such men, for they only argue for toleration in cases where individuals cannot be convicted of error through wantonness and stubbornness, due to the heinousness of their actions or opinions or their turbulent and proud behavior. In such cases, they propose forbearance. However, to think that all manner of things should be tolerated, including all forms of blasphemy, is a grave mistake. Anyone who has propagated this notion should bear the weight of guilt upon them. If they do not repent, they will be held accountable on Judgment Day. The plea is simply that all those who agree with us in fundamental doctrine and worship and conduct themselves in a peaceful, humble, and meek manner should receive forbearance from their brethren. Why should this hinder peace among us? Can we not live in harmony and enjoy one another's company without casting blame on those who advocate for complete tolerance or accusing others of persecution because they do not tolerate everything? This demonstrates that one can suffer in matters of religion justly and righteously. However, the limitations I previously mentioned should be observed.

Now, on the other hand, to convince individuals that they may unwittingly cause others to suffer for the sake of righteousness, you might question who would subject someone to such suffering. It seems unlikely.

To that, I respond that even the devil himself would never cause the people of God to suffer solely on the grounds of righteousness. If the devil were to instigate persecution against the saints, he would provide some pretext for their suffering. You will never find an instance where the devil denounced individuals purely for their righteousness. He always assigns some other name to bring suffering upon religious believers. For example, when the devil desired the Jewish people to suffer, Haman approached the king and informed him that it was not in the king's best interest to tolerate such individuals. Haman portrayed them as rebellious, constantly opposing the government. He incited the king against the Jewish people, who constituted the only church of God at the time, based on their alleged opposition to the government. He did not acknowledge them as God's chosen people; it was their opposition to the government that he emphasized. This pattern persists throughout history. When the Apostle Paul endured suffering, it was not due to righteousness but because he was considered a troublemaker, a fomenter of sedition, and responsible for turning the world upside down. In the early days of Christianity, all the troubles in various regions were attributed to the Christians, and they suffered under this label, as if they were responsible for all the turmoil. In a similar vein, when pagans set dogs upon Christians, they would dress them in animal skins to provoke the dogs to attack. This is the harsh treatment that the people of God have repeatedly encountered. They seek to walk righteously before the Lord, and there is such beauty and excellence in righteousness that people dare not persecute them under that name. Consequently, they attach some other name, create false accusations and slanders, and use that as a pretext to inflict suffering upon them. Hence, the saints may suffer for the sake of righteousness at the hands of wicked individuals without being aware of it. I had intended to further explore this by way of conviction, to expose the hearts of those who oppose the people of God for the sake of righteousness, even though they may not realize it. It would be beneficial to restrain certain individuals and perhaps prompt them to reflect if they could only recognize that it is for righteousness' sake. However, time constraints prevent me from elaborating further at present, so we shall let this matter rest.

# SERMON XXXIII

## Reasons why righteousness must expect to suffer

"Blessed are they which are persecuted for righteousness' sake,
for theirs is the kingdom of heaven." - Matthew 5:10

John preached with a tone of terror, proclaiming that the axe was now at
the root of the tree. Christ's preaching, on the other hand, conveys His
doctrine by revealing the blessings bestowed upon those who embrace it. In this
lengthy sermon, Christ begins with blessings that surpass the comprehension of
reason, both collectively and individually. He starts with the poor in spirit and
concludes with those who are persecuted. "Blessed are the poor in spirit, and
blessed are they that are persecuted."

Righteousness itself incites opposition from the hearts of men and leads
them to persecute it. Scripture provides abundant evidence for this fact. Take,
for instance, the case of Cain, who, as Scripture tells us, "was of that wicked
one and slew his brother. And why did he slay him? Because his own works
were evil, and his brother's righteous." Cain attacked his brother solely because
his own works were evil and his brother was righteous. It was for the sake of
righteousness, marking the first instance of persecution in the world. I will

mention another Scripture: 1 Peter 2:19. "For this is thankworthy, if a man for conscience toward God endure grief, suffering wrongfully." Here, suffering is solely due to conscience toward God. There is no need to cite further examples.

The reasons for this are as follows:

Firstly, righteousness itself opposes the corruption of men's hearts. It stands in the way of their sinful inclinations, and men can endure much in every aspect except when it challenges their corruptions. Righteousness opposes each man's corruptions in its own unique manner. While a godly person can endure anything, except when it is against righteousness, wicked individuals can bear much (for some possess patient and tranquil spirits), but not when it opposes their corruptions. This, they cannot tolerate.

Secondly, carnal hearts cannot comprehend righteousness. They witness people fervently professing righteousness but fail to understand it. Righteousness remains an enigma to them, as expressed in 1 Peter 4:4: "Wherein they think it strange that ye run not with them to the same excess of riot, speaking evil of you." They find it strange that you do not engage in the same sinful excesses as they do.

Thirdly, righteousness condemns the world. Just as Noah condemned the world, those whose righteousness surpasses others expose the shortcomings of the rest. This condemnation occurs both within their own consciences and through the observations of others. They cannot bear being condemned, even if it is only partially or by those who perceive their deficiencies in comparison to the righteousness achieved by others. Their hearts become filled with resentment.

Fourthly, righteousness compels individuals to remain steadfast in their principles, regardless of changing times. Regardless of how circumstances may shift, if righteousness is deeply ingrained in the hearts of men and women, it will motivate them to adhere to their principles and continue on their chosen path, even if heaven and earth were to collide. The truth is, there is no way to avoid suffering unless one possesses principles that can bend in accordance with the times. Those individuals, I assure you, will steer clear of suffering. Some people possess remarkable wit in devising distinctions that enable them to adapt to any situation. They have a distinction for one set of circumstances, another for different circumstances, and a third for yet another scenario. However, if righteousness prevails in their hearts, they will remain steadfast in their course. As the times change, opposition will inevitably arise. The wind does not oppose weathercocks; it simply turns them in its direction. But if something is fixed and unyielding, the wind will bluster against it. Righteousness maintains a harmonious relationship between the heart and God, regardless of which way the wind blows. Therefore, it must face the blustering winds of opposition. Those who adhere to their principles are viewed by the world as being stubborn, whereas God and their own consciences recognize that it is the principles of righteousness within them that keep their hearts steadfast with God. Consequently, they must endure suffering.

Fifthly, righteousness signifies a special claim of having a closer relationship with God than others, which the world cannot tolerate. When individuals walk in righteousness beyond others, it reveals to the world that these individuals lay claim to a special connection with God. This provokes the world's fury, and thus righteousness must anticipate suffering.

By way of Application:

Firstly, we can observe the wickedness of the world that opposes righteousness. Righteousness, which should make the world enamored by its beauty, is the very target of ungodly men. Righteous individuals should be regarded as the greatest blessings in the world. If the world truly understood, they would consider righteous individuals who reflect the image of God to be as valuable as the sun, moon, and stars, if not more. However, such is the wickedness of the world that it directs its wrath and hatred towards them, persecuting them.

Secondly, when righteousness is persecuted in the world, do not deem any cause unjust or unrighteous simply because it faces persecution. Do not assume that a cause or its proponents are unrighteous because they are persecuted. On the contrary, persecution can be an indication of righteousness. If we were to judge based on this rule, even Christ himself and his apostles would not be considered righteous, and their cause would not be deemed righteous. It is crucial not to pass such unjust judgments.

Thirdly, one must be cautious not to place excessive reliance on a righteous cause, thinking that it will be sufficient to shield them from suffering. No, this is a misconception. Many people believe that as long as their cause is righteous and they conduct themselves well, they will be spared from suffering. However, the truth is that one's cause may be good, their character may be virtuous, and they may handle their cause admirably, yet they may still experience suffering. Therefore, be prepared for suffering.

Lastly, if righteousness must endure persecution, let those who profess righteousness take care not to provide any other grounds for persecution apart from their righteousness. The world will persecute you no matter what, even if you are righteous. Troubles will come your way. Therefore, since you are destined to encounter opposition in the world, be mindful not to suffer as evildoers. Do not let your suffering be a result of actions that your conscience tells you are not right. The people of God must walk with utmost care in the midst of the world, for there will always be something they must endure. They should avoid adding to their sufferings. I have often contemplated that when those who profess religion live among carnal and wicked individuals, due to their commitment to religious principles and their readiness to suffer for them, they need to be the most inoffensive in all matters. They should be willing to serve all men to the best of their ability with a clear conscience. By doing so, they can demonstrate that whenever they oppose others, it is solely out of conscience and not stubbornness. This way, when they stand against anything that goes against them, they can prove that their opposition arises from conscience rather than stubbornness. This applies to all who profess religion, urging them to be willing to serve others and be flexible in doing good. They should convince others that if there is anything they cannot yield to, it is because they cannot, not because they will not.

Now, let us turn to the main point: "Persecuted for righteousness."

You may ask, how is it possible for people to oppose those who do good? Surely, there must be something else behind it. Swetonius recounts an incident about Tiberius who desired to have a virgin strangled. Some informed him that it was against Roman law to treat a virgin in such a manner. In response, he ordered the virgin to be defiled before being put to death. Similarly, the world treats righteousness and righteous causes. They have something in their consciences that tells them they must not oppose what is righteous. Therefore, they defile righteousness and attempt to distort its true meaning, enabling them to oppose it more freely.

However, there are certainly individuals who persecute righteousness without being aware of it themselves. Many individuals, if fully convinced that something is righteousness and a just cause, would not oppose it. Yet, they may still oppose righteousness. They can manipulate circumstances to create a semblance of freedom from opposition, while God sees that their hearts are against righteousness.

Firstly, all individuals in the world naturally have hearts opposed to righteousness. Therefore, where a new nature is absent, there will be opposition to righteousness. As a result, most people still possess a natural inclination against righteousness. If we were to enter the most despicable place and ask each person, "Do you hate righteousness?" they would vehemently deny it. However, the undeniable truth is that all individuals are naturally enemies of righteousness. Therefore, there are certainly those who are against righteousness without their own awareness.

Secondly, individuals with great intellects, who have the ability to comprehend things profoundly, may still be opponents of righteousness. Some may argue, "What about scholars, learned men? They know whether something is good or not. If they knew it was good, they would never oppose it." Such reasoning is mistaken. Certain individuals can go against their consciences. Furthermore, those with the greatest intellects do not always grasp the full understanding of Christ's teachings. The scribes and Pharisees were the most knowledgeable individuals during Christ's time, yet they were the greatest adversaries of Jesus Christ.

Thirdly, even individuals who are morally righteous can oppose righteousness. For example, the scribes and Pharisees were morally righteous. The same applies to Paul, who persecuted the church and displayed great animosity towards them. What was Paul like during his days as a persecutor? He was not a drunkard, adulterer, or blasphemer, at least according to the prevailing standards of that time. In fact, Paul himself attested to his blamelessness concerning the law (Philippians 3:6). Before his conversion, Paul led a morally upright life, and no one could accuse him of any evil deeds. Yet, he fiercely persecuted righteousness. Similarly, Trajan, known for instigating the third of the ten early persecutions, was considered the most morally upright and just among all emperors. He was praised for treating his subjects as he would wish to be treated if he were a subject himself. Moreover, when giving a sword to an officer, he said, "Use this sword for justice. But if you see me commit injustice, use it against me" (to his own officer). Despite being morally just, Trajan was a deadly enemy of Christians and a abominable persecutor. It is not merely one's nature that determines whether they will oppose righteousness, as even those with a gentle disposition can become fierce and furious opponents when they come face-to-face with righteousness. Titus Vespatian, for instance, was renowned for being a delight to humankind, and yet he was a staunch enemy of the people of God.

However, some may argue that these individuals opposed righteousness due to their different religious beliefs, even if they had a gentle disposition.

Fifthly, moreover, a man or woman can be devout in their religious profession and still be a great persecutor, sometimes even the greatest. Those who are deeply devout in their own way tend to be the most vehement persecutors of those who follow a different path. We have an example of this in Acts 13:50. When Paul preached and faced opposition, it was the devout and honorable women, along with the city's chief men, who incited persecution against him and Barnabas, driving them out of their territory.

However, you might ask if there is any example of a godly person persecuting another. If you ask me to find an example of a godly person with true piety persecuting others, I would struggle to provide one. I would need to search from Genesis to Revelation to find such an example. The only instance that comes to mind is King Asa, who, in a fit of rage, struck and imprisoned a prophet when he delivered God's message to him. It is worth noting that Scripture describes King Asa as a godly man. Therefore, persecution becomes even more dangerous for those who engage in it.

Secondly, the persecution endured by the righteous is more grievous because it is unparalleled. Although in the next verse, I will demonstrate that it has been the fate of God's people to face persecution, I cannot find any evidence in the entire Bible that godly individuals suffered at the hands of other godly individuals in a consistent manner. Therefore, if we find ourselves in an era where the godly suffer at the hands of the godly, it is an unprecedented time, unlike anything previously recorded. We have never read of such a situation in the entire Word of God. The persecution they face is the most severe.

If you ask how we can discern those who oppose righteousness without their own awareness, I would first tell you that the Scriptures make it clear that men can oppose righteousness and godly individuals, thinking they are serving God. In John 16:2, Christ foretells that his disciples will suffer at the hands of those who believe they are doing God a service by killing them. But you may ask, how can we identify them?

Firstly, we can recognize them when they oppose something under the banner of righteousness without examining or understanding it. As soon as there is a semblance of righteousness, they vehemently attack and oppose it before even examining its reality. This is a dangerous sign that their hearts are against righteousness. To illustrate this, let's consider a simile: imagine a man who sees a broad seal and immediately tramples it underfoot without further investigation. Would this man not be charged with felony, if not treason? He might argue that he didn't know what it was, but the response would be that he should have examined it. Likewise, when something is presented as righteousness and has an appearance of religiosity, it may indeed not be right. However, it is essential to withhold judgment until it has been thoroughly examined. If a person opposes something with only a pretense of righteousness, one must be certain that it is indeed a pretense and not righteousness. Therefore, whenever one intends to take action against others (particularly in religious matters) or align with those who oppose, it is crucial to have a solid foundation, thoroughly examine the matter, and be able to provide a rationale for opposition. One must be able to say, "I oppose this, and here are my grounds and reasons for doing so. I have examined it and found it to be contrary to the will of God."

Secondly, when a person becomes more loose in their conduct, they become more opposed to a particular way. Conversely, if they become better and more restrained, they develop a more favorable opinion of that way. This is highly suspicious and suggests that what they oppose is righteousness. Let me clarify with an example: individuals exhibit fluctuations in their behavior; sometimes they are much better than at other times. Even individuals with profane principles and wicked tendencies may experience moments of conscience and restraint, driven by common gifts that keep them in check. However, when these restraints fail to hold against the overpowering force of their corruptions, they break free and act against their consciences. Therefore, we must examine their hearts. How do they feel about a cause or person when they are at their best? Perhaps they begin to think favorably of such individuals and causes at that time. Yet, when their lusts are most intense and overpowering, they become the hottest and most vehement opponents of those same individuals and causes. This is highly suspicious, indicating that it is righteousness they oppose. Here's the logic behind it: if they were opposing something evil rather than good, the better they become, the more they should oppose it. Conversely, the worse they are, the more they oppose it, suggesting that what they oppose is not evil but rather good. Consider this: when you are healthy, strong, and inebriated at a tavern, you scorn, mock, and speak against certain individuals. Now, suppose the hand of God rests upon you, and you find yourself on your sickbed, apprehending that you are nearing the end of your earthly existence, about to face eternal judgment from God. Are those individuals still as loathsome to you as they were when you spoke against them in the tavern? If you spoke against them because they were wicked, the closer you come to facing God's judgment, the stronger your aversion towards them should be. However, we often find the opposite to be true. Many individuals who would not consider themselves persecutors of righteousness speak against those individuals more vehemently when their lusts are inflamed by wine, food, pride, strength, and good health. They do so more passionately during those times than they would on their sickbeds when they are about to stand before the Lord to give an account. This discovery confirms that they are persecuting righteousness, regardless of their initial pretenses.

Thirdly, individuals who oppose others under the pretext of faults they themselves were once much guiltier of before professing religion and righteousness can be identified. Oddly enough, they were able to tolerate those faults when they were more deeply mired in them. Yet now, they find themselves unable to bear with those same faults.

For instance, let's say someone starts to profess their religion more than before. Now, your hearts are against them, but how? You make some pretence that they committed some fault, and that's why you oppose them. But I appeal to your consciences: weren't they more faulty before they made such a profession of religion? Yet you were more tolerant of their faults back then. Your consciences tell you that your servants, children, and spouse were more disobedient then, yet you were more patient with their faults before their profession. Therefore, it is righteousness that is opposed, rather than anything else.

Fourthly, another way to recognize opposition to righteousness is when people are partial in their opposition. They can stand by it and even defend it, but they are not as severe against others who are guilty of equally or greater faults. Surely, then, it is righteousness that is opposed, rather than the faults that are claimed.

Fifthly, when people rejoice upon hearing of faults in those who profess religion, when they are glad to have that pretense and find joy in having something to use against them, it is an indication that righteousness is what they truly hate. If it were evil that they hated, upon discovering that someone who professes religion has committed a scandalous act, their hearts would mourn, realizing that religion has been wounded. However, when you find joy upon hearing of such an evil act committed by someone who professes religion more than others, it is a sign that it is righteousness that your hearts are against. If you claim to be troubled by the discovery of such a person's falsehood, then if your spirit is right, you would mourn and lament over the sin that has been committed.

Sixthly, you would be concerned with repairing the breach that has been made in the profession of religion. When someone reveals their falsehood, showing great zeal in their profession but later becoming scandalous, and you realize the damage it has caused to religion, your response should be to strive to compensate for it by being more devout yourself. However, this is not the case with many people. Therefore, it is righteousness that their hearts are most opposed to, rather than anything else.

Seventhly, when those who oppose what is good find their greatest strength in aligning with the worst sort of people, the rabble and the refuse of society, it is a warning sign to be cautious. It is righteousness that you oppose.

Eighthly, when individuals know in their consciences that they have ulterior motives in their opposition, when they examine things according to their conscience and realize that their motives are selfish, driven by self-interest, it is evident that their opposition is motivated by such self-respect. Certainly, if false ends drive us, it is not righteousness that we are motivated by. The wrath of man does not accomplish the righteousness of God, and the corrupt desires and false motives of individuals cannot achieve righteousness.

There are various other signs that could be given, but I would like to conclude with a word of exhortation, urging people to be cautious about what they oppose. There are many things I had considered speaking about in terms of exhortation. People should be wary of their opposition. It is the time when Christ is opposing Antichrist more than ever before. Therefore, although Christ was patient towards persecutors in the past, they should not expect the same patience now because it is a time of tearing down the man of sin. Christ is more active and stirring now. We see Christ in action more than before. Christ has risen, and if Christ is risen, his enemies must be scattered. So, even though much was overlooked in the past, now that Christ is active and stirring, be cautious about opposing what is good. Furthermore, in these times, there is more light and revelation than before. There are more professors of religion now than ever before, which means there is a greater danger of opposing the saints. Moreover, we are currently in a period of discovering and searching for the ways of God that we were previously unaware of. In such times, when we start professing things that we previously opposed, shouldn't we rise above opposing those who do not do the same things we do? Lastly, let's consider that England has been guilty of the sin of persecuting righteousness, perhaps more than any other kingdom. We should be cautious because we ourselves have been persecuted in the past. We have made significant professions of faith lately, and we have committed ourselves to the way. When we align ourselves with the saints and become part of their community, we need to be wary of persecution.

Lastly, in these times, it is futile to persecute because there is so much light and revelation. Many people not only make professions but also have a genuine work of God within them. Persecution will not prevail now. In Revelation 14:13, it is written, "Blessed are they who die in the Lord or for the Lord." The Spirit says, "Write it down from now on." Flesh and blood may not reason that those who suffer for the Lord are blessed, but the Spirit confirms it. The judgment of the Spirit differs from the judgment of the world.

# SERMON XXXIV
## Principles for Suffering

"Blessed are they which are persecuted for Righteousness' sake,
for theirs is the kingdom of heaven." - Matthew 5:10

I won't dwell on what has already been discussed. Instead, I will present some principles for suffering, that is, certain considerations that may assist God's people in being willing and able to endure suffering for the sake of righteousness. We don't know what God may call us to face, and to some extent, everyone who is godly experiences suffering at some point in their lives. Therefore, the first principle to equip Christians for suffering is to view ourselves as sent into the world for the purpose of bearing witness to the truth. That is the primary principle. It should be seen as the great end for which we were born and continue to live - to be witnesses of God and His truth. If it was Christ's purpose and He regarded it as the reason for His coming into the world, then we have every reason to consider it ours as well. In John 18:37, it is clearly stated, "To this end was I born, and for this cause came I into the world, that I should bear witness unto the truth." It is a significant scripture, and those who profess to be Christ's disciples should make good use of it. If the purpose of our birth and existence is to eat, drink, and live splendidly in this world, then we have missed the mark. We were born for a higher and nobler purpose - to bear witness to God's truth. If that was the purpose of our birth, then it is fitting for God to call us to bear witness in any way, whether through doing or suffering. We should be willing to do it, for we fulfill the purpose for which we were born in doing so. Above all, witnessing for the truth through suffering is the most glorious witness. As Cyprian said concerning the persecuted martyrs, "They confessed with a glorious voice." When people confess the truth with words that come from their hearts, God accepts it. But when they bear witness to the truth through suffering, it is a glorious profession of the truth and a Christian fulfills the purpose for which they were born. That is the first principle for enduring suffering.

The second suffering principle is this: it is better to lose for God than to enjoy for ourselves. If Christians firmly establish these principles within themselves, they will find it easy to endure anything for the sake of Christ. It is better for a person with wealth to lose it for God than to enjoy it for themselves. It is better to lose our liberties for God than to enjoy them for ourselves. It is better to lose our reputation, honour, pleasure, and delights for God than to enjoy them for ourselves. I recall that Pliny, in his Dedication Epistle to Vespatian, spoke of a heathen, Cato, who professed that he took more joy in giving up his estate for the cause of justice than in what he possessed. Shall a heathen profess to find more joy in what he sacrifices for the sake of justice than in what he possesses? Shouldn't Christians consider it even better to part with anything in order to honour God and serve Him, rather than to enjoy it for themselves? When someone is called to suffer, they should consider what they may have to give up. For example, they might think, "I have wealth, and I could live comfortably. Should I lose it now for this cause?" But my friend, if you consider it as loss for God, it becomes the most valuable part of your wealth. If a person loses a limb for their country, that part of their body is considered more beautiful than any other. I recall a story from Ecclesiastical Histories, which tells of Constantine entering a council and seeing a man who had lost his eye for the sake of his faith. Constantine immediately approached him and kissed that place, considering it the most beautiful part of his face. Christians should view it in the same way and give thanks to God not only when they have wealth, credit, esteem, liberty, or life, but especially when they are called to part with these things for the sake of God. In losing these things for God, I am now a happier person than I ever was in my life while possessing them. This may seem mysterious and puzzling to those with worldly hearts, but only those who are truly gracious and godly understand the meaning of this principle.

Thirdly, whoever suffers for God is in a better position than their persecutors. For instance, when you read about the martyrs who were brought before their persecutors, the persecutors appeared grand, sitting in their splendid attire, speaking freely, enjoying themselves fully, and commanding respect from the people. They seemed impressive. But a group of poor Christians, coming out of prison, stood before them, trembling and dressed in rags, and defended their lives. Many poor people might think that these wretched individuals, standing in such a pitiable condition in the eyes of the world, are in the worst state, while the persecutors are fortunate. However, a Christian sees things quite differently. They perceive the persecutors as the most miserable, wretched, forsaken, and ruined creatures, while the saints are viewed as the most glorious beings. The Holy Ghost's judgment of the suffering saints is evident in Hebrews 11:37, "They were stoned, they were sawn asunder, were tempted, were slain with the sword, they wandered about in sheepskins, being destitute, afflicted, torment- ed." Although flesh and blood may consider them miserable, mark what the Holy Spirit's judgment is: "Of whom the world was not worthy." The suffering saints who wandered in sheepskins and goatskins were so blessed that the world was not worthy of them. The persecutors, on the other hand, were vile. I recall the description of Antiochus Epiphanes, who, despite being a powerful prince, is called a vile person because he persecuted the saints. The Spirit of God refers to those who were persecuted as individuals whom the world was not worthy of.

Fourthly, it is far better to suffer for Christ than to suffer for sin. This con- sideration holds significant power. When you are called to endure something for the cause of Christ, you may think, "The Lord might have left me to suffer as much for my sin, for my wickedness, as I am now called to suffer for Jesus Christ. I may be required to endure the loss of a portion of my wealth. But I could have faced conviction for my sin and had my estate taken away by the hand of Justice. I am in prison, but I might have been imprisoned for my wickedness. My life is in danger, but God could have allowed me to commit a sin that would have led to my life being taken by the hand of Justice. How much better is it for me to stand here and suffer for Christ, which I could have suffered for my sin? Even in the face of danger, I testify my allegiance to Christ. I might have faced peril through my sin. Oh, how blessed it is to suffer for Christ rather than the alternative!" This consideration carries great weight.

Fifthly, God may make me suffer against my will. If I find any reluctance in myself to come forward and suffer for Christ, I may be forced to do so against my own desires. What comfort will I have then? How much better is it to suffer freely and willingly for Jesus Christ than to be compelled to suffer, in which case there will be no exercise of grace, but I will be merely passive? I remember a story from the Book of Martyrs about a blacksmith who played a role in converting another person to the truth during King Edward's reign. However, during Queen Mary's reign, the persecutors arrested the converted individual. The blacksmith, who was the cause of the person's conversion, wondered how he had managed to escape persecution. He sent word to the persecuted individual, confessing that what he had said was true, but he could not bear to burn. However, later on, by some accident, the blacksmith's house caught fire, and he burned to death in his own home. So, whether he wanted to or not, Christ made him burn. How much better it would have been for this man to burn for Christ! If you are unwilling to suffer any loss of your wealth for Christ, He can make you suffer. He can set fire to your houses or take away your possessions through providence. He can afflict you with diseases and afflictions. If you are reluctant to risk yourself for Him, He can impose greater evils upon you than those you were called to suffer for His name's sake. Consider this: God can make you suffer, whether you like it or not. It is far better, therefore, to willingly and readily offer ourselves to suffer for Jesus Christ.

Sixthly, no creature possesses any good in it unless it is enjoyed in God and used for God's purposes. This is the sixth principle for enduring suffering. When God grants me the use of a creature and I enjoy it in God's love and favor, then there is some good in it. If I can utilize it in any way to honor and glorify God, then it brings true comfort. However, if these two aspects are absent in any creature enjoyed by anyone in the world, then there is no good in it; it is merely an empty shell. For instance, you may have certain comforts in a creature, but do you experience the presence of God in them or enjoy them for God's sake?

If so, then they are good. Without this, they are nothing but emptiness; they are filled with nothing but wind. Now, if I am called to suffer for the cause of Christ, it is as if a loud voice from Heaven speaks to me, saying, "This creature that you are now called to part with in order to bear witness to My truth, you can no longer enjoy Me in it, nor can you further use it to honor Me. However, in parting with it, what was previously good in the enjoyment of it now holds goodness in the act of letting it go." This is the sixth principle, and if we truly embrace it, how easy it would be to let go of any creature comfort for the sake of Christ.

Seventhly, every suffering experienced by the saints is ordered and predetermined by God. God determines the timing, the type, the duration, the instruments, and every aspect of the suffering. You can see this in the book of Revelation, where it is stated, "Satan shall cast some of you into prison for ten days." Only some will be cast into prison, not all, and their lives will be spared. Furthermore, it will only last for ten days. This consideration greatly strengthens the suffering saints. Just as it provided strength to Christ, knowing that all His sufferings were predetermined, it also provides strength to the saints. Therefore, as Christ said, "Shall I not drink the cup that my Father hath given me to drink?" He was referring to His sufferings. In the same way, everyone called to suffer for the truth should reason with themselves and suppress any rising rebellion against those sufferings. Shall I not drink the cup that my Father hath given me to drink? It is a bitter cup indeed, to be hated by friends, to suffer loss of estate, liberty, and all outward comforts, to live a miserable life in the eyes of the world. But shall I not drink the cup that my Father hath given me to drink? This is the seventh principle.

Eighthly, whenever we suffer for Christ, Christ suffers with us. We partake in His sufferings, and He partakes in ours. As stated in Isaiah 63:9, "In all their affliction he was afflicted." This realization brings great support and comfort. Just as it is comforting to think that friends sympathize with us and are affected by our sufferings, know that Jesus Christ sympathizes with you in your sufferings. He suffers as much as, if not more than, you in all your sufferings. It is said of Moses that he considered "the reproach of Christ greater riches." The awareness that these sufferings belong to Christ is useful in various ways to assist the soul in suffering. It not only assures us that Christ will pity and have compassion on us, but also that Christ, suffering alongside us, will help us bear our sufferings. Why? Because they are His own sufferings. Therefore, He will order and moderate your sufferings. Whenever you suffer in the cause of Christ, Christ bears the weightier end of the burden. This realization is a mighty help in the face of suffering and provides support.

Ninthly, suffering seems more evil in imagination before it occurs than when it actually arrives. Many who have been imprisoned for a just cause have professed that imprisonment was not as difficult to endure as they had imagined. Likewise, the loss of wealth and friends, although terrifying before it happens, often does not appear as harsh and grievous when actually experienced by the saints.

Tenthly, the least sin contains more evil than the greatest afflictions. It is a poor choice to prefer the least sin over the greatest affliction. If suffering is presented to you, and you fear it, finding it terrible, consider that the least vain thought in your mind is a greater evil than all the torments inflicted by persecutors in the world. You may find this hard to accept, but it is indeed a riddle, just like my text itself. It is not surprising that we speak things that carnal hearts cannot understand. However, those to whom God has revealed the dreadful evil of sin cannot help but be aware, to some extent, that there is more evil in any single sin than in any afflictions. Therefore, they would rather endure all the torments devised by the world than willingly commit even the slightest known sin. Perhaps some of you trivialize sin and are easily led to commit it at every little temptation. But however lightly you regard sin, those who are the saints of God, who understand the true nature of sin, would prefer to endure all the torments imaginable rather than willingly commit even one known sin. There is undoubtedly a significant difference between your perception and theirs. I implore you, brethren, to remember this tenth principle, and I urge those who remember or grasp these principles to help others with them. Lay them upon your hearts and keep them close at hand for the time when God may call you to suffer for His truths.

But the text holds much significance: "Blessed are those who are persecuted for the sake of righteousness." There is a profound blessing in suffering. We can add as an eleventh point that suffering for Christ is a great blessing, and that's the focal point of the text. It is a gift from God. He has given it to you not only to believe but also to suffer. It is a greater gift to be enabled to suffer for Christ than to be enabled to do anything else in the world for Him. Even if Christ were to enable you to perform miracles or raise the dead, it would not be as great a gift as having a heart willing to suffer for Him. Anyone to whom Christ grants a suffering heart should know that they have received a great gift from Him. You may consider it excellent to be able to pray, but it is even more excellent to be able to suffer. I recall reading about a martyr who, when called to argue for the truth, said, "I cannot dispute for it, but I can die for it," and that is more significant. It is more valuable to be able to suffer for the truth than to preach or practice it. It is a blessed thing. The Scriptures are abundant in illustrating the blessedness of suffering. In Acts 5:41, they rejoiced because they were counted worthy to suffer shame for His name. In Luke 6:22-23, Jesus encouraged His disciples to rejoice and be glad when they faced persecution. In 2 Corinthians 11:23, the apostle Paul listed his sufferings and considered them as his glory. He boasted about the sufferings he endured for Christ, not about his knowledge or honors. It is indeed a blessed thing to suffer for Christ. In 2 Corinthians 12:10, Paul declared that he took pleasure in infirmities, reproaches, necessities, persecutions, and distresses for Christ's sake. It is delightful and pleasant to suffer for Christ. Tertullian, in the primitive times, said, "Your cruelty is our glory, our blessedness." Paul desired to know nothing but Christ, and not just Christ alone, but Christ crucified. To suffer for righteousness' sake is a blessed thing. Now, there are many things that could be said about the blessedness of suffering, but I will present a brief overview of the blessings found in persecution.

Firstly, if God gives you a heart to suffer for Him, it serves as a clear evidence of the truth of your faith and the strength and genuineness of your grace. You testify to the world that you genuinely love Christ and that your graces are strong and powerful. You prove that you are not a hypocrite who will fall away in times of trial. You demonstrate that you have the Spirit and strength of Christ within you, and your graces are genuine. This is a blessed thing, providing evidence before everyone, including your own conscience, that your heart is sincere in its devotion to Christ.

Secondly, there is great honor in suffering. Ignatius said, "I would rather be a martyr than a monarch." Moses chose to suffer with the people of God rather than enjoy the pleasures and riches of Egypt. Moreover, when Chrysostom spoke of Paul's commendations, he emphasized his sufferings as a significant part of his praise. He even stated that if he had to choose between hearing Paul speak from heaven or from prison, he would prefer to hear him speak from prison. Suffering for Christ is highly honorable before men, angels, God Himself, the Church, and all the saints. In the primitive times, there was a tradition of honoring martyrs by going to their chains and kissing them. It is indeed honorable to suffer for Christ.

Thirdly, suffering is the highest and greatest development of one's abilities, graces, and comforts. It is the ultimate test and the means to reach the highest potential. The people of God have always been most eminent in grace during times of persecution. The Church has been most fruitful when watered with the blood of the saints. The saints' graces are more fragrant and flourish in times of suffering. The breathings of holiness and the experience of heaven on earth are heightened during times of suffering. Suffering is the highest opportunity to make use of the graces and comforts bestowed upon believers.

Fourthly, those who suffer are under many blessed promises. If you suffer with Christ, you will be glorified with Him. There are numerous excellent promises made to those who suffer for the cause of Christ. It is easy to spend hours recounting these promises. Suffering is accompanied by blessed comforts. The martyrs expressed joy and found pleasure in their sufferings. They considered it a most blessed thing. The presence of the Spirit of Glory and of God rests upon those who suffer for Christ. The Spirit provides comfort, guidance, and illumination.

Fifthly, as stated in the text, the kingdom of heaven belongs to those who suffer for righteousness' sake. This encompasses the blessings of the gospel that believers receive in this life and the eternal kingdom of glory in heaven. The kingdom of heaven includes the blessings of righteousness, peace, joy, and all the good that the gospel offers. Those who suffer for Christ will partake in these blessings in an eminent and special manner.

But then, secondly, the kingdom of heaven. This refers to the portion of the kingdom that Christ will have before He surrenders it to the Father. Those who suffer for righteousness' sake will have a prominent share in this blessing. To me, it is evident from Scripture that there is a kingdom that Christ will possess before He gives it up to the Father. In 1 Corinthians 15, it is mentioned that on the last day, Christ will hand over the kingdom to the Father, and God will be all in all. However, the Scriptures speak of the kingdom of Christ as a promise to the saints before the kingdom of the Father. In Revelation 3:21, it says, "To him who overcomes, I will grant to sit with Me on My throne, as I also overcame and sat down with My Father on His throne." Take note of this Scripture; it clearly indicates that there was a throne of Christ that the saints would sit upon after their victories. While Christ presently rules the world and His Church through the scepter of His Word and Spirit, there is another time referred to in the Scriptures as a reward for their sufferings and triumphs. During that time, they will sit on His throne, just as He sits on His Father's throne. You might argue that this will happen in heaven. But there, it is plain that Christ will surrender the kingdom to the Father, and God will be all in all. However, there is another kingdom of Christ promised to those who overcome, and those who suffer will have a special share and participation in it, as revealed in the book of Revelation. This book was written to encourage the saints during the Antichristian times of persecution. You will discover that Christ promises that they will reign on the earth. In the 20th chapter, where Christ speaks of a kingdom He will possess for a long time, it is particularly mentioned in verse 4 that those who were beheaded and refused to worship the Beast or receive its mark, openly or secretly, were the people Christ specifically targeted when He ascended to His kingdom. In the Gospel of Luke, Christ encourages His disciples in the path of suffering for Him, saying, "You are those who have continued with Me in My trials. And I bestow upon you a kingdom, just as My Father bestowed one upon Me." Additionally, in 2 Peter 3:13, it is stated, "Rejoice to the extent that you partake of Christ's sufferings, that when His glory is revealed, you may also be glad with exceeding joy." Though you are currently sorrowful, despised, and trampled upon, when Christ appears in His glory to claim the kingdom for Himself, He will undoubtedly acknowledge and honor those who have suffered for Him. His first action will be to recognize and exalt them before the entire world. Yes, you endured difficult things in the worldly kingdom, but there is another kingdom where you will be honored. In Revelation 7:14, it says, "These are the ones who come out of the great tribulation, and washed their robes and made them white in the blood of the Lamb." They will be glorified. I recall reading about Emperor Carus, who, upon hearing that Agrippa suffered for his cause before becoming emperor, immediately replaced the chain with which Agrippa was shackled by offering him a gold chain of equal weight. Likewise, when Christ comes to claim His kingdom, His first act will be to summon all those who have suffered for His sake and apportion them a proportionate measure of glory. Tertullian said, "The greatest reward follows the greatest contest, strife, and suffering for Jesus Christ." I also remember reading about Gordius, a martyr, who, when about to suffer, told his persecutors that if they reduced the suffering intended for him, he would be at a loss. Thus, when the general judgment arrives, oh, the embrace of Jesus Christ, embracing those who have suffered for Him! He will place white robes upon them and seat them on His throne. They will judge their judges and the twelve tribes of Israel. Not only the apostles but all the saints will sit with Christ, judging the wicked and the ungodly on that day, ascending with Him in glory and enjoying the fruits of their sufferings. Blessed are those who die in the Lord. It may as well be read, "Blessed are those who die for the Lord," for they rest from their labors, and their works follow them. The apostles and others clearly saw this truth. In 2 Corinthians 4, towards the end, it says, "For our light affliction, which is but for a moment, is working for us a far more exceeding and eternal weight of glory." This is one of the most eloquent expressions ever written by any author in the world: the exceeding, excessive, eternal weight of glory. And our sufferings, which are but light and momentary. But you might ask, "Isn't this a legalistic approach to finding encouragement in our duties or suffering, hoping for heaven?"

Honestly, for those who believe they have reached such a level of grace that they can do all things purely out of love for God, without any consideration for their own good in heaven, I do not know if Scripture supports such a notion. The Scripture encourages even those who are most eminent in grace to find their encouragement in the hope of heaven, in what they do or suffer for Jesus Christ. You may argue that it is true, we are allowed to do so, but wouldn't it be better if we could do it without such encouragement?

No, I find that even Christ Himself was encouraged in this way, and there is no greater example of grace than that of Christ. Hebrews 12:3 tells us to consider Him who endured such hostility from sinners against Himself, lest we become weary and discouraged in our minds. And in the preceding verse, it says, "Looking unto Jesus, the author and finisher of our faith, who for the joy that was set before Him endured the cross, despising the shame, and has sat down at the right hand of the throne of God." Christ endured the cross and disregarded the shame because He saw the joy set before Him. He had the joy of sitting at the right hand of the Father before Him. It is even noted as one of the fruits of Christ's sufferings that He is seated at the right hand of the throne of God. Christ, in the midst of His sufferings, had the assurance that after enduring some sufferings here, He would soon sit at the right hand of the Father's throne. And it is this assurance that helped Him endure His sufferings. If Christ Himself makes use of this encouragement, it is indeed foolish and prideful for anyone to think they have no need of it.

But now, after discussing these matters, I had intended to provide only a brief application for you. Only, you can see from what has been said how the stumbling block of the cross is removed. Oh, store up these things that have been presented to you, that have been spoken to you on this day in the name of Christ. You never know when you may need them; keep them in your hearts for times of suffering so that you may have them readily available. Just as people prone to fainting keep their aqua vitae bottles and similar things to help them in their fainting spells, so should you store up these truths that can assist you in overcoming moments of weakness. It should be of no consequence to you whether you experience times of prosperity or times of persecution. Regardless of which way the world goes, a Christian should stay steadfast in their path, focusing solely on fulfilling their duties, regardless of the outcome. The worst that can happen is persecution, but even that will contribute to your glory and aid in your future happiness. Blessed are those who are persecuted for the sake of righteousness.

# SERMON XXXV

## Some Points from what has been said about the blessedness of persecution

"Blessed are they which are persecuted for Righteousness' sake,
for theirs is the kingdom of heaven." - MATTHEW 5:10

W e have already preached several sermons on the topic of persecution, explaining what it is and when someone is persecuted for the sake of righteousness. We have also discussed how individuals may be guilty of persecuting others for righteousness' sake without realizing it. Last time, we explored the blessedness that accompanies suffering persecution. But I will not dwell on that; instead, I will proceed. However, for verse 10, I will offer a few points by way of application based on what has been said about the blessedness of suffering persecution. It is a blessed thing to endure persecution, not only because blessedness and persecution can coexist, but also because a person is blessed precisely because they are persecuted. The world finds it difficult to comprehend how blessedness and persecution can be intertwined, but among all the saints in the world, those who are most persecuted are the most blessed.

This paradox may confound the world, but it emanates from the words of Christ and, as we demonstrated in our previous sermon, it holds true.

Now, let us consider the implications.

From this, we see the excellence of a Christian's state. Even in their worst condition, they are blessed. Moreover, the worst condition they can experience actually enhances their blessedness. Therefore, their state is truly exceptional. Through their sufferings, they gain something valuable. Just as the philosopher's stone is praised for transforming all things into gold, so too does grace in a Christian possess the power to turn their losses, sufferings, and the contempt and insults cast upon them into blessedness. Consequently, it is evident that godly individuals are not foolish for willingly enduring so much in God's cause. They understand what they are doing because they know how it contributes to their blessedness.

Secondly, it is futile for worldly people to believe that they can dissuade the saints from following Christ through persecution. You may be opposed to servants, friends, relatives, neighbours, or even your spouse, and you may think that you can compel them to act differently. Perhaps you intend to make them suffer losses in certain areas to force a change in their behavior. However, this is a great misconception. Persecution tends to strengthen, rather than weaken, the resolve of the saints. It enhances their virtues and raises them above you and your persecution. I recall a story in which Modestus, an officer of the Emperor, was advised not to meddle with Basil. The reasoning was that Basil was superior to him. Similarly, carnal and wicked individuals believe that persecution would discourage others from following any religious path. They assume that they can discourage them by subjecting them to suffering. It is true that if others were motivated by the same principles as you, they might be discouraged by persecution. However, because you are conscious of the base principles upon which you operate and are aware that persecution would discourage you, you mistakenly believe that others operate on the same principles. You are mistaken. Their principles are higher and nobler. Therefore, even though persecution may discourage you, it will not discourage them. As Jeremiah 23:27 states, "Which think to cause my people to forget my name by their dreams which they tell every man to his neighbour," we can apply this passage to the context of persecution. Just as the false prophets' dreams could not make true saints forget God's name, persecution cannot cause the faithful to deviate from the ways of God. On the contrary, they perceive blessedness in those ways. You may attempt to divert them from any path, but by subjecting them to suffering, you inadvertently make them even more blessed.

Thirdly, if suffering persecution is such a blessed thing, how base and vile are those hypocrites and apostates who forsake God out of fear of persecution! How far beneath true Christians they are! One rejoices in persecution, blesses God for it, and considers it an enhancement of their glory. They are strengthened and encouraged to persevere in the ways of God. On the other hand, you view it as such a great evil that you would abandon God, Christ, your conscience, the truth, your profession, and even the saints themselves, rather than endure suffering in your material possessions, your freedom, or your reputation. This is especially true if the danger becomes greater. You possess a base and vile spirit. You do not understand the things of God if you are so fearful of persecution that you are willing to sacrifice the greatest riches rather than wholeheartedly trust in God. Persecution could have blessed you, yet you prefer to risk losing your portion in God and your inheritance in the Almighty. Instead, you are willing to sacrifice your conscience and subject yourself to the eternal wrath of God. You are a foolish slave to your desires if you would forsake Christ and His cause due to fear of persecution. Christ Himself said that those who suffer persecution are blessed.

Fourthly, Christians should strive to firmly establish themselves in this truth to prepare for persecution. Look to Christ and see Him proclaiming this blessedness. Consider all the points that have been discussed, particularly the glory of the kingdom of Heaven. Meditating on this glory, if you can make it real to your soul, will impart courage to your spirit. It will elevate you above worldly concerns, causing you to view everything beneath you with disdain and contempt. Just as Christ, when He contemplated the joy that awaited Him, despised the shame and regarded it as something insignificant, so too will the genuine sight of the glorious things in the kingdom of Heaven make you more courageous. If you have experienced even a glimpse of the glory of the things in the Kingdom of Heaven and regard them as certain and real, how easy would it be for you to endure anything in the world? The passage in Hebrews 10:32-34 is noteworthy in this regard: "But call to remembrance the former days, in which after ye were illuminated, ye endured a great fight of afflictions; partly whilst ye were made a gazing-stock, both by reproaches and afflictions; and partly whilst ye became companions of them that were so used. For ye had compassion of me in my bonds, and took joyfully the spoiling of your goods, knowing in yourselves that ye have in Heaven a better and an enduring substance." How were they strengthened to joyfully endure the spoiling of their goods? Pay attention to the text: "knowing in yourselves that ye have in Heaven a better and enduring substance." Note the phrase—it does not say that you have heard it said, but rather knowing in yourselves. The Holy Spirit revealed it to their souls to assure them and establish their hearts in this truth. When you know it within yourself, when the Spirit of God certifies it to your soul, you will be able to suffer the spoiling of your goods with joy. I must confess that all I have preached about this matter will never enable you to suffer with joy merely by hearing it from me or others. It is only when you know it within yourself, having a certain and assured knowledge of it through the Spirit of God revealing it to your soul, that you will be able to suffer with gladness. Just as Joseph said to Jacob, "Regard not the stuff, for the riches of Egypt are yours," so too does a gracious heart, when it comprehends the riches of Heaven and the joys of eternity, view earthly possessions as mere trinkets and rubbish. Such a heart is prepared to endure any loss and withstand any inflicted evil.

Fifthly, if suffering with Christ is such a blessed thing, then how immensely blessed is it to reign with Christ! Take a Christian at their lowest, cast them into prison, bind them with chains and shackles, yet they remain a blessed individual. Strip away their food and clothing, let the malice and rage of all the devils in hell and all people in the world inflict whatever evil they can upon them, and still they are blessed. If they are blessed in their current state, how much more blessed will they be when they reign with Christ? They will wear a crown upon their head, stand before the Father, Jesus Christ, and the angels in glorious robes, sit with Jesus Christ to judge the world, and reign with Him forever. Oh, how blessed they will be then!

Sixthly, let us not hold a low or disdainful view of those who suffer. Let us regard them as honourable and blessed. Do not shy away from them. It is common in the world that when someone suffers for a righteous cause, others abandon them and are wary of associating with them. Oh, what wickedness this is! It is like a herd of deer that remain together until the hunter shoots one of them. As soon as the other deer see the blood, they push the wounded one away and refuse to accompany it any longer. Such is often the case in this wicked world. Those who profess religion may be content to join and associate with those who prosper in the world. However, if God's providence singles out one person for greater suffering than others, all those who were previously close and intimate with them withdraw and barely acknowledge them. This is a wicked and accursed thing. Why do you refuse to acknowledge them now? Do you consider them to be in a worse condition than before? No, now they are made blessed. I recall Ignatius saying when he felt his bones crunching in the mouths of wild beasts, "Now I begin to be a Christian." Thus, he truly begins to be a Christian. It is a sign that God regards him as more distinguished than you, for he is called to suffer. Therefore, do not be ashamed of those whom Christ glories in and declares to be blessed. It is quite remarkable that we read of John in Revelation 1:9, where he speaks of himself and boasts in being the companion of the saints in tribulation. He says, "I, John, who also am your brother and companion in tribulation, and in the kingdom and patience of Jesus Christ, was in the isle that is called Patmos, for the word of God and for the testimony of Jesus Christ." John glories in being the companion of others who suffer for the cause of Christ. He does not boast by saying, "I, John, an apostle, the beloved disciple of Christ, who lay in His bosom," but rather, "I, John, your companion in tribulation, banished to the Isle of Patmos for the word of God and the testimony of Christ." John takes pride in being the companion of those who suffer for the cause of Christ. Likewise, the passage in Hebrews 10:33 states, "Partly while ye became companions of them that were so used." It is a useful note to remember for the day when the saints suffer. Be willing to acknowledge them and do not feel any shame in doing so. I will mention one Scripture regarding glory in suffering: even Christ Himself glories in suffering. When He revealed His glory to Paul in Acts 9, note what He said: "I heard a voice saying, 'Saul, Saul, why persecutest thou me?' And the Lord said, 'I am Jesus whom thou persecutest: it is hard for thee to kick against the pricks.'" By persecuting Him, Saul was kicking against the pricks. He was persecuting not the saints, but Christ Himself. Christ claims them as His own. I remember another Scripture where Jesus speaks of Himself and says, "Jesus of Nazareth."

Nazareth was the place where He was scorned, and yet Christ glories in that title, "Jesus of Nazareth."

Seventhly, and finally, if those who suffer persecution are blessed, then it behooves the saints to endure their sufferings with meekness and gentleness. Do not display any anger or passion in your sufferings. Why? Because you are blessed in your suffering. Let those who are cursed in their suffering have their hearts enraged, but for those who are blessed in their suffering, let their hearts be calm and serene. Do not be troubled by your sufferings. Carry yourselves in a manner even more composed than your persecutors. I recall reading about Socrates advising people on how to behave meekly toward those they suffer from. He said, "If you encounter someone in the street whose body is more afflicted than yours, will you be angry with them because of their physical condition?" Similarly, when you meet those who wrong you, it is the ailment of their souls. Therefore, do not allow your spirits to rise against them. Instead, have compassion on them. This was the commendation given to the martyrs—to have pity on their persecutors and pray for them, just as Stephen did. This is truly Christlike. However, I am not inclined to proceed further on this point. Let us move on to the next verse.

"Blessed are you when people insult you, persecute you, and falsely say all kinds of evil against you because of me." - MATTHEW 5:11

After speaking generally about persecution, Christ now gives a specific instance of persecution, namely, the persecution of the tongue. He says, "Blessed are you when people insult you and persecute you, when they revile you and falsely accuse you of all kinds of evil because of me." The main point conveyed in this verse is that the saints should anticipate ill treatment from wicked individuals while they live in this world, enduring reviling for the sake of Christ.

To revile means to reproach with detestation, to verbally attack, to accuse with evil intent, and to engage in quarrels and harsh language. The English word "revile" originates from the Latin term that denotes vileness, treating someone as if they are base and contemptible, unworthy of regard. In 1 Peter 2:23, the same word is used in reference to Christ: "When he was reviled, he did not revile in return." Though not the exact same Greek word, it conveys a similar meaning. There are several key points to consider here:

1. Note that the saints should expect this ill treatment from wicked

individuals due to their allegiance to Christ.

2. It is blessed to suffer reviling when it is for Christ's sake and based on false accusations. The saints are blessed in their sufferings when people revile them and speak all kinds of evil against them, lying about them. They should expect whatever wicked men and hell can conceive to be cast upon them. Numerous scriptures attest to the reviling endured by saints throughout history. It is not a novel occurrence, but I will postpone discussing it until we reach the next point, where it is mentioned that the prophets also faced such treatment. It suffices to say that the saints should expect reviling from wicked men because of the hatred they bear towards them. Malice is inventive in devising false accusations when there is hatred. If wicked individuals cannot physically harm the saints, they will resort to harming them with their tongues. Every wicked person harbours animosity towards the godly and will readily attack them verbally. It is impossible for anyone to live a godly life without enduring the tongues of men. While a person can live in such a manner as to avoid physical harm from wicked men, they can never escape their tongues because anyone can use them. Proverbs 16:27 states, "A worthless man plots evil, and on his lips there is like a scorching fire." If a wicked person cannot find any real evil in the godly, they will dig for it or fabricate it. They view the godly with disdain and provoke them with their speech. Wicked people perceive the ways of God as irrational and fail to comprehend their underlying principles. Consequently, they regard the godly as hypocrites. If a wicked person were to engage in the same actions as the saints, they would indeed be hypocritical because they lack the principles to sustain such conduct. Since they do not comprehend the principles that motivate the saints, they accuse them of hypocrisy, falsehood, and revile them with derogatory names. Moreover, they perceive the godly's righteous ways as a condemnation of their own actions, which further fuels their contempt. The godly claim a stronger connection with God than the wicked, and this is intolerable to them. Thus, they employ all possible means to discredit and demean the godly. If they fail to do so, the godly's righteousness would elevate their status in

the eyes of the world, which the wicked envy because they themselves are dishonoured and disgraced. Sanballat and Tobiah, for instance, endeavoured to cast reproach upon Nehemiah for this very reason. They feared that the construction of the Temple in Jerusalem would diminish the status and popularity of their own Temple in Samaria. If the Temple in Jerusalem were built, people would naturally be inclined to go there. Hence, they launched numerous accusations against Nehemiah to prevent the honour and reputation of their Temple from declining. This behaviour is typical of individuals engaged in wickedness that deviates from God's ways. Whenever someone introduces a stricter path that appears to be more devout, it stirs their hearts with bitterness. They resort to calumny, reproach, and every possible means to undermine the esteem of those individuals. They reason that if the latter gain prominence, their own standing will diminish. Those who are fervent in the work of reformation must expect reviling. Zechariah 3:2-3 recounts how Satan stood at the right hand of Joshua the high priest to resist him. Joshua, who played a crucial role in the work of reformation, stood before the Angel of the Lord clad in filthy garments, symbolizing reproach and reviling. Satan sought to hinder Joshua by tarnishing his reputation. Those who are zealous in the work of reformation are often hindered by reproach and reviling. Satan employs this tactic because reviling and reproaching are more grievous to a person of integrity than imprisonment, loss of possessions, bodily pain, and even death. Some individuals have endured imprisonment, loss of wealth, and the threat of death, yet faltered when faced with reviling and reproach. The devil has prevailed through this means when he could not succeed by other forms of opposition. Recognizing the profound effect of reviling on a person of integrity, Satan employs it as a last resort, hoping it will succeed if other methods fail. Therefore, the saints must expect reviling and reproach.

Yeah, sometimes God has a hand in it, allowing them to be reviled and reproached. God sometimes chastises his people through the reviling of wicked men, though it eventually turns into a blessing for them. However, I won't discuss that here. I will focus solely on reviling for the sake of Christ. So, by way of application:

When any of you begin to profess religion, be prepared in advance. Under stand that even your closest friends will be ready to revile you. Expect reviling within your own families. And if you encounter reviling in the ways of God, don't be surprised. Upon professing religion, you must anticipate reproaches and contempt being cast upon you. Prepare yourselves, young believers, so that you may not be led astray when you face reviling.

Furthermore, let the saints strive to walk more diligently because of this. It is crucial that you give no cause for reviling. But if you are reviled, let it be solely for the sake of Christ. Oh, it is truly remarkable when Christians can live in such a way that, even when their enemies seek to find fault, they have no reproach except for their zealous devotion to God. And if others revile them, it should only be because they revile them for nothing more than their faith in Christ. Don't suffer as fools; do not let the saints revile other saints. It is enough that the ungodly revile the saints. Professors of religion should not add to their burden. Don't bind me, as Sampson said, and let not those who are considered godly revile me. Oh, let not the godly make the lives of fellow believers grievous in any way. Although Christ will turn it into a blessing, it is still very difficult for the saints to endure reviling, especially from those who are also godly. David mentioned in one of the Psalms how he was reviled by his neighbors—those who ate bread with him at his table, his friends and close acquaintances. In this, David was a foreshadowing of Christ, who was betrayed by his intimate friend Judas. People of God should be cautious about tarnishing one another's reputations, for surely the devil delights in it. There is no greater joy in hell than when one godly person reviles another. You become a source of entertainment even for the devils themselves. Such behavior has become increasingly prevalent in recent years. People of God should not revile the wicked, let alone fellow saints. I recall reading about Memnon, Darius' general, who, when soldiers in his presence reviled Alexander, struck one of them on the head with his lance and said, "Sirrah, I pay you to fight against Alexander, not to revile and insult him." When you see any work of grace, beware of reviling.

Now, we could raise the question: Why should we not speak ill of wicked people who do evil? This question can either be addressed here or when we come to the second part of the application, which discusses the blessedness of those who are reviled. In that section, we will explore how the saints should conduct themselves, not reviling in return. Those who suffer reviling are blessed in many ways. I won't mention the numerous scriptures that support this (such as 2 Corinthians 12:10 and Hebrews 11:26), but I will highlight some of the blessings that come through enduring reviling.

Firstly, by enduring reviling, they perceive a significant distinction that God has made between them and others. They may think to themselves, "I could have been among the revilers, but instead, I am reviled for the sake of Christ. Oh, what a blessed thing it is! I, who have as wicked a heart as anyone, could have been left to join the ranks of those who revile the saints, yet I am the one being reviled. The difference is immense."

Secondly, those who are reviled increase in grace through this means; it does not hinder them in any way. It is said of Luther that he was nourished by the reproaches wicked men cast upon him. Indeed, God allows the reviling of wicked men to make the saints more fruitful, just as casting dung upon the earth makes it more fertile. Therefore, they are blessed. They never grow more than when they are most reviled.

Thirdly, those who are reviled are blessed because Christ claims all the reproaches cast upon them. Christ regards them as his own. He takes care of their names and will honor them. Christ will reward them for every reproach and every derogatory name cast upon them will receive great rewards in heaven. Therefore, they are blessed.

So, if it is a blessed thing to be reviled for Christ, then those who are reviled should not seek to defend themselves by reviling in return. Why would you revile in anger? Why say, "I am reviled, who can bear it?" What harm will you gain from it? Christ says you are blessed in enduring reviling, so you can be more patient under it. Indeed, the more patient you are, the more Christ will acknowledge you. As Psalm 38:12-15 says, "Those also who seek my life lay snares for me; those who seek my hurt speak of destruction and plan deception all day long. But I, like a deaf man, do not hear; I am like a mute who does not open his mouth. I have become like a man who does not hear and has no arguments. For I hope in you, O Lord; you will answer, O Lord my God." The less we listen to reviling, the more God will listen. If we listen too much, God will close His ears. God's people know how to defend themselves without resorting to reviling. Indeed, there are many people who bicker in the streets, and if someone throws dirt at them, they will throw dirt back. That's their only means of defense—to throw dirt at one another. But those who have integrity do not stoop to such low tactics. Instead, they use other weapons. However, you might say, don't we find in Scripture that when people are wicked and vile, the Scriptures speak ill of them and use contemptuous names for them? Can't we do the same with those who deal wickedly and sinfully? Can't we expose their foolishness, shame them in front of the world, and seek to humble them by emphasizing their wrongdoing? But is this reviling again?

Indeed, we read about Christ in 1 Peter 2:23. His example is set before us. "When he was reviled, he did not revile in return; when he suffered, he did not threaten, but continued entrusting himself to him who judges justly." However, please observe two things: Firstly, consider what the Scripture does in certain cases. Secondly, note the rules that should be observed to distinguish it from reviling.

Certainly, the saints should not revile in return. This must be laid as a foundation and principle. Yet, they may rebuke others sharply. For instance, in Titus 1:10, the apostle speaks of the Cretans as liars, calling them "unruly and empty talkers and deceivers, especially those of the circumcision." He insists that their mouths must be stopped. Similarly, it is mentioned that "one of their own prophets has said, 'Cretans are always liars, evil beasts, lazy gluttons.' This testimony is true. Therefore rebuke them sharply." Rebuke them in a cutting manner. Rebuke them to the point of causing a sting. John, known for his loving spirit, said that if he were to come, he would remember the deeds of Diotrephes, who maliciously gossiped against them. Paul, when dealing with Elimas, looked at him and said, "You are a child of the devil." And Christ, when dealing with the Pharisees, called them a "brood of vipers." The key for a Christian lies in knowing how to address others, speaking sharply but not resorting to reviling. To conclude this exercise, I want to help you deal with wicked people or religious professors. You should deal with them straightforwardly without reviling. Therefore, observe these rules.

First, if a person is guilty of what another charges them with, then I admit that even if the other person is wicked and sinful in their accusation, the guilty person should patiently bear it and not rebuke the passionate accuser. For instance, when Shimei approached David, calling him a "bloody man" and reviling him, David, who was burdened by guilt at that time, did not utter a word in response to Shimei's wicked intention. David remained silent because he was guilty and dared not speak a word. He humbled himself under God's hand. So, if your conscience tells you that you are guilty, be cautious. Even if others speak ill of you with an evil spirit, be careful not to retaliate.

Secondly, you must not react immediately. Suppose someone has done something against you intentionally, and you are not guilty. Firstly, if you are guilty, then say nothing and humble yourself before God. But if you are innocent, it is not appropriate to immediately confront the unjust accuser with harsh language. Take time to consider and pray over it. Examine your own heart. Those who respond with foul language as soon as they hear someone accusing them of wrongdoing are prone to the sin of reviling instead of offering a just defense or reproof of what is wrong in others.

Thirdly, you may rebuke others for their sins, but the rebuke should be sharp only if the sin is willful, not out of weakness. You should consider whether the sin is a result of weakness or willfulness. If it is a sin of weakness, you should show compassion. Do not use harsh language, as Jesus did when he rebuked Peter, saying, "Get behind me, Satan." Peter's action was a sin of weakness, not malice, but because his words had such grave implications, Jesus responded sharply. However, when the offense is due to weakness and lacks such significant consequences, you must be gentle. But if someone has said something that displeased you, and you immediately respond with sharp words, you will become a reviler.

Fourthly, even if the offense is great, if it has been repented of, we must not deal with others sharply. It is common for those who revile the saints to attack them for the slightest weakness and even for sins they have repented of. They bring up past things from the time of their ignorance when they did not know God to make them appear odious. But if the offense has been repented of and buried by the Lord, we must do the same.

Fifthly, if the sin is secret, we should not reprove it in front of others or use harsh language. If God has kept it secret, you should not reveal it in the presence of others. Revilers, on the other hand, will promptly expose any secret matter to cast reproach upon those they love to revile.

Sixthly, do not show favoritism in using harsh language. Many carnal and wicked people will speak harshly against a professing Christian for any wrongdoing. But if one of their companions commits a worse offense, they will not utter reviling words against them. This is a sign that you are not reproving according to the way of Christ when you are partial in your reproaches.

Seventhly, ensure that your harsh language does not exceed the matter at hand. That is reviling. Do not disregard the rules we have previously discussed.

Eighthly, pay attention to the disposition of your spirit. It should not be driven by passion, revealing that you are angry. When you speak about the wrongdoing of others, maintain a calm spirit. Reviling arises when people become heated and say things without restraint. So, when you examine your words and realize that you have spoken certain things and that the person in question is guilty, what should you do? It is not appropriate to reproach them in a passionate manner. Keep your spirit calm and strive to quell all passion when you reprove your brethren.

Ninthly, avoid seeking revenge through your words. It is not enough to say that someone deserves it. You may speak about their actions, not out of hatred for their sin or with the intention to do them good, but out of a spirit of revenge. Shimei, as mentioned earlier, reviled David even though what he said was true because he did it out of a spirit of revenge. However, there are instances where sharp words can do someone good. For example, when dealing with Cretans as described in Scripture, cutting remarks can be more suitable and tend to their benefit.

Tenthly, consider whether some individuals respond better to gentle approaches rather than harsh ones. If you find that a soft and gentle approach will have a positive effect on them, then use that method instead of being sharp.

Eleventhly, the sharper you are in your dealings with others, the more you should pray. I appeal to you based on the previous rule and this one. When you deal with individuals whom you are exasperated against, doesn't your conscience tell you that reasoning with them in a fair manner would be more convincing than being sharp? In such cases, you should examine yourselves and make sure that you convince them through this approach. Pray fervently for them. Pray for them more than ever, especially when you are sharpest towards them. Let your conscience testify that you can bring them before the Throne of Grace and sincerely pray for them. If they are wicked and ungodly, you can even pray against them, just as Paul did against Alexander the Coppersmith.

Twelfthly, another rule to consider is that when someone acknowledges their wrongdoing, be ready to reconcile with them. Even if you have reproved them sharply, if they are willing to acknowledge their fault, be ready to reconcile and thank God for them. But if you revile others, and they come to acknowledge the wrongdoing you spoke against, yet you are even more against them, that indicates that you are a reviler. On the other hand, if you have shown grace, and the other person acknowledges their mistake, you would join with them, bless God for them, and be more united with them than ever before.

Thirteenthly, speaking ill of another person and being glad that you have something evil to say about them constitutes reviling. This does not align with reproving sharply according to God's will. Instead, it reveals that you value your personal advantage more than God's honor. When dealing with an adversary, if there is something evil that you have to address, charge them according to the nature of the offense. Also, be sorrowful that God has allowed them to fall into such sin. Mourn over it and appeal to God. Do you do this when you revile others or speak ill of them? No one will admit to being a reviler. They will claim to have just cause to speak ill. But even if you have just cause, are you genuinely sorry that there is just cause? Does it truly grieve your soul that this person is steeped in so much evil and that you have such an advantage against them? If it is so, then there is no fear of reviling.

Fourteenthly, when people speak ill of others without being called upon to do so, it indicates their guiltiness. Such individuals are in danger of committing the sin of reviling. Therefore, observe these rules, for the human heart is unruly. By doing so, you will know how to conduct yourself in a Christian manner when dealing with others who deserve sharp reproof. You may reprove them sharply without reviling them because the person who is falsely reviled for Christ's sake is blessed.

# SERMON XXXVI

## A Word of Use to Those Who Are Reviled

"Blessed are ye, when men shall revile you, and persecute you, and shall say all manner of evil against you falsely for my sake."
- Matthew 5:11

This final rule of our Saviour for blessedness is the most perplexing to human nature. To be blessed when persecuted and reviled, and even more blessed because of it, is a riddle to flesh and blood. That's why Christ elaborates on it, devoting three verses to this point while others receive only one. We have already discussed persecution and the condition of the Saints, explaining wherein the blessedness of persecution lies. Since few will admit that they persecute for righteousness' sake, we offered some convictions to help people recognize that their persecution of godly individuals is rooted in righteousness. We also explored the promise that the kingdom of heaven belongs to those who endure persecution.

Last time, we addressed a specific form of persecution: the persecution of the tongue through reviling. "Blessed are ye when men shall revile you." The word used for reviling means to reproach someone, casting their evils in their face with detestation. The condition of the Saints is such that they can expect to be reviled and reproached in the world, as we have shown from Scripture. Consider the examples of persecution against the Prophets. As for the use of reviling, I discussed it last time. The hatred and malice in the hearts of ungodly people cause them to despise the Saints. While not everyone can physically persecute them, everyone has the liberty to revile them. The devil knows that reviling is a powerful way to weaken them in their faith. Many spirits cannot bear reviling, and it becomes a heavy and burdensome affliction. The devil realizes that when he cannot prevail through persecution, he often succeeds through reviling. Reviling is a severe evil that deeply affects people's spirits. We made several general applications, such as when individuals embrace their religious profession, they should anticipate reviling and ill language. Parents, relatives, friends, acquaintances, and employers may all revile them and come up with names to mock them. Be prepared for this. Furthermore, be careful in your conduct so that they find no grounds to revile you. Saints should also avoid reviling one another, as it is a grievous matter. The psalmist lamented this in Psalm 31:11, "I was a reproach among all mine enemies, but especially among my neighbours, and a fear to mine acquaintance: they that did see me without fled from me." He complained not only about the reproach from his enemies but also about the reproach from his neighbours, which troubled him greatly. It is more sorrowful for the Saints to suffer reviling from one another than from prelates. Do you not bind me, as Sampson said? The godly will say the same to their fellow brethren. There is great blessing in enduring reviling. Just as a farmer enriches his soil by spreading dung on it, God makes His Saints fruitful by allowing wicked people to cast reviling upon them. Why is it such a blessedness? Consider it a blessed thing that when you are reviled for Christ's sake, you could have been reviled for your own wickedness. Blessed are ye, for there is a great reward; your reward is great in heaven. The Lord cares for your reputation while you endure reviling. The lesson we discussed last time is this: if it is such a blessed thing to be reviled and to suffer for Christ, then it should teach the Saints not to revile in return when they are reviled. Why should they? Reviling has been transformed into a blessing.

Again, we must not revile others. We spent a great deal of time the last day discussing how to charge others with the evil they are guilty of, deeply yet without reviling. Titus 1:10 and 13 warn about unruly and vain talkers and deceivers, especially those of the Circumcision. The word translated as "sharply" means "cuttingly." If there are people in the world who may be rebuked, it is the Cretians, whom the Apostle calls liars. However, it is not safe to rebuke someone immediately when they provoke you. When the matter concerns ourselves, we can avoid turning reproof into reviling by deliberating on it. If the sin is secret, we must not publicly speak ill of others. It indicates a love for reviling when one seeks to unearth and publicly declare secret things with evil language. If God keeps them secret, you should not reveal them. Moreover, do not take pleasure in offences. Mourn for them. Ensure that any language you use is founded on the evil committed by those individuals, and that you do not do it with passion or a desire for revenge. Instead, do it with a gentle and quiet spirit, motivated by love for the truth. The more you speak against someone and charge them with wrongdoing, the more you ought to pray for them, especially if you sense any presence of God in them. If they have any trace of godliness, do not speak against them except in prayer. If these rules were observed, praying for others with as much fervor as you speak against them with bitterness, your conscience would be clear of reviling. But let us not proceed further with what we discussed last time.

A few more words on this point in general.

If those who are reviled are blessed, then the Saints should not be deterred from their path by reviling. When Christ tells you that you are blessed, what great harm is it when people call you names and speak evil of you, and you can bear it? Those who truly understand what Christian religion means should not be swayed or disheartened by reviling. Do not settle for the thought that since you embraced the Christian religion, you have been subjected to scorn, reproach, and reviling. I remember a learned man using this analogy: it would be dishonourable for a soldier to be thrown off his horse by a mere gust of wind. Everyone would laugh at it. Likewise, it is dishonourable for someone on the right path or in a just cause to be swayed by the reproaches of wicked men, which are as insignificant as puffs of wind. People are willing to endure reproach for their sin, shame, and any name to fulfill their desires. Will you not be willing to endure nicknames for the cause of Christ? Remember that Christ has delivered you from eternal reproach (Daniel 12:2: "And many of them that sleep in the dust of the earth shall awake, some to everlasting life, and some to shame and everlasting contempt"). Also, remember that Christ takes care of your reputation, and there are numerous promises to vindicate your righteousness like the noonday. Do not think of diverting from the way because of reviling, but rather pray to the Lord. Let me provide you with a few Scriptures to guide the godly when they are reviled. One is found in Psalm 109, the beginning of which says, "Hold not thy peace, O God of my praise. For the mouth of the wicked and the mouth of the deceitful are opened against me: they have spoken against me with a lying tongue." David, who was a type of the Church, suffered greatly, experiencing various forms of suffering and reviling. In verse 3, he says, "They compassed me about also with words of hatred; and fought against me without a cause." What does he do then? In verse 4, he says, "But I give myself unto prayer." The original Hebrew reads, "But I pray." Prayer is his refuge and help. Similarly, in Job 16:20, Job says, "My friends scorn me: but mine eye poureth out tears unto God." Psalm 57:2-3 says, "I will cry unto God most high; unto God that performeth all things for me. He shall send from heaven, and save me from the reproach of him that would swallow me up. Selah. God shall send forth his mercy and his truth." David expresses similar sentiments in other passages, affirming that he finds help in heaven and therefore does not need to revile or become discouraged on his path. Nehemiah was reproached while engaged in his work, but he did not cease his work.

Lastly, if those who are reviled are blessed, then certainly those who are revilers are cursed. It is a blessed thing when godly people are reviled for Christ, but what do you think of those who, instead of suffering for reviling, are themselves revilers? Oh, beware of them. There are no more bitter revilers of religion than those who are apostate professors. When you see someone who was once a zealous professor fall away and turn against the faith, remember Rabshakeh's apostasy. He was the worst reviler of all. Truly, those who revile the godly are in a truly cursed condition. People may pray against them, as Nehemiah did (Nehemiah 4:3-5). Be cautious and avoid reviling, even if it is done unknowingly. It is a most dangerous thing. You may argue that you do not revile the godly because of their righteousness, but because they are hypocrites. For that, I will present this Scripture (Mark 3:22): "And the scribes which came down from Jerusalem said, He hath Beelzebub, and by the prince of the devils casteth he out devils." They did not revile the godly by saying, "We speak ill of them not because they have the Spirit of God, but because they are associated with Beelzebub." Therefore, note this: it is a dangerous thing to charge hypocrisy or any wickedness when it is actually from the Spirit of God. I could show you various Scriptures, such as Psalm 59 and 57, but especially Psalm 59. When you speak contemptibly of the saints, the Holy Spirit speaks contemptibly of you. God restrains their hands, or else they would do more. They go about grieving in the streets. So, let us continue with the text: "Blessed are you when men revile you and persecute you." Here, persecution comes into play once again.

First, from the repetition in this passage (for nothing in Scripture is in vain, and even in repetitions, there is a reason), we learn that those who suffer persecution for Christ's sake are blessed, and their posterity is blessed too. Christ pronounces blessedness on those who endure persecution for His name's sake. It can be a great comfort to anyone whose ancestors suffered persecution. Christ will acknowledge them and their posterity more readily. Suppose a poor, ragged beggar comes to your door, and someone tells you, "This man's father lost everything for your sake. His grandfather lost his life for your cause." Would you not reward this child, knowing they are the offspring of the father or grandchild of the grandfather who suffered for you? Perhaps you are currently experiencing persecution, and though you are pronounced blessed, you do not see the blessedness. Yet, there is a double blessing reserved for you in the future. Those who currently have reviling spirits would become persecuting spirits if they were given power. Oh, let us pray that the Lord restrains them.

Secondly, and furthermore, it is worth mentioning that some people can bear harsh words but cannot bear persecution. They do not care what others say about them in words because words do not cause physical harm, but if they have to suffer the loss of something, such as their possessions or imprisonment, then they are quick to falter. We should not only be willing to endure hurtful words but also to endure harmful actions. When people speak all kinds of evil against us, it is indeed remarkable that such a statement would be made about the Disciples, those who were to be sent out. They may have been considered a little too strict, but it is quite extreme for all manner of evil to be spoken of them. Yet, as Saint Paul says, "We are the off-scouring of the world" (1 Corinthians 4:13). According to some interpreters, this phrase refers to the dung carts, as everyone brings their dirt and throws it into their carts. Thus, Paul is saying, "We are the off-scouring of the world, and we are the dung carts. There is no one who does not have some dirt or another to cast upon us." The Apostle alludes to the expiation practices among the heathens. When certain condemned individuals were brought forth with garlands on their heads to be offered as sacrifices to Neptune, it was customary to say, "Sis pro nobis peripsema" (be thou a propitiation for us). Therefore, if the Apostle had said, "We are as detestable in the eyes of the people as those condemned individuals who were offered up as expiation," it means that we are now loaded with curses and revilings, just as those individuals were. Blessed are you when they speak all manner of evil. Some can bear certain reproaches but not all reproaches. We must be willing to submit to whatever God calls us to, all manner of evil. It may be that some suspicions have a basis, but we must not reproach people based on mere suspicion. However, even if we do not go beyond speaking evil due to a suspicion, the people of God must expect that wicked men will revile them.

Secondly, they will revile them with the kind of evil that is most contrary to them. For example, those who are the most sober and temperate must be willing to be reviled as drunkards. Those who are the most chaste must be willing to be reviled as unchaste. Those who desire peace above all else and do not wish to cause trouble, except as duty requires, must be considered as troublemakers in the state and the church. They must be willing to suffer the very evil that they detest. Yes, whatever evil any wicked men are guilty of, the godly are charged with it. When Nero set fire to Rome, the Christians were blamed for it. All kinds of evil are attributed to them. Why should they speak all manner of evil? Even if they are not guilty of it, it would be cleansed away, and the shame would fall back on those who cast it upon them. But they will spread the evil far and wide, and many will hear of the reproach but will not hear of the justification or the answer to the reproach. Therefore, boldly and strongly, they will speak all manner of evil, even things that are as far removed from the truth as the East is from the West. They will seek to cause it to stick by casting it upon them. Whoever can remove it by speaking all manner of evil, let them do so. From this, we should learn not to judge the saints based on what we hear about them. It would be an immeasurable wrong for us to think that men are guilty based on whatever is cast upon them. We would wrong the generation of the righteous if we were to entertain even the slightest thought of guilt based on the reproaches that circulate. Moreover, the godly should strive to refute all the evil that is said about them, as stated in 1 Peter 1:15: "But as he which hath called you is holy, so be ye holy in all manner of conversation." It seems that the wicked labour to revile with all manner of evil cast upon you, and you should labour in your entire conduct to manifest all holiness. That is the way to answer all manner of reviling.

Thirdly, furthermore, blessed are you when they revile you, persecute you, and speak all manner of evil falsely, lyingly. It is a strange statement that some make. They say, "If I were guilty, it would not trouble me as much, but for them to accuse me when I never even thought of it, that must surely trouble me." Brethren, even the best of all the saints have some evil in them. Therefore, we should strive to conduct ourselves in a manner that if people revile us, they will not hit the mark. We are aware of our own faults, but we should keep them hidden from the world's eyes. How shameful it is for those who profess godliness to give just cause for reviling. If men's mouths are opened and it turns out to be true that you are a professor of religion, and your conscience tells you that you are worse than they accuse you of, you are in a sad condition when you have a reproving conscience within you. You may speak of men's revilings, but what does your conscience say? Men may speak some evil of you, but your conscience speaks even more evil of you. Secondly, consider this: if what they reproach you for is true and not false, it is God's just hand against you. God spits in your face and shames you through the reviling of others.

Fourthly, you are the ones who harm religion. You give valid reasons for people to revile you. Professors who live scandalously, who make a great show of religion, are the ones who do the greatest harm of all people on earth to religion. God will demand retribution for all the sufferings of his other saints from your hands. You do more harm to religion than all the persecutors in the world. A Christian who professes religion and gives just cause for reviling does more harm to religion than all the revilers in the world. The reason is that persecutors only make people afraid to profess religion, but those who live scandalously affect people's consciences, causing them to hate religion. Now, is causing people to hate it not more detrimental than making them afraid to profess it? Therefore, take heed of yourselves. If people speak any evil of you, may it be false. But if they speak it with just cause, then you cannot complain to God; you are cut off from that privilege. However, if you are reviled falsely, then you can enjoy that privilege, as you can read in Jeremiah 15:15: "O Lord, thou knowest: remember me, and visit me, and revenge me of my persecutors; take me not away in thy long-suffering: know that for thy sake I have suffered rebuke." If anyone suffers for your sake, you consider yourself obligated to defend them. Likewise, the Spirit helps our infirmities, as mentioned in Romans 8:26: "Likewise the Spirit also helpeth our infirmities: for we know not what we should pray for as we ought: but the Spirit itself maketh intercession for us with groanings which cannot be uttered." It is comforting to know that the Lord takes note of your sufferings when you suffer for Christ's sake. Christ loves you, he has promised to help you, and he is committed to helping you because you suffer for his sake. Therefore, continue and count yourself blessed for his sake. Certainly, if you are willing to suffer for his sake, he will be willing to suffer for your sake. When you suffer anything for Christ, who is infinitely worthy, he is worthy of everything you have. What has he done for you? Has he not done more for you than you have done for him or can do for him?

Sixthly, a very important lesson to learn is that blessed are those who have all manner of evil spoken falsely for my name's sake. When you are reproached for Christ's sake, you are blessed. However, when Christ is reproached for your sake, even though he is not in a position to merit anything, having finished the work, he may still experience suffering and have shame cast upon him because of your wicked and ungodly life. This is a cursed, cursed thing. It is to bring Christ down from heaven to suffer again. Did Christ not suffer enough? Why do you want him to suffer more for your sake? Do not add to his suffering but suffer as much for his sake as he has done for yours. As written in Romans 2:24: "For the name of God is blasphemed among the Gentiles through you, as it is written." See how God is reviled, how his name is blasphemed because of your actions. When you walk scandalously, the name of God is reproached. If a professor of religion faces any temptation to sin, consider this: if you give permission to that sin, you trample on the name of Christ. You trample on Christ himself. "You trample on me," says Christ. Will you continue to permit sin even though the name of God lies before you? Oh, hard-hearted wretch, who knows that the name of God lies there and yet tramples on it! It follows in the twelfth verse: "Rejoice, and be exceeding glad." True Christians should not only consider themselves blessed but also rejoice and be exceedingly glad. In Luke 6:23, it is stated: "Rejoice ye in that day, and leap for joy: for, behold, your reward is great in heaven: for in the like manner did their fathers unto the prophets." Leap for joy, skip and leap for joy when you are reviled for Christ. It is not fitting for true Christians to manifest any kind of sorrow under any suffering for Christ. When we suffer for our sins, we may express sorrow, but when we suffer persecution for Christ's sake, Scripture does not call for mourning, weeping, or humiliation. Instead, it calls for rejoicing and blessing God for being counted worthy to suffer for him.

# SERMON XXXVII

## Saints should be careful not to suffer for evil genuinely

Rejoice, and be exceedingly glad, for great is your reward in heaven; for so persecuted they the Prophets which were before you. - Matthew 5:12

The final rule of blessedness is the suffering of persecution and reviling for the sake of Christ. Blessed are those who endure such suffering. We have discussed persecution in general and reviling in particular, and the blessedness that comes from enduring either persecution or reviling. Even when people speak all kinds of evil against us—evil that seems unlikely and baseless—they still dare to fasten all sorts of accusations upon us. But let the saints be careful that no genuine evil is spoken of them, for that is a grievous matter. They are not blessed in such circumstances. Rather, they are blessed when false accusations are made against them for the sake of Christ's name, not for their own desires or lusts. Christ will acknowledge them in those cases. Indeed, Christ has a special regard for those who suffer anything in his cause, including having their names wounded. He will bind up that wound. In Jeremiah 15:15, we read, "O Lord, thou knowest: remember me, and visit me, and revenge me of my persecutors;

take me not away in thy long suffering: know that for thy sake I have suffered rebuke." When you suffer for your own lusts and passions, you suffer because of your own wickedness. But when it is for the sake of the Lord, then you can approach prayer with comfort. Be cautious that Christ does not suffer for your sake in the sense of suffering for your sins and wickedness. Isn't it enough that Christ has suffered for your sake in a meritorious manner? Instead, suffer for Christ's sake, but do not let Christ suffer for your sake.

Moving on to verse 12, "Rejoice, and be exceedingly glad." Rejoice, leap, and skip for joy. In Luke 6:23, we find the following words: "Rejoice ye in that day, and leap for joy: for, behold, your reward is great in heaven: for in the like manner did their fathers unto the Prophets." It should bring great joy to the saints when they are reviled and persecuted for the sake of Christ. This is a clear indication that they are on the path of Christ, that they belong to Christ, and that they have advanced far enough to become sufferers for him. Rejoice in that. The good deeds you do are good for you, but not as much as when you suffer. When you are reviled, the Spirit of God and glory rest upon you. As stated in 1 Peter 4:14, "If ye be reproached for the name of Christ, happy are ye; for the spirit of glory and of God resteth upon you: on their part he is evil spoken of, but on your part he is glorified." It is not sufficient for the people of God to merely be patient in their suffering; they must also be reproached. Moses regarded the reproaches for Christ as greater riches than the treasures of Egypt. Persecutions for the sake of Christ are riches to a truly gracious heart. Therefore, rejoice.

First, how can I rejoice when it is an affliction? If anyone is afflicted, let him pray. I confess that when our affliction comes as a chastisement for sin, mourning is necessary. However, I never find the Scripture calling for mourning from the saints who suffer for the cause of Christ. Though it is an evil in itself, it does not call for mourning. While God may send other afflictions as a result of the sins of his people, we do not find God charging his people with suffering for his cause and affliction for their sin. When we come to suffer for the cause of Christ, God has a further purpose beyond afflicting us, one that does not require mourning. Rejoice and leap for joy. Why? Because great is your reward in heaven. You will be rewarded for your suffering. Every speck of dirt cast upon you will be transformed into a pearl, enhancing the glory of your reward and your happiness. The happiness that the saints will experience is called a reward, not a reward based on merit, but a reward of free grace. Just as a father intends to leave an inheritance for his child but promises certain rewards to encourage him to attend school, not as a matter of merit but out of his free love for the child, the Lord chooses to call all the glory in heaven a reward. The suffering we endure for the sake of his name, though tainted by sin, serves as encouragement for us poor creatures who now live in hope of a reward. And great is your reward; it is abundant, a substantial reward. There is undoubtedly a difference in the glory of heaven. Those who suffer the most will receive the greatest reward. They shall receive a significant reward because they suffer greatly. This serves as an encouragement during times of suffering. There is undoubtedly a distinction in the rewards for suffering. They shall receive a great reward. It is worth noting that Christ does not specify the exact reward they shall receive. He does not mention specific rewards because they are so great that they cannot be limited or adequately expressed. We are unable to comprehend them. Instead, Christ simply states that it is a great reward. Surely our hearts are too limited if we attempt to establish boundaries for God's mercy. When we think in terms of "if God is merciful to us, then we shall be happy," our spirits are too narrow. The mercy of God is a profound concept. No carnal heart in the world limits God's mercy to the extent that it limits its own obedience. However, it may hold certain expectations for ultimate contentment. A gracious heart is so expansive that no specific thing can satisfy it. This is why a gracious heart will never limit itself to any duty but will immerse itself in an infinite ocean of service to God. The expectation that such a soul has from God surpasses all finite goods. Therefore, Christ says, "Great is your reward." He does not name any specific reward.

Again, great is your reward in heaven. It may be that you will receive no reward here on earth. As long as you live on this earth, you will be reviled and persecuted. This will never end. It is possible that your entire life will be spent enduring this, so look for your reward in a higher place. Personally, I didn't care much if I was persecuted by some and honoured by others. However, it may be that you will be reviled by the wicked and disapproved of by the righteous. As a result, you may not receive any reward here on earth. But you must expect it in the afterlife. I confess that sometimes the Lord does reward them here on earth by honouring them in the consciences of those who reviled them. However, if that doesn't happen, if you receive nothing here, you must wait for it until you reach heaven, where you will receive a full reward. The saints are willing to do so; they are willing to wait for all their reward until they come to heaven. We see such a reality and certainty and glory in heavenly things that we are willing to wait. When it comes, it will make up for everything. A carnal heart is not willing to wait; it wants something tangible in the present moment. But the saints have the willingness to wait for what comes afterward; they have the ability to look beyond the veil. What is this? In 2 Peter 1:9, it is written, "But he that lacketh these things is blind, and cannot see afar off, and hath forgotten that he was purged from his old sins." Wicked people are short-sighted; they can only see things that are right in front of them. They cannot see far off; they cannot see heaven. They consider earthly things as realities. But the saints view earthly things as vain and empty, and they see heavenly things as reality. The people of the world engage in transactions with God for small things; they seek immediate satisfaction for their carnal hearts. They do not understand the true nature of these things, for they only seek little from God. However, the saints of God engage in transactions with God for eternity, for glory, for a kingdom, and for a crown. They are willing to wait until afterward; they do not care what happens to them here as long as they have the kingdom of heaven in the future. There is a difference between the service that God requires from men in the world. The Lord has some who serve him, and they must receive immediate payment. God says, "You shall have it, and that is your portion." When he has given you some outward satisfaction in the world, that is all you are likely to have forever. But the saints of God are not concerned about what they will receive. They are willing to serve him no matter the outcome. Although they may not receive the immediate payment that others receive in the world, their reward in heaven is great. The reward in heaven is substantial, a great reward. In Psalm 57:2, it is written, "Power from on high," meaning glorious power, great power. In Jeremiah 25:3, it is stated, "Surely there is a reward for the righteous." Regardless of what they encounter here, surely there is a reward in heaven. In Psalm 119:89, it is written, "For ever, O Lord, thy word is settled in heaven." There is certainly a reward for the saints. One indication that there must be a great reward is that from the beginning of the world until now, they have suffered so much on earth. God must take some time to distribute his infinite treasures, visibly too. Certainly, the power of God will match his grace and mercy to work mightily and reveal the infinite riches of his grace in rewarding. Therefore, there is a reward for the saints, and especially for the suffering saints.

Secondly, there must be a great reward in heaven for them because the Lord gives the greatest portion of the earth to the wicked, even to the dogs. There are higher things for the saints. If the earth is so excellent that God gives it to his enemies, what does he have for his own saints, those who are dear to him, his children who suffer for him? When we consider this world, when we see its canopy adorned with stars and witness the glory and wealth of the earth, and then contemplate to whom this belongs—namely, the enemies of God, those whom God hates—the entire Turkish Empire is but a crumb, something that the master of a household throws to his dog. Surely, then, what shall the saints have! Therefore, when you see the wicked prosper, reason in this way: "Is it indeed true that wicked people have so much here? Then what shall the saints have, those who suffer for him?"

Thirdly, another proof is that the hopes of the saints are elevated and raised, and this is done by the Holy Spirit. Their hopes for great things must not fade because they are raised by the power of the Holy Spirit. In Romans 15:13, it is written, "Now the God of hope fill you with all joy and peace in believing, that ye may abound in hope, through the power of the Holy Ghost." The hopes of the saints are raised by God and by the power of the Holy Spirit. If God and the Holy Spirit have undertaken to raise their hopes, surely those hopes must not be insignificant. The object of their hopes is undoubtedly magnificent, as it is the glory of God and the glory of the Holy Spirit that elevates their hopes. Surely, these are glorious hopes. When great men, captains, and princes take a title for themselves based on something, it indicates their high regard for it. The hopes of the saints are such that God takes a title from them; he is the God of their hopes. Surely, their reward must be a glorious reward, the one they hope for.

Fourthly, it must be a great reward because it was prepared for them before the foundation of the world. God has been preparing glory for his people from all eternity. Surely, the work that God has been preparing since eternity past will be exceedingly glorious.

Fifthly, another proof is that whenever it comes, it is for the purpose of God declaring to men and angels what his infinite power is capable of elevating a creature to and what his infinite mercy is able to bestow upon a creature.

We are chosen to the praise of his rich and glorious grace. If this is God's purpose in choosing us—to manifest the power of his grace and what that power means—then this is the reward for you, to what a height an infinite God is able to raise poor creatures. Great is your reward in heaven.

Lastly, it must be a great reward because it is the fruit of the purchase made by the blood of Christ, a purchase that was so costly. Therefore, it must be of equal value and worth that the blood of Christ deserved. Just as sin cries out for more and more wrath to be poured upon it for all eternity because sin deserves it, the merit of Christ will cry out for you if you do not receive to the utmost capacity that a creature is capable of. Isn't there enough here to encourage us in suffering? This reward is such that Christ has gone ahead to prepare. In John 14, it is mentioned as one purpose of his ascension into heaven, to make all things ready for his saints and disciples when they come. If you ask me what it is, well, should I tell you about the blessed vision of God, the enjoyment of God, communion with God, communion with the Father, Son, and Holy Ghost? The Scripture speaks only briefly about the glory of the soul because it wants us to reason from that which is more tangible. If the Scripture tells us that the body will shine like the sun in the sky, then what will the soul do? The soul is capable of communion with God. So, keep in mind that every time you suffer something, you are exercising your faith in that glorious reward. "Blessed are you when you suffer for righteousness' sake and when men revile you, for great is your reward" (Matthew 5:10-11). The person being addressed changes; first, "Blessed are they," and then, "Blessed are you." The reason for this change is that Christ seems to be directing himself to those disciples whom he sent out to preach the Gospel. Just as he spoke to all those who would profess the Gospel, saying, "Blessed are they who suffer for righteousness' sake," now he says, "Blessed are you."

Take note of this: the ministers of the Gospel should expect to experience suffering from the evil and wicked world. As Jesus said, "I send you out as sheep among wolves." The ministers of the Gospel are engaged in a direct battle against the kingdom of Satan like no other people in the world. It is a peculiar statement we find in John 17:14, "And have given them thy word; and the world hath hated them, because they are not of the world, even as I am not of the world." Immediately after receiving the Word, the world hates them. The more they possess the word of truth, the more the world hates them. You know what Christ said about Paul during his conversion in Acts 9:15-16, "But the Lord said unto him, Go thy way: for he is a chosen vessel unto me, to bear my name before the Gentiles, and kings, and the children of Israel: For I will shew him how great things he must suffer for my name's sake." If he goes to bear the name of Christ, then he must endure great suffering.

Secondly, the ministers of the Gospel are more visible and under constant scrutiny compared to other people. They must be cautious as they are constantly watched and targeted.

Thirdly, the ministers of the Gospel have no physical weapons to defend themselves; their only defense is spiritual. A magistrate can defend himself because he possesses the sword, but a minister cannot. Ministers confront people's desires, especially their beloved lusts. If a minister preaches in a general manner and does not strike at their lusts, all is well. However, if they address their lusts directly, they cannot bear it and revile the minister.

Fourthly, the devil knows that he can cause great harm by tarnishing the reputation of ministers and diminishing their esteem among the people. Although he may not succeed in certain areas for a long time, he can make the ministers appear despicable and incite people to speak evil of them. Let us recognize the wickedness of this world. Even though the ministers of God bring the greatest blessing by proclaiming the riches of God's grace in the blessed Covenant, and should be accepted as messengers of the divine, this wicked world harbours enmity towards them. Ministers should be careful to walk circumspectly so that no grounds for objection can be found against them.

Lastly, strive to uphold the true honour that Christ has entrusted to you in the ministry of the Gospel. You know how concerned and protective Jesus Christ is of the honour and esteem of his ministers. Therefore, you must not accept an accusation against an elder without two or three witnesses. Rather than believing and spreading accusations without evidence, all godly individuals should make every effort to uphold the honour of faithful ministers, treating their reputation with care and demolishing anything that could prejudice them.

"For so persecuted they the Prophets."

It is neither strange nor new that you encounter persecution and reviling. You should not consider it a strange thing, as Peter mentions in regard to the fiery trial. Consider these three aspects. First, the history of how the Prophets, throughout time, faced persecution, particularly the ministers of God. He does not say that the same happened to the saints but to the Prophets.

The second aspect is to demonstrate where the power of the argument lies, that you should rejoice and be glad because the Prophets were persecuted.

Thirdly, we should consider the practical implications of the suffering of the Prophets. From Abraham onwards, you know the hardships they endured. Isaac also suffered, as did Moses, who faced reproach, as mentioned in Hebrews 11. David, in Psalm 35:15, said, "But in mine adversity they rejoiced, and gathered themselves together: yea, the abjects (or as it is in the Hebrew, the smiters) gathered themselves together against me, and I knew it not; they did tear me, and ceased not." The Church in Psalm 79:4 declared, "We are become a reproach to our neighbours, a scorn and derision to them that are round about us." Job was called by the basest of people. In Job 16:9-10, it is written, "He teareth me in his wrath, who hateth me: he gnasheth upon me with his teeth; mine enemy sharpeneth his eyes upon me. They have gaped upon me with their mouth; they have smitten me upon the cheek reproachfully; they have gathered themselves together against me." Nehemiah 2:19 tells us that when Sanballat the Horonite, Tobiah the servant, and Geshem the Arabian heard of Nehemiah's work, they laughed them to scorn, despised them, and questioned their actions. Isaiah suffered similar mockery, as described in Isaiah 28:13, "But the word of the Lord was unto them precept upon precept, precept upon precept; line upon line, line upon line; here a little, and there a little; that they might go, and fall backward, and be broken, and snared, and taken." The Prophet Isaiah was even sawn asunder, and he endured scorn for his ministry. The Hebrew word used to describe how the prophets were addressed implies a kind of scorn shown to them despite their elevated status as prophets. Ezekiel and Jeremiah also suffered, as did Christ Himself and the apostles, martyrs, and reformers. Those who played significant roles in the work of reformation faced contempt, reviling, and scorn. Tertullian wrote about the Christians in his time, how they were labeled as enemies of the state, accused of meeting secretly at night, extinguishing candles, and engaging in immoral acts, worshiping an ass's head, mocking them as foolish people. Chrysostom was banished by the Empress and faced much scorn. Augustine also endured reviling in his time. When I previously discussed the persecution of the disciples, I focused on their specific sufferings, but I postponed discussing the sufferings endured by eminent Christians who played a key role in religious reformation. Calvin, who was instrumental in the Church of God, was said to have been eaten by worms and accused of calling on the devil, despite his gentle nature and peaceful death. Similar accusations were made against Beza, claiming he desired lordship, was stubborn, and had an unforgiving spirit. Such accusations fulfill the prophecy of speaking evil of others. It is reported that Beza lived without bitterness, remaining calm even when enemies attempted to provoke him with a violent spirit. He remained as tranquil as a person without a gall bladder. This illustrates how it has always been the way of wicked men to oppose those who have contributed to good and reformation with great earnestness and zeal, particularly during the time of Queen Elizabeth. Those who opposed the hierarchy of the Church faced mistreatment from the bishops. Therefore, do not consider your names to be more precious than theirs. Why should you expect an easier journey to heaven than they had? Why do you assume that God should favour you over them? Remember that the same spirit of darkness still prevails. Keep your hearts close to God and Christ, and ensure that you suffer only for the sake of Christ. In that case, rejoice and be exceedingly glad, for great is your reward in heaven. This is how the prophets who came before you were persecuted.

# SERMON XXXVIII

## Some Arguments for the Encouragement of Saints in Suffering

"For so persecuted they the Prophets which were before you.
We are the salt of the Earth, but if the Salt have lost his savour,
wherewith shall it be salted, it is thenceforth good for nothing
but to be cast out, and to be trodden underfoot of men. You are
the light of the world." - Matthew 5: The latter part of verse 12

In order to strengthen his disciples against persecution and reviling, and to help them in their suffering, our Saviour, among other things, tells them that they are no worse off than the prophets who came before them. "For so persecuted they the Prophets which were before you." The point is that considering the sufferings of the servants of God in the past should serve as an encouragement for us in our own suffering. First, we will look at the history of the great hardships endured by the prophets, disciples, and saints who came before us. Secondly, we will examine the argument for rejoicing under persecution. Lastly, we will consider the practical implications of the persecution endured by the prophets. I will only cover the first aspect and proceed to the second. Where does the strength of this argument lie? There are five distinct strengths or rather five arguments within it.

Firstly, the same spirit of wickedness that opposed the prophets still prevails. The spirit of truth that is opposed is the same spirit of Satan. You can see that you are facing opposition, but it is merely the old spirit of Satan, the same spirit of wickedness that has appeared before, that is now opposing you.

Secondly, this shows that even those who are beloved and precious to God may suffer hardships. You cannot deny that the prophets were beloved by God, and yet they suffered as much as you. They were despised and reviled just like you. Therefore, do not be troubled by it, but rejoice and be glad.

Thirdly, if God were to deal differently with you than He did with others in the past, it might discourage you. However, they endured the same sufferings as His servants of old. God will lead you to heaven along the same path that He led His servants in the past.

Fourthly, this is the way in which God has brought all His servants to heaven. Why should you think that God will provide you with an easier way than He did for others? The prophets themselves suffered such things. What makes your flesh or your name superior to theirs? It is most intolerable that we, who are so base and insignificant, and who do so little in the service of God, should consider it too much to do anything for His cause, especially when those who were better than us endured greater suffering.

The fifth argument is that although the prophets suffered, the truth of God prevailed. Some may question what will become of God's truth if the prophets are imprisoned and persecuted. Do not be overly concerned about that, for the prophets themselves suffered, yet God preserved His truth. They became instruments of great good through their suffering. Consider these five points together, and you will understand the power of the argument.

Now, let us consider how we can apply the sufferings of those who came before us. Firstly, if those who were the most eminent servants of God endured such hardships, then we, who experience little suffering amidst prosperity, must examine whether our prosperity is accompanied by the love of God. Do we receive prosperity as a sign of God's love? Those who were most beloved by Him did not enjoy ease and contentment as we do. Therefore, we must examine whether the prosperity we enjoy is truly a manifestation of God's love. Many believe that God loves them more because they have more. But this is not the case. If God does not deal with you as He did with other saints, you should examine how you experience that prosperity. When reading about the precious saints of God and realizing that they have accomplished more in one week than you have in a whole year, any person living in luxury and comfort should question, "Does God love me more than them? Is this all that I am destined to have?"

Secondly, if the prophets were called to suffer in the past, then if we are called to endure less suffering, let us be more diligent in active obedience. Hearing about the sufferings of the prophets would pain your heart. Reading the book of martyrs would be very instructive. I will focus on one particular use of it. When you hear of their suffering, think to yourself, "God called them to suffer passively, enduring the rage and tortures devised by wicked men. But God does not call me to suffer in such a fearful manner. Surely, I must give God the glory of my strength. Let me spend it in praying, honoring, and worshiping God, just as others did when they endured torments from wicked men. Since we owe God the glory of our names, the glory of our wealth, and the glory of our lives, if God does not receive it through suffering, we should freely give it to Him through acts of service. Think about how they lay on the cold earth in prison. When engaging in any form of service, whether it be prayer, reading, or hearing, and it begins to cause discomfort to your flesh, why would you cease your service to God because your flesh is uncomfortable? What did the martyrs endure in the flesh? It is a shame for you to abandon the service of God because it causes some discomfort to your flesh."

Thirdly, when we consider the sufferings of those who came before us, it should lead us to curb our excessive indulgence of the flesh. Even though we have an abundance to satisfy our physical desires, let us moderate it. We read that often the prophets and martyrs lacked bread and necessary provisions. Should I then abuse God's creations through excessive consumption? During Ahab's time, the prophets were content with bread and water. Should I be excessive in my eating and drinking? Those of you who spend whole nights engaging in immoral and self-indulgent activities such as revelry, drunkenness, gluttony, and excess, solely seeking pleasure for the flesh and caring only to satisfy your lusts, check your hearts in these ways.

The fourth use is to prepare for suffering. Although we are not presently called to suffer, we must not be complacent. We should not assume that we will always enjoy the peace we currently have. The prophets endured difficult trials, and we should expect to encounter the same.

The fifth and final use is this: Surely, God has received little support from the world throughout history in upholding His truth. The world has proven itself to be wicked, persecuting and tormenting His saints and prophets. Therefore, the Lord owes little to this world. The world has set itself against God, and it will not be long before the Lord shatters this sinful world.

Thus, we have concluded with that portion of Christ's sermon, the Beatitudes, the various blessings that Christ bestows upon the saints who fulfill their duties.

Verse 13: "You are the salt of the earth."

Here begins a new topic. First, Jesus informs His disciples about blessedness. They will come to recognize their own blessedness. Having shown them their blessedness, regardless of how the world perceives them, in the eyes of God, they are blessed creatures. Now, He explains to them the service they must perform in the world. This service is indeed a significant part of blessedness as well. From the context, note that those whom God places in a state of blessedness are suitable and capable instruments for great service in His name. Once the soul is satisfied with this understanding—that the Lord has shown mercy upon me, cast a favorable gaze upon me, and granted me a state of blessedness—no matter what the world may do to me, they cannot take away my blessedness. Oh, how suitable such a person is to serve God! In the subsequent words, we find the greatest task to which the apostles were called in the world.

Secondly, "You are the light of the world." This statement is especially relevant in light of what Christ had just told them about persecution. He assures them that they will suffer greatly and encourages them to be willing to endure. Why? Because they are called to the greatest works to which God has ever summoned anyone. Regardless of what people say or how they revile, God will undoubtedly reward them. "You are the salt of the earth, and the light of the world. If you were to shrink back out of fear of suffering, what would become of everything? Indeed, the consideration of one's role in the world is a powerful argument to carry one through any difficulty, encouraging them to persevere. It is akin to a general who approaches some officers in the army and informs them that the battle is intensifying, urging them to hold their ground for the welfare of the entire army, even the welfare of the entire kingdom depends on them. Such words would instill courage in anyone, as they recognize the great responsibilities resting upon their shoulders. Now, says Christ, even if you face persecution, continue in your ways, for you are the salt of the earth, you are the light of the world. Therefore, press on. You are the salt of the earth. I must admit that nearly all interpreters understand these words as applying only to the disciples, specifically the apostles who were sent to preach to others. However, not everyone holds that view. One learned interpreter states that he sees no sufficient reason to restrict these words solely to the apostles, providing two reasons for this broader interpretation.

First, all the preceding words apply generally to all Christians: the poor in spirit, those who mourn, the meek, those who hunger and thirst for right-eousness, the merciful, the pure in heart, the peacemakers, and those who are persecuted and reviled. These qualities pertain not only to the apostles but to all Christians. Why, then, should this statement be an exception?

Secondly, the subsequent verse, verse 16, applies to Christians, as evident from Philippians 2:15: "That ye may be blameless and harmless, the sons of God, without rebuke, in the midst of a crooked and perverse nation, among whom ye shine as lights in the world." You are the ones who are the lights, shining in the world.

Thirdly, a further reason can be found in the latter part of verse 13: "But if the salt have lost his savour, wherewith shall it be salted? It is thenceforth good for nothing, but to be cast out, and to be trodden underfoot of men." Christ is clearly speaking to the multitude. Luke 14:25-34 provides a comparison. "And there went great multitudes with him, and he turned and said unto them: Salt is good, but if the salt have lost his savour, wherewith shall it be seasoned?" There-fore, according to this learned interpreter, both the preceding and following statements apply to Christians. "You are then the salt of the earth."

First, all Christians who possess the truth of the Gospel and demonstrate it through their lives and conduct, they are the salt of the earth. In an elevated sense, those who proclaim the truths of the Gospel to the world, they are the salt of the earth. What does this mean? It is a straightforward metaphor employed by Christ, as people in that region frequently used similes. There is profound significance in God's intention behind this expression. Firstly, in Scripture, salt is associated with wisdom. Colossians 4:6 states, "Let your speech always be with grace, seasoned with salt, that ye may know how ye ought to answer every man." When you speak, ensure that your words are always filled with wisdom. In Mark 9:50, Jesus declares, "Salt is good, but if the salt have lost his savour, wherewith will ye season it? Have salt in yourselves, and have peace one with another." Conduct yourselves wisely in all matters. This meaning was commonly understood in those times. Salt was almost universally regarded as a symbol of understanding and wisdom. It was said that the Greeks were the salt of the nations because Greece possessed almost all forms of knowledge, and that was considered the salt of the nations. They would frequently use salt to represent the works of human understanding. I have read that in Italy, if someone were to throw salt at another person, it would be considered a disgrace and mockery, as if to imply that the recipient lacked wit. The Latin language also reflects this notion, as they say, "One who is foolish lacks salt." Scripture uses the term "unsavory" to describe something tasteless or foolish due to a lack of salt. For example, in Job 1:22, it states, "In all this Job sinned not, nor charged God foolishly." Furthermore, in Job 6:6, it poses the question, "Can that which is unsavory be eaten without salt? Or is there any taste in the white of an egg?" Thus, both Scripture and common usage in former times associated salt with understanding and wisdom. Now, when Christ says, "You are the salt of the earth," He means that, first and foremost, they are the ones proclaiming the Gospel, the ministers who bring wisdom to the world. They are tasked with declaring the message that will make people wise unto salvation. Without the Gospel, nothing in the world can make people truly wise, for without knowing Christ and the Gospel, their foolish hearts remain in darkness. However, through your ministry, you are to reveal to them God's divine will concerning their eternal state, enabling them to attain wisdom for eternity. You are the salt of the earth, for the world continues in its foolish ways until the Gospel reaches them. The majority of people, without the preaching of the Word, what goals do they set for themselves in life? And even if they do set goals, they are not the right ones. They are far from seeking to enjoy God in His Son Jesus Christ, and they are far from employing the correct means to attain this end. The world is driven by passion, following the dictates of their corrupt desires. Thus, they lack the wisdom to conduct themselves for the purpose of eternity. However, you are the salt of the earth, who will cause people to reflect upon their lives and consider why they were born and what their purpose in this world is. They will come to recognize their ultimate goal and begin to ponder and weigh things. When your teachings begin to penetrate their hearts, they will acquire wisdom where there was once only folly. Consequently, when people interact with the saints, they will learn wisdom, engage in meaningful discussions, and have their hearts seasoned with wisdom. All the wisdom of human learning in the world cannot make people wise unto salvation. The principles of philosophy may impart wisdom, but Scripture tells us that the world, through its wisdom, does not know God. That is the first aspect: the Gospel brings wisdom wherever it is proclaimed, teaching people to be truly wise for their salvation.

Secondly, salt adds savour to things. This is the second aspect to consider about salt. Salt has the property of enhancing the taste of food and removing any unpleasant moisture that diminishes its flavour. Salt imparts savour to almost everything we consume. It's as if Jesus is saying, "Naturally, people's hearts lack savour. Despite having remarkable abilities, their speech and actions are unsavoury. Imagine encountering people who have never heard the Gospel preached; you will find their spirits unsavoury, knowing little of God. A godly person cannot bear to spend much time among them. The unsavouriness of their hearts makes all their religious practices unsavoury. Whatever duties they perform for God, there is nothing pleasant in them. It's like unsavoury food to you. For all those living without the Gospel, without its transformative power in their hearts, all their religious acts are as unappetising to God as unsavoury food is to you. Now, says Christ, you will go and preach the Gospel to make their hearts savoury. Then their acts of worship will be pleasing to God, and their presence will be delightful to the saints. Previously, a person without the Gospel prevailing in their heart could not appreciate the company of the saints. But when the Gospel reaches them, they can appreciate their conversations, pray sincerely, and perform other duties with genuine devotion. (Matthew 16:23: "But he turned, and said unto Peter, Get thee behind me, Satan: thou art an offence unto me: for thou savourest not the things that be of God, but those that be of men.") When we present the most excellent and glorious truths of God in the Gospel, they fail to appreciate them because their hearts lack savour. Hearts devoid of the Gospel's influence are preoccupied with worldly matters. (Romans 8:5: "For they that are after the flesh do mind the things of the flesh.") However, when the ministry of the Gospel reaches them, they will savour things differently than ever before.

Thirdly, "You are the salt of the earth." Salt preserves and prevents putrefaction. This is why Numbers 18:19 mentions "a covenant of salt" that lasts forever. It signifies a covenant that retains its potency, virtue, and strength over time. Without salt, meat or fish putrefies, losing its original nourishment and deteriorating until it becomes entirely devoid of any value in nourishing the body. Likewise, when we make covenants with God, they may initially appear vigorous and strong, but after a few days, they lose their power. They resemble flesh or fish that, with time, loses its palatability and becomes less suitable for nourishment. However, adding salt can restore their edibility. Similarly, our covenants, though initially robust and vigorous, lose their effectiveness over time. Oh, they were not covenants of salt! I fear that the covenants we have made, both private and public, lack the enduring quality of salt. Yet, when the Lord makes covenants of salt, He remembers them, and their strength and vigour remain unchanged even a thousand years later. Many people only utilize their souls to preserve their bodies from putrefaction. "You are the salt of the earth," means that while the rest of the world descends into putrefaction due to the evil in their hearts, worsening and perishing eternally (1 John 1:5: "This then is the message which we have heard of him, and declare unto you, that God is light, and in him is no darkness at all."), the preaching of the Gospel serves as a preservative. It prevents the hearts of men and women in the world, devoid of the Gospel's doctrine, from becoming putrid, rotting masses. These hearts would undoubtedly perish. The entire world is in this condition. However, when the Gospel reaches them, it preserves their hearts from putrefaction, preventing them from rotting away. It is called the "wholesome word" because it maintains the spiritual health of their hearts. "You are the salt of the earth" means that you preserve them from putrefaction, ensuring that your lives are not corrupt but instead sweet and savoury for the Lord. When you combine these three aspects, you can understand the significance of the rule that every sacrifice offered to God must be seasoned with salt (Leviticus 2:13: "And every oblation of thy meat offering shalt thou season with salt; neither shalt thou suffer the salt of the covenant of thy God to be lacking from thy meat offering: with all thine offerings thou shalt offer salt."). You may think this expression is insignificant, but it repeatedly demonstrates the necessity of salt in every sacrifice. No matter the type of offering—whether it's a grain offering, an oil offering, or an offering of flour—salt must be present. (Mark 9:50: "Salt is good: but if the salt have lost his saltness, wherewith will ye season it? Have salt in yourselves, and have peace one with another.") The meaning is that whatever sacrifice you offer to God, including yourself (Romans 12:1: "I beseech you therefore, brethren, by the mercies of God, that ye present your bodies a living sacrifice, holy, acceptable unto God, which is your reasonable service."), it must contain salt. Your spiritual life must possess a savoury spirit that is pleasing to God, one that appreciates godly things. It must be free from corruption and putrefaction. Only then will your offering be acceptable to God. Otherwise, your sacrifice will be offered to His justice, and you will be salted with the fire that cannot be quenched. Thus, you can grasp the meaning of Christ's words: "You are the salt of the earth." The preaching of the Gospel initially causes great discomfort in corrupt hearts until their vices are subdued, until the Gospel conquers their corruptions. Compare the last few verses of Mark 9 with any passage from the Old Testament, and you will find that the expression of God's wrath against sinners is more severe in Mark than in any other Old Testament text. The curse of everlasting fire and unquenchable worm is unparalleled (Mark 9:48: "Where their worm dieth not, and the fire is not quenched."). Other texts proclaim, "For this cause cometh the wrath of God upon the children of disobedience" and "You are the children of wrath." The wrath of God is directed against all unrighteousness. If a person were to deliver only one sermon in their lifetime to make sin abhorrent, it would be more fitting to choose a passage from the Gospel than from the Law. The Gospel reveals the true nature of people outside of Jesus Christ, what price was paid for their souls, and emphasizes the necessity of mortifying our lusts. The Gospel possesses a power that surpasses the law in effecting mortification. For instance, in this sermon, Jesus teaches that if a person looks at another with lust, they have already committed adultery in their heart. The ministry of the Gospel has such authority that it prevails over all these sins. Hence, it is called the salt of the earth. Salt is also used medicinally and as a remedy (2 Kings 2:21-22: "And he went forth unto the spring of the waters, and cast the salt in there, and said, Thus saith the LORD, I have healed these waters; there shall not be from thence any more death or barren land. So the waters were healed unto this day, according to the saying of Elisha which he spake."). Salt is a great gift of nature and is referred to as the very balm of nature.

The first use of the Ministry of the Gospel is to demonstrate its great excellence. It is the salt of the world, the very essence of nature's healing power. Therefore, we should value it, for without it, the world would be distasteful to God. Just go to those streets where the Gospel is not preached, and witness the rotten putrefaction that prevails there. Even if the Gospel does not convert their souls, it still removes some gross corruptions and civilizes them. Give me any place where the Ministry of salt is present, and you will find that, for the most part, there is less wickedness. Those who oppose it grow even worse against it. Oh, cherish the Gospel! I recall the 60th chapter of Isaiah, where the Holy Spirit speaks of the saints who flock to the preaching of the Word. They are likened to doves, as doves are drawn to a salt stone. They have a great affection for salt stones. The salt stone of the Gospel entices not birds of prey like rooks or ravens, but those with dove-like spirits. They find that the Gospel does them good. It is the Gospel that gives savour to all things. They can say, "Before I heard the Gospel, my heart lacked savour. But since the Gospel reached me, I have never tasted anything so delightful." Some may consider it unlucky if salt spills, but truly, the overthrow of the Gospel is a sign of great calamity. It spells disaster for the Christian world, just as the absence of salt brings harm. Not everyone can bear the Gospel; they prefer only sweet things, even if it leads to their decay. Isn't it better to be preserved with brine than to rot with sugar? The Ministers of the Gospel must apply salt. Sometimes it needs to be rubbed in. Some people's hearts derive no benefit from the Word because they are unsavoury and refuse to take it in. The Ministers must rub it in through application. Merely presenting the Word to the people accomplishes little; it must be rubbed in through application.

Secondly, this serves as an exhortation. If the Ministry of the Gospel is of such excellent use, then be cautious not to reject it. When the preaching of the

Gospel first arrives in a place and is received, it brings abundant goodness to the soul. But if people allow their lusts to prevail, it does little good for them. The Lord permits them to perish eternally. This holds the power to restore those who stink, but not always. Take heed, young ones, for you are not yet so corrupted that the application of salt cannot heal your souls. When poor people in the countryside go to the market, they always bring home salt for the benefit of their families. Do the same. The Doctrine is the salt; bring it home. There are many unsavoury words in your families. When you hear the Word, take some salt home and apply it. Husband to wife, wife to husband, parents to children, and let the servants and everyone say to one another, "Were not these doctrines preached today against the evil ways in which we walk? Surely they will restrain us from our wicked courses." So, if you commit a sin, apply salt to your heart immediately, and it will prevent it from staining. If God has applied it once, we must apply it again and again. We must apply it every day, or else our hearts will become unsavoury. Remember that when salting meat, if there is a part that is beginning to corrupt more than the rest, you rub more salt there than in other places. Likewise, observe your precious corruptions and think, "I have some lusts and sins that are more dangerous than others. There is a lust that is likely to overcome me. I will apply the Word there. I will find Scripture that speaks most against that sin and lay it to my heart." For example, suppose someone has an inordinate affection that seeks to satisfy the lust of the flesh. There is a place in their heart that is prone to putrefaction. Apply some salt there. Let me give you a few grains of salt to apply to that spot. Job 31:1-2 says, "I made a covenant with mine eyes; why then should I think upon a maid? For what portion of God is there from above? and what inheritance of the Almighty from on high?" He means that if he does not make a covenant with his eyes and allows them to wander for the satisfaction of his flesh, he will have no portion in the Almighty. Whenever he yields to his eyes' desires for the satisfaction of the flesh, he will venture to apply salt to that place. Another Scripture for the sin of uncleanness is Proverbs 22:14, which says, "The mouth of a strange woman is a deep pit: he that is abhorred of the Lord shall fall therein." The one abhorred by God will fall into the deep pit. There are many Scriptures in the New Testament for this as well. For instance, 2 Peter 2:9 says, "The Lord knoweth how to deliver the godly out of temptations, and to reserve the unjust unto the day of judgment to be

punished: but chiefly them that walk after the flesh in the lust of uncleanness."
Apply this salt to your hearts, you who walk in the lust of uncleanness, and it will
help remove impurity from that place. To those who allow themselves to indulge
in the lust of the flesh, Romans 8:13 says, "For if ye live after the flesh, ye shall
die: but if ye through the Spirit do mortify the deeds of the body, ye shall live."
In other words, anyone who gives themselves the liberty to satisfy the lusts of the
flesh and makes it their chief contentment will perish forever. These Scriptures
contain powerful teachings to eradicate the corruptions of the heart. When you
attend the Ministry of the Gospel, you will eventually discover that the Word
uncovers your particular sins. Go home and rub them with salt. Labour to kill
and mortify your sins. The Ministers of God cannot do it as effectively as you
can. Christ speaks here in similes so that you will remember. You have occasion
to remember when salt is on your table and when you salt your meat. If I don't
salt my meat, it will putrefy and become unsavoury. Likewise, my heart cannot
appreciate or savour anything without the Gospel. Without salt, I cannot offer
any sacrifices that are pleasing to God. The Doctrine of the Ministry of the Word
acts as salt for the benefit of our spiritual nature.

# SERMON XXXIX

## How believers are described as unsavoury

"You are the salt of the earth, but if the salt loses its savour, wherewith shall it be salted? It is thenceforth good for nothing but to be cast out and to be trodden underfoot of men. You are the light of the world." - Matthew 5:13

We read in Scripture that sometimes salt makes the land barren where it is sown, as in Judges 9:45. "And Abimelech fought against the city all that day; and he took the city, and slew the people that were therein, and beat down the city, and sowed it with salt." Excessive salt on the land can render it barren. The same can happen to many of our hearts. We receive a constant sowing of the salt of the word, yet there is no fruit. Instead, our hearts grow barren. There seems to be a curse on the ground that has salt sown on it. Likewise, there is a curse on the hearts of those who live under the ministry of the word, who hear these blessed truths preached to them and yet remain unfruitful.

Now, let's consider the phrase, "If salt loses its savour, wherewith shall it be seasoned?" This can apply either to believers who carry the truths of the

Gospel in their lives to some extent (Luke 14:25, compared with verse 35), or to ministers if they have lost their savour and need to be salted again.

Speaking briefly about believers who have knowledge of many Gospel truths and have expressed and embraced them for a time, they have been of great use in towns, parishes, and families where they have lived. They have served as salt, and many have benefited from their knowledge and the excellent gifts they possess through the Gospel. However, some of them lose their savour. True grace in the heart cannot be lost, but the abundance of truths and gifts acquired through the Gospel can be lost. Many believers who were once fervent and zealous, bearing fruit and benefiting all who encountered them, have now lost their savour. There is no longer the same vitality and liveliness in their duties and performances. They have become flat and cold, lacking passion in their duties and merely going through the motions. Little good can be gained or expected from them. When you converse with them, you find that many have become unsavoury. They have mingled base lusts with their profession and zeal, losing their power. They have become earthly, with their corruptions prevailing over the salt. Though they seemed restrained for a while, their corruptions gained power over the truths they once understood and publicly professed. Consequently, they have lost all their vigour and become formal in their duties. Their savour is gone. This describes those who have made a profession of faith but have lost their savour. People may remark, "How they have changed! They were..." If salt loses its savour, how can it be seasoned? How can this condition be restored? It is not impossible, but it is rare for a former zealous believer who has now become flat and cold to be restored. It is a rare occurrence. Hebrews 6:4 states, "For it is impossible for those who were once enlightened, and have tasted of the heavenly gift, and were made partakers of the Holy Ghost, etc." This passage does not explicitly mention the sin against the Holy Ghost, but it presents a more general warning, leaving individuals in dreadful fear, cautioning them not to fall away. Let such individuals be careful not to nurture any corruption. Rarely do we see anyone restored or returning after falling away from their profession of faith. Why is this so? When they had experienced truth and witnessed its effect on others' hearts, it did not have a similar impact on their own hearts. They understood these truths years ago, but for many, they only awaken their consciences, stir their hearts, humble their spirits, and reveal the wretchedness of their natural state. However, when a formal believer who has fallen away from the truth hears such things, they have gained power over their conscience. There is little efficacy in their lives to overcome it. How can they be seasoned when the salt has lost its savour? As a result, they are considered unuseful members in the Church or society. They are almost good for nothing. A believer who is not fruitful is of no value. When salt loses its savour, it becomes entirely useless, unlike other things such as broken money that can still serve a purpose for a goldsmith. Salt, on the other hand, is utterly worthless. The same applies to believers who apostatize from the truth. There is no more miserable creature than an apostatizing Christian. They are worthless, as neither God nor man will trust them anymore. They had been zealous in their faith but have now fallen away. God no longer trusts them, and people do not trust them due to their unfaithfulness to God. Those who are not useful are cast out from people's hearts. There was a time when you rejoiced to be in their company, considering it a privilege. But now, you regard them with contempt. They wander as poor wretches forsaken by God and man because they are of no use to the world, nor are they esteemed or valued within the Church. On the contrary, they do harm wherever they go. God often takes away their gifts. When they professed their faith, they possessed gifts from God, but now they cannot pray as they once did. A secret curse accompanies everything they do. During their youth and when they initially made their profession, they received gifts from God for the edification of others. But now, God has withdrawn His presence, taking away their gifts. They have turned away from God, experiencing a tremendous change. They roam as burdens to towns and families, being trodden underfoot. Few do more harm than those who were once fervent in their profession of faith but later fell away. They view the name of God as contemptible, and God regards them in the same light. They become stumbling blocks and discouragements to young believers who are starting their journey with God. When God begins to work in their hearts, the apostates harden the hearts of the wicked. Once considered great in the Church of God, they have now fallen away, leading others to think that religion is merely a fancy or a passing whim. They become discouragements to weak individuals, causing them to wonder, "What will become of me if even those who were once eminent in their profession fall away?" Oh Lord, how can I persevere? You are discouragements to others who previously made a profession but have grown complacent, vexed to see young believers showing more fervour than themselves. The truth is, they should examine their hearts and ask, "Have I lost my savour? Have I become more sluggish? Is it not just for God to take away my esteem and reputation within the Church?" They should be willing to cry out, having apostatized from the truth, just as one did, "Tread upon me, tread upon me, unsavoury salt. Let everyone tread upon me. It is just for all of God's servants to tread upon me." I beseech you to consider this if you are beginning to make a profession of faith and have experienced the work of God in your hearts, especially those of you who are young and still have a taste for savoury things. When temptation comes, consider the dreadful condition of those who apostatize from their profession of faith. While you are young, you may believe that you will hold fast to these truths of God that you currently embrace. However, you do not know your own hearts.

I now address the issue concerning Ministers. According to most interpreters, they are considered the valuable individuals in society, often referred to as the "salt of the earth." However, when Ministers lose their zeal and effectiveness, they become unsavory. Initially, their preaching is powerful and zealous, but as they face worldly temptations and gain comfortable positions, their commitment weakens. Their sermons become flat, lacking the impact they once had. They avoid addressing matters that challenge people's hearts and consciences and instead prefer preaching easy, general truths that don't trouble anyone. Their teaching loses its saltiness, adopting a flattering and superficial tone. They even mix their own inventions with the truth and indulge in superstitious practices. To someone with genuine grace in their heart, this kind of preaching is unpalatable.

It is worth noting that many Ministers who were initially reluctant to preach become fervent and fierce when speaking against those who preach the true Word of God. Such preachers are what Christ refers to as unsavory. When Ministers become lazy and sluggish in their ministry, they have lost their savour. It is nearly impossible for a Minister who has deviated from the truth of the Gospel to be restored. While I won't say it's impossible, it is a rarity. Firstly, their pride prevents them from being taught by others or acknowledging their errors, even when their consciences convict them. Secondly, their corrupted natural abilities are employed to resist the truths of God that could benefit them. It is like a person with a sore on their body; the body's nourishment goes toward feeding the sore. Similarly, their wickedness prevails, and there is a curse from God upon them. The recovery of such Ministers is highly unlikely. How few Ministers who were once wicked and malign return, and only when compelled to do so.

Therefore, we should not be offended when we witness learned individuals behaving in certain ways. Instead, we should learn from it and understand the dreadful consequences of sinning against the light. If I were speaking to an audience full of young Ministers who are currently full of vigor and enthusiasm, I would caution them to take these words to heart. Those who are currently perceived as savory should strive to maintain that savour until the end. Even as their natural abilities may decline, they should display a light and fervor of spirit, demonstrating love for God and providing wholesome counsel based on their experiences. Blessed are those who possess these qualities. However, it is most miserable for those who were once fervent in their youth as Ministers to become unsavory and remain unrecoverable. They are henceforth good for nothing.

What should be done with them? If they are placed in congregations of good people, it will only dampen their spirits and grieve their hearts. If they are sent to congregations where the people are wicked, it will only worsen them. Moreover, there is usually a curse from God upon their abilities and gifts, and they are seldom trusted due to their unfaithfulness to God. I recall a Papist commentator on Malachi 2:3, who remarked that such Ministers are good for nothing and shall be cast out and trodden underfoot. "Behold, I will corrupt your seed and spread dung upon your faces, even the dung of your solemn feasts, and one shall take you away with it." What will become of those who are unsavory? Some may pity them, but it is the just judgment of God that they shall be trodden underfoot. Even those who once flocked to their sermons now find no use for them in the Church. The more discerning among them reject them, casting them out of their hearts. There may be much evil in people's hearts when they withdraw from those who preach savory truths, but in general, all true believers reject them and hold them in low regard. They may preach good things, but their words are disregarded. They are utterly useless. The Lord desires that they be cast out and trodden underfoot, despised. There is no group more deserving of contempt than Ministers whose ministry has turned from savouriness to unsavoriness. This is the just judgment of God upon them. Scripture provides evidence of this. For example, in 1 Samuel 2:30, the Lord God of Israel says, "I said indeed that thy house and the house of thy father should walk before me forever. But now the Lord saith, Be it far from me; for them that honour me, I will honour, and they that despise me shall be lightly esteemed." These Ministers valued their own status more than God's honour. No group sets their own honour above that of Ministers. God declares that they will be lightly esteemed, trodden underfoot, and cast out. Another passage is found in Hosea 4:6, "My people are destroyed for lack of knowledge: because thou hast rejected knowledge, I will also reject thee, that thou shalt be no Priest to me, seeing thou hast forgotten the Law of thy God, I will also forget thy Children." Trimelius noted that there is one extra letter in the word "thee," emphasizing the strength of God's rejection. It signifies that this is not an ordinary rejection, but a powerful one. The fulfillment of this Scripture is evident in the present circumstances. Once triumphant, the Prelatical Priests are now scattered and cast down. In Revelation 3:21, it is written, "To him that overcometh will I grant to sit with me in my throne, even as I also overcame, and am set down with my Father in his throne: He that hath an ear, let him hear what the Spirit saith unto the Churches."

Let us acknowledge the righteousness of the Lord and recognize His hand in these events. Let us also appreciate the goodness of the Lord, who has stirred up our leaders to remove unsavory Ministers. It is a clear sign of the unsavoriness of people's spirits that they could still tolerate such ministry and consider it superior to the current ministry. This disposition reminds me of a scripture in 2 Corinthians 11:20: "For ye suffer, if a man bring you into bondage, if a man devour you, if a man take of you, if a man exalt himself, if a man smite you on the face." People endured hardships and exploitation under those Ministers, even facing the confiscation of their possessions. Yet, despite all they suffered, their hearts still clung to those Ministers rather than those who preached the Gospel truths for the salvation of their souls. I am astonished by this disposition of people's spirits.

Indeed, many today would rather tolerate anything from unsavory Ministers than be offended by faithful Ministers of God. This is indicative of unsavory spirits.

Lastly, if I were to address young Ministers, I would provide them with a guiding principle to maintain their honour. The best way to uphold their honour in the manner that God has appointed for them is through the savoriness of their Ministry and their way of life. Even if wicked individuals in taverns mock and slander them, when they find themselves on their deathbeds, their conscience will compel them to speak differently of the Ministers. Therefore, Ministers should not fret or be distressed when they lose their reputation. Instead, they should consider whether they have lost some of their savor and strive to be savory. If they succeed in being savory, they need not strive for honour, for God will honour them.

Augustine speaks about this excellently. A person cannot be trampled upon unless they are inferior or subordinate to someone else. However, if their heart is fixed on heaven, even though they may suffer physically, they are not subordinate to anyone. This principle can be applied in the following manner: a person should not willingly submit themselves to the desires of others. In their teaching, they should surpass the satisfaction of fleshly desires, and their doctrine should be founded on the Gospel. Their life should be characterized by heavenly and holy conduct. By doing so, they cannot be trampled upon, and their reputation will surpass all attempts to tarnish it. The very memory of those who have been esteemed in the past, even in recent times, is remarkably savory. They lived above the approval of others, and therefore, they could not be trampled upon. God has ensured that their names endure from generation to generation. Therefore, Ministers and Christians alike should strive to maintain their savor if they wish to avoid being trampled underfoot by others.

# SERMON XL

## Being the Light of the World is a Great Honour

"You are the light of the world. A city that is set on a hill cannot be hidden." - Matthew 5:14

To be the salt of the earth and the light of the world is a tremendous honour that God bestows upon His Ministers, as well as His Saints to a lesser extent. After foretelling the sufferings His Disciples would encounter, Christ reassures them about the significant role the Lord has assigned to them. He conveys the message that despite reviling, persecution, and the spreading of false accusations, they should persist in their mission. "You are the salt of the earth, you are the light of the world." Only those who possess the qualities mentioned earlier—being poor in spirit, mourners, meek, hungering and thirsting for righteousness, merciful, pure in heart, peacemakers, and persecuted—truly deserve this honour. In the previous verse, which we concluded last, we explored how the Ministers of the Gospel serve as the salt of the earth. Those who share the likeness of salt in their Ministry must also resemble light in their Ministry. The more provocative a Minister's words are to a congregation, the more convincingly they should speak. If they are salt, they must also be light. "You are the light of the world." This statement is almost as exalted as any proclamation about mankind could be. For a few humble fishermen to be called the salt of the earth, responsible for preserving it from decay, and the light of the world—what greater honour could be bestowed upon men? Luther remarked on this passage, describing it as an exceptional calling and a greater honour than any other, to be the salt of the earth and the light of the world. Light is an extraordinary phenomenon, and our understanding of it remains limited. This exposes human ignorance, demonstrating that man has little reason for pride. Two of the most vital aspects of life—light and life itself—are subjects on which we struggle to articulate adequately. The most excellent things are often referred to as light: God Himself is light according to Scripture, and the highest expression of His glory is light. Christ is light; He is called the light of the world. The angels are light, the Word is called light, grace is light, the saints are called light, comfort is light, God's favour is the light of His countenance, prosperity is light, deliverance from evil is light, and even heaven itself is light. However, when Christ speaks of being the light of the world, it specifically refers to the Gospel and its Ministry, and then extends to the saints according to their kind and degree. The saints, too, serve as the light of the world, but the Gospel and its Ministers are explicitly identified as the light of the world. It is as if Christ is saying, "As you go forth into the world, you will become bearers of the glorious Gospel, and this Gospel that you are taking to the world is the light that will illuminate it. You are like heavenly luminaries that scatter light upon the Earth." Therefore, we can infer the following: The entire world remains in darkness until the Gospel reaches them. Kingdoms, countries, towns, families, individuals, souls—all dwell in darkness until the Gospel arrives.

Firstly, the world dwells in darkness. Scripture portrays man's natural state as darkness. Before the Gospel is preached in any location, the inhabitants do not know God. "For after that, in the wisdom of God, the world through wisdom did not know God, it pleased God by the foolishness of preaching to save them that believe" (1 Corinthians 1:21). Even the most intellectually gifted individuals remain in darkness until the Gospel reaches them. It is astonishing to observe the meager and misguided thoughts people naturally possess about God—the infinite, glorious, supreme being. Foolish hearts are shrouded in darkness; they are ignorant of the path of light, the standards of light. Prior to the arrival of the

Gospel, people are unaware of the proper way to worship God. They engage in vain worship, worshipping God according to their own imaginations and inventions. They are ignorant of the purpose of human life, unaware of the ultimate happiness and glory that humanity can attain. This knowledge is only accessible through the Gospel. In their natural state, people fail to comprehend their own condition; they possess limited knowledge of sin, original corruption, and the separation between God and mankind. They remain oblivious to God's ordained path for reconciling the world to Himself—a profound mystery that has eluded the rulers of this world, only to be revealed through the light of the Gospel. They know nothing of the great work of Mediation or the Covenant of grace—the second Covenant God established with humanity. They lack understanding of the extraordinary nature of grace. Consequently, individuals in their natural state are immersed in darkness, disconnected from a profound understanding of God. They allow the great and glorious aspects of God to pass them by without grasping hold of them, wandering aimlessly without direction. "But he that hateth his brother is in darkness and walketh in darkness and knoweth not whither he goeth, because that darkness hath blinded his eyes" (1 John 2:11). They tread the path of darkness, engaging in the works of darkness, stumbling at every turn, stumbling even at the ways of God. Every scandal causes them to despise God's ways, and every reproach reinforces their negative opinion of God's ways. Individuals in their natural state find themselves in a wretched condition, deluding themselves with false comfort and a false sense of light. They possess no more understanding than a child born and raised in the depths of a dungeon. Thus, wicked individuals are naturally akin to prisoners in a dark cell, presuming they possess spiritual sight while remaining blinded by their carnal eyes. Furthermore, their path is fraught with danger; they remain uncertain about what awaits them with each step, fearing they may plunge into perdition.

Furthermore, they are under the dominion of darkness due to the darkness within their own spirits. Consequently, the spirit of darkness and their own spirits align and harmonize. It is questionable whether the devil would tempt anyone in any other way than by presenting external temptations if it weren't for the sinfulness of our hearts. When he tempted Adam in his state of innocence, we only read of him using serpents and similar suggestions. When he tempted our Saviour Christ, he did not attempt to tempt Him spiritually but resorted to external temptations, such as taking Him to the top of a mountain. Therefore, in the absence of sin, the devil, or the spirit of darkness, cannot align with the spirit except by presenting evil through external objects. However, those who dwell in darkness and have their spirits immersed in darkness can align with the Prince of darkness. The devil not only presents outward temptations to wicked individuals but seems to merge with their spirits. This is the misery of natural men.

Lastly, the entire world is so enveloped in darkness that if left to themselves, they will be consigned to everlasting darkness. Many may believe that they are not in darkness, but as Christ said, "If ye were blind, ye should have no sin: but now ye say, We see; therefore your sin remaineth" (John 9:41). The more convinced people are that they are in the light, the more glaring their sin becomes. No one can accurately judge their natural state because they are in darkness, let alone judge spiritual matters. Let us not rely on the judgment of men based on their great intellectual abilities when it comes to spiritual matters because their foolish minds are clouded in darkness. Just as dark vaults are home to toads and repugnant creatures, the same can be said of dark hearts. "Have respect unto the covenant: for the dark places of the earth are full of the habitations of cruelty" (Psalm 74:20). It is no wonder that people are so fierce and obstinate, for their hearts are dark abodes of cruelty. Before the Gospel reaches them, people are in darkness, and where the light of the Gospel does not shine, the devil, the prince of darkness, rules both outwardly and inwardly. In some places where the Gospel is unknown, people worship the devil in visible forms. This natural darkness is in direct opposition to God, for God is light. It is detestable to God, and the darkness in the hearts of men is not merely the absence of light, but an active opposition and hatred towards light. All the darkness in the world cannot overcome the illumination of even the smallest candle. The light of the tiniest candle triumphs over all the darkness in the world. However, the darkness within man's heart not only lacks light but actively opposes and despises it. Their darkness is the shadow of death, a hellish darkness that not only leads to hellish darkness but is itself the beginning of hell within their hearts. It is no wonder that men rely on vain hopes and supports for their eternal salvation. "You are the light of the world." Therefore, the entire world dwells in darkness.

This is the natural state of man—darkness. The Gospel brings light into the world. The Gospel, in its Ministry, is the light. Firstly, Christ Himself is the preeminent light. Just as the scattered light in the universe eventually converges into the sun, all light and illumination come from Christ. Thus, Christ disperses light throughout the world through the Ministry of the Gospel. "He was not that light, but was sent to bear witness of that light" (John 1:8, 9). Every person who enters the world and possesses any light receives it from Christ, who is the true light. John, although a significant light in his own right, was sent to bear witness to the true light. This is the task of the Ministry—to bear witness to that light. However, Christ Himself is the true light. "Then spake Jesus again unto them, saying, I am the light of the world: he that followeth me shall not walk in darkness, but shall have the light of life" (John 8:12). Christ is the light; He is the Gospel. The Gospel is simply the doctrine of Christ, the good news concerning Jesus Christ that has entered the world. That is the Gospel, the light that brings illumination to the world. First and foremost, light is a most beautiful thing. "Truly the light is sweet, and a pleasant thing it is for the eyes to behold the sun" (Ecclesiastes 11:7). There is no object more worthy of love, more delightful than beholding the glory of God shining through the Gospel. There are sweet things to behold, and it is pleasant to behold that light. When a poor sinner who has lived in darkness all his days finally has his eyes opened to see the light of the Gospel, he stands in awe and wonder, amazed at the things he sees. The conversion of a sinner is akin to bringing a poor man out of a dungeon where he was born and suddenly exposing him to the glorious creatures of the world—the earth, the stars, and mankind. He cannot help but stand amazed. The same is true of the conversion of a sinner. Examine whether you have found the light to be lovely and captivating, whether your heart has been filled with wonder upon seeing things you have never seen before. Just as light reveals, the nature of light is to uncover things. "But all things that are reproved are made manifest by the light: for whatsoever doth make manifest is light" (Ephesians 5:13). The Gospel, which you bring into the world, reveals great things. What does it make manifest? It reveals God Himself. Those who lived without knowledge of God now see Him as God. They behold God in the face of Jesus Christ. The light of the glory of God truly appears to them. The Apostle Paul, speaking of the light that shines in the hearts of those whom God has worked upon, says, "For

God, who commanded the light to shine out of darkness, hath shined in our hearts, to give the light of the knowledge of the glory of God in the face of Jesus Christ" (2 Corinthians 4:6, 7). The light surpasses the eyes; it shines in the heart. It is transformative. It transforms those who were once darkness into light itself. "For ye were sometimes darkness, but now are ye light in the Lord" (Ephesians 5:8). The light of the Gospel is an increasing light, growing as the times and ages of the Gospel progress. It is not all revealed at once but gradually increases in the souls it reaches. It is an everlasting light, the very beginning of the light of glory. It is impossible to comprehend until it is seen. If one were to speak about light to blind men, expounding on its qualities, could they truly grasp the concept of light without ever having seen it? They cannot comprehend its excellence until they see it. Similarly, we can speak of the Gospel as light, but until you see it for yourself, you will never truly understand it or know its excellence. This light of the Gospel is not conveyed except through the Ministers of the Gospel. The Ministers are the light of the world. Thus, it is the duty of Ministers to shine in their doctrine and burn in their conduct. Through their teachings and way of life, they should display the light of the Gospel wherever they go. "He was a burning and a shining light" (John 5:35). If Ministers fulfill their role as they should, they will be shining and burning lights. They bring light through their doctrine and their lives. The purpose of the Ministry is to open people's eyes and turn them from darkness to light, from the power of Satan to God, that they may receive forgiveness of sins and an inheritance among those who are sanctified by faith in Christ. The end goal of the Ministry is to open people's eyes, to turn them from darkness to light. The Gospel ushers in the day of grace and salvation in its Ministry. As the preaching of the Gospel reaches a place, so does the day of grace and salvation. When God removes the light of the Ministry, the day of grace and salvation also departs. "He saith, I have heard thee in a time accepted, and in the day of salvation have I succoured thee: behold, now is the accepted time; behold, now is the day of salvation" (2 Corinthians 6:2). When God sends a faithful Minister to a place, He brings light to that place. Then the light of the Gospel shines, and the day of grace and salvation arrives. As long as God sustains the light of the Ministry of the Gospel, the day of grace and salvation persists. However, once that light is extinguished, the sun sets. "You are the light of the world." We possess this light in earthen vessels, but it is the lamp that shines with the light of the knowledge of God.

The message would be very rare if I had to address a gathering of Ministers. I would tell them the importance of being filled with light themselves, having knowledge of the Mystery of salvation. When they come to preach, they should come with the radiance of the Gospel, allowing it to shine upon them. They should come like Moses descending from the mount, his face aglow with light. Similarly, Ministers should come with their light shining, spreading its beams to the souls wherever they go. Some souls will be grateful for the light that enters their lives, and the Minister's duty is to share light with the people, presenting the whole counsel of God without holding anything back. John was a burning light, consuming himself to give light to others. Ministers should also devote themselves and expend their efforts to bring light to others. They should have compassion for those who dwell in darkness and guide them towards the light. Ministers should recognize the significant task they are sent to accomplish, which is to carry light to those who sit in darkness. In their Ministry, Ministers should ensure it is full of light. They should be cautious not to mix it with their own human inventions or dilute it with unnecessary elements. Some preachers tend to incorporate their own ideas, but the more human invention is mixed with preaching, the less light it gives. It is the simplicity and purity of the Gospel that illuminates the soul. Ministers should be mindful not to let their personal passions dictate their preaching.

Moreover, there is a special providence of God over faithful Ministers. If they remain faithful, they can expect God's special providence to protect their lives and guide their paths because they are light. In Revelation 1:16, it is said, "He had in his right hand seven stars, and out of his mouth went a sharp two-edged sword, and his countenance was as the sun shines in its strength." These stars, representing the Ministers, cannot be plucked out or fall because Christ holds them in His right hand. Whenever Christ desires light to shine in a place, He sends out a Minister to provide that light. Some Ministers may shine more brightly than others, while some may only offer a dim light. Those who had light in their youth but have succumbed to worldly desires have extinguished that light within themselves.

Ministers should rejoice in the knowledge acquired by the people. It is not fitting for Ministers to be vexed when the people gain knowledge. They should be like light that shines on refuse without defiling itself. Ministers should strive to do good to all, even to the worst of people, and adapt to their circumstances without becoming contaminated. If a Minister engages in conversation, it should be to illuminate others, but they must be cautious not to be tainted by such interactions.

Learn to value the Ministry of the Gospel because it is the light of the world, bringing the light of God to the people. Be grateful that the Gospel has come among you and that God, in His mercy, has shown favor to your generation. Though many seek to extinguish the light, God keeps His chosen Ministers in His right hand. As long as the light of the Gospel continues to shine, it signifies God's goodness towards His people. Be willing to sustain the charge of maintaining the light. Light is invaluable; one would rather give ten thousand pounds than be without it. In Chrysostom's time, the people cherished the light of the Gospel that he preached to them. They believed it was better for the sun to withdraw its beams than for Chrysostom's mouth to be silenced. John was a burning and shining light, precious in his ministry. Therefore, Herod should not have hesitated to spare John's life when he made an oath. We should esteem the light as a tremendous blessing. Consider if we lived in a place where the sun had never appeared during our lifetimes. If, at the appointed time, the sun were to rise in all its glory, we would be amazed. Yet, since we see the sun every day, we fail to appreciate it fully. Similarly, the Ministry is undervalued because it is ordinary and commonplace among us. However, if it were not so common, we would prize it more. We should rejoice in the light of the Gospel. If we truly valued it as we should, it would bring a profound change to our hearts. The enjoyment of the Gospel compensates for any affliction. Isaiah 30:20-21 affirms this: "And though the Lord give you the bread of adversity and the water of affliction, yet shall not thy teachers be removed into a corner any more, but thine eyes shall see thy teachers. And thine ears shall hear a word behind thee, saying, 'This is the way, walk ye in it,' when ye turn to the right hand and when ye turn to the left." Despite facing hardships, having teachers who convey the Ministry of the Gospel is a compensation. While the Lord may provide adversity, the presence of faithful teachers remains, guiding and instructing the people. Although affliction may come, it cannot compare to the reward of having access to the light of the Gospel.

Trouble may arise when Ministers are removed from a place without immediate replacement. This results in darkness unless the Lord provides a substitute.

# SERMON XLI

## The Relevance of the Ministry of the Gospel

"You are the light of the world. A city set on a hill cannot be hidden. Nor do men light a candle and put it under a bushel, but on a candlestick, and it gives light to all that are in the house." - Matthew 5:14, 15

Next, if the ministry of the Gospel is light, let us open our hearts to receive that light. In the morning, we open our windows to let in the light. Likewise, let us open our hearts to receive the light. 2 Samuel 23:4 says, "And he shall be as the light of the morning, when the sun rises, even a morning without clouds; as the tender grass springing out of the earth by clear shining after rain." Set aside our previous notions and embrace the light of truth. In Your light, we shall see light. Don't let the world obstruct this light from reaching our eyes. Let us never be content until we experience the glorious light of the Gospel shining on our hearts. Lord, You have said that Your Gospel is light. When will that light shine into my heart? Furthermore, walk in the light when you have it. In John 8:33, they answered Him, "We are Abraham's descendants and have never been in bondage to anyone. How can You say, 'You will be made free'?"

Let us all encourage one another to go to the house of the Lord and resolve to walk in the light of the Lord. Isaiah 2:5 says, "O house of Jacob, come and let us walk in the light of the Lord." Whenever you come to hear the ministry of the Gospel preached, resolve within yourself, "Lord, I come to receive light into my soul, and I am resolved to walk in that light which You will reveal to my soul. It is time to arise while the light of the Gospel shines upon us." Isaiah 60 begins with "Arise, shine; for your light has come! And the glory of the Lord is risen upon you." For behold, darkness shall cover the Earth, and gross darkness the people; but the Lord will arise over you, and His glory will be seen upon you. The Gentiles shall come to your light, and kings to the brightness of your rising. Now, this light is not given to us for mere amusement; it is given for work—for the work of our souls. Understand that the work we have in this world is of infinite consequence, concern, and value. Therefore, while we have the light, we must make use of it. It would be better a thousand times over if you had never been born than to lose the light and leave your work undone. Let us cherish our light, walk in it, and know that the work God has assigned us in this world is precise and must be done with exactness—especially the great work of making peace with God for eternity. In twilight, one may be able to perform some tasks without precision, but when a work requires exactness, we need abundant light to carry it out. Now, the work we have to do in relation to God and our eternal destinies is exacting; therefore, we need great light. So walk in the light. There are many dangers and byways that can lead us astray; therefore, walk in the light. Our time for our work is short—the time we have to prepare for eternity is brief, uncertain, and fleeting. Therefore, we must make use of the light.

Again, every step taken in darkness leads us astray. Every step you have taken on your way to heaven before the light of the Gospel reached you, you have bewildered yourself, gone astray, and deviated from the path. There will be no comfort for you on your sickbed like that of those who have walked in the light and made use of it to do their work. Therefore, those who are far from walking in the light and are opposed to it are rebuked. Although the light may be a pleasant thing, it is not good for sore eyes. Those guilty of adultery, those who love the works of darkness and the ways of sin, do not care for the light because it exposes and reveals both them and their wickedness. That is why they love darkness—the light scorches them. Just as some people find the rising sun scorching and hurl darts at it, cursing the sun, this light will scorch the consciences of many individuals. Those who are confused do not love the light. Likewise, feeble individuals prefer to keep the light away during their sickness. Thus, it is a sign of weakness when people cannot tolerate the light. The same goes for those who love to gratify the lust of the flesh or rather the deceitfulness of the flesh. They desire to continue in a secure way and would gladly have the light extinguished. It is dangerous for people to sin against the light. As stated in Job 10:22, "Before I go to the place from which I shall not return, to the land of darkness and the shadow of death, a land as dark as darkness itself, as the shadow of death, without any order, and where the light is as darkness." The light is as darkness to them. Many shut their eyes against the light, even though it dazzles them. The Lord causes His truths to dazzle their spirits, but they shut their eyes and turn away from it. That's how they shut their eyes against it. Job 24:13 says, "They are of those who rebel against the light; they do not know its ways nor abide in its paths." These are the people who rebel against the light. So that this Scripture may not be verified in many of you, take heed that your conscience is not forced to claim this Scripture as your own—saying, "This is the person, this is the woman who rebels against the light." The Lord has caused them to come and live in places where the light of the Gospel is gloriously manifested, yet they not only turn away from it, but the light follows them, and they flee from it. When you rebel against light, you rebel against God, for God is light. Rising against any light in your heart is rising against God. Furthermore, know that by rebelling against the light, you aggravate all your past sins. In the time of ignorance, God overlooked them. But now, if you do not repent, the axe is poised at the root of the tree. It makes your sin greater than that of the heathens. None of the heathens have such an aggravation of sin as you have because you live under the light of the Gospel. John 3 states, "And this is the condemnation, that the light has come into the world, and men loved darkness rather than light." This is the ultimate condemnation. There is no greater condemnation than rebelling against the light. By choosing darkness over light, you willingly blind yourselves. Shall a base desire be chosen over the glorious and blessed God who shines in the Gospel? The Lord is pleased to reveal Himself in the Gospel, where the beauty and excellence of God are displayed. Yet, when this light dazzles your eyes, you still prefer a base desire over that shining light.

You shall be condemned without a doubt, and your sins will intensify your condemnation. It's as if to say, those who live as if there is no God in the world, even if they are profane and ungodly, if only they had embraced the light when God sent it among them, then their souls might have been saved forever. But it is this very thing that will make your torments exceedingly terrible—that the light has come into the world, and you sin against that light, choosing darkness instead of light. You may say, "I am unable to do anything by myself." Yet, you still choose darkness over light. Those who rebel against light, those who sin against light—it is just for God to take it away from them. It is just for God to remove the Gospel from them. There is a threat pronounced against you in Micah 3:6. "Therefore you shall have night without vision, and you shall have darkness without divination; the sun shall go down on the prophets, and the day shall be dark for them." It would be the most dreadful judgment in the world for God to take away the light after He has been pleased to test a nation with it. It would be a curse for future generations.

And furthermore, if you live under the light of the Gospel and choose darkness instead of light, that is, if there is a particular sin that your soul clings to and you reject the light because it exposes that sin of yours, there is a tremendously sobering Scripture in 2 Corinthians 4:3: "But if our Gospel be hid, it is hid to them that are lost." Oh, may you take this Scripture to heart, may it pierce your spirit like a dart! Lord, how long have I lived under the preaching of the Gospel, and what do I truly know of it? Is it hidden from me? If the Gospel is effective for salvation, should it not also bring illumination? It is a grave judgment when God allows a people to remain spiritually blind in the presence of the light of the Gospel. Some individuals have experienced the light of the Gospel shining upon them and have turned away from certain base desires they once had. But I come and, as the Lord knows, they are hidden from me. "But if our Gospel be hidden, it is hidden to them that are lost." Furthermore, know that your end will be eternal darkness. You love darkness, and darkness shall be your ultimate destiny. Therefore, consider this as an exceedingly dreadful matter—rebellion and sinning against knowledge. What you now sin against will haunt you in the future. The Holy Spirit regards it as a special sign of sincerity to embrace the light. Those who are capable of beholding the light, those whose ways are such that they can appeal to God, testifying that they walk in the truth—here is one who is capable of beholding the light. Cursed is that contentment that cannot coexist with the light.

Let us learn from what Christ says—that the ministers are the light of the world—and let us learn to kindle our own candle at this light. The Scriptures refer to a person's conscience as their candle. Proverbs 20:27 states, "The spirit of man is the candle of the Lord, searching all the inward parts of the belly." The spirit of man is the candle of the Lord; it has the ability to sustain its burden. But who can bear a wounded spirit? The spirit of man is the candle of the Lord. God has placed a conscience in every man and woman, and that conscience is a candle—it possesses some light. If you desire enough light to examine the condition of your soul, you must light your candle at the Word and carry those truths and the light you have encountered there into your conscience. Search into the depths of your heart and all your ways. Do not be afraid to bring the light into every corner. When the minister sheds some light into the consciences of individuals, he cannot expose every secret sin. The souls of men have the light of truth shining upon them, but there are some corners of the heart that remain untouched by the light. Thus, if a person takes a candle, they can explore every corner of the house and peer into every crevice. You have been hearing the Word, and the Word has convicted you, yet there are many secret sins that the Word has not exposed. Therefore, you should light your candle and search every corner of your heart, casting out all your sins there.

"You are the light of the world." This applies to the ministers in both their doctrine and conduct. The doctrine of a minister is one witness, while conscience is another. If they both agree, they must both be light. Likewise, Christians in their conduct can be considered the light of the world. Philippians 2:15 states, "That ye may be blameless and harmless, the sons of God, without rebuke, in the midst of a crooked and perverse nation, among whom ye shine as lights in the world." Proverbs 4:18 says, "But the path of the just is as the shining light, that shines more and more unto the perfect day."

In every family where there is a godly man or woman, their godliness and holiness become a light—a light that troubles many. The light present in a righteous son may convict the parents, as well as in a righteous servant. Everyone should strive to shine in the place where God has placed them, to manifest this light. Your hearts should be detached from all other things and consider this as the purpose for which you live—to display the beauty and excellence of God's name in the places where you reside. "You are the light of the world," and it follows that:

"A city that is set on a hill cannot be hidden."

Some interpreters apply these words not only to the Church of God but to all saints as a spiritual community. Indeed, the Holy Spirit refers to the Church as a city. Psalm 46:4 says, "There is a river whose streams shall make glad the city of God, the holy place of the tabernacle of the Most High." Psalm 48:8 states, "As we have heard, so have we seen in the city of the Lord of hosts, in the city of our God: God will establish it forever." Psalm 87:3 proclaims, "Glorious things are spoken of thee, O city of God." Ezekiel 40:2 describes a vision where the prophet is brought into the land of Israel and set upon a high mountain, where he sees the framework of a city on the south. This is the law of the house, upon the top of the mountain; the entire boundary around it shall be most holy. Behold, this is the law of the house. While it is true that the Church is set on a hill, signifying unity in gathering together, I do not believe this is the primary focus of Christ's message. Rather, it is to emphasize the eminence of the Gospel. You are sent into the world to preach and administer the ordinances of the Gospel, to go forth publicly. The eyes of all men will be fixed upon you. Therefore, you must be mindful of your ways, for the eyes of all men will be upon you. Just as a city set on a hill cannot be hidden, and if there is any time of danger, that city is immediately discovered, so you must go and preach in the world. You must not expect to remain concealed, as some possess a sordid spirit and would rather hide and be of no use than to appear publicly and be useful for Christ. No, says Christ, you must not expect to hide and be safe. Instead, you must be willing to be the object of the world's attention. Luther remarks on this passage, "Therefore, you must not conceal any of the truths of God. You must go and preach them plainly, without considering the reproach or shame in the world. Disregard poverty, riches, hatred, favor, life, or death. The Apostles and Christians professed truths that the world saw no reason for, and that drew the world's attention. Tertullian likewise comments on this passage, asking, 'How is it that our Lord compares us to a city on a high hill?' He explains that when our desires are aroused, all the ministers of God and Christ—those who have been placed in positions of eminence—should strive to live blamelessly, for the eyes of men are upon them. Our Saviour Christ uses this as an argument for ministers to walk precisely in their ways and to let their conduct shine before men, knowing that all eyes are upon them. It is incumbent upon all ministers and Christians to live blamelessly, as the eyes of men are upon them. Therefore, live blamelessly, taking care that when others observe you, they do not witness any base or sinful behavior. This will bring dishonor to Christ and to yourselves.

Furthermore, Christ's statement that ministers and Christians are in the sight of all should remind the godly to uphold the honor of the Gospel ministers. But above all, Christ aims to highlight this: a city set on a hill. "I am sending you to preach. Do not concern yourselves with your own comfort, but rather proclaim my truths and administer my ordinances publicly."

Note: It is the duty of all ministers and Christians to present all duties and ordinances to the fullest extent possible, for all the world to see.

Therefore, whoever privately engages in any ordinance, such as preaching the Word, when they could do it publicly, undoubtedly goes against this Scripture. However, I do not want you to hinder people in public and then complain about them in private. The apostles preached publicly; they came and preached in the Temple, but they were not allowed to break bread there. They did as much as they could publicly.

Like a city set on a hill that cannot be hidden, neither do people light a candle and put it under a bushel. Instead, they put it on a candlestick, and it gives light to everyone in the house.

You have received some light, but your light is like that of a candle. If a person has a candle, the way to preserve it is to put it under a bushel; then it will not burn out as quickly as it would if placed on a candlestick. It is true, says Christ, that some of you have a vile spirit that leads you to think that revealing what you have may cause envy or opposition, and it will require a great deal of effort and trouble. Therefore, you would rather hide your gifts and talents under a bushel, partly out of pride, as you are unwilling for others to know what you know. Our Saviour says that if you have any gifts, abilities, light, or knowledge, use them to the fullest, even if it means exhausting yourself. This is the exhortation for ministers and all people. No one who has any light can be of much help if they keep it to themselves. It is very easy for a person with gifts and talents to be idle, especially if they have a steady income. But Christ says, where did you light your candle? Has God given you more light than others, and do you think you should have more ease than another? If you have any abilities that qualify you for service to God, bring them all forth and be of public benefit in the place where God has placed you. This applies not only to ministers but to all people. All the gifts you have are God's talents, and you will be held accountable for all of them. Know that sins of omission are just as accountable before the Lord as sins of commission. Oh, that people would consider this: if there is something evil in the place where I live, and I have the means to prevent it but choose not to, I am guilty of the evil that is done. If God has blessed many in their trade, and they have acquired wealth and live a comfortable life, but then abandon their trade, leading an idle existence with little usefulness to their families, having enough income each year, why should they not bother to engage in activities that could benefit the public? You may find pleasure in such thoughts, but they are truly sinful before the Lord. If you have any talents to offer to the Lord, do not hide them under a bushel but showcase them in the places where you are so that others may benefit from them. Sometimes, a servant may shed light on the family, but above all, the heads of households, the masters, if the Lord has bestowed such talents upon you, do not keep them hidden, but fully utilize them for the good of all people.

FINIS.

# WE HAVE RUINED

## *God*

## MY JOURNEY OUT OF RELIGION

## &

## INTO UNCONDITIONAL LOVE

### BY REV. DR. SHERI PALLAS

*Social Butterfly Media, LLC*
30 N Gould St., Suite R, Sheridan, WY 82801

Printed in the United States of America.

Book design by Social Butterfly Media, LLC
Cover design inspired by Fahi M and finalized by Timothy Pallas

*We Have Ruined God: My Journey Out of Religion and Into Unconditional Love*
For more information, or to book an event, contact: Rev. Dr. Sheri Pallas
SheriPallas.com

Print - Paperback: 979-8-9902457-8-5
Print- Hardcover : 979-8-9902457-9-2
EPUB: 979-8-9902457-7-8
Kindle: 979-8-9902457-5-4
Audio: 979-8-9902457-4-7

Library of Congress Cataloging-Publication-Data
First Edition: April 2024. Updated March 2025.